Honest to Genesis

A Biblical and Scientific Challenge to Creationism

With best wishes!
Margaret Towne
Jeremiah 33:2-3

Margaret Gray Towne

PublishAmerica
Baltimore

ISBN: 1-59286-497-X
PUBLISHED BY PUBLISHAMERICA, LLLP
www.publishamerica.com
Baltimore

Printed in the United States of America

"A product of mature faith, biological learning, critical thinking and theological skill, this valuable work also has the merit of being eminently readable. Margaret Towne's book demonstrates with great clarity, as well as abundant charity, how easily evolution and a robust Christian faith can get along. And it does so in a style accessible to a wide readership. I would recommend this book to parishioners, students, biology teachers, seminarians and anyone else who wants an accessible introduction to one of the most important issues of the day."

John F. Haught
Landegger Distinguished Professor of Theology
Georgetown University

"A very important book for Christians and great insights for scientists. Margaret Towne teaches us how to integrate modern science with a solid Christian faith."

Jack Horner
Regent's Professor of Paleontology
Montana State University

"Margaret Towne, science educator and biblically devoted Christian, has produced a remarkable work that does not merely promote a scientific worldview or defend a Christian faith grounded in the scriptural witness. Focusing on the seemingly perennial controversy over evolutionary theory, she demonstrates how the scriptural tradition about creation, fittingly interpreted, can be enriched by scientific findings about the history of creation. As well, she shows how evolutionary science, far from antithetical to a Biblical faith, enables the Christian to understand more deeply the dynamic ways of God in creation. And throughout she gives witness to the Biblical injunction that the Christian is to love God with all one's mind."

James B. Miller
Senior Program Associate
Program of Dialogue on Science, Ethics and
Religion
American Association for the Advancement
of Science

"In this unique and much-needed contribution to the creative and responsible discussion of evolution and Christian faith, Margaret Towne brings together her training in both biology and theology and her faith as a Christian to offer educators, pastors, scientists and seminarians a dependable, fair, comprehensive, and engaging resource for healing and deepening understanding. I am delighted to recommend *Honest to Genesis* to all fair-minded and serious readers in "science and religion" and I will look forward to using it in my seminary courses."

Robert John Russell
Founder and Director, The Center for Theology and
the Natural Sciences
Professor of Theology and Science in Residence
The Graduate Theological Union, Berkeley, CA

"In this timely and very accessible book teachers of all kinds will find an invaluable resource for helping their students move beyond the stark impasse of always having to contrast the theory of evolution with the Christian faith. Margaret Gray Towne has written a passionate, brave book that reveals the damage done to the church, and to the Christian faith in general, by the excesses of the Creationist movement. This book is the gripping tale of the journey of someone, both scientist and Christian believer, from a deeply committed faith to also embracing evolution. In achieving this integration Towne points the way beyond the extremes of creationism and materialist evolutionism, and in doing so shows us that the voices of science and faith, rightly conceived, can go together seamlessly."

J. Wentzel van Huyssteen
James I. McCord Professor of Theology and Science
Princeton Theological Seminary

*Dedicated to
my husband, Reverend Vernon William Towne,
and our remarkable daughters, Cheyan and Jannay*

Acknowledgements

Over the years, colleagues, friends and mentors have given insight and supported this effort in countless ways. It may have had its beginnings when my Southfield High School biology teacher, Suzanne Robinson, took me from Detroit to a quarry in Ohio to gather fossils. Four years with Henry van der Schalie at the University of Michigan Mollusk Division expanded my understanding and answered as well as triggered many questions.

Robert Fellenz, Gary Conti, Tom Roll, and Jack Horner served on my doctoral committee at Montana State University and guided my journey, providing unique and challenging opportunities. Research from my dissertation is incorporated into this book, especially in Chapter Six. Colleagues Ken Olson, James B. Miller, Wentzel van Huyssteen, Frederick Brown, Dawn Neuman, Paul Schollmeier, Edward Kraybill, Jay Clymer, Tucker Dempsey, Peter Hess, Tom Warne, Michael Fuchs, Peggy Fuchs, Marvin Shaw, David Lehmann, and Philip Hefner all gave significantly.

I recognize the contribution given by the Juniata College "J. Omar Good Distinguished Visiting Professor" board: Nancy Rosenberger Faus, W. Clemens Rosenberger, Thomas Pheasant, and Earl Kaylor as well as President Thomas Kepple and Provost James Lakso. They provided me with numerous opportunities to present this material in the classroom, at seminars, over coffee, and in many and varied denominational settings. Former Juniata President Calvert Ellis, decades earlier, graciously granted me a leave of absence from teaching biology to attend seminary.

Special thanks to Katherine Henrikson and Cheyan Towne who edited and gave many valued suggestions and to Gwen Fukumoto, Jeffrey Patterson and Margaret Lydic for their specialized expertise. My husband, Vernon Towne, a Presbyterian minister, regularly provided theological as well as general support and encouragement.

Others whose influence will never be forgotten include my sister, Rosemary Cotton, my parents, David and Margaret Brown Gray, Jannay Towne, John Cotton, Bonnie Price, Martin Price, Renee Lucas, Kay Quast, Betsey Ellis, Fran Wylder, Norma Ashby, Catherine Taylor, Adrienne Horger, Gerry Jennings, Arlene Parisot, Artamarie Barclay, Molly Ettenger, Christy Dowdy, Betty Ann Cherry, Lydia Sarandan, Pat Lofton, Marie Torres, Dorothy Jean McKay, and the board of the Presbyterian Association on Science, Technology and the Christian Faith. I thank my students who shared, questioned, and honestly grappled with these significant issues.

Finally, I must point out that the numerous conferences I have attended sponsored by the Science and Religion Course Program, the Center for Theology and Natural Science, the American Association for the Advancement of Science, and the American Scientific Affiliation, as well as many creationist seminars gave a broad overview as well as in-depth insight into these significant questions on origins and purpose.

TABLE OF CONTENTS

This is what the Lord says—
Your Redeemer, Who formed you in the womb:

"I am the Lord who has made all things,
Who alone stretched out the heavens,
Who spread out the earth by myself."

Isaiah 44:24 NIV

PREFACE

All Nature is but Art, unknown to thee;
All Chance, Direction, which thou canst not see;
All Discord, Harmony, not understood;
All partial Evil, universal Good.

Alexander Pope, An Essay on Man, *Epistle 1*
Vol III, Mack, Maynard (Ed.), New Haven,
Yale University Press, 1950, pp. 50-51.

Why this book? For most of the 20th Century, American Christendom was divided over how the creation accounts in Genesis should be interpreted. Much confusion, discord, and even animosity resulted. This division continues and can be attributed to two major causes. First, many Americans are not well grounded in science. They are not familiar with its definition, its purposes, its limitations, and its operations. More specifically, they are not informed of the technical rationale and supporting data of evolutionary theory. Second, many Christians do not know how to appropriately read the many genres of the ancient and, in some cases, puzzling and mysterious literature in the Bible. They are not aware of the scholarly means of interpretation that can be applied to the scriptures which pertain to creation. These factors have led to much confusion concerning the subjects of creationism, "creation science," evolutionary theory, evolutionary naturalism and materialism, the Christian Doctrine of Creation, intelligent design, the origin of life, and the origin of the universe.

Variety of opinion as to the appropriate means of interpreting the Bible's creation accounts contributes to considerable perplexity. Many young people are confused and often become disillusioned as they learn one thesis about origins from loving parents, pastors, and church school teachers and another from respected instructors in biology, geology, or paleontology classes in high school or college. Conflict arises as they attempt to integrate what they are taught in the science classroom with what they learned in the church school classroom. The need to be loyal to the latter can result in ignoring rational thinking and observable data, leading to a faulty knowledge base. If, on the other hand, they choose to side with rationality, departure from the faith may be a logical, albeit unnecessary, outcome. Either way, everyone, including the church, loses. It must be candidly admitted that the kingdom of God is endangered rather than furthered by the internal discord engendered by the creationism/evolution conflict. If these issues could be resolved, much gain would accrue to the cause of Christ.

An additional motivation for writing this book came because I, a Christian, have traveled the scenic, circuitous, and often arduous journey to evolutionary understanding and I feel the experience could have been eased if the data had been comprehensively presented in a manner that was scholarly yet sensitive to my religious apprehensions. It is my sincere desire that this book will help clarify issues for questioning Christians, both young and old.

That misinformation and misunderstanding are extremely common with respect to these subjects became apparent in the numerous interviews conducted and questionnaires collected while I was gathering data for a dissertation on whether Christians employ critical thinking as they form or modify belief on creationism and organic evolution. Also, a lack of clarity on these issues has been manifest in countless discussions I have had with Christians over many years, and with students in my biology classes as well as colleagues across the departments of the university. Inaccuracies abound on websites and in varied publications and videos. In short, surprisingly few are well informed about the science or the theology that relate to the controversy surrounding evolution and creationism. Encouragement to write this book came from my doctoral committee at Montana State University who recognized the need for clarification of these issues in a medium that could be understood by the layperson in both science and theology.

This book addresses many of the factors and much of the data that are pertinent to what has become a serious controversy within the Christian church at large, and has rippled into the classrooms and courtrooms of the broader culture. Specifically, this is a handbook for searching, thoughtful Christians, educators and pastors, young people, parents, students, and seminarians. It should also give insight to public school teachers, school board members, museum personnel, textbook authors and publishers, and other interested parties who find themselves curious about or embroiled in creationism/evolution issues. It targets those who desire to understand how a Christian can hold the evolutionary view yet affirm God as the omnipotent Creator, and it seeks to assist those who sincerely search for resolution to the confusion that surrounds these subjects.

To help the intended readers, technical terms are briefly explained within the text. Modern evolutionary theory is presented and the means of integrating its data with the Christian scriptures are explained. Many assertions and criticisms of evolutionary theory by creationists, which are presented in their publications, debates, videos, and seminars over the years, are confronted. I am deeply saddened to have witnessed much pain resulting from the division within the Christian world because of the belief disparity that has been nourished by the error of creationists' belief. Yet I declare my respect for the deep faith and commitment demonstrated by these Christians and warmly include them as my brothers and sisters in the Lord. We have much in common as will be noted in Chapter Eleven.

The opposite perspective of creationism is evolutionary naturalism/ materialism. The tendency of some scientists to incorporate this atheistic philosophy into their world view and then, knowingly or unknowingly, inappropriately attach it to the science of evolutionary theory is exposed and discussed. This has no doubt interfered with many Christians' attempts to integrate the scientific basis for evolution with their understanding of biblical teaching. The discipline of evolution is a science, not a philosophy or religion, and I profoundly disagree with scientists who masquerade evolutionary naturalism as philosophy within science.

It is time that the issues are addressed for the common reader: What is science? What is meant by evolutionary theory? What are its claims? What data support it? What are its present enigmas? Is there a basis for "creation science"? Why is it not accepted by most scientists, even those who are avowed Christians? What important questions have creationists not answered? What is evolutionary naturalism or materialism? What is meant by "Intelligent Design"? What are the methods of and bases for scriptural interpretation in modern biblical scholarship? How can the data from biology, geology, and paleontology be integrated into a Christian paradigm? How can one maintain the Christian faith and be honest to Genesis as well as to observable data and the rational theories of modern science?

I am concerned that Christianity has lost respect in general, and from the scientific community in particular, because of this conflict. It is unknown how many searchers have been discouraged from the Christian faith because of it. I also regret the pain that inquiring Christians must endure as they honestly struggle with these issues in their search for truth. Some experience ostracism and the alienating judgment of their peers, and many admit to carefully avoiding discussions on these subjects for fear of consequences. Intellectual bondage is not a hallmark of authentic Christianity.

Along with their devotional Bible study, most pastors and church leaders seek a broad, scholarly foundation in the scriptures. This training is typically received at seminary. Those in authority who guide the laity attempt to understand a very ancient book written in several foreign languages over a period of a thousand years by numerous authors, some known and some unknown. They try to understand its application to the many technical aspects of a question such as evolution. There remain seminaries, Bible schools, and many books and curricula that do not teach a scriptural interpretation that is consistent with the voluminous data of modern evolutionary theory. When pastors are not informed then parishioners cannot become acquainted with the means available to correlate these important disciplines.

For more than a century, mainline Protestant and Catholic seminaries have been teaching a scriptural interpretation that facilitates the integration of evolutionary theory with the biblical creation accounts. Few institutions, however, offered courses that integrate specific subjects of modern science, such as evolutionary theory, with revealed biblical truth although this is definitely improving. An insufficient grasp of these complex subjects may explain why few of their graduates address these issues in their congregations. Possibly they fear the conflict that may ensue as parishioners' beliefs or means of interpretation are challenged, or the risk involved, which may even endanger their jobs. Time, and other priorities and interests may also explain this omission. This book seeks to fill this void, introducing the reader to these important subjects and presenting an overview of many significant issues.

It must be noted that scientists devote lifetimes to the complex discipline of evolutionary theory and theologians commit their lives to the scholarship of biblical interpretation as well. This effort will hit many of the high points but it in no way claims to be an exhaustive treatment. It is a beginning and the numerous references included can lead the reader deeper into these significant and interesting subjects.

Pastors may have made valiant attempts to explain evolutionary theory in light of modern biblical interpretation but congregants have not availed themselves of these opportunities. Mainline denominations have published excellent study materials and other literature that are designed for those who inquire in these areas. As can be seen from the reading lists at the end of most chapters, there are many books written by scientists and biblical scholars. Comprehensive videos from various sources are also available. Appendix G includes societies and journals for ongoing information. There is a need for more scholarly sophistication of biblical interpretation, admittedly a very deep and challenging discipline, in the pews across the denominations, in cathedrals, and in independent churches.

I sincerely hope that all who have questions on how evolution can be integrated with the Christian faith will openmindedly, courageously, humbly, and prayerfully consider the tenets they are about to read. They may grasp a new perspective and will be more informed of the data from both the scientific and theological viewpoints. The good news is that there is compatibility and no cause for concern. There is a marvelous consistency between God's amazing Word (the Bible) and God's awesome works (nature).

Science is tentative. It may be demonstrated tomorrow or farther into the future that a wholly different paradigm explains origins and development. For almost a century and a half, however, the vast majority of scientists, including those who are Christians, have seen the data of evolutionary theory to be compellingly persuasive. Furthermore, biblical scholarship over the same period has demonstrated how this body of scientific evidence can be appropriately integrated into the Christian world view. We must continually be open to new information as well as new revelation, being sensitive and honest in assessing how the data gained through modern science relates to the faith.

I was raised in a branch of Christianity where deeply committed Christians modeled Christ's compassion and self-sacrificial love by positively influencing their world. They were faithful to the scriptures as they understood them. There was a strong indoctrination into what was perceived as truth on various theological issues. Autonomous thinking or consideration of alternative belief positions even on peripheral questions was generally not encouraged. Questioning or entertaining doubts could be perceived as lack of faith so most passively accepted the established biblical interpretations of the elders and leaders. Also, the priority of many of those devout Christians was living the faith and loving in God's name, and there was less time or inclination to dwell on theological issues.

Even though Genesis 1 and 2 were generally taken literally and most would have called themselves biblical literalists, they did not interpret all of the scriptures literally. For instance, while God was believed to be a spirit they had no trouble with such phrases as "God breathed" in Genesis 2:7 (as though God had muscles and lungs), or "the eye of God" (Deuteronomy 11:12), or "With my outstretched arm I made the Earth" (Jeremiah 27:5). They knew these texts were figurative. It is a beautiful image that Abraham's descendants were to be as numerous as the stars in the sky and the sand on the seashore, but this cannot be interpreted as a literal promise (Genesis 22:17). Even though Jesus taught "If your right hand offend you, cut it off" (Matthew 5:30), his followers did not do that. Nor did anyone sell all that they had and give to the poor as Jesus instructed an inquiring young man (Matthew 19:21). They knew what Jesus meant when he said "I am the door" (John 10:9) or when the Psalmist (92:15) declared "The Lord is upright; he is my Rock." These passages were not to be taken literally. They had profound, powerful, theological, figurative messages! The images buried in Daniel and other Old Testament prophets or Revelation were given nonliteral, symbolic meaning. Obviously, not all of the scriptures were to be taken literally. How was it decided that Genesis 1 and 2 *had* to be interpreted as relating to literal, scientific, historic events and could not have been seen as containing profound theological messages instead?

The interpretation of pre-scientific writings that originated thousands of years ago in languages from far and extinct cultures presents considerable challenge, and most beginners employ a literal approach. A degree of instruction is necessary to recognize the Bible as a composite of numerous types of literature, each needing to be interpreted appropriately and some even requiring significant scholarship to be understood. Just as Shakespeare's play *Hamlet* is read differently than the poem "Casey at the Bat," or the fictional story of Eliza Doolittle in *My Fair Lady* is interpreted differently than a historical account of World War II, so the prophecies of Ezekiel are read differently than the love poems of the Song of Solomon, the laws of Deuteronomy, the histories of I and II Kings, the parables in the Gospel of Mark, the personal letters of Paul, or the origin stories in Genesis.

High school students routinely need to be instructed in how to read the classics of English literature. Similar formal training is generally required for accurate exegesis (interpretation) of any literature especially if it was written long ago and in a different cultural setting. Many Christians are not acquainted with the scholarship associated with biblical exegesis or do not appreciate that such expertise has value. Some reject it, believing that too much questioning or analysis of the scriptures might be detrimental to the faith. This can result in Christians accepting without question the dogmatic and authoritative interpretations that have been established by their particular wing of the church and they do not consider, nor are they encouraged to consider, the insights of other theologians and biblical scholars. They are bound and loyal to a tradition rather than a truth.

There is something powerful and safe in traditional belief that makes even the consideration of a novel idea almost impossible. However, elevating the teachings and interpretations of former pastors and teachers above their present counterparts can be perceived by some as closemindedness, fear, or even idolatry. Confined thinking that requires conformity to one interpretation which is heralded as "The Truth" leaves no room for personal development and God's progressive revelation and ongoing activity in the world. As God was introduced to ancient Israel and then unveiled more character through Christ, God has continued to reveal this divine will and work down through the centuries. Besides the insight gained through conscientious and rigorous study of the scriptures, another most profound medium through which this revelation has come is modern science, the careful study of God's workmanship.

Thinking Christians must be open to considering whether the pre-scientific accounts of Genesis 1 and 2 might indeed be not just records of literal happenings, but profound and powerful theological theses; revelations from the God of the universe who was beginning to be made known. Those who hold to biblical literalism often express the concern that if some parts of the Bible are not taken literally, then other parts such as their security about salvation and the promises of Jesus are threatened. The good news is that that fear is unfounded. The key is in recognizing the various literary genres and appropriately interpreting them. Truth will prevail.

In the mid 1960s, after earning two degrees in biology, I sought theological training and discovered that the seminaries in my milieu did not accept women. That led to my enrolling at an institution which some labeled "liberal." I wasn't in that academic community long before I realized that the mind was recognized as a significant creation of God and its exercise was vigorously encouraged. A disciplined mind, the faculty held, could be used to the glory of God. The Christian faith and the scriptures were seen as strong enough to endure questions and they were not exempt from challenge or doubt. Scholarship within the faith was regarded as honest and profound enhancement, not elevated above faith but integrated into it. I was impressed with the deep spiritual commitment as well as the brilliance and academic humility of the faculty. They were on a search for God's truth. There was no distinction between the men and the women with respect to their gifts and exercise of them, their opinions and/or means of faith expression. As a young woman, I found it a fertile environment for growth.

Students at that seminary were encouraged to become informed and reflect on all sides of issues and prayerfully and autonomously draw conclusions. That inevitably resulted in some heterogeneity of belief on the peripheral issues of the faith within the student body and alumni, and inclusiveness and tolerance were fostered within the whole community. No one had an edge on truth. This dynamic bred openminded, expectant interaction, and maturity in faith resulted. In an affirming community students honestly assessed their beliefs, sometimes with considerable pain as the need for change was acknowledged and addressed. It was not easy for individuals to recognize and admit that a loving parent, pastor, Sunday school teacher, church, denomination, or they, themselves, were wrong on an issue.

While I knew that those in my religious heritage had taught me much truth, I became aware that their interpretation of the scriptures dealing with women, which led to discrimination against them at seminary, was wrong. They were forgiven, but this realization led me to subject other areas of their biblical interpretation to closer scrutiny. If they didn't see the need to adapt an ancient literature, which was written in a patriarchal culture, to a modern

21

society, what other areas of oversight might there be? I came to suspect literalism.

I look back on the people in the Christian community in which I was raised with deep affection and gratitude. Their committed, Christ-centered living and enthusiasm for the faith were exemplary. They sincerely tried to please their Lord and I know He will say of them "Well done, good and faithful servants." I treasure the examples they were to me of costly grace and committed faith and am grateful for the priority they gave to scripture memorization. I yearn at this point for a Christianity that unites this genuine Christ-like living and love for God's word with the academic rigor and informed scholarship of trained scientists and theologians. I long to see an attitude of tolerance and humility which comes from the unique, inclusive love modeled by our Lord. This would be the best of all worlds. It would enable Christianity to meet the challenges that perpetually arise in a complex, changing, scientific, and highly technical world. Without this mindset, the faith offered by Jesus Christ may be seen as dogmatic, narrow, prideful, divisive, dated, and unattractive or even amusing to those who are educated and acculturated in this scientifically based era.

I have taught biology on the college level for over 25 years at institutions varying from a community college to an Ivy League university. Countless students have asked me how I could be a minister's wife or call myself Christian and believe in evolution. There is much about the subject of evolution and its relationship to the scriptures that is not resolved in many minds. In their attempt to deal with apparent disparity, some Christians have to separate their academic pursuits from their faith, leaving the scientific issues of the week outside the sanctuary door. There is a need for honest dialogue and wholeness. One college student said, "I find it easier to ignore the church as I pursue my major in geology."

Besides contributing to an integration of the truth of scripture with the truth of modern science, an additional desired outcome of this book is to in some way facilitate unity within the parts of the Christian world that have historically been divided on these questions. Such division disserves our Lord, encouraging conflict and distracting us from the good news, hope, service, and love for the Lord which unites Christians.

It is further hoped that this effort will lead to more careful scholarship, more tolerance for alternative views on peripheral issues, more inclusiveness, and where necessary, courageous belief modification among the people of God. Christians may never be able to agree fully on these issues, but above all we must practice the love, forgiveness, and forbearance that honors our Lord. An "us" and "them" mentality among the people of God is not consistent with Jesus' teaching "that they all may be one" (John 17:21). We must cease to allow the more peripheral question of how we got here to interfere with the more central questions of why we are here, how we must live, where we are going, whom we serve, and how we respond to God.

Great is our Lord, and of great power: his understanding is infinite.
Psalms 147:5

In both the domains
of nature and faith,
you will find
the most excellent things
are the deepest hidden.

Erasmus, *The Sages*, 1515
Erasmus of Rotterdam (~1466-1536)

Preparing for the Journey

Chapter One

The pathway was here also exceeding narrow, and therefore good Christian was the more put to it; for when he sought, in the dark, to shun the ditch on the one hand, he was ready to tip over into the mire on the other; also, when he sought to escape the mire, without great carefulness he would be ready to fall into the ditch. Thus he went on, and I heard him here sigh bitterly; for besides the danger mentioned above, the pathway was here so dark, that oftimes, when he lifted up his foot to go forward, he knew not where or upon what he should set it next.

John Bunyan, Pilgrim's Progress,
The Fourth Stage

His candle shineth on my head, and by his light I go through darkness. Job 29:3

Before setting off on a trip a wise traveler devises a plan and, unless going on a serendipitous outing, has a destination in mind. For the Christian on this particular journey, prayer asking for insight, the revelation of truth, and the courage to go where that truth leads is most appropriate. Other indispensable preparations that will profoundly enrich this journey include acquiring skills in careful thinking, gaining a historical perspective on the pertinent issues, and receiving training in biblical interpretation. Instruction in each of these areas is included in the chapters that follow.

The thesis and purpose of this book is to justify the position of theistic ("theos" = God) evolution (change over time). While most people are aware of the two extreme positions, atheistic ("a theos" = without God) evolutionary naturalism/materialism, which denies a creator God, and the creationist belief in a six, solar day, young Earth creation by the creator God, many are not aware of a third position, theistic evolution. It acknowledges and honors God as creator yet holds that this creative activity occurred over billions of years within the parameters of natural laws and the mechanisms of evolution, all originating with, designed, or freed by the Creator. This paradigm affirms the biblical Doctrine of Creation yet respects and incorporates the rational data from modern science. To establish the foundations for theistic evolution the data for evolutionary science as well as the basic tenets of modern biblical scholarship are included.

The God of the Bible is here acknowledged as Creator, a position taken on faith based on the holy scriptures, which are regarded as true. That this God indeed created cannot be scientifically substantiated, nor can it be disproved, as this is a belief position based on faith. Many hold that the indescribable beauty, intricate complexity, amazing order, and infinite size of the natural world are tangibles that point without question to an omnipotent creator. It is a religious doctrine or belief, yet a valid way of knowing to millions of people, from youth to esteemed scholar.

The position of theistic evolution recognizes the data of science and respects the use of reason in answering questions. It, without apology, employs the mind, one of the Creator's greatest accomplishments. It respects the information that comes by way of the scientific method and the senses, which are gifts from God. This position integrates the data from scripture with the data from the rocks as well as from within cells into a meaningful and exciting thesis that has great potential to enrich faith.

Preparing for the journey of bridging God's works with his word includes becoming familiar with definitions of some pertinent terms and theses.

Christian Doctrine of Creation

Most Christians adhere to the doctrine that the God they worship was prior to the material universe. This God is the originating creator of the universe and of life itself. This belief is known as the Christian Doctrine of Creation and it is based on numerous Old and New Testament references (many of which are included in Appendix A) which affirm God as omnipotent creator. Furthermore, since Jesus Christ is a part of the godhead, it is believed that he, too, was present and active in creation. This is proclaimed, among other references, in the first chapter of the Gospel of John: "In the beginning was the Word (Jesus) and the Word was with God and the Word was God. All things were made by Him" (Verses 1 and 3). An additional magnificent reference to Jesus Christ as creator can be found in Colossians 1:15-17: "He is the image of the invisible God, the firstborn over all creation. For by him all things were created: things in heaven and on earth, visible and invisible, whether thrones or powers or rulers or authorities; all things were created by him and for him. He is before all things, and in him all things hold together."

It is important to note that the Christian Doctrine of Creation does not express *how* God created, but attests to the fact that God *did* create. Theistic evolutionary belief does not negate this important doctrine. It affirms that God indeed is the creator and confers on God all the honor, reverence, glory, majesty, and acclaim that that deserves.

Theistic Evolution

It is most regrettable that creationists only recognize the two extreme positions, evolutionary naturalism/materialism and creationism. They fail to inform lay people of this third option which integrates the Christian Doctrine of Creation with modern science. Because belief in theistic evolution credits God as creator, is supported by scripture, and recognizes the data from science which rationality finds hard to dispute, many thinking Christians have seriously considered and eventually embraced it. The mainline Protestant denominations, Catholics, and many Muslims and Jews have affirmed the validity of this overarching position, some for over a century.

Theistic evolution enables scientists and other questioning Christians to be honest both to Genesis and to geology, to God's word and God's works. It includes belief in a creator God who designed, freed, and sustains creation and who has accomplished this through natural laws over millions of years through evolutionary mechanisms, some known and some not yet understood. Theistic evolutionists accept descent with modification (change over time) caused by mutation, genetic variation, and species isolation as reasonable and partial explanations of the origin of species. They deny any idea that such descent was not governed in some way or blessed with a freedom by a divine creator. How this creator, whom Christians and Jews identify as Jehovah, God, works is believed to be capable of being, at least in part, rationally explained. As the early Hebrews were limited by their lack of scientific understanding, we also experience enigmas. The Creator's purposeful yet permissive, freeing, sustaining, guiding involvement is not completely understood and is accepted by faith based on the assertions of scripture. Much has been revealed in the past century, however, and new insights accrue daily. Evolution can be viewed by the scientist and the Christian as an awesome God working through dependable laws. This is an expanded insight when compared to the colorful creation stories of a pre-scientific culture in the ancient Middle East.

Theistic evolution allows the data of science to be seen in light of an omnipotent creator who honors us by sharing details of his ways and laws. It gives order, meaning, and security. Dependability, not capriciousness or whimsy, reigns. It triggers the desire to seek and rewards with the exhilaration of finding. Our God has blessed us, first of all with the gift of reason, and second, with explanations provided by the dedication and persistence of scientists over the centuries. Third, we are profoundly indebted to theologians who interpret these events in light of the truth of the God whom we have always trusted and known. Just as this God was progressively revealed throughout scripture, peaking with the incarnation and resurrection of Jesus, God continues this dynamic relationship in the present, enhancing our understanding yet preserving mystery and reverential greatness.

This new idea leads to awe, delight, worship, and thanksgiving to a God who cares to share insights with us. It enables the faith of the ancients revealed in scripture to be wholly integrated and relevant to a post-modern culture! There is no reasonable foundation for insisting on the mythical stories of Genesis whose truths are profoundly theological rather than scientific. Theistic evolutionists integrate their scientific knowledge of evolution with their faith in an omnipotent creator God. Millions of them are in churches, temples, cathedrals, mosques or synagogues across the globe on Sunday mornings or other days or times of worship. Many are in the pulpits, serving on mission fields, or can be found on seminary and university faculty. Polls reveal that over 40% of Americans hold this position. The numbers would be much higher in other Western countries where Christian fundamentalism is not as dominant.

Among Christians, data show that there is a strong correlation between level of education and belief in theistic evolution. The higher the level of education the more likely one will confirm this position. This is because evolutionary data are not generally fully presented and understood until the college experience. Christians with this belief are also found more often in less authoritarian religious settings which allow autonomous thinking and where rationality is recognized as a valid way to mold belief and arrive at truth.

Furthermore, theistic evolutionists are active in their communities and churches or synagogues, bettering society, and leading upright lives as are creationists. Their beliefs in evolution have in no way influenced or driven them to immoral or irresponsible living, which some suggest are outcomes of such belief. Affirming evolution as a scientific thesis is irrelevant to their character, morality, lawfulness, and faith expression. As dependable law operates in mathematics, engineering, agriculture, medicine, astronomy, pharmacology, architecture, and physics, so it operates in biology and geology. God is the consistent and dependable originator of these laws and with God rests the unveiling and liberating potential of history.

Theistic evolutionists believe the omnipotent creator's majesty and power are not reduced to suggest that billions of years were employed in accomplishing the grand task of creation. Some claim this model is more awesome, remarkable, logical, and consistent with God's timeless existence and character of order, reliability, and trustworthiness than for God to merely speak and thus create an instantaneous and unexplainable complex entity. They are honored that through science, little by little, this Creator shares creative mechanisms with humankind. These have come through inventions such as the telescope and electron microscope as well as through genetics, radiometric dating technology, fossil finds, the anatomy and physiology of DNA, molecular biology, and biochemical pathways. Theistic evolutionists acknowledge God's power and even God's voluntary abdication of that power as natural laws are freed to unfold, and they are humbled by the insights. The time required to form the vast universe and life as we know it often results in indescribable awe and worship as such reality is contemplated.

Theistic evolutionists do not affirm a literal interpretation of the Genesis creation accounts. They respect the scriptures as inspired by God but recognize the scholarship of higher criticism and apply it to their biblical interpretation. They are as consistent in searching for and considering the scholarship in theology and the Bible as they are in seeking it in science. The scriptures answer the "Who?" and "Why?" which are theological questions. They look to science to explain the "How?" and "When?" questions. The creation accounts in Genesis 1 and 2 are interpreted figuratively and theologically rather than literally, scientifically, and historically. Overwhelming support for this interpretation comes not only from the data of the rocks, such as their configurations, dates, composition, and fossils but also from the fields of molecular biology, comparative anatomy, biogeography, embryology, genetics, biblical archeology and history, and biblical exegesis (interpretation) and language.

Theistic evolutionists appreciate the Bible as a compendium of many types of literature including prophesy, law, history, letters, poetry, proverb, song, parable, and genealogy. They hold that not all of these literary works should be read and interpreted in the same way. Some can be taken literally, such as the historical records in I and II Samuel, and some must be seen figuratively, such as images in the Song of Solomon or Revelation. The challenge for all who deal with the Genesis creation accounts is to discern the correct means by which these two chapters must be interpreted. This is the goal of any sincere seeker of biblical understanding.

Theistic evolutionists do not claim to understand fully God's role or plan in creation and how power or creativity have been released to the natural and dependable laws which have been designed. God may have granted an independence whereby natural laws rule rather than taking the role of a coercive director. God's design may be a self-unfolding universe. The verity that God is creator is accepted and while many previous unknowns have become known it is recognized that God's ways and thoughts may never be totally understood ("For my thoughts are not your thoughts, neither are your ways my ways, declares the Lord. As the heavens are higher than the earth, so are my ways higher than your ways and my thoughts than your thoughts" Isaiah 55:8-9). There is an optimism, however, that God will continue to reveal insights through scientific inquiry and religious openness.

Theistic evolutionists all credit God as creator over long periods but it must be noted that there is variety of belief or expression within this group. Some of the positions are:

1. Plants and animals evolved but humans were created separately and directly
2. Over long periods God may have intervened within the created order in a variety of times and places such as in (1) above; progressive, old Earth creation
3. God specifically designed each organism but each one came into being over long periods of time through natural evolutionary processes; preprogramming
4. God directly controls evolution, maybe at the level of mutations
5. The designer God triggered life on Earth and set it loose conforming to and bound by natural laws which God formulated, freed and/or controls
6. God allowed a self-directedness to take place in nature leading to novelty and variety and it includes death, suffering and extinction
7. God planned the unique environment on the Earth and designed chemistry so that life as we know it could arise and change through natural means
8. Other options or combinations of the above

Those who hold to theistic evolution vehemently reject the thesis that life's origins and evolution were totally the result of random, chance processes, devoid of any original divine design, control or liberty. These Christians, weighing thoughtfully the data from science and yet committed to the Christian Doctrine of Creation, view evolution as a process of the creator's invention and intention. This insight expands their understanding of the creator's power, omniscience, and limitless potential for action or inaction over the eons. In no way does this belief position diminish the creator's awesome power. It leads many to deeper worship as they gain understanding of dependable natural laws and experience the delight that it engenders. Indeed, Christian biochemists are awed at molecular intricacy and complex metabolic pathways as are geologists as they survey the vistas at Glacier

National Park or the Peruvian Andes, or physiologists who study kidney nephrons and lung alveoli, or the ecologists who research the biotic (living) and abiotic (nonliving) components of a coral reef, cave, or geothermal spring. Science can trigger Creator worship!

Since Christians fear the loss of meaning and against all rationality will defend beliefs that threaten meaning, it is essential that the theistic evolutionary position be carefully delineated to include the thought that God is in charge, is allowing his ultimate plan to be fulfilled, and is the omnipotent and ongoing creator liberator. God is active, not passive, present not distant. Creativity is ongoing, not complete. Some have suggested that the genetic manipulation that is now practiced may be God allowing humans to be "co-creators"!

Theistic evolution gives thinking Christians a freedom to accept evidence from the senses without fearing that any such data will threaten the truth or the God of the Bible. God's world and word are consistent. One does not deny nor negate the other. Divine order is continually displayed in the complexity and beauty in nature and the abiding care of a loving sustainer prevails. Children taught this model respect their God-given environment and recognize their responsibility in living lives that honor this Creator's handiwork. They also are blessed with the freedom to fearlessly open their minds to evidence and novelty. Theistic evolutionary belief in no way interferes with one's faith journey, in fact it can enrich it.

Theistic evolutionists acknowledge that the omnipotent creator God could have created in a spoken word in six solar days, or in one millisecond, for that matter. God is *God*. But to them the data of science show that God worked differently, over long periods of time, and through natural processes. They reject the thesis that God created the universe with the appearance of age as some creationists affirm (Adam being minutes old yet a man, trees in the Garden of Eden having growth rings yet being minutes old, the universe appearing to have begun billions of years ago yet being only thousands of years old). This appearance of age is called the omphalos argument and to some the idea suggests a deception by the creator. To theistic evolutionists the heavens will forever declare the glory and dependable character of God and the firmament will continually reflect the Creator's handiwork (Psalm 19:1).

Anthropic Principle

Scientists and theologians are aware of a number of critical considerations which, when taken together, produce a series of basic requirements as to how the universe and the Earth must be in order that we happen to be here to contemplate them and ourselves! To many it appears more than coincidental that the very precise conditions for life, and intelligent life at that, came by chance. "Anthropos" means humankind in Greek. This principle suggests that the universe was designed such that ultimately humans would appear and thrive.

The particular size of the Earth and its distance from the sun and moon determines the gravitational force that in turn holds the atmosphere in place at the surface. The atmosphere protects from ultraviolet light, which helps maintain a surface temperature between 0 and 100 degrees Celsius. This is the range within which water, a primary constituent of life, is in a liquid and therefore useable state, rather than in a gaseous (steam) or solid (ice) form. If any of these factors or physical laws were altered in the minutest way, life as we know it would not exist.

The laws of physics, chemistry, and biology are so mutually supportive and inter-related that to many honest and open minds it is hard to believe it all just happened without design. Events from the Big Bang until the present were so intricate that if even a small change in force or temperature had occurred it would have resulted in an entirely different universe, no doubt disrupting the delicate and fragile balance that supports life. Many believe that a totally naturalistic approach to explaining the universe is inadequate and that a theistic viewpoint with an explanation that transcends naturalism or holds to a God designing laws within which the universe and life operate is required. It would seem that the chaos at the beginning of the universe was somehow guided, liberated, planned, or destined by an omnipotent Mind. In 1802, William Paley, an Anglican priest, introduced "the argument from design." He contended that something as complex as a watch presupposes a watchmaker. An ordered Earth, he reasoned, must have a designer. All assumed the designer was the God of the Bible.

Scientists believe that there is an explanation for all phenomena in the universe; however, there are phenomena that science cannot as yet explain, such as the explosive birth of the universe. At present science's pursuit backwards ends at the moment of the Big Bang. It may be that the mystery which began the universe will never be untangled. This is where the biblical beginning becomes most profound: *In the beginning....God (Genesis 1:1)*. It would seem that the Bang required a Banger!

Some have suggested that if it is difficult to believe in a creator God it requires even more faith to believe that this magnificent universe and life as we know it could have arisen through chance processes alone. The probabilities for such organization are so minuscule that spontaneous creation of the universe and life, including the human brain, linguistic ability, abstract thought, religious insight, musical and artistic gifts, complex personality, and moral capability would have to be described as miraculous, which approaches theologians' creation doctrine. The anthropic principle holds that probabilities against chance are so vast that the only alternative explanation is a creator God. Some would say the belief in a universe randomly evolving with life originating outside of a divine intelligence is the most daring proposition in the history of science.

Teleology

This term comes from the Greek "*telos*" meaning purpose or end and it is the search for directedness or a goal in nature, final cause. It attempts to answer the "why" question. What is the universe and life "for"? Why are they here? Scientists look for mechanistic, physicochemical, natural explanations for natural phenomena. They seek to answer the "how" question. The religious look to the remarkable structure of wings, eyes, cellular biochemical pathways, the beauty of the sunset, or the refined adaptability of plants or animals to their unique environments and hypothesize a supernatural power who is expressing premeditated design or who has allowed the freedom of natural law to result in complex life. The interrelationships between orchids and their pollinators, for example, seems too complex and gives evidence for a purposeful designer to many.

Many ask "Why did God do it? What was God's purpose?" Some have suggested that humans, who have the ability and choice to worship the Creator, may have been the ultimate purpose of creation.

Origin of Life

Presently, three possible explanations are offered to answer the universal and enigmatic question "From whence did we come?"

1. Special, miraculous, abrupt creation by a supernatural being
2. Spontaneous generation, life from non-life, by chance over millions of years (evolutionary naturalism/materialism)
3. Naturalistic spontaneous generation over millions of years as directed, freed, or somehow programmed by a designer Creator (theistic evolution). This thesis is theology's response to Darwinian evolution.

Spontaneous generation, the thesis that life abruptly arose from non-life, was clearly disproven by Pasteur in 1861. At that time the only alternative was special creation. Very little scientific attention was given to the subject until Oparin, a Russian, and Haldane, an Englishman, suggested in the early decades of the 20th century that life spontaneously generated and then evolved in the ocean in a reducing (no free oxygen) atmosphere. They proposed that organic (carbon-based) compounds were synthesized by ultraviolet light energy. Molecules would accumulate in a warm environment and somehow minimally organize. Given enormous amounts of time and a vast area, it seemed reasonable that somewhere the conditions would be conducive to molecular organization, sooner or later. More complexity would follow with specialized cell organelles such as nuclei, chloroplasts or ribosomes, all having a membrane. The sun's light enabled photosynthesis (putting together with light energy) to occur resulting in an alternative kind of energy (chemical bond energy). Carbon dioxide and water were put together to form sugar. Oxygen would be a byproduct of photosynthesis and it would facilitate cellular respiration (the removal of chemical bond energy from sugar). It is conceivable that an original spontaneous generation could have occurred under specific circumstances but since they are no longer extant, such generation, according to Pasteur, is inoperative today.

What *evidence* do scientists have for original spontaneous generation? Earth's early atmosphere was no doubt reducing (without free oxygen); atmospheres of other planets today are also reducing. Fossil remains of primitive micro-organisms have been found and simple organic molecules have been synthesized in the lab. The content of sedimentary rocks has been analyzed and there are reduced minerals in the sand. Fully oxidized beds of iron, not older than 1.4 billion years, have been found.

Precambrian fossils on the Minnesota/Ontario border have been dated at 1.9 billion years. The oldest fossils found to date, filamentous cyanobacteria-like microbes, come from rocks in the Pilbara Supergroup in Northwestern Australia and in the Swaziland Supergroup in Eastern South Africa. These fossils are found in rocks dated 3 - 3.5 billion years. Not only are these fossils old but quite advanced, suggesting that evolution occurred at a faster rate than would have been formerly predicted.

A major problem with this model of spontaneous generation is the massive jump between the warm ocean soup and the simplest fermenting (anaerobic=without needing oxygen) bacterium. There is a huge chasm between what we know about the origin of organic molecules (such as amino acids that compose proteins, sugars that compose complex carbohydrates, and nucleotides that compose DNA), and protocells and the earliest cells.

We assume the steps that would fill this void are numerous and complex, yet the time from the planet's formation to their development is a fairly short period, geologically speaking. It was approximately the same period of time that it took for the next step of protocells to become eucaryotic cells (advanced cells with distinct membrane-bound nuclei and organelles). Generally, most cells excluding bacteria are eucaryotic today. Currently there is significant support for the model that early life could have arisen in deep sea volcanic vents getting energy from heat or chemical reactions instead of from the sun.

There is evidence in microfossils and living models to support the process from protocells to eukaryotes, but no demonstrable evidence for the first process, molecules to life, and scientists are pessimistic that such data will be forthcoming. While there is evidence for the formation of the planet and the steps to eucaryotic cells, imagination combined with some laboratory experiments fill the middle era. DNA, which encodes protein recipes, had to acquire the ability to replicate. The step from replicating a molecule to a cell is thought by some to be the biggest step in all of evolution, larger than the progression from a protozoan to humans. Yet over three billion years were available for these sequential steps to have commenced and progressed. Once molecules reached a certain level of complexity, natural selection rather than chance would have been operative. Some of the record might have been in the rocks but rocks also evolve by becoming heated, worn, metamorphosed or displaced. The older the rocks, the more chance of change or destruction, and therefore the fewer there are of these. Thus the record is forever lost.

Scientists have produced microspheres in the laboratory. These are protein-like polypeptides (chains of amino acids) that have a double layered boundary similar to the double layered membrane of micro-organisms. They have been seen to independently assemble. These structures, not what we'd call living, do illustrate the influence that physical forces can have in synthesizing molecules.

It has also been demonstrated that less-refined proteins than the complex ones identified today could have performed the same biochemical processes. Experiments reveal that carbon-containing molecules of varying complexity can synthesize naturally. The research in this area is fascinating and no one knows what might be elucidated in the future.

It must be noted that even if scientists were to synthesize complex organic molecules or protocells in the laboratory it would still not prove that the original origin of life followed in that particular manner. Because there are so many unanswered questions pertaining to the origin of life and the complexity of early life, and since little is known of the evolution of the intricate chemistry of so many metabolic pathways of the cell's physiology, many feel that the only explanation is the mysterious and miraculous guiding influence of a master intelligent Designer.

Whether answers to these dilemmas will come remains to be seen. More is known today than a decade ago. Explaining what is yet unexplained by invoking a supernatural act by an omnipotent creator, a phenomenon called the "god of the gaps," is vulnerable to being negated when valid empirical explanation eventually is offered. There is a history of this very pattern in the past and as mysteries which at one time were explained by miraculous intervention have indeed been resolved scientifically, this god is forced to retreat. This thesis of explaining what is not yet understood with miracle can quench rational inquiry and squelch scientific endeavors which seek to find rational explanation. Because something is as yet unexplained does not mean it is unexplainable.

There definitely are areas of science that are unclear and may remain so. However, remarkable data are being generated even as we write and many biochemists at present cannot conscientiously relegate the sequences to an intelligent design umbrella. They are optimistic that light will be shed on these questions and explanations eventually offered. Either way, God is seen by the Christian as the original author, designer, or freer of life whether the mechanisms are eventually revealed or remain forever concealed.

It is extremely important to understand that the subject of life's origins is distinctive from the subject of evolutionary change. These two disciplines must be separated in the discussions that pertain to evolution and creationism. The former concerns biochemists, paleobiologists (those who study ancient life), micro and molecular biologists. The latter concerns these scientists as well as those who specialize in such biological fields as genetics, comparative anatomy, physiology, embryology, and biogeography as well as geology and paleontology.

Without doubt scientists have much more substantiating data on descent with modification (evolution) than they do on life's origins (abiogenesis). Authors or speakers who do not distinguish between these two subjects perpetrate a deception, muddy the waters, and contribute to the misunderstanding that prevails among the masses. They suggest that since data on origins is minimal, it in turn weakens evolutionary theory. Nothing is further from the truth. Indeed, evolutionary data stand on their own, separate from origins research. Even if origin of life research never progresses beyond where it is at this time that dilemma must be distinguished from the quite separate question of whether descent with modification, change over time, evolution, has occurred. How life started is not yet clarified but there is an enormous amount of data that tell where life subsequently went, and such data accrue daily.

Origin of the Universe

Those who study the universe and its origin specialize in astronomy, physics, chemistry, and mathematics. While a subject of much interest, it is also distinct from evolutionary inquiry which centers on the fields of biology, geology, chemistry, and paleontology and is the main thesis of this book.

Data from telescopes have informed us that the universe is expanding. The rates of such expansion can be determined and scientists can extrapolate backwards and arrive at numbers that represent the beginning of this expansion. They call this beginning the Big Bang and at present the data suggest that it occurred approximately13.7 billion years ago. No one has an explanation for this "bang" or explosion and some believe that its cause(s) will never be understood. The age of the Earth is determined to be approximately 4.5 billion years, the sun having been formed prior to that. The oldest rocks identified on the Earth, in Northwest Territories, Canada, are dated at about 4.03 billion years. Cosmology, the branch of astronomy which studies the origin, structure and evolution of the universe, lies outside the mission of this book. The reader is encouraged to pursue this fascinating area of inquiry.

Additional Reading

Barrow, John D. & Tipler, Frank J. (1986). *The anthropic cosmological principle*. Oxford/New York: Oxford University Press.

Davies, Paul (1982). *The accidental universe*. Cambridge, NY: Cambridge University Press.

Davies, Paul (1992). *The mind of God: The scientific basis for a rational world*. New York: Simon & Schuster.

Davis, Percival & Kenyon, Dean H. (1993). *Of pandas and people: The central question of biological origins*. Dallas, TX: Haughton Publ. Co.

Ferguson, Kitty (1994). *The fire in the equations: Science, religion, and the search for God*. Grand Rapids, MI: Eerdmans Publ. Co.

Jaki, Stanley (1989). *God and the cosmologists*. Washington, DC: Regenery Gateway.

Margeneau, Henry & Varghese, Roy A. (1992). *Cosmos, bios, theos*. LaSalle, IL: Open Court.

Miller, Jonathan (1982). *Darwin for beginners*. New York: Pantheon Books.

Mixter, Russell (Ed.). (1959). *Evolution and Christian thought today*. Grand Rapids, MI: Wm B. Eerdmans Publ. Co.

Morris, Simon Conway (1998). *The crucible of creation: The Burgess shale and the rise of mammals*, Oxford: Oxford University Press.

Ratzch, Del (1986). *Philosophy of science: The natural sciences in Christian perspective*. Downer's Grove, IL: InterVarsity Press.

Rolston, Holmes III (1987). *Science and religion*. Philadelphia: Temple University Press.

Ross, Hugh (1992). *The fingerprint of God*. Pasadena, CA: Reason to Believe.

Schopf, J. William (1999). *Cradle of life: The discovery of Earth's earliest fossils*. Princeton: Princeton University Press.

Templeton, John M & Herrmann, Robert L. (1989). *The God who would be known*. New York: Harper & Row.

Templeton, John M. (Ed.). (1994). *Evidence of purpose: scientists discover the creator*. New York: Continuum.

Towne, Margaret G. (1995). *The influence of critical thinking on Christians' belief and belief change with reference to the polarities of creationism and organic evolution*. Doctoral Dissertation, Montana State University.

Foundations in Critical/ Careful Thinking

Chapter Two

Every truth has two sides; it is well to look at both, before we commit to either.
"The Mule" Fables Aesop (~620-560 B.C.) Greek Fabulist

Then he opened their minds. (Luke 24:45)
Prepare your minds for action. (I Peter 1:13)

Necessity for Critical Thinking

Traveling can be exciting, surprising, mind stretching, and risky, especially if the route ventures into new territory. A journey toward understanding the bases for evolutionary theory and how they integrate with the Christian faith requires a prayerful and open mind, one that is fearless, trusting that God is dependable and will faithfully lead into truth.

God has endowed us with minds which, although limited, are remarkable and can be used and trained for God's glory. The skills of critical (careful or disciplined) thinking can be very helpful in dealing with varied data, opinion, and interpretation. This is true especially when conflicting and numerous interpretations surround a particular thesis and it is difficult to discern which perspectives are more valid or credible. When the various dimensions of the complex issues of creationism and evolution are considered, the employment of clear thinking helps resolve many of the perplexities. It is certain that without the rigor of disciplined thinking the confusion and dissension that prevails with respect to these subjects will continue. The awesome human mind, without doubt a pinnacle of the created order, is therefore called into duty. Refusing to use the mind for any reason rejects one of the most astounding achievements of the created order.

It is the opinion of many that traditional education in the United States could have centered more on teaching students how to think, and to challenge and allow them to think for themselves. They have been fed a multitude of facts which were to be memorized and have not been informed as to how these facts were arrived at or if there were alternate means of interpreting them. They weren't encouraged to thoughtfully question. Sometimes there just wasn't time for that. Students should be instructed as to how to gather and assess data rigorously and then honestly go wherever it leads. They should be able to identify and admit error, recognize bias, consider all sides, and to humbly acknowledge a limited understanding of complex subjects. It is easy to unknowingly harbor prejudices and misinterpretations and often difficult to identify and acknowledge these weaknesses in thinking especially if one has been carefully indoctrinated into a discipline and only given one perspective. Rigorous training is required for the mind's fullest potential to be realized. The good news is that from pre-schools to graduate schools this is changing within our culture.

Many people prefer to have an authority of some kind tell them how to think rather than to persistently gather information from all sides and weigh it objectively for themselves. It takes a lot of time and effort to sift through all of the data on a subject and the easiest thing to do is just accept the conclusions of those who are either chosen or by default have become our authorities. Such secondhand conclusions may or may not have been based on informed and objective thinking.

Most concur that we do not often think about how we think (a discipline called metacognition) nor are we even aware of the level of expertise we have attained at careful thinking. Yet a Christian who recognizes that his or her mind is one of God's greatest creations and prayerfully uses it with skill and discipline can contribute considerably toward resolving many of the issues which cause conflict and confusion within Christendom. The lack or fear of careful thinking has more than once been detrimental to the church and dishonored its Lord in the past as will be noted in Chapter Five. Conscientious thinking is a prerequisite for resolving the conflicts which surround the creationism/organic evolution controversy. Contemporary Christians owe it to their Lord to develop and employ quality thinking as they weigh questions which seriously impact the kingdom.

Some selected, significant attributes of a careful thinker are here presented. While the reader considers the numerous theses throughout the present volume, a regular review of these characteristics can be a profitable exercise. Are these qualities being conscientiously employed? The reader is encouraged to apply these critical skills to this text and its assertions and conclusions. No one thinks in a critical manner consistently and flawlessly and the reader's peer review is welcomed. Everyone has biases. No author, scientist, or reader is free of them. We all need to continually improve our thinking skills.

Characteristics of Critical Thinking

Unbiased, Nonprejudicial

The person with this quality comes with an open mind. She has not previously formed an opinion and she works hard at listening objectively and weighing the data fairly from all sides. Her conclusions are based on the data, not on others' opinions or previous indoctrination, for even respected authorities may be biased. All sources are considered, all ideas evaluated and questioned with equal vigor. It is almost impossible to be totally objective but she can improve on this skill and learn to recognize when she is and when she is not practicing it. She must be determined to follow courageously and honestly where the data lead no matter where that might be and she must commit to rejecting prior belief, no matter how treasured, if it is not consistent with observed data.

Reserving Judgment

This quality enables the thinker to resist jumping to conclusions until all of the data are in, not always embracing the first approach that is presented. It is a natural tendency to prematurely form opinion based on minimal information and hearsay. Training and effort are required to develop the skill of patiently reserving judgment. In some situations a conclusion can never be formed because all of the data will not be available. Therefore it is necessary to be resigned and disciplined to living in a state of uncertainty or suspended judgment. A person may be uncomfortable in that position but it is a perfectly valid place to be if one is a critical thinker. A statement like "At this time I just don't know enough to form a conclusion" is a profound, honest and humble statement. It is absolutely permissible, respectable, scholarly, and necessary at times to admit, "I do not know."

Thinking Autonomously

This is the ability to think on one's own, to claim the freedom and exercise the responsibility of drawing conclusions from one's own experience and rigorous learning. No loyalty is promised to another person or institution, and there should be no guilt in practicing this independence. The inalienable right of autonomous thinking or having free will should be granted persons in church settings as well as in academic, political, family, or social environments.

A trained and disciplined (two basic qualities) critical thinker who considers all dimensions of a particular dilemma can enjoy emancipation from others' authoritarian views. This person is not cowed by dominating traditions, entrenched or outmoded interpretations, particular mindsets, or persuasive individuals and can take the risks associated with being a self-directed thinker. Such risks may include exclusion from the group, which can occur when an individual's conclusions differ from the group at large. Courage is often required. Autonomous thinkers regularly become aware of their limitations and recognize the need for others' input. They are free to thoughtfully choose appropriate authorities who help in weighing alternatives.

Many Christians use the phrase *"personal relationship with Jesus Christ."* That infers a unique relationship. Each of us is special, having a distinctive genetic endowment and original life experience. Our particular friendship with the Lord is unlike anyone else's. It is personal and it should therefore not be forced into a mold that has been designed by others. When everyone is expected to be and believe alike, the personal is denied and an *"identical relationship with Jesus Christ"* is inferred. Actually, Christians have a combination of both a personal and communal relationship with Christ. They enjoy the shared fellowship and communion of other believers as well as maintain a distinct and personal relationship with Christ, an autonomy which should never be eroded. It is interesting to contemplate the relationships Jesus enjoyed with various people: Peter, Thomas, Lazarus, Mary and Martha, the woman at the well, those he healed, those he comforted. Each was special, personal, unique.

Thinking Rationally

This quality eliminates points of view based on weak reasoning, prejudicial or insufficient data, stereotypes, distortions grounded in emotions, dogmatism, outmoded traditions, and illogical conclusions. The rational thinker identifies these conditions and honestly calls them what they are. This demands questioning, examining, probing, comparing, gathering evidence, analyzing, even doubting, and sometimes making painful judgments. As with autonomous thinking, yielding to rationality requires intellectual courage, one of the premier qualities of an accomplished thinker.

Understanding

When a thinker understands, he doesn't parrot back what someone else has said without knowing what it means. He can reword a concept and express it in his own way. He is grounded in the bases and rationale required for a conclusion. Understanding often requires integrating a variety of disciplines, which necessitates a solid foundation in each. It often demands intensive research on the subject which may take months, years, or even a lifetime.

Evaluating the Credibility of Sources

There are many opinions and interpretations offered on the controversial subjects of creationism and organic evolution. A thinker in this arena should question the credentials and expertise of a source. The seeker is not impressed by degrees alone but considers which degrees, from which institutions, the source's experience, associations, world view, possible biases, credibility, or whether he or she has an agenda. Is the source trying honestly to inform or is there attempted manipulation toward one position? Are all sides presented or just one viewpoint? Does the source expose the weaknesses and enigmas of all sides? Is she open to new perspectives or immovable? Does she claim to have "all truth?" In regard to printed matter or lectures, is a forum provided for interaction, discussion, questions, or peer review? This subject is treated in more depth in Chapter Three.

Does the source speak only to the data or does he label, or in any other way personally denigrate those of opposite opinion? Does he instill fear and discourage autonomous thinking? Critical thinkers must exercise the right to throw out any sources who they have fairly judged to be incompetent, dominating, biased or manipulative.

In the areas of creationism and evolution much interdisciplinary expertise is required. Someone with a doctorate in science and no formal study in religion, theology or biblical studies may be quite naïve and uninformed about significant aspects pertaining to these issues. Conversely, someone with credentials in theology may not be qualified to speak to scientific concerns. This is an interdisciplinary area where it is mandatory that authorities have training across the disciplines.

Avoiding Oversimplification and Generalizations

The critical thinker acknowledges the complexity of a problem and recognizes that simple, superficial answers are insufficient. She clarifies issues and avoids sweeping, unsubstantiated generalizations.

A Healthy Attitude Toward Error: Humility

Admitting that longstanding beliefs can possibly be incorrect is a requisite for growth in any discipline. The responsible thinker graciously and honestly acknowledges misconceptions or erroneous conclusions or beliefs and moves on. Just as maturity is noted when children see the falsehood of the Santa Claus myth so should Christians grow in their understanding of spiritual things.

Having the humility and courage to acknowledge error and subsequently to modify belief are routine outcomes for the serious, maturing thinker. This passion for truth leads to growth and is exciting, liberating, and honoring to our Lord! The Apostle Paul is a premier example of this. He took an about face on the Damascus Road, moving from a position of persecuting Christians and affirming the death of Stephen to becoming one of Christianity's greatest evangelists. The church in the past admitted it was wrong in assuming the Earth was flat and the center of the solar system. Its practice of collecting indulgences and its affirmation of slavery were recognized as inappropriate and terminated. Individuals and organizations regularly become better informed, grow, adapt, and change.

Christians can determine to make the Bible and the faith relevant to the contemporary world. There are many dynamic Christian environments that encourage this kind of inquiry and independent thought and those who are serious about careful thinking might seek them out. Some say they are "reformed yet always reforming" as they gain new light from scripture. Searching Christians with open minds, praying hearts, and the courage to go where the data lead are welcomed to this study.

Not long ago I spoke on the telephone with my 88 year old father who was in a nursing home. He had just finished reading an article in a Christian magazine. "You know, the author's view is different from what we were always taught," he said. After a pause came, "In fact, it is quite radical!" Another pause and he declared "But you know, I think he's *right!*" I cannot but admire in this elderly Christian the critical thinking qualities of intellectual courage, humility, and honesty, as well as his openmindedness. It is not easy for many to admit, at any age, that they do not have all truth, that they are wrong. This welcoming of a new perspective instead of fearing it is a model for the whole church so that we can rightly divide the word of truth. "Do your best to present yourself to God as one approved, a workman who does not need to be ashamed and who correctly handles the word of truth" (II Timothy 2:15).

Welcoming Novel Ideas: Openmindedness

The thinking of Christians in the past should always be prayerfully and fairly considered, however individuals must claim the right to think independently or listen to new heralds as a God-given right and use that right to honor God in any way they can. Accomplished thinkers are willing to entertain other viewpoints without reacting defensively. Fresh approaches to thinking often result in growth and new insight and this should be encouraged throughout Christendom. God is active in the world and has progressively revealed truth through the centuries. God shows us "new and hidden things which we have not known before" (Jeremiah 33:3). Jesus himself was a new idea and he, too, met with severe opposition. Modification of tradition or the status quo is usually threatening and therefore resisted.

The Freedom to Doubt

Traditionally, the Christian world has not always affirmed questioners or doubters. Doubt is often seen as a negative quality in the religious setting, yet through doubt a person is forced to think and often through thinking one arrives at truth. Furthermore, scripture affirms that "great is the *mystery* of godliness" (I Timothy 3:16). No one understands it all perfectly. Doubt and questioning are normal responses of conscientious thinkers. Authoritarian environments prevail in many religious settings with established views on various issues, and sometimes little affirmation is given to those who wish to independently and carefully think, even in areas that are not central to the faith. Requiring individuals to conform to and strictly abide by beliefs that are peripheral to the faith for inclusion into a church, organization, or institution is not uncommon. Conformity is rewarded when individuals express the accepted position on homosexuality, abortion, evolution, the death penalty, the role of women in the church, dancing, biblical inerrancy, type and time of baptism, dispensationalism, and a host of other issues. Tolerance for belief disparity or doubt is often quite limited within church settings. Exclusion prevails for those who cannot conform, and there is bondage rather than liberty of thought. Yet many recognize the truth that "he or she who never thinks, never doubts!"

The Affective Domain: Employing Emotion

Accomplished thinkers exhibit certain attitudes, states of mind, commitments, and passions. These affective qualities, along with the rational ones, are essential to the application of higher order thinking in real life settings. Such qualities as humility, courage, integrity, perseverance, humor, and curiosity are requisite in the practice of careful thinking. Critical thinkers appreciate creativity, see the future as malleable and open, not static, and have the self-confidence to endure or even welcome change. They exude a sense that life is full of possibilities. They do not think that they "have arrived" and "have all truth." Their Christian experience is seen as a journey. With God as their guide they may experience new and exotic places!

Additional Reading

Adler, M. & Van Doren, C. (1972). *How to read a book.* New York: Simon & Schuster.

Barnet, Sylvan & Bedau, Hugo (2002). *Current issues and enduring questions* (6th ed.). Boston: Bedford/St. Martin's.

Baron, Joan & Sternberg, Robert (1987). *Teaching thinking skills: Theory and practice.* New York: W. H. Freeman Co.

Barry, Vincent E. & Rudinow, Joel (1990). *Invitation to critical thinking* (2nd ed.). New York: Holt, Rinehart & Winston.

Beyer, B. K. (1987). *Practical strategies for the teaching of thinking.* Boston: Allyn & Bacon.

Bloom, Allan (1987). *The closing of the American mind.* New York: Simon & Schuster.

Brookfield, S. (1987). *Developing critical thinkers.* San Francisco: Jossey-Bass.

Chaffee, J. (1985). *Thinking critically.* Boston: Houghton Mifflin.

Conway, David A. & Munson, Ronald (1997). *The elements of reasoning* (2nd ed.). Belmont, CA: Wadsworth Publishing Co.

de Bono, E. (1993). *Teach your child how to think.* New York: Viking Penguin.

Ennis, R. H. (1962). A concept of critical thinking. *Harvard Educational Review, 32,* 81-111.

Dewey, J. (1933). *How we think.* New York: DC Heath.

Freire, P. (1973). *Education for critical consciousness.* New York: The Seabury Press.

Gardner, Howard (1999). *The disciplined mind.* New York: Simon & Schuster.

Hitchcock, D. (1983). *Critical thinking: A guide to evaluating information.* New York: Methven.

Hoagland, John (1984). *Critical thinking.* Newport News, VA: Vale Press.

Hull, J. M. (1985). *What prevents Christian adults from learning?* London: SCM Press.

Kelley, David (1998). *The art of reasoning* (3rd ed.). New York: W. W. Norton & Co.

King, P. M. (1992). How do we know? Why do we believe? Learning to make reflective judgments. *Liberal Education, 78,* 2-9.

Meyers, C. (1986). *Teaching students to think critically.* San Francisco: Jossey-Bass.

Mezirow, J. (1991). *Fostering critical reflection in adulthood: A guide to transformative and emancipatory learning.* San Francisco: Jossey-Bass.

Moore, Brooke (1989). *Critical thinking: Evaluating Claims and arguments in everyday life* (2nd ed.). Palo Alto, CA: Mayfield Publishing Co.

Norris, Stephen P. & Ennis, Robert H. (1989). *Evaluating critical thinking.* Pacific Grove, CA: Midwest Publications.

Paul, R. W. (1993). *Critical thinking: How to prepare students for a rapidly changing world.* Santa Rosa, CA: The Foundation for Critical Thinking.

Penaskovic, Richard (1997). *Critical thinking and the academic study of religion.* Atlanta: Scholars Press.

Pelikan, J. (1965). *The Christian intellectual.* New York: Harper & Row.

Resnick, Lauren (1987). *Education and learning to think.* Washington, DC: National Academy Press.

Ruggiero, V. R. (1975). *Beyond feelings: A guide to critical thinking.* New York: Alfred.

Sire, James W. (2000). *Habits of the mind: Intellectual life as a Christian calling.* Downers Grove, IL: InterVarsity Press.

The NIV (New International Version) Study Bible (1995). Grand Rapids, MI: Zondervan Publishing House.

Who Are Your Authorities?

Chapter Three

We should believe nothing in either sphere of thought which does not appear to us to be certified by solid reasons based upon the critical research either of ourselves or of competent authorities.

Alfred North Whitehead, Science and the Modern World. *(p. 184)*

The subjects of creationism, organic evolution, science, scripture interpretation, faith, and belief encompass a tremendous amount of information with technical data and terminology from several disciplines. Years of dedicated study are required for one to become knowledgeable and expert on these issues, thoroughly grasping and sifting all the subtle arguments and myriad explanations. Very few have the time, training, or inclination to personally pursue these subjects in depth and therefore most rely on others who weigh the data, clarify and interpret for them. The sources they follow become their authorities, and they must be evaluated and chosen openmindedly, thoughtfully, and very carefully. It is insightful to all who search for an understanding of these subjects to identify the authorities who have influenced their beliefs to date.

Inherited/Inadvertent and Chosen Authorities

There are two general kinds of authorities: (a) inherited, or inadvertent, and (b) chosen. Inherited authorities are those who inadvertently, or by chance, enter our lives. They teach and influence us without our having consciously chosen them for that purpose. Parents, siblings, grandparents, neighbors, teachers (including Sunday school teachers), pastors, the media such as TV or the local newspaper, or even friends can be this kind of authority. A father may be a wonderful parent but quite ill informed about cars, yet we will listen to his opinions on cars because he is an intelligent and respected parent. A grandmother may be an extremely loving person who teaches us about the Bible and we listen, not because we have chosen her as an authority on the scriptures but because we dearly love her, recognize her as a committed Christian, and know she would not knowingly deceive us. We assume that since she is wise in many areas her knowledge must be dependable here, too.

A pastor or seminary professor whom we highly esteem as a gifted man or woman of God may teach us about evolution yet if that person is not trained in science he or she is probably unqualified to speak authoritatively on that subject. Conversely, doctorates in science who are not sophisticated in biblical scholarship can be equally unqualified as authorities on the biblical interpretation of creation accounts. In all of these instances authorities may be heeded, not because of their proficiency in knowledge of cars, the Bible, theology or evolution, but because they are present in our lives, care about us, are respected and liked, even loved. They automatically gain and claim authority status without question.

Chosen authorities, on the other hand, are those whose credibility on a particular subject has been consciously evaluated and we have chosen to listen to them based on valid criteria. We can ultimately agree or disagree with their opinions but we know that they have a recognized expertise on a subject and their opinions are judged worthy of consideration. These authorities are not chosen because they are particularly loved or have any other sentimental attachment but because in that particular area they are deemed worth listening to. They may be authors, teachers, scholars, journalists, or everyday people who have a recognized expertise. It is important to note that a chosen authority can indeed be a parent, sister, pastor, or friend, but they have been chosen as authoritative for a particular area and did not inadvertently gain that status.

Many people go through life almost exclusively with inherited authorities who are never questioned. Seldom, if ever, do these individuals choose new authorities and replace the old ones. The thought never occurs to them. They are not skeptical of the opinions of the members of their family, friends, neighbors, congregants at church, TV evangelists or radio preachers, various authors, or colleagues in the workplace. They do not challenge local or national policies, religious leaders, or the teachers or professors to whom they have been assigned. They are at the mercy, so to speak, of the influences that just happen to have come into their lives.

Others, realizing that critically thought-out conclusions cannot be arrived at individually in so many areas of life, seek expert opinion, carefully choosing who their authorities will be based upon the training, demonstrated expertise and reputation those individuals have achieved. They personally choose these authorities, always retaining the option to throw them out at any point. They freely challenge, question, or doubt the information they receive. They request substantiation and a rational basis for assertions. Those who choose their authorities understand the necessity at times to exclude the opinions of significant people in their lives such as parents, spouses, teachers, or pastors because they honestly and objectively recognize them as being ill equipped to address certain issues.

Christians must be especially careful choosing authorities. By our very culture much of our religious training as children comes from inherited authorities whom we have not chosen: parents, grandparents, Sunday school teachers, pastors, camp counselors, a particular denomination, authors, or the radio or television personalities who have gained the airwaves at that specific time. As we mature we should consider their qualifications in various areas and, if necessary, replace them with more competent authorities, and we should replace them without guilt. We should seek out those with opposite opinions and honestly consider their data and conclusions. Any environment that does not encourage such an effort must be seriously challenged. It may be coercive, narrow, dogmatic, or dominating and rely on fear to retain allegiance.

This kind of discernment should be exercised when considering authorities on the subjects of evolution and creationism. We are bombarded with perspectives from a variety of sources and it is not easy for the layperson to decide whose opinions should be considered. We tend to give credence to those in the faith, regardless of their qualifications, rather than scientists who may not be Christian, assuming that Christians would not deceive us or have an agenda. We sometimes prefer those we judge to have a close walk with God over those who demonstrably understand the scholarship on this subject yet are not particularly devout. We might not be aware of those who are subtly trying to persuade us and we can fall for arguments that have been cunningly designed. We may choose incompetent authorities who are readily available over those who we would have to pursue with effort and time.

Since most of us are not expert theologians or accomplished in the specific fields of science pertaining to evolution and creationism, the positions we take usually depend upon the authorities who have entered our lives. If we fail to assess them carefully, we may incorporate beliefs that are without basis; this can be detrimental to the credible witness of the church.

Choosing Authorities

1. Inquire about the credentials of potential authorities. Are they well informed scientifically as well as theologically? Note that many who write as authorities on the subjects of creationism and evolution are either not trained in science or not trained in theology. Many are not trained in either. Few have a grasp of both disciplines from a professional perspective. Have they personally studied this material and originally and

critically considered it or are they just parroting THEIR authorities? Academic credentials in fields other than theology, biology, chemistry, anthropology, geology, or paleontology do not insure a deep knowledge of these issues. Medical doctors, dentists, lawyers or doctors in many other disciplines have not been formally trained in the specifics of these particular scientific and theological issues. It is always possible, however, that a person has become expert on these subjects outside of his or her formal education. The point is that degrees alone should not impress. One should ask which degrees, from what institutions. A doctoral degree represents training in depth in a specific area but it does not ensure expertise in other fields. A cardiologist is a layperson in geology or theology. Paleontologists and geologists are laypersons in theology. Some would-be authorities claim doctorates from unaccredited or even nonexistent institutions.

Inquirers should ask what training has been received that would equip authorities in this specialized area. It is of interest if their training comes from religious institutions that require unanimity of belief, for they may never have been exposed to alternative data or encouraged to consider opposing perspectives. They may not have been encouraged to think autonomously on these questions. Some Christians have been home schooled, then attended church related schools, and have been indoctrinated into one perspective. They may never have been exposed to the data of modern evolutionary theory or to other theological interpretations and therefore are not qualified to be spokespersons for these significant issues.

2. Has their scholarship been subjected to and withstood rigorous peer review by both the scientific and theological communities? Anyone can write a book and pay for its printing. Having a book published does not mean that it has withstood broad editorial review. Note the publishers of books. Some organizations own their own publishing house so their books and journals have not been exposed to extensive critical review. Articles in scholarly, reputable journals are vulnerable to the challenge of peer review and often considerable interaction is generated in subsequent issues of the journal or in other forums. Look for opportunities for responses to assertions or critique opportunities in writings being considered. Many religious organizations that have a particular agenda do not provide a forum for critical reader response. When there is never dissent, be wary.

3. Do they assume certain conclusions without having valid scientific data to support them? This is where the astute seeker, for example, can spot the scientist who goes beyond science and inserts philosophy into a thesis suggesting there is no purpose or creator and that everything got here by pure chance. On the other hand, creationists claim supernatural miracle for explanation. Neither claim can be demonstrated empirically. They are philosophical or religious beliefs, not science, and they should be recognized as such.

4. Is absolute truth claimed on the subject? These issues encompass many areas where dogmatic statements cannot be made, areas that are not and may never be completely understood. Do they freely disclose the uncertainties and limitations of their model? Do they come as seekers or knowers? Judgment should be reserved for anyone who claims to have it all together without question. Intellectual humility and honesty are important qualities for authorities to possess.

5. Do potential authorities encourage autonomous thinking or do they expect that their thinking will be affirmed without question? Are they eager to suggest sources that present all sides of the question or do they discourage such balanced research?

6. Do they offer only two options; (a) six-day, young Earth creationism or (b) evolutionary naturalism, which holds that there is no God, no design, and we got here by chance? There is a third position: theistic evolution. Those who are uninformed about this option or who purposely avoid it should be seriously questioned. Do they squelch this perspective out of fear? If they are open to truth, why do they fear? Do they understand that a theistic evolutionary position in no way negates the need for a savior?

7. Are they able to let the facts stand on their own or do they have a prior belief to which the facts must conform? Can they go wherever the data lead or must they fit the data into a preconceived model? Do they come with a prior belief in a <u>literal</u> reading of the Bible and then force all data into that model?

8. Do potential authorities have an open mind towards new data or the reinterpretation of old data? Are they closed-minded about even considering a figurative, theological interpretation of Genesis 1 and 2? Are they in bondage to "the old-time religion" and how they've always thought? Do they have a bias for the teachings of past Bible teachers and

preachers, suggesting that they had more truth than modern biblical scholars? Are they unwilling to even listen to a new viewpoint?

9. Do authorities being considered belittle, label, or question the spirituality of those who hold other opinions? Do they argue against the people rather than against the ideas of those people?

10. Do they expose and admit past errors? Do they freely correct these errors in journals, seminars, books, and debates, intent on the truth, or do they ignore them?

11. If they are scientists, do they acknowledge the limitations of the scientific method? Do they know when they have left the arena of empirical science (capable of being demonstrated or observed or substantially inferred) and have entered philosophical naturalism? Are they impatient with doubters? If they are theologians, do they understand where science begins and its requirements for supporting data?

Christians have a responsibility in this complex world to be honest to data, open to new perspectives, and willing to admit error. Additional data or new interpretations of old data can be met with an open mind, not dominated by prior belief to which the new ideas or data must conform. They must honestly weigh all the information available and with intellectual humility be willing to reserve judgment if conclusions cannot be drawn. They may need to exercise courage and honesty by modifying belief if the data demand it. Actually, this is growth! They must be deeply committed to using their minds as well as their hearts on important subjects that have the potential to be destructive and divisive within the Christian milieu. They must prayerfully and carefully choose proper authorities.

God the creator will not be inconsistent with God the author of scripture. Sometimes alternative scriptural interpretation is necessary as God's progressive revelation becomes clear, often presented through the medium of new scientific insights. A critical thinker is perennially free in the future to replace authorities if the data so dictate. Loyalty resides with the truth. Unquestioned loyalty to people, a cherished era, prior belief, a particular biblical interpretation or translation, or a denomination or institution represents bondage. Loyalty to truth is liberating. "The truth will set you free" (John 8:32).

> *Read not to contradict and confute,*
> *nor to believe and take for granted...*
> *but to weigh and consider. —Francis Bacon*

Belief and Faith

Chapter Four

Facts can be rejected if they don't fit with our beliefs.
Anonymous

In the English language the terms faith and belief are often used interchangeably. Definition distinctions between these two concepts have become quite blurred. Other words, such as opinion, knowledge, and even religion are also used as synonyms for faith or belief. It is not uncommon for someone to ask "What is your religion?" and mean "To what faith do you belong?" These questions often equate with "What do you believe?" or "What is your opinion?" Is one's belief or religion based on faith or opinion or knowledge or all three? Is there a difference between faith and belief?

Belief

Since the primary subject of this book, theistic evolution, is a belief position, upon what basis is it formulated? This question could be asked of creationism or evolutionary naturalism as well. Is empirical (derived from actual observation or experimentation) knowledge a necessary undergirding for a belief position, or is faith enough? What directs us, often subconsciously, to attitudes, opinions and belief positions? These are important questions. Since the conflict between creationism and evolution is quite divisive it is worth analyzing how such diametrically opposed conclusions can be drawn by equally conscientious Christians. How could two sincere, intelligent, devout, searching Christians arrive at opposite destinations? What are the bases for their conflicting conclusions?

If an individual requires rational, empirical data to hold a particular belief position, such a person will embrace a conclusion if adequate support is provided and reject it if it is unsubstantiated, even if it is affirmed by a supposed authority. If another person does not demand evidence but is willing to base a belief on an authority's statement, or be influenced by an authority's charisma, then it is clear that the foundations for belief in these two situations are quite different. The latter is based on faith in the opinion or conclusion of an authority rather than on personally observed data that leads to an autonomous conclusion. If the authority who influences one individual has a faulty base and the other individual accurately interprets valid data, then it is easy to see how two searching Christians could end up with opposing views.

Creationist belief originally was solely founded on the authority of a literal reading of the scriptures, and until the 19th Century most accepted that means of biblical interpretation with regard to origins. When scientists found data that appeared to contradict the literal biblical assertions many Christians began to base their belief on observable evidence rather than upon faith in an ancient, prescientific, literal authority. This duality continues: creationists cannot extricate themselves from affirming the authority of a literal interpretation of Genesis 1-11, and other Christians base their belief on observed or inferred scientific data, diligently searching all the while for the nonliteral, profound, *theological* messages of the early chapters of Genesis.

The culture respected and was dominated by science in the 20th Century and many have seen the validity of scientific methodology. Creationists try to correlate the Genesis accounts with a scientific perspective and have even coined the term "creation science" to give authenticity to their endeavors. They attempt to convince others of their beliefs by 1) trying to demonstrate them empirically with scientific proof, 2) attacking or ignoring evolutionary evidence or dwelling on what has not yet been proven and hoping to win, so to speak, by default, or 3) claiming the literal authority of Genesis by faith, sometimes against all reason. Chapters Nine and Ten seek to show that they fail at both 1) and 2), and are left with option 3), which is dealt with in Chapter Six.

The scientific culture recognizes the human mind as a phenomenal tool for answering questions that have haunted the species from time immemorial. It demands rigorous rationality, objectivity, and grounds for belief, and respects the data that can be gleaned through scientific method. It places less value on beliefs formed apart from these tools, which are often arrived at subjectively. They are vulnerable to the whim of the interpreter and often include unexplainable and untestable theses.

In this information-laden society new data often require change of belief. The 20th Century saw more change and demanded more adaptability and thought revision than any other period of history. Persons of eighty years can trace back to a time before antibiotics and vaccinations, cell phones, jet travel, television, computers, freeways, the space age, roller coasters, genetic engineering, organ transplants, weather science, nuclear and biological weapons, worldwide communication and innumerable other phenomena that significantly impacted life and enlarged world views. That dynamic era provided both the excitement and the pain of change. Some changes were helpful and easy to accept such as dishwashers, air conditioning, and innovations in medicine. Others, such as legal and technological complexities, new terminologies and procedures, were not as welcome. Expansion, modification or elimination of theological, ethical, moral, or other belief positions were often resisted, sometimes vigorously. Racial and gender equality, for example, required much effort for some.

The Christian church was not free from change in the 20th Century. Novel means of expressing faith and of understanding how God is at work in the world, fresh challenges in meeting its commission to interpret the life and teachings of Jesus, and integrating new technologies into the presentation of the ageless tenets of the faith demanded much adaptation. Innovative types and times of worship, new liturgies, massive evangelistic campaigns, culturally inclusive hymnody with exotic accompaniments, myriad biblical translations, new architecture, televised church, and women in leadership caused adjustment and in some settings were met with resistance. There is comfort in the old and familiar. It becomes harder and harder to find consensus when everyone is at a different adjustment level with respect to perpetual change.

If within Christendom unanimity of belief is beyond the realm of possibility then the conflict among Christians can somewhat be ameliorated by all parties acknowledging that variety of belief and faith expression is extant and with humility and Christian grace admitting that no group has all truth. Reconciliation may also come if all accept their position as that of seekers and not always knowers. There would no doubt be less attack and dissension if Christians agreed to disagree. This increased tolerance for belief disparity would engender more unity within Christendom. Bonuses from such inclusiveness include individual growth in love and understanding and a positive witness to the non-Christian world that love indeed rules.

Christians who are trained in science may be more prone to require empirical evidence for a belief position on subjects such as evolution and creationism. They may also need more tangible evidence to commit to the religious life because the culture in which they have been immersed demands a knowledge base for conclusions and commitments. They look to the historical church which has withstood persecution for centuries and yet prevails. They see the self sacrificial living of many devoted Christians as witness to a power beyond themselves. They are aware of the positive influence that Christianity had on the formation of our democratic culture and laws such as those that endorse respect for the individual. Hospitals, relief organizations, and institutions of higher learning that came out of the faith commitment of many are recognized. The scriptures are respected as a remarkable compilation of writings that have universal application and relevance throughout the centuries. They acknowledge the historical Jesus.

With this base it is easier to take the required step of faith to recognize this Jesus as Lord and Savior.

Other Christians, through different training, may not require these foundations for their religious beliefs. They will more readily accept the assertions of certain authorities without question or respond to emotional appeal. Most Christians do not require that their faith or beliefs be grounded on provable evidence, for it is the very nature of faith to step out without being able to understand everything.

Many other factors play a role in the way one comes to belief, such as genetics, myriad life experiences in the home, culture, or church, and psychological factors, some subtle, some obvious, and some undescribed. The time of life one is in, particular friends, or even world events can wield significant influence on belief positions.

Those who study the creationism/evolution controversy are interested in what factors contribute to different ways of thinking. Among those that have been noted are comfort zones whereby the seeker chooses a belief that has the least stress or novelty and demands minimal adjustment or change. A new idea is automatically rejected and tradition and the familiar remain at all costs. Some are convinced that they already have the truth and nothing else needs to be considered.

Many people form opinion or belief based upon the authority who happens to introduce the paradigm to them first. It has been shown that a likable, familiar, affirming, friendly presenter may win converts to his or her position merely on the basis of communication skills, charisma, and personality, regardless of the data. Some follow a dominating, assertive, confident authority especially if they have been accustomed to authoritarian pronouncements. They are vulnerable to the conformity often insinuated by this method of instruction. Others form belief after a mindful, critical assessment of the data, and distinguish the messenger from the message.

The attitude that seekers bring to new material is significant. Those who have been indoctrinated with beliefs that are seen as ultimate truth will resist new data. Individuals who fear new perspectives, or are unwilling to expend the time and effort to consider new paradigms, or who have significant people in their lives who they know will be displeased if they stray from an established belief may subconsciously reject new perspectives and authorities. Others, who enjoy a freedom to think autonomously and are affirmed in belief change, who have a passion for truth and who do not fear where it leads, will have less stress in change, may find it exhilarating and even welcome it.

Many religious milieus have well-constructed belief parameters demanding conformity, and adherents tend to respond to them in a routine fashion. They willingly assent to subscribed tenets and are discouraged from any irregularity of belief that might arise from autonomous thinking or new data. Other religious environments encourage conscious choice and affirm alternate belief especially on less critical issues. A particular religious acculturation often subtly and unknowingly dictates how an individual responds to new information.

People regularly believe things that are not true or disbelieve things that are true. For centuries a flat Earth and geocentrism (the Earth as the center of the universe) was accepted by the masses, both untrue. Individual point of view is often mistaken for reality. Belief is often ungrounded and subjectively developed. As individuals and in groups facts can be unknowingly confused with hearsay and valid data with the interpretations of unqualified authority figures.

Belief tends to be dominant over evidence based knowledge in some religious circles. This is understandable because some tenets which are basic to the faith are indeed accepted by faith. Jesus as the Messiah, Savior of the world, is accepted by faith. In parts of this journey we walk by faith, not sight (II Corinthians 5:7). However, religious belief is often reduced to accepting what those around us believe, with little demand for grounds. It is clearly exemplified in the interfacing of evolutionary theory with biblical origin stories. Differing perspectives are not sought and beliefs are protected from objectivity and reason. This condition is supported by what is perceived to be faith: belief without evidence. It is almost intimated that the weaker the evidence and the stronger the belief then the greater the faith! A pastor friend has a framed poster on his wall which states, "He died to take away our sins, not our minds!"

One theory that speaks to belief formation centers around the terms mindfulness and mindlessness. They can be summarized in the following manner:

Mindlessness	Mindfulness
Automatic response to environmental cues, knee jerk response	Reasoned judgment
Minimal cognitive involvement	Processes information

Routine response; less opportunity for change	Open to novelty; less stable, often resulting in change
Dogmatically indoctrinated	Given freedom for autonomous thought; conscious choice
Opinions formed without evidence; superficial; emotionally held opinions	Long and thoughtful inquiry; deep
Judgmentalism	Judgment

Palmerino, Langer and McGillis, 1984

If religious settings do not encourage mindfulness, then many Christians will be exercising mindlessness in their faith choices. Their fervent beliefs may be confused with knowledge or proof. Knowing is different from believing. If the reasons are strong and proven, one knows. If evidence is lacking or incomplete, one believes. Justification is required for knowledge, but not always for belief.

The astute reader will appreciate the way this relates to critical thinking. A culture that is deficient in encouraging students to require justification for what they are taught will suffer as mindlessness flourishes. A religious setting that discourages questioning, doubt, or alternative interpretation and rewards blind faith produces passive learners who do not and cannot grow. Too often, what we believe is a mirror image of what those around us believe. Collective delusion can occur in a culture.

Faith

Within the Christian milieu faith and belief are often used interchangeably. Individuals are described as "believers," which infers they are people of faith or religious. Yet the two words have distinctive origins, etiologies and definitions. Faith is described by many Christian authors and theologians as a word of action. It differs from belief in that beliefs vary from religion to religion or denomination to denomination; they are tenets to which one gives intellectual assent. Beliefs can be arrived at easily, although not always, and be held with little risk, although not always. Faith, on the other hand, demands action, commitment, risk, struggle, quest, engagement, participation, and sometimes the willingness to give one's life. We hear about "Bible-believing churches." What about "Bible-*faithing* churches?"

It is not surprising that the eleventh chapter of Hebrews in the New Testament, a text traditionally referred to as the "faith chapter," includes many action verbs: offered, pleased, built, obeyed, went, made, spoke, conquered, administered, prepared, worshipped, chose, received. Faith is associated with action. It requires and is authenticated by deeds and is made complete by what we *do*, not by what we believe (James 2:22 "Faith without works is dead."). Faith is constant, a state of ultimate concern, not whimsical or subject to feelings.

Faith is where we put dreams and our best energy. For it we pour out our lives and realize our most sacred hopes. It is our source of serenity and courage. It defines our centers of value. It is routinely sustained by a religious tradition and grounded in a source beyond ourselves. It is what makes life meaningful, the quality of human living. It is what gives strength in daily life and carries us though the darkest night of perplexity and sorrow. The phenomenon of faith crosses religious barriers and is consistent in many and varied life and cultural settings.

Unlike faith, belief is subject to change. Ironically, in some settings in the present religious milieu belief appears to be valued more than faith. What one believes is more significant than whether one has lived a life of faith. The absence of the expression and fruitfulness of faith is forgiven far more quickly than what is perceived as faulty or doubtful belief. Parents will rigorously check out the beliefs of a young man their daughter brings home. If they conform he is accepted even though faith expressed by a life of service or sacrificial commitment is missing. They are often less accepting if the latter is present, yet there is disparity of belief.

Belief positions on the theory of evolution, theistic evolution, and creationism are extremely important within some Christian settings. They can personally divide Christian brother from Christian sister and impact the unity of a family, friendship, church or denomination. They are seen as important enough to terminate a pastor's ministry, break up relationships, or risk a witness of disunity within the body of Christ throughout the world. Some suggest that if Christians were half as concerned about demanding and living lives of self-sacrificial faith that honors their Lord as they are about beliefs on origins, that Christianity would be much stronger and far more appealing to a world that yearns for academic honesty and rigor, tolerance, inclusion, hope, good works, purpose, and something for which to live and die.

Additional Reading

Braithwaite, R. B. (1991). An empiricist's view of the nature of religious belief. In E. D. Klemke (Ed.), *To Believe or Not to Believe: Readings in the Philosophy of Religion* (pp. 446-457). New York: Harcourt Brace Jovanovich.

Cartwright, D. (1972). Achieving change in people: Some applications of group dynamics theory. In G. Zaltman, P. Kotler & I. Kaufman (Eds.), *Creating Social Change* (pp. 74-82). New York: Holt, Rinehart & Winston.

Easton, W. B., Jr. (1957). *Basic Christian beliefs*. Philadelphia: Westminster Press.

Crocker, J., Fiske, S. T. & Taylor, S. E. (1984). Schematic basis of belief change. In R. Eiser (Ed.), *Attitudinal Judgment* (pp. 197-226). New York: Springer-Verlag.

Doob, L.W. (1940). Some factors determining change in attitude. *Journal of Abnormal and Social Psychology, 35*, 549-565.

Festinger, L. (1964). Behavioral support for opinion change. *Public Opinion Quarterly, 28.* 404-417.

Fowler, J. W. (1981). *Stages of faith: The psychology of human development and the quest for meaning*. San Francisco: Harper & Row.

Freire, P. (1973). *Education for critical consciousness*. New York: The Seabury Press.

Gordon, G. N. (1971). *Persuasion: The theory and practice of manipulative communication*. New York: Hastings House.

Helfaer, P. M. (1972). *The psychology of religious doubt*. Boston: Beacon Press.

Highlander Research and Education Center: An approach to education presented through a collection of writings. (1989). New Market, TN.

Hoffer, E. (1963). *The ordeal of change*. New York: Harper & Row.

Hull, J. M. (1985). *What prevents Christian adults from learning?* London: SCM Press.

Insko, C. A. (1967). *Theories of attitude change*. New York: Appleton-Century-Crofts.

James, W. (1956). *The will to believe and other essays in popular philosophy*. New York: Dover.

Karlins, M. & Abelson, H. I. (1970). *Persuasion: How opinions and attitudes are changed*, (2nd ed.). New York: Springer.

Kelly, H. H. & Volkhart, E. H. (1952). The resistance to change of group-anchored attitudes. *American Sociological Review, 17*, 453-465.

Kiesler, C. A., Collins, B. E. & Miller, N. (1969). *Attitude change: A critical analysis of theoretical approaches*. New York: John Wiley & Son.

Kitchener, K. S. & King, P. M. (1991). Reflective judgment: Concepts of justification and their relationship to age and education. *Journal of Applied Developmental Psychology, 2*.

Lawson, A. E. & Worsnop, W. A. (1992). Learning about evolution and rejecting a belief in special creation: Effects of reflective reasoning skill, prior knowledge, prior belief, and religious commitment. *Journal of Research in Science Teaching, 29* (2), 143-166.

Lindquist, J. (1978). *Strategies for change*. Berkeley, CA: Pacific Sounding Press.

Lord, C. G., Ross, L. & Lepper, M. R. (1979). Biased assimilation and attitude polarization: The effects of prior theories on subsequently considered evidence. *Journal of Personality and Social Psychology, 37* (1), 2098-2109.

McCroskey, J. C. (1969). A summary of experimental research on the effects of evidence in persuasive communication. *The Quarterly Journal of Speech, 55*, 169-176.

Mezirow, J. (1990). *Fostering critical reflection in adulthood: A guide to transformative and emancipatory learning.* San Francisco: Jossey-Bass.

Morley, D. D. (1987). The role of importance, novelty, and plausibility in producing belief change. *Communication Monographs, 54,* 183-203.

Palmerino, M., Langer, E. & McGillis, D (1984). Attitudes and attitude change: Mindlessness-mindfulness perspective. In J. R. Eiser (Ed.), *Attitudinal judgment* (pp. 179-193.). New York: Springer-Verlag.

Paul, R. W., 1993. *Critical thinking: How to prepare students for a rapidly changing world.* Santa Rosa, CA: The Foundation for Critical Thinking.

Poole, M. (1990). Beliefs and values in science education: A Christian perspective (Part I). *School Science Review, 71,* 25-32.

Popper, K. R. (1979). *Truth, rationality, and the growth of knowledge.* Vittorio Klostermann Frankfurt am Main.

Reynolds, R. A. & Burgoon, M. (1983). Belief processing, reasoning, evidence. *Communication Reviews and Commentaries, 7,* 83-104.

Rokeach, M. (1960). *The open and closed mind: Investigations into the nature of belief systems and personality systems.* New York: Basic Books.

Watson, G. (1972). Resistance to change. In G. Zaltman, P., Kotler & I. Kaufman (Eds.), *Creating Social Change* (pp. 610-618). New York: Holt, Rinehart & Winston.

Wright, P. H. (1966). Attitude change under direct and indirect interpersonal influence. *Human Relations, 19,* 199-211.

Zaltman, G., Kotner, P. & Kaufman, I. (1972). *Achieving change in people: Some applications of group dynamics theory.* New York: Holt, Rinehart & Winston.

Historical Perspective

Chapter Five

Traditionally, the Bible was the means by which the world was perceived. Following the Enlightenment, the world became the means by which the Bible was understood.

Theologian Brevard Childs, Interpreting the Bible Amid Cultural Change, *p. 201*

Introduction

When misunderstanding prevails, a historical perspective can often clarify issues by explaining their origins and the factors that have led to present day conflicts. This chapter seeks to briefly outline some of the events that have contributed to the disagreements over origins which are seen within the Christian world. Hopefully such insight will contribute to their resolution.

Science, the attempt to understand the natural world by rational means using the senses, is a search for knowledge. Carved seasonal records on bone go back 30,000 years and cave paintings make it apparent that prehistoric humans were astutely aware of natural events. The megalithic structures of Stonehenge in Great Britain were designed and arranged ~1,900 B.C. These provide evidence of sophisticated mathematical and astronomical insight. From time immemorial, we wanted to *know!*

Religion combined with astronomy can be detected over and over in the early history of science. Egypt, China, India, and regions of Central America and the Middle East all have archeological support for this duality. Astronomy reigned for thousands of years, practically alone. Regularity of planet movement and star positions as well as extraordinary events such as comets generated many questions and attempts at explanation. Everyone had access to the night sky laboratory. Since the heavens were believed to be the home of the gods, and heavenly events were perceived to influence the Earth, they were carefully observed and recorded. This observation and description laid the foundation for early science. Then came explanation, often involving interpretation.

Before scientific method underpinned with reason was delineated in the 16th Century, capricious gods, magic, folk inventions, and ancestral beings prevailed as explanations for the natural world. Inquiring minds require explanations and if none are available, then superstition and ideas generated from religion fill in.

Throughout history when individuals or tribes questioned the origin of the universe and of life they generated their own explanations. Many cultures credited ancestral beings or spirits with creation and these beliefs were usually intertwined with prevailing religious concepts. Origin myths are preserved in many cultures. They are alike in their attempt to explain. The explanations are varied and colorful and reflect the vast potential of human imagination combined with diversity of culture.

Cosmogony is the study of the origin and development of the universe, including the galaxies and their solar systems, often using stories (Greek: "kosmos"= order). It refers to origins in a neutral manner, whereas "creation" implies a creator and purposeful action. Cosmology, on the other hand, is a branch of astronomy that studies the origin, processes, and structure (space, time) of the universe. In their own way ancient people were involved in these disciplines, and a colorful record remains of their attempts to make sense of the world in which they lived. From the very beginning they asked: "From whence did we come?" Along with being puzzled by the origin of life and of themselves, that question encompassed the origin of the Earth, stars, sun, and planets, plants and animals. Always underneath hovered the question for meaning: "Why are we here?" This questioning gave birth to philosophy, the love of wisdom. Science was not far behind.

There are records of origin myths in Sumerian (ancient culture of 2nd millennium B.C. in what is modern Iraq) texts which suggest that the first humans grew from the Earth as do grass and trees. Some such stories assume matter and water were present and that life arose by varied means from these pre-existing substances. An example of this is seen in the most ancient of the two Genesis (Chapter 2) creation accounts where man was created from dust and woman from a man's rib. Creation from nothing, ex nihilo, with the spoken word, in the more recent Genesis (Chapter 1) record, was a less common idea.

All of the variations in cosmogony and the origin of life represent attempts to render life and the cosmos comprehensible and meaningful to human understanding. Myths were sometimes intertwined with ritual. The creation epic, *Enuma elish,* dating back to at least the First Babylonian Dynasty (~1,830 - 1,530 BC), for instance, was recited at the New Year's festival. The progression from magic/myth/ritual to ritual/tradition/customs/religion to science can be followed.

While the seeds of science can be traced far back in history to China, India, and Greece, very little is found in ancient Israel. The early Hebrews believed that the universe and life on Earth were the handiwork of a miracle working Creator. Besides Genesis, the writings of Job show the Israelites questioning, arguing, and trying to explain the mysteries that were observed in the natural world. By contrast, earlier civilizations such as the Babylonians were excellent astronomers and they, the Egyptians, and the Sumerians laid the groundwork in science for the Greeks. They also profoundly influenced the Hebrews' ideas on origins. The Hebrews were known for their imagery, poetry, depth of thought, and beauty of language. The Greeks were more technical, rational, practical, and scientific.

While scholars today recognize myth in Genesis 1 and 2, and can even trace some of its origins back to the aforementioned *Enuma elish*, it is important to note that the Israelite origin stories had distinctive character. Their one creator God (monotheism = one God) was transcendent, before and above nature, and benevolent. These are most unique concepts compared with other cosmogonies which included many gods (polytheism), who were often temporal and feared.

Early Science: Greeks/Romans

Science thrives in a cultural and political environment that is conducive to the free exercise of the senses and nourishes rational thought. The ancient Greeks lived at a time when intellectual curiosity and independent thought were able to flourish. They were free from the religious and political restrictions that often hamper the development of natural philosophy.

The Greeks were among the first to note that there were causes and predictable effects that could be explained. They gave birth to the science of logic, which saw thinking progress from reliance on myths, legends, and religious conviction to reliance on observation, the senses, questions, and scientific scrutiny. It is most interesting that as far back as the 6th Century B.C., Thales of Miletus (~640 – 546), perhaps the first Greek philosopher, proposed that the cosmos and Earth had come from natural rather than supernatural or mythical processes. He believed that water in its three states held the key to understanding the origin of observed phenomena. This thesis explained the fossil sea animals that had been discovered inland. He also taught that all material things in the universe had a purpose. Intertwined with theology, this purposeful belief position is termed teleology, and it exists to this day. Thales' ideas of order and purpose became identifying characteristics of classical Greek science.

Many ancient Greek philosophers invented creation myths or explanations. Thales' disciple, Anaximander (610-546/545 B.C.), was an early thinker who developed a cosmology and a systematic, philosophical view of the world. He reasoned that because life is closely related to moisture it must have originated in the sea and that animals could be transformed from one kind to another, all land animals having originated from marine organisms. Interestingly, Anaximander challenged Thales' ideas on water as a basic substance of matter and this critical response gave birth to peer review which is fundamental to science. Empedocles (~490-430 B.C.) believed that animals could be composed of combinations of pre-existing, transformed parts, and that Earth, air, water, and fire were the components of the universe.

Pythagoras (~580-~500 B.C.), the father of mathematical physics, which characterizes physical experience through numerical relationships, formulated principles that laid the groundwork for Western rational philosophy. Hippocrates (460-377 B.C.) initiated reasoned thinking from a medical perspective, rejecting the thesis that disease was caused by divine disfavor toward human error. He insisted that it was caused by natural phenomena, not supernatural beings or forces. Aristarchos of Samos (310-230 B.C.) even suggested that the sun was the center of the universe! Euclid (323-285 B.C.) founded geometry.

Plato (427-347 B.C.) and Aristotle (the first great biologist, 384-322 B.C.) attempted to find natural explanations for observable events. Aristotle thought a lot about the relationships among organisms and was perplexed at some which seemed to be ambiguous in identity (sponges looked like plants yet they ate food as did animals). He attempted to classify nature in an orderly manner, starting with nonliving matter, progressing to fungi, mosses, higher plants, primitive animals, and ending with humans and spiritual beings. All the way to the 18th Century, Aristotle's hierarchical continuum (Great Chain of Being) or ladder of nature (Scala Naturae), which represented links from the most imperfect (inanimate matter) to the most perfect (humans and spiritual beings), was the dominant belief. He saw purpose, teleology, in all parts of nature including the organs of living things.

Aristotle held the theological position that the stars and planets were divine and thus perfect, and moved in perfect, unchanging circles. The Earth was not divine but was at the center. The ultimate cause of all celestial movement was a prime, or unmoved, mover, which existed apart from the universe. This was God, the creator. Aristotle was a phenomenal observer who questioned process, structure, development, and purpose. Experimentation, common in modern science, involves design and the modification of structures, conditions, or activities. It was not a part of his modus operandi for it was considered unnatural to change things and the results would have been invalid. Observation, not experimentation, characterized Greek science.

In spite of the sophisticated thinking of many Greek scholars, most people in early Greece and down through the centuries believed that otherworldly, capricious beings, gods and goddesses, intervened erratically and unpredictably in nature and in the lives of humans, causing or curing disease or influencing any number of other activities. It was thought that planets exerted influence on life on Earth, a belief system known as astrology.

Superstitions surrounded not only stars, planets and living things, but later on, fossils and geological formations as well. Fossils were believed to have grown inside the Earth, the results of mystical forces flowing through rock. Some credited fossils with magical powers, such as keeping milk from going sour or serving as good luck charms. They have been found with human skeletons in ancient burial grounds. Where there was no rational explanation, humans devised their own mystical ones. Anthropology is rife with records of these varied and imaginative attempts to explain. Whale and mammoth tusks have been claimed to be unicorn horns!

Greek culture waned as a result of turmoil within its city-states and the eventual overthrow from without by Philip II of Macedon and his son, Alexander the Great (356 – 323 B.C.). While Alexander succeeded in establishing the Greek language in the East and the Greek culture was introduced into distant parts of Asia, a general decline in scientific progress occurred. The Roman Empire, while it benefited from Greek thinking in science, did not share the same fervor for inquiry and therefore contributed very little to its advancement. Science's doom was sealed when the Roman Empire was destroyed in the 5th Century A.D. by repeated barbaric invasions. The stage was set for the Middle Ages, which began at Rome's fall in 476 A.D.

Philosophy during these troubled years was kept alive by the works of Augustine (354-430) who, just before the fall of Rome, claimed that scriptural authority was greater than the ability of the mind and therefore knowledge would be based on its proclamations rather than on any human insight or rationality. The world of the senses was not recognized as valuable. Nature and its patterns or mechanisms had an insignificant role. The natural world was important at creation but now there were other things to attend to, primarily the spiritual dimension.

Boethius (~480-~525), in turn, challenged Christians to join faith with reason. Scholasticism was a philosophical system of medieval Christian thinkers that was profoundly influenced by this scholar and author. Its leaders attempted to integrate the Christian faith and its traditions, revelation, and authority with reason and realism in order to attain truth as much from the intellect as from the faith and scriptures. It challenged the mystical and contemplative groups to include more intellectual rigor.

Middle Ages

Most scholarship in the Western Empire during the Middle Ages occurred in monastic settings. Monk scribes copied writings of ancient thought in scriptoria, writing centers associated with monastery libraries. These handwritten materials enlarged the libraries and contributed considerably to the perseverance of Greek language and thought. Magnificent illuminated manuscripts of secular materials as well as the scriptures remain as astonishing evidence of the efforts and genius of these illuminators (artists who decorated and/or drew miniature paintings, often with gold), rubricators (those who added color, especially red), and calligraphers (those who were skilled in beautiful lettering). Instruction, including the established learning of the Greeks, continued in the monasteries. The Benedictine order was distinguished for its emphasis not only on worship and service but also on reading and study. The Byzantine Empire in the East, centered in Constantinople, was stronger than the European West during this period and it contributed much to the preservation of ancient knowledge and traditions.

The utter hopelessness that was felt at the demise of Roman civilization was relieved by the Christian message of faith and hope in a better world beyond, a conviction of salvation from the perils and disappointments of the present natural life experience. This theology kept the people from succumbing to despair and helped them weather the next eight hundred years. Although sustaining, this spiritual mindset was not one in which science could thrive and grow. Its dominant thesis of the world beyond would have to be slowly but surely eroded before scientific thought, which deals with the present, could resume.

It is of interest that in the 7th Century, the Arabs, inspired by their new Islamic religion, established the Islamic Empire, which flourished for about 500 years. The Arabs respected the ancient science of the Greeks, believing it was one way of glimpsing God. They incorporated astronomy, astrology, and the philosophical works of Plato and Aristotle into their culture, translating the Greek writings into Arabic. What is more, while Europe was scientifically regressing, by the 9th Century the Arabs were adding to this body of knowledge, building astronomical observatories, seeing progress in medicine, and inventing algebra.

Renaissance

The process of change began in Europe around the 11th and 12th Centuries when cathedral schools and universities were founded. Increased trade and navigation aided by the invention of the compass, agricultural productivity, economic prosperity, and technical innovation stimulated the progress that followed. It was a period of peace. These factors, including the support of the church, led to the rebirth of scientific, independent, and rational thought. The studies of mathematics, medicine, and classical literature reappeared.

Interestingly, in the 12th Century at the school at Chartres Cathedral in France, scholars taught a symbolic interpretation of Genesis and the innovative idea that the work of creation was still in progress. Hints at the evolutionary paradigm appeared that early, even though into the 14th Century most continued to believe that all organisms were created at the same time. Aristotle's Great Chain of Being, or hierarchy in nature, from the lowest forms to plants, animals, humans, and spiritual beings, was still the predominant paradigm. There was no thought by most that one species might have evolved into another.

The school at Chartres Cathedral played a most significant role in emancipating minds that previously were bound to imagining a more limited image of God and nature, a view that thrived in the traditional milieu of the Middle Ages. Secular, independent, empirical thinking, which had been almost abandoned since the Greeks and Romans, was reborn and the philosophical groundwork for modern science was established. The study of nature was given a pre-eminence unknown up to this period. Ancient scientific writings were assembled into a library from which the master teachers could gain insight and inspiration. It was most appropriate that the church, which had been the seat of learning in its monastic orders throughout the Middle Ages, would help bridge the era of stoic otherworldliness with lively inquiry, rational investigation, and a celebration of the senses.

The clerics who taught at Chartres were not about to divorce the natural world from God's world. They viewed the laws of nature and their growing understanding as being within the divine design, a unity. They were open to a more figurative interpretation of the Genesis creation accounts. All of this innovative thinking attracted strong critique. Their insistence that nature possesses intrinsic creativity, orderliness and autonomy and their suggestion of natural law that could be studied and understood upset traditionalists who perceived nature as being passive and mysterious. Change is always resisted by some. Many point to this controversy as initiating the historic conflict between science and theology, which continues in various settings to this day.

Historians maintain it was not science that triggered and fostered the wedge between faith and reason, but the fearful religious who forced the chasm by resisting new ways of thinking and waged a skirmish which has been all out war at times. The idea of a unity of all knowledge grounded in a confident faith could not yet be grasped and continues to evade many even into the present era.

Roger Bacon (~1220-~1294), a philosopher and educational reformer as well as a Franciscan friar, was convinced that being familiar with the things of the world would help theologians in their understanding of scripture and in confirming the Christian faith. Indeed, knowing the world would help in knowing the Creator! Among his many interests were optics, astronomy, and alchemy and he dreamed of machines that could fly and motorized ships! Bacon ardently pursued and extolled empirical science, basing conclusions on experimentally derived data. He was ahead of his time. Modern science didn't catch up with him for several hundred years.

Petrarch (1304-1374), an Italian priest, is considered the founder of humanism. Humanistic thought embraced that which elevated man's relationship to God particularly as it encouraged free-will and a personal desire for truth and justice. Seeds were sown that would eventually bear fruit during the Reformation. Petrarch promoted the study and translation of the Latin classics and helped to re-establish the Socratic tradition of repeated questioning to elicit truths which were assumed to be present in all rational beings. He also heralded independent thinking, morally, spiritually, and intellectually and encouraged the self-knowledge and individualism that would become central to Renaissance thought. Poetry was seen as therapeutic and a powerful influence on virtue and right living.

The enthusiasm generated for the classics during this period resulted in a revival in Latin, Hebrew, and Greek studies. There was a renewed interest in the scriptures and their analysis, which laid a groundwork for textual criticism and the rational, critical approach to studying literature, including the scriptures. Reasoned thinking and a questioning attitude were considered fundamental to an individual realizing his or her full human potential and enjoying the richness of unlocking the secrets of knowledge.

In the middle of the 15th Century, moveable type and an oil-based ink were invented in Germany by Johannes Gutenberg. The Bible was his first project. Paper technology and bookbinding also advanced, facilitating information dissemination. Prior to that time all writing was handwritten (manu-script). The mass production of the Bible led to extensive cultural and religious change in the centuries that followed. Books in the languages of the people proliferated. Universities multiplied throughout Europe. Humanistic tenets encouraged people to think autonomously and choose their own destiny. A quest for learning flourished.

The liberty of thought and action during this period established much of the intellectual and moral attitudes of Western culture. Concurrently, there was a weakening of the dominant ruling forces of church and empire and inevitable conflict simmered as a result. From this was born the Renaissance, a transition period between the Middle Ages and the Modern period.

The Renaissance, which lasted from approximately the 14th through the 16th Centuries, is noted for the rebirth of science. By the 15th Century, as a consequence of extensive exploration beyond their own borders, Europeans were overwhelmed by the variety and size of newly discovered continents and astounded by their bizarre and numerous plants and animals. They became aware of biogeography, the discipline that studies the distribution of species. New questions confounded them. Why, for instance, were similar appearing species found in correspondingly similar environments that were separated by vast oceans or mountain ranges? The ostrich from Africa, the rhea from South America, the emu from Australia, and the moa from New Zealand were all large, flightless birds. What explained their similarities and yet their isolation from each other? How did they get to such remote regions from Mt. Ararat after the flood? Why did these birds, which couldn't fly, have wings?

Reformation

Beginning in 1521 the Christian church experienced the Reformation under the leadership of Martin Luther and later John Calvin. This was a byproduct of the Renaissance. Calvin's extensive biblical commentaries helped the Protestant laity, many of whom were literate and who were now free to read and independently interpret the scriptures. The newly synthesized Protestant theology became established. The monolithic, external authority of the Catholic Church was challenged and the exercise of autonomous judgment by the individual was affirmed. This led to critical questioning and skepticism, all authority being subject to the inquiries of emancipated minds. Books were prevalent. The Bible was no longer exempt from critical, personal or scholarly assessment.

Scientific Revolution

The Renaissance also contributed to what would be called the Scientific Revolution. In Italy, Copernicus (1473-1543), and later Galileo (1564-1642), enjoyed an environment that inspired intellectual inquiry and encouraged experimentation. By that time physical science and its practical applications were well established. Minds as well as emotions, human needs, the search for happiness, esthetics, and the sense experience were all affirmed. The Copernican Revolution initiated modern science. Natural processes could be explained by understandable natural laws.

Artists reflected the dynamic yet harmonious spirit of the times. Many, such as Leonardo da Vinci, Giotto, and Michaelangelo, studied nature. Plants, animals, geology and, above all, the anatomy and physiology of the human body were incorporated systematically, three dimensionally, and sensually into their work. Even spiritual and sacred art was set in a realistic, physical setting rather than in an ethereal one. What was more, art was used to teach the sciences such as anatomy, botany, and zoology. Vesalius' art poignantly demonstrated this progression. The interplay and creativity between art and science was significant in the Renaissance and was seen in a variety of settings such as mapmaking. This duality was epitomized by Leonardo's mastery.

In the late 15th Century Leonardo da Vinci expressed wonder about seashells that were found in layered rocks of Italy's high mountains, hundreds of miles from the sea. The explanation at that time was the biblical flood. da Vinci questioned how some shells, which were thin and fragile with two articulated halves, could be so intact for having been swirled and battered in catastrophic floodwaters. Others were broken, obviously moved after death. He concluded that fossil shells were deposited under a variety of circumstances. He also wondered why, if they all were laid down during that flood, some rock layers had shells and others had none. Noting the annual silting of rivers, he innovatively postulated that the strata were deposited during many events over long periods of time.

New ideas and revolutionary thinking continued into the 16th Century. It was an era of foment as the metaphysical (abstract, supernatural) thinking patterns of Western Christianity were challenged and modern science gained its foothold. In the middle of that century Copernicus proposed the theory of heliocentrism, which put the sun at the center of the solar system. Up to that time it was believed that the Earth was at the center of the universe (geocentrism) with humankind being the pinnacle of life on Earth, tenets that seemed to be supported by the Bible. Heliocentrism was considered heretical by the Roman Catholic Church, which at the time continued to hold powerful influence in the culture. Copernicus, and then Galileo, challenged the cosmogony of the scriptures. The concept of a finite Heaven and Earth began to be replaced by an infinite universe.

By the late 16th Century geologists became aware of additional fossils in sedimentary beds that were exposed by erosion or excavation. As they examined older to younger layers an increase in structural complexity of the plant and animal fossils was noted. Lower layers were presumed to be older, and those strata closer to the surface, younger. What explained this progressive complexity? What was more, lower layers had organisms that were different from any living things at that time. Why were they unique and what accounted for their demise? Why were present species not represented in the early fossil record?

Science was defined apart from religion, being freed from biblical constraint. With the liberation of the mind it was inevitable that eventually the Bible itself would be the object of challenge, as fair game for rational inquiry. This is why the 17th Century is considered one of the most revolutionary periods in history. Science was beginning to wrest power from both the religious and political establishments, explaining phenomena apart from theological reference. It threatened design by providing answers for mysteries that until that time were credited to God's omniscience. Up to then truth was pursued through a metaphysical analysis of the nature of things. The revolution of the 17th Century abandoned this method in favor of reason, demonstrated facts, experimentation and the dependability of natural laws. In response, the church burned heretics who attacked traditional Aristotelian thought, those who claimed, for example, that the sun wasn't perfect after all, but had spots.

In 1609, the telescope was developed. Worlds never even imagined were seen. Questions never imagined were posed. Mountains could be observed on the moon, satellites were seen circling Jupiter, the Milky Way had an infinite number of stars! Galileo was the first to use the telescope and he collected data that suggested that the Earth revolved around the sun, supporting Copernicus' assertions. What forces enabled the Earth to go around the sun?

It is most significant that many devout scientists of this era were inspired by their faith to do science. Scientific inquiry was seen as a form of worship; understanding the universe would bring scientists closer to its Creator. Much has been written about the profound influence Christianity had on science because of this motivation. Robert Boyle (1627-1691), chemist and physicist, and John Ray (~1627-1705), naturalist and systematist, saw scientific inquiry as a means to relate to God. Descartes (1596-1650), philosopher and mathematician, formulated the so-called first law of mechanics; he was convinced that the laws that he was discovering were God's laws. Johannes Kepler (1751-1630), an astronomer noted for his principles of planetary motion, agreed with Copernicus' heliocentrism and the beliefs that the Earth rotated daily on its own axis and revolved annually around the sun. He saw that planets orbited in ellipses, not the perfect circles or uniform motion held by Aristotle. Kepler is remembered for declaring "O God, I am thinking Thy thoughts after Thee."

Isaac Newton (1643-1727) discovered the second law of mechanics and the law of universal gravitation and showed how the discoveries of Galileo, Hooke, Kepler, and Descartes, and his own work were inter-related. This synthesis further ushered in the era of modern science. Everything had the potential to be explained! Everything made sense! Other scientists who contributed during this time were Harvey, Pascal, Locke, Spinoza, and Francis Bacon.

Even though much change in thinking was occurring among scholars at this time the cosmology of the populace was still the cosmogony of Genesis. It was based on faith and the conviction that Genesis was literal truth. The transition from biblical to modern scientific cosmology wasn't easy for some and has not been attained by many even to this day. In 1616 church authorities were threatened by Galileo's support of Copernican cosmology which appeared to contradict the scriptures and he was admonished to abandon the Copernican system and not teach it orally or in writing. In 1633, the Catholic Church sentenced him to house arrest the last eight years of his life because it was felt that he had gone too far on these issues in his book *Dialogue Concerning the Two Chief World Systems.* Galileo's struggle for the freedom of inquiry, unhampered by tradition or authority, was significant to the progress of the scientific revolution.

The resistance of the church in acknowledging heliocentrism paralleled its earlier reluctance to recognize a spherical Earth. It insisted on literal scriptural interpretation, demanding a young Earth and a six, solar day (24 hour) creation. Having been wrong in the past, it needed to recognize that the progress of knowledge requires belief modification and other types of change. As with the prophet Jeremiah (33:2-3 "Call unto me and I will show you great and hidden things which you have not known before") God also promises to show *us* great and hidden things that we have not yet known. This requires an openness to novel perspectives, the humility and honesty to admit error, and the courage to adapt to new truth.

Robert Hooke (1635-1702), a microscopist who first described cells, expressed frustration as he experienced the authority of the church interfering with scientific discovery. He felt it was a "vain thing to make experiments and collect observations, if when we have them, we may not make use of them; if we must not believe our senses, if we may not judge a thing by trials and sensible proofs – but must remain tied up to the opinions we have received from others..." (Greene, 1959).

In 1650, Archbishop James Ussher of Ireland published his calculations of the Earth's age based on numbers and generations recorded in the Bible. He estimated the generations since Adam by counting through the "begats" in the Old Testament and suggested that the creation week took place in 4004 B.C., giving the Earth an approximate age of 6,000 years. These numbers went unchallenged until the rise of geology in the mid 18th Century. Many accepted them into the 19th Century, even as evolutionary theory and extensive geological evidence pointed to a much older Earth. Young Earth creationists affirm these numbers today although some extend the Earth's age up to 10,000 years.

Enlightenment

In the 17th and 18th Centuries Europe witnessed an intellectual movement called the Enlightenment. Nurtured by the fruits of learning during the previous centuries, new ideas regarding God, nature, reason, and man were proposed. They impacted art, law, government, philosophy, politics, and religion. Humankind was encouraged to pursue knowledge and strive for intellectual freedom and personal happiness. Authoritarian regimes continued to be challenged and critical, skeptical inquiry was affirmed. Optimism enveloped the liberated minds of this period. Hope for progress, fulfillment, justice, reformation, and virtue fed the intellectual leadership. Human reason was freed from traditional, fettered, dictated conservatism. These new currents of thought contributed to revolutions, which displaced much of the old order. The Declaration of Independence of the American colonists, which affirmed individual freedom, rippled to the French, profoundly influencing their thinking.

This environment affected the way in which scientists addressed their discoveries. Natural laws would explain all mystery and reason could ultimately explain these laws. Humankind would have control as nature's mechanisms were understood. Ecclesiastical authority and spiritual revelation were seen by some as unnecessary and even as impediments.

In 1705, astronomer Edmond Halley, applying Newton's laws, predicted that a comet, which had last been seen in 1682, would reappear in 1758. When Halley's comet returned on Christmas night of that year, long after the deaths of both Halley and Newton, the authenticity and power of mechanistic explanations inspired astronomers to search for a rational understanding of the stars. Thinking people could not ignore this means of unwrapping the shroud of mystery that enveloped much of the natural world.

In 1721, French philosopher Montesquieu expressed the belief that present species had arisen from a few early species and that differences could develop in animals over time. Buffon (1707-1785), one of the greatest naturalists of the period, considered but subsequently rejected the idea of possible descent of several species from a common ancestor. He was curious about the horse possibly being related to the ass and thought in terms of explaining natural events naturally rather than supernaturally. Erasmus Darwin (1731-1802), Charles' grandfather, suggested that species were interrelated and that animals may possibly change in response to their environments, passing these changes on to their offspring. (Note his remarkable evolutionary poetry in

Appendix F.) The groundwork was being laid for Charles Darwin's thesis, which would surface in the mid 19th Century.

Cuvier (1769-1832) analyzed fossil bones and concluded that numerous animal types had become extinct and that there seemed to be an evolutionary (change with time) progression in the biological world. He observed that mammals with grinding teeth have hoofed feet and those with cutting/piercing teeth have clawed, padded feet. This insight which held that there is a correspondence of anatomical parts was a significant breakthrough. He also proposed the theory of catastrophism, suggesting that there were many species created in the beginning but catastrophes like the flood during the time of Noah destroyed large numbers of these forms. He noted the gaps in the fossil record as well as among living organisms. Believing species were unchanging or fixed, it was proposed that there were fresh creations after each catastrophic extinction with the most modern species being the result of the most recent creation.

William Smith (1769-1839), a surveyor and geologist, mapped coal mines in England and worked on canals that had been dug as part of the support base for the industrial revolution. He observed similar sedimentary layers over large areas and interpreted this phenomenon as an organization in rock formation, a concept not noted to that point. This inferential data (arrived through observation rather than experimentation) led him to presume an ancient Earth and enabled him to predict the composition of more distant formations, sight unseen. He concluded that rocks containing similar fossils were approximately the same age. The orderliness, rationality, and dependability of nature was becoming clear.

Geologists James Hutton (1726-1797) and Charles Lyell (1797-1875), in their respective studies of the Earth's rock layers and their associated fossils, postulated uniformitarianism. This suggested that the slow and gradual forces such as wind, water, erosion, and ice that shape the modern world also operated on the ancient Earth. Observing soil being washed into lakes by rivers, they reasoned that in the past streams wore down continents and deposited their sediments into the sea in the same manner. Uniformitarianism, requiring long periods of time, contrasted with catastrophism which could cause change in a hurry.

Hutton held that the Earth's surface had been formed from older rocks that had been disrupted, upheaved, convulsed, heated, and exposed to erosion. Sills (igneous rock of volcanic origin intruded between beds of sedimentary rock), and dikes (once molten, igneous rock that intruded into fissures in older rock) provided evidence of subterranean heat that would cause the Earth to expand in places, resulting in uplift and new continent formation. The thesis that the history of the rocks occurs in cycles over long periods of time was in contrast to the prevailing belief that the Earth had a recent beginning and its composition and topography at the beginning were quite similar to that at present.

Hutton postulated that rocks were reduced to sediment by slow processes such as weathering. The sediments in turn were transported by wind and water to new sites and deposited, often forming layers. Over time this sediment could be compressed to a new type of rock which, if buried by more rock, could be heated, would melt, and flow back to the Earth's surface as lava, subject once again to weathering processes. Hutton, agreeing with Smith, concluded that rocks on the bottom were older than those on top (Law of Superposition).

Hutton's view of the Earth's history seemed contrary to the scriptural account. He felt it was inappropriate for religion to explain natural history yet he believed that nature was subordinate to a wise and omniscient God. Scientific inquiry flourished during this period and the church lagged in adapting to the challenges of innovative theses. Scientists did not enjoy the freedom of going where the data took them without feeling some pressures from the religious community.

Lyell proposed dividing the geological system into groups, characterized by the kinds of fossil shells in rock layers. He was the source of the names Eocene (dawn of recent), Miocene (less of recent), and Pliocene (more of recent) which are still used in reference to the geological column. Both Hutton and Lyell established a foundation for the idea that the Earth was millions of years old and in a state of constant change.

Lamarck (1744-1829) noted a sequence towards complexity in the biological world. He also thought the world was much older than the 6,000 years that seemed to be described in the Bible. He postulated that the variations observed within the living world came as a result of the inheritance of acquired characteristics. This meant that an organism's body could undergo modification during its lifetime through the use or disuse of structures and that an individual could in turn pass these new traits on to its offspring. For instance, it was suggested that giraffes have long necks because in their ancestry individuals had to stretch to reach high branches and, little by little, they acquired the characteristic of a longer neck, which they passed on to their offspring. Lamarck reasoned that this process could result in great variety in animals over time. His hypothesis has long been disproven as geneticists have demonstrated that hereditary information is contained and transmitted in the sex cells and is not subject to alteration by behavior or anatomical modification in a lifetime.

Increased global travel expanded naturalists' awareness of new forms, many resembling organisms with which they were already acquainted. The idea that species might have arisen from common ancestors continued to erupt. In 1802, William Paley's "argument from design" was presented. It held that a complex Earth assumes an intelligent Designer. In 1809, Lamarck's theory of orthogenesis was published. It held that species arise from nonliving sources, or spontaneously generate, a thesis fully disproven in the 1860s by Louis Pasteur.

More fossils were discovered, some of organisms that resembled living species and some of very different types. The causes of extinction were debated. It was suggested that organisms had changed. Furthermore, since not many modern species were represented in the fossil record, it was believed that they were relatively new on the scene and not part of the original created stock.

At the same time, systematists (those who classify), comparative anatomists, and embryologists were becoming aware of similarities among different species. Anatomists studying the structure of vertebrates such as birds, amphibians, reptiles, fish, and mammals, noted similarity in their body plans. They saw parallels between the human arm, the front leg of an antelope, alligator or frog, the flipper of a whale, and the wing of a hawk or bat. These limbs were all unique with distinctive functions, yet they shared many common anatomical features such as skeletal, muscular and other tissue arrangement, location, comparative size, and embryology. They questioned whether these relationships were significant. In addition, they noted that some snakes contained bones corresponding to the pelvic girdle to which leg bones generally attach. They wondered why snakes had these bones when there was no apparent need for them. What had the Creator in mind?

In spite of these confounding questions, for the most part up to the 18th Century biblical creationism went unchallenged. There was little reason for ordinary folk to reject the literal presentation given in the Old Testament. During the 19th Century naturalists tried to reconcile the accumulated evidence with traditional explanations that did not allow for change. Yet observing the forces of wind, rain, temperature, and volcanic eruptions on the Earth's surface, the time required for sedimentation in river deltas, and the rate of erosion along seashores and river courses, geologists became quite convinced that the Earth was much older than Archbishop Ussher's 6,000 years, a value that had been almost universally accepted.

The 19th Century was distinguished by a surge in technology, which is science applied for humankind's benefit. This disciplined progress led to substantial change. The steam engine had arrived. Railways proliferated. Travel broadened outlook as the traveler was exposed to new areas, people, thinking, and histories. The exchange of ideas pricked imaginations and innovation exploded. The learned dogmatism of the past was challenged and defeated in countless settings.

Meanwhile, many scientists suspected that organisms developed through inheritance from ancestral organisms and that there were relationships between species because of a common ancestry. See Appendix F with Erasmus Darwin's poetry published in 1803! This was the world into which the Englishman Charles Robert Darwin (1809-1882), Erasmus' grandson, entered.

Darwin's Theory and Mechanism

In 1831, as a young man of 22, Charles Darwin was selected to be the naturalist on a cartographic (mapping) expedition aboard a 90-foot long ship, the *H.M.S. Beagle*, which sailed around the world, a five-year journey. He studied plants, animals, and fossils on many continents and islands and in distant seas and was exposed to remarkably diverse geological features. This experience played a pivotal role in the development of his thinking on the nature of life on Earth.

Before leaving on his journey, Darwin, as well as most people of his time, thought that species of living things were unchanging, or immutable, a concept referred to as the fixity of species. Few were aware of extinction and most believed that the living things on the Earth were the kinds that God had created in the beginning during the six days of creation week.

While on his worldwide journey, Darwin read a book by Lyell, *Principles of Geology*. It introduced him to uniformitarianism, the idea that geologic processes presently at work on Earth have been at work in the past. Rain and wind have been slowly eroding mountains and the washed-down sediments have accumulated in stratified layers in the valleys and on the bottom of lakes, rivers, and seas. Gradually, mountains arose from plains and the seafloors. Catastrophes such as floods, earthquakes, landslides, drought, hurricanes, tsunamis, and volcanoes which punctuated these slow and gradual processes were also acknowledged. Uniformitarianism required eons of time which would bother those who remained loyal to the biblical timetable of an Earth 6,000 years in age.

Darwin asked: If the Earth is millions of years old, as seen by its geology, then could changes have slowly been occurring in life forms over this time expanse just as change to the Earth had occurred? Could species evolve (slowly change)? How?

Darwin noted remains of an extinct, cow-sized glyptodont in Argentina. Armadillos, while much smaller, are the only living animals that resemble glyptodonts and, interestingly, they live in the same regions in which glyptodont fossils were found. Darwin pondered: Is it possible that glyptodonts were early relatives of armadillos? These two animals were both armored, yet they were quite different in size. He observed a similar condition with giant, twenty-foot high fossil sloths and modern sloths in South America, and an extinct hippo-sized rodent, *Toxodon*. It seemed more than coincidental that the geographical area where these extinct animals lived supported anatomically closely related relatives today. Was this not evidence for change over time?

Darwin also noticed that areas that had similar climates, such as parts of North and South America, and Africa, had distinctive plants and animals, yet the respective organisms had many similarities. It seemed that they had been patterned or selected by their parallel environmental stresses and developed similar characteristics, a phenomenon later termed parallel evolution.

The *Beagle* anchored five weeks at the Galapagos Islands, volcanic cones about 600 miles west of Ecuador. Darwin saw that tortoises varied quite perceptibly from island to island. He reasoned that all the tortoises were related, having come from the same stock on the Ecuadorian mainland, but the populations had undergone selective change in a variety of ways as they were isolated for long periods on separate islands. Over time, various characteristics were selected for in the different island settings and each tortoise population changed enough that individuals from one island could not breed with those on other islands. The result was speciation, the origin of new species. This phenomenon has come to be called divergent evolution.

Darwin also observed divergent evolution in the finches on the Galapagos Islands. On one island the birds had large, strong bills for cracking cactus seeds. He concluded that the characteristic had been selected for in past generations. On other islands a long bill enabling the finch to probe for insects had been selected for, while on a third island the birds had bills designed for eating cactus flowers and fruits. Darwin postulated that what he had observed and concluded on the Galapagos Islands was a miniature model of how radiating species populated the whole Earth, adapting to various niches yet being related through common ancestry.

In the years following his circumnavigation of the globe Darwin attempted to integrate the data he had gathered and the observations he had made with his knowledge of geology and biology. He formulated theories on the diversity of life and how living forms related to each other and documented the change that occurred in various species. He noted that breeders could select for preferred qualities in pigeons and in a comparatively short time end up with bizarre forms. He wondered if similar selection occurred in nature, of course taking much longer. He researched, questioned, mulled for decades, and eventually came to some profound conclusions. Assuming his theory would generate controversy, he postponed its announcement for more than a decade after he had originally expressed it in an unpublished essay.

Darwin's theory was based on (a) competition, or struggle for existence, (b) the data from fossils that pointed to species change, and (c) the observations he had made of domesticated breeding and the changes that could be achieved through artificial selection. He felt his theory gave cohesion to a variety of facts and disciplines which to that point were unexplained and appeared unrelated.

Darwin was profoundly influenced by the writings of Thomas Malthus, a clergyman and economist. Malthus noted that more individuals are born than there are resources to support. The numbers of frog or insect eggs, pollen grains or seeds that are produced, for instance, vastly exceed the numbers of individuals that survive to reproduce. There is a struggle for existence where competition for food, shelter, territory, and mates ensues. Darwin concluded that those that survive must have some special adaptation or competitive edge, some genetic endowment perhaps, that gives them an advantage over their peers. Maybe it would be a slightly different coloration giving better camouflage, or the ability to run or swim a bit faster, or endure a colder or drier environment. This selection by nature would explain the variations of species seen on different islands or in different environments on land.

The idea of natural selection also shed light on the extinction of species that were apparently not as fit, especially when environments changed. Those that had the best genetic endowment for a particular habitat tended to survive and reproduce. They in turn passed on these preferred qualities to their offspring. Those less well adapted succumbed prior to reproductive maturity and their particular characteristics would thus be eliminated from the population. A population evolved as its heritable traits were selected for or against through successive generations, corresponding to environmental change over time.

Darwin was forced to finally present his ideas publicly when another naturalist, Alfred Russel Wallace, developed the identical theory based on his own observations in Malaya, part of present day Malaysia. These two scientists independently concluded that natural selection was at least one force behind the variety of life forms on Earth. They simultaneously presented their work on change over time, descent with modification, or evolution, to the Linnean Society of London in 1858. Darwin published *On the Origin of Species* in 1859.

Darwin and Wallace suggested, first of all, that change had occurred, and secondly, that it was the result of natural selection. Since then, some of the factors that operate in natural selection have been identified such as mutation (genetic change), geographical isolation, environmental variations, and genetic recombination. While the change of species over time had been suggested prior to their work, their revolutionary offering was an explanation for this change, natural selection. Darwin also proposed a gradual, common descent whereby several species trace back to a common ancestor. This thesis gave a rationale for the formation of new species and what was observed in the fossil record. It was a concept in opposition to fixity of species. Darwin completed the Copernican Revolution. Even the history of organisms could be *explained*.

Since ancient times it was noted that sea levels rose and fell, that fossil marine animals occurred in displaced areas such as in mountainous regions, that valleys were carved by rivers and that sediments from this erosion were deposited by those rivers in distant valleys and in the sea. Stratification was observed and correlated with time sequence. The ancients realized that the Earth was not static but dynamic, and they categorized organisms on the basis of unique structural qualities. However, none of this data was synthesized. There was no understanding of their interconnectedness. That is what evolutionary theory provided. It is the overarching rationality for all of this observation. It unites all of biology and integrates it with paleontology and geology.

During the 20th Century, genetics provided detailed evidence of evolutionary change. Darwin's natural selection thesis combined with genetic theory, including macroevolution (development of new species) and population genetics, as well as paleontology, systematics and mathematics, has become the Modern Synthetic Theory of Evolution, sometimes called the Modern Synthesis. Theodosius Dobzhansky presented this integration in 1937. Julian Huxley and Ernst Mayr further substantiated it in the 1940s. Subsequently, molecular biology has undergirded this theory even more.

In 1912, Alfred Wegener (1880-1930) proposed the theory of continental drift, which suggested that the continents were not fixed but in a constant state of movement across the Earth's surface. Wegener pointed to the more than coincidental match between the east coast of South America and the west coast of Africa and the correlation of rocks between Tasmania, Australia, and Antarctica. Although rejected at first by the scientific community, by the 1960s his theory was accepted and much empirical and inferential data has accrued since to affirm it. Data supplied by those who study earthquakes supported this hypothesis, as did the conclusions of geologists who compared the strata and fossils between continents such as South America and Africa. Continental movement explains the distribution of many fossil species throughout the world as well as the biogeographical distribution of living forms. Measurements of contemporary continental drift can be mathematically demonstrated. This is another field that has added to the accumulating support for evolutionary theory. Earth movement data also affirm an ancient, not young, planet.

With the continual flow of new knowledge during the last two centuries, not only in biology and geology, but also in physics and astronomy, inevitable change occurred with respect to the definitions and perceptions of science and religion. Scientific progress contributed to modifying the attitudes of fear and subjection toward God the Creator to the more positive perspectives of admiration and awe. Science was self-critical, empirical, and tentative, being subject to testing and challenge. The natural world was perceived more and more as being the product of impersonal forces subject to dependable laws. The religious would affirm that the Creator designed these laws, which gave explanation as to *how* he created.

Religion, which included worship, ceremony, comfort, hope, purpose, personal belief, and commitment, differed from science especially in its yielding to dogmatic authority and its rejection of self-criticism and autonomous thought. Its mysticism, faith, and contentment with not always being able to know or understand set it apart from the scientific mindset.

The Church's Response to Darwin

Evolutionary theory brought some unsettling questions. Continual change, unpredictable events, extinction, predation and struggle for survival appeared to have little or no divine guidance. What then was the Creator's role? These questions persist for Christians to this day and require faith, trust, openness, deep thought, humility, and contentment with uncertainty.

Church folk in the 19th Century responded to these revolutionary ideas in several ways. Some, who understood and were impressed and honest with the data, were open to considering that this was possibly how God had created. They began to see the records in Genesis 1 and 2 as stories with theological meaning rather than as literal historic events. Others resisted these new ideas and what they considered to be heretical interpretation of scripture. This, despite the inevitable belief changes in Christendom that resulted from the scientific investigation of Galileo on the position of the Earth in the solar system. To them this new theory threatened to diminish the role God had in the miracle of creation and to cast doubt on the reliability of the Bible. Evolution required more time than that allowed by Archbishop Ussher's calculation, which was printed in the margin of the King James Bible and was a value to which many readers gave inspired status.

Evolutionary theory challenged the literal authority of Genesis and advocated the critical thinking qualities of skepticism and objectivity derived from scientific investigation. Thomas Henry Huxley (1825–1895), Darwin's spokesperson who was often referred to as "Darwin's Bulldog," defended evolutionary theory from the criticism of the Anglican Church.

Eventually, many Christians honestly acknowledged the scientific support and openmindedly and objectively reassessed their own belief base and world view. They recognized evolution as a mechanism through which God allows life to operate, an application of his created natural laws, and a means of expressing divine freedom, direction, novelty. With some discomfort they modified their interpretation of the creation accounts in Genesis, seeing them as theological theses and not scientific summaries. They were aided by the discipline of biblical criticism that theologians had developed during the 19th Century. It provided scholarly grounds for new means of biblical exegesis (interpretation).

What bothered many Christians during the late 19th and early 20th Centuries was perhaps not evolution per se, but the accompanying proposition held by some that there was no set goal either by God or nature and that the universe and humans got here randomly, by chance. They feared a lack of meaning. Pre-Darwinian theories of evolution had included a goal-directed process. This additional implication threatened the Christian Doctrine of Creation for some and definitely challenged the literal accounts of creation as recorded in Genesis. From these decades arose the damaging and erroneous impression that biblical Christianity and this area of modern science were inherently opposed to each other. Religion and science were and are not in conflict. What was and is in conflict is modern science and the prescientific beliefs of the ancient Hebrews. Science, to this day, cannot speak to purpose, values, and meaning. Religion will always be required to answer these significant questions. Science will remain a limited way of knowing. It studies the natural, not the supernatural, world.

Mainline Protestants, Catholics, and Reformed Jews acknowledged evolutionary theory as valid science and integrated it into their faith for most of the 20th Century. They concur with C. A. Simpson, who in 1952 asserted with respect to evolution:

> If this world is not God's world, even the most frenzied arguments could not make it so. But if it is God's world, we do not need to be afraid of anything it actually reveals. All life is growth, and in growth there are often growing pains. But these are profitable. It is not the man of faith but the man of secret doubts, which he is trying to smother, who will be afraid of unfamiliar facts and will try to drown them out with clamor. Whoever really

believes that he is moving in God's world will go forward steadily to meet even its dismaying revelations (p. 462).

In 1941 the American Scientific Affiliation was founded by five scientists who were Christians who were concerned about relating the scientific world of that time to the Christian faith. This organization has grown in influence and numbers with members in 43 foreign countries. In 1959, Pope Pius XII affirmed evolution as being compatible with the Christian faith. Pope John Paul, in 1981, asserted the theological rather than the scientific validity of the Genesis accounts of creation. In 1996, Pope John Paul II declared that "fresh knowledge leads to recognition of the theory of evolution as more than just a hypothesis."

Presbyterians maintain that God alone is Lord of the conscience and their official statements affirm the rights of individuals to form belief on matters that respect religion, recognizing and accepting the diversity of belief regarding creation and human origins. The Episcopal Church holds that God could have created in any manner God wished and it specifically rejects the rigid dogmatism of the creationist movement. The United Church of Christ asserts that the book of Genesis, written in a prescientific age, should not be regarded as a book of science since that obscures its theological purposes; the church rebukes the creationist movement for insinuating this confusion. Appendix C includes other responses to evolutionary theory by Christians.

In spite of the fact that many in the religious community have come to terms with the theory of evolution, a large number of Christians continue to reject its data. They tend to belong to the group of Christians called fundamentalists who can be found in pews across the denominations, as well as in independent churches.

Fundamentalism/Creationism

Fundamentalism within Christianity arose in the first decade of the 20th Century with the publication in Chicago of some pamphlets, "The Fundamentals," which were distributed to 3,000,000 people. Five fundamentals of Christianity were outlined: the infallibility and inerrancy of the Bible, Christ's virgin birth, his substitutionary atonement, resurrection, and imminent second coming. The pamphlets were underwritten by two wealthy laymen from Los Angeles and authored by a distinguished group of conservative, interdenominational, Protestant theologians from Great Britain and the United States. They were broad in subject matter, rhetorically moderate, expressed conviction, and demonstrated intellectual depth. The pamphlets were sent to pastors, evangelists, professors and students of theology, and various other leaders in the Christian world. They were a response to what was seen as modernist tendencies in American religious and secular life. The tenets of biblical criticism and evolution were of primary concern. Some say the term "fundamentalist" was used prior to this period but many historians suggest the pamphlets launched the fundamentalist movement.

After 1920, fundamentalists became less moderate and more militant when they waged a holy war to save American civilization from the modern, liberal trend they perceived and the subversive impact that they believed the theory of evolution was having on the culture. They convinced Arkansas, Mississippi, Oklahoma, and Tennessee legislators to pass laws prohibiting the teaching of evolution in the public schools. The 1925 Scopes trial in Dayton, Tennessee, grew out of this legislation. It pitted evolutionists against creationists as John Scopes was found guilty of teaching evolution in the public school, an illegal act.

Fundamentalists tend to be deeply committed in their faith, strong on evangelism, and serious about their call as Christ's witnesses on this Earth. Some in this devout group might also be described as being (1) resistant to and fearful of change especially if it is perceived as "modernism," (2) strict biblical literalists and inerrantists, (3) defenders of traditional values and interpretations, (4) fervent in the belief that they alone have "the truth," (5) anti-intellectual and generally less well educated, and (6) intolerant of ambiguity and uncomfortable with uncertainty. For some, emotion may be stronger than reason, skepticism is discouraged, modern biblical scholarship is rejected, and there is fear that challenge to the scriptures might even be blasphemous.

Young people acculturated in this milieu are often protected from "the world," which includes its higher learning, questioning mentality, critical thinking and search for new knowledge, and even the mainline denominations of Christendom. Many are not acquainted with autonomous thinking nor are they encouraged to have intellectual curiosity. Emancipation often comes when they enter college. For some this can be very traumatic. Those who do not go to college tend to retain the dogma they have been taught and it is extremely difficult for them to understand that there are other valid ways of thinking, interpreting scripture or, more specifically, dealing with science as it relates to the scriptures.

In the decades following the Scopes trial, evolution was not consistently taught in the public schools, and biology textbook publishers, bowing to sales pressures, reduced or eliminated evolutionary rationale or data. Several generations were therefore academically uninformed about this theory and most of their education in this area came from the religious sector, which itself was generally untrained in the field. The higher education of many of the religious leaders was received in Bible schools, church related colleges, or seminaries where evolution, if taught, was vehemently opposed. Some leaders had no higher education. During the mid 20th Century some fundamentalists suggested that evolution and biblical criticism were part of a Communist plot.

As a result of Sputnik's success in 1957, the United States' program in science education was reformed and the National Science Foundation wrote and published the *Biological Science Curriculum Study* which presented evolution in a thorough manner for the first time in forty years! Fundamentalists challenged these texts in the courts and that war continues with periodic battles and skirmishes throughout the country.

The majority of contemporary Christians who actively support creationist organizations come from churches where evolution is still considered a threat not only to the faith but also to the culture. "Evil-ution" it is cunningly called. It is blamed for divorce, abortion, crime, drug addiction, prostitution, pornography, juvenile delinquency, illegitimacy, child abuse, and numerous other ills or perceived ills in American culture today. These beliefs are held so firmly that ecclesiastical separatism is encouraged and even seen as a test of true commitment. This contributes to the division that is seen within modern American Christianity. It must be noted that creationists can be found in pews and pulpits across independent churches and the denominations. They are not limited to conservative, evangelical, or fundamental churches.

Throughout the 20th Century, a variety of creationist organizations arose. Their colorful history includes periodic splintering, usually over fine points of doctrine. Some have waned, some have disbanded, and others have flourished. Their variety reflects the disparity of belief within creationism as well as purpose (see Chapter Nine and Appendix G, which lists some of these organizations).

Young Earth creationists conduct their research, produce web pages, and market their literature, videos, and tapes through several of these organizations. The leadership present seminars in churches, parochial schools, universities, and in civic auditoriums across the country and throughout the world. They organize field trips and participate in debates. Courses are available, even degree programs. Many materials are published from their own publishing wings. Their sincerity, zeal, and regular reference to the scriptures convince the scientifically and theologically unsophisticated layperson that what they propound is truth. Some have academic credentials and some do not. A few itinerant creationists in recent years have claimed invalid credentials.

It must be noted that most creationist leaders do not have theological credentials. They may have advanced degrees in science or other areas but they have never grappled with these issues in a scholarly milieu from a theological perspective. They have never had exposure to means of biblical interpretation except what they were taught in their particular wing of the church. This lack of theological sophistication is glaring to those who deal with these issues on a scholarly level. Laypersons tend not to question its absence. However, this subject matter deals with *science* and *religion*. A respected authority should have expert training in both.

I have attended eight creationist seminars in churches or civic auditoriums in three states in recent years. One speaker had a PhD in biology, taught at a state university, had been a Christian for six years, and admitted that what he knew of theology he had learned in his local church in the past six years. A second had a PhD in geology and no formal theological training. A third had a Masters in biology and no credentialed theological training. He graciously credited his father with teaching him the Bible. Two claimed doctorates from two institutions that are physically nonexistent. One had a three year certificate from a Bible college and no formal scientific training. None of these folk apparently understood the need to be better equipped to authoritatively represent these very difficult, diverse, and complex questions dealing with multiple fields of science as well as theology. It will never be known if their perspective might have been altered if they had sought a well-balanced, credentialed education in these varied fields. What is also most disheartening was that the laity and pastors of those host churches did not seem to recognize that their guest speakers were inadequately trained. This is why the subject of authorities, as discussed in Chapter Three, is so significant.

While some creationists have been politically organized, influencing textbook publishers, state legislators, and local and state school board decisions, others have established private schools, produce home schooling curricula, books, pamphlets and videos, and have radio programs and web pages. At least one organization offers a degree program and some encourage research.

In recent decades proponents of creationism have suggested that the biblical creation accounts can be supported and proven scientifically. They call themselves "scientific creationists." They do "creation science," a term held to be an oxymoron by most in the scientific community. Spontaneous creation by the miraculous word of a supernatural Creator cannot be explained or demonstrated through natural laws or inferred by supporting data under which science is bound. Neither can the gathering of pairs of all terrestrial animal kinds which have ever lived into an ark in the Middle East, survival for a year on that floating vessel, and the redistribution of those animals around the globe afterwards.

In 1968 the Supreme Court of the United States declared any law that banned the teaching of evolution in the public schools to be unconstitutional. Since then creationists have fought for "balanced treatment," which would require the teaching of creation science whenever evolution is taught in the public schools. In 1981 the "Balanced Treatment for Creation-Science and Evolutionary-Science Act" was signed into law in Arkansas. This law was overturned in 1982 as unconstitutional. Creation science was seen to be dogmatic, absolutist, and not subject to revision. Its conclusions are not arrived at through scientific method but are claimed in ancient religious literature. These qualities identify it as a religious viewpoint rather than as science, which is tentative and always subject to falsification, modification, or if need be, abandonment.

In 1987 the Supreme Court of the United States ruled unconstitutional Louisiana's "Creationism Act" which forbade the teaching of evolution in public schools unless creation science was also presented. The agenda of the original legislators was recognized as religious and the court held that such teaching would be a masked form of religious instruction and that it would give an advantage to a doctrine that rejects the factual basis of evolution.

Generally, the courts have ruled against the elimination of evolutionary theory and have found "creation science" inappropriate in the public school science classroom. But creationists continue their opposition and their tactics have become more sophisticated, making their offensive attack against modern science a perpetual threat. For example, Alabama requires a disclaimer in biology textbooks which says that evolution is a theory, not fact. Kentucky, Illinois, Oklahoma, and Florida, among other states, have avoided the word "evolution" from the biology context. Ohio modified its standards to include the word at the end of 2002. Some creationists have asserted that evolution is a theory in crisis and that evolution and religion are incompatible, both not true.

In August 1999 the Board of Education of the State of Kansas declared that local school boards could decide whether evolution and Big Bang cosmology would be taught in their systems and that an understanding of these subjects would not be required for students to meet the state's science education standards. Are local school boards qualified to design course content? Would English, history, physics, mathematics, music, or Spanish teachers allow lay, elected school board members to determine what their courses should cover? Was there an agenda here? The panel, dominated by religious conservatives, succeeded in giving evolutionary education a setback. Many felt this was most regrettable, for students without this training would be less prepared for higher education than their contemporaries, and the level of ignorance on these subjects would rise, exacerbating the conflict among Christians. Interestingly, after heated discussion both state-wide and nationally, in August of 2000 Kansas voters rejected three Board of Education candidates who supported removing evolution from the science curriculum the year before, a strong statement in support of a modern scientific curriculum. In February of 2001 the Kansas Board of Education reversed the 1999 vote and restored the Theory of Evolution and Big Bang cosmology to state school standards.

At the same time that Kansans were debating the significance of teaching evolutionary theory in their schools, legislators in Illinois, Oklahoma, Arizona, West Virginia, Idaho, Nebraska, Texas and many other states were also studying various proposals dealing with the same subject. In 2002, Ohio educators and politicians grappled with these issues for most of the year. Some describe these conflicts as a creationist assault on science education. There is tremendous concern by some that the serious study of God's works (science) will undermine God's word, so attempts are made to eliminate such study. Theistic evolutionists, on the other hand, maintain that God and the Bible are strong enough to handle the search for truth in nature.

Creationism has deep religious foundations and ramifications. It requires supernatural intervention and miracles. It is based on the origin stories of the prescientific Hebrew people of 3,000 years ago. Their stories were partially borrowed from stories of earlier cultures. Creationists must admit that it is not appropriate to teach such dogma in a science classroom where curricula are founded on the scientific method and observable or inferred data. Also, there are numerous creation models besides those found in Genesis 1 and 2. Examples would be the Mandan, Blackfeet, Wyandot, Onandaga, and Washo Native American origin stories, as well as those of Polynesian, Chinese, African, Hindu, and Siberian cultures. A genuine and fair balanced treatment on origins would necessitate the study of more than just the Judeo-Christian creationist thesis. Such a curriculum emphasis would be more religious than scientific and it could be appropriately incorporated into the discipline of comparative religion rather than science.

Intelligent Design

Much has been heard about the Intelligent Design Movement since the 1990s. This thesis holds that there is intelligence behind the created order which is reflected in the fine-tuned universe such as in DNA or in intricate cellular metabolic pathways. Proponents of this idea maintain that cells or cell structures such as flagella are too complex, irreducibly complex, they say, to have arisen through evolutionary mechanisms. An intelligent designer must have been involved somehow or given direction at various points and it is claimed that this can be demonstrated scientifically and should be included in public school science curricula. The intelligent design supporters as yet do not clarify how the designer intervenes. Is it sporadically, miraculously, predictably, or routinely? This negates the tenets of evolution which hold to natural selection of random but advantageous changes over time. Some suggest intelligent design is a variation of the old "god of the gaps." If it cannot be explained, it must be a miracle. Yet science is, little by little, explaining complexities and resolving questions and in time many more of them will no doubt be understood, just as science has explained unknowns in the past. Some questions, indeed, may never be explained scientifically, but natural law, not miracle, seems to be operating.

The intelligent design thesis also fails to explain why disease causing microbes, imperfect eyesight, or nonfunctional wisdom teeth exist. Are some things designed and others not? Why have most organisms which have ever lived gone extinct? Is that poor design? Could the designer work through evolutionary mechanisms? Why does a designer allow predation, infant mortality, volcanoes, earthquakes, death? Those adhering to the intelligent design position have not as yet produced experimental, peer-reviewed data which support their point. Since they wish to have it incorporated into public school curricula, most of the leaders of this movement are careful not to identify the designer but some authors have asserted that the Intelligent Designer is indeed the God of the Bible. They explain that pain and death are the result of human error, sin, and are not to be blamed on the designer. This is a theological position, not a scientific one.

Bridging Science and Faith

Many Christian leaders and scholars of the 19th century attempted to integrate the new scientific revelations (God's works) with the Hebrew scriptures (God's word) and this effort continues. Scientists who pioneered this interdisciplinary thinking included Harvard botanist and devout Christian Asa Gray, geologist Charles Lyell, minister and natural science lecturer Joseph Hooker, and Henry Drummond. This has led to the position of theistic evolution (see Chapter One), which integrates the science of evolution with the theology of Genesis.

In 1965, Ian Barbour, physicist and Christian theologian, published *Issues in Science and Religion*. This significantly contributed to a movement of dialogue between science and religion in the contemporary setting. Since the 1980s, the John Templeton Foundation has underwritten many projects worldwide that facilitate the interchange between science and faith. College and seminary courses have been designed and taught, and conferences, lectures, and journals proliferate. A very exciting and lively interdisciplinary exchange is going on! Education in both science and theology, an open mind, intellectual humility, and a conviction that with God's grace such unity can occur, appears to be the key.

Along with all of the progress intellectually and culturally that resulted from the Renaissance, the Reformation, the Enlightenment, and the Scientific Revolution, this liberation also delivered the Bible into the hands of laypeople who were then free to read and interpret it apart from dictatorial church authorities. A steady stream of new translations has put the Bible into the language of the people, and with the help of the Holy Spirit, individuals experience God speaking directly to them. The book has come alive for the common man and woman who now have the prerogative to personally study and interpret the word of God. While this has been a rich blessing to millions over the centuries, inevitably this freedom of personal interpretation has resulted in some misinterpretation. People who have not been taught how to rightly interpret or exegete these ancient writings are free to conclude any number of things and they can, in turn, influence others with their falsehood. The literal rendering of Genesis 1 and 2 is an example of inaccurate interpretation of scripture (as will be discussed in Chapter Six) and it has contributed to widespread division and acrimony among Christians. Many would hold that it has disserved the cause of Christ in the culture, especially among those who study natural science.

The Bible is not an easy book to read, having been written and edited thousands of years ago by numerous prescientific people in obscure languages not presently spoken. Much of the accurate meaning is buried in the ancient Hebrew and Greek and requires scholars to decipher. Even the most devout cannot be certain that they understand the original and subtle meanings of a culture far removed in time and place. This is evidenced by the numerous translations now available, each set of translators attempting to do their best in relating the original message. This is further discussed in the following chapter.

The historical drama of the interaction of creationism and evolutionary theory continues. This book attempts to give insight into some of the issues that surround this conflict and to help in its resolution. Intellectual humility and spiritual conscientiousness dictate that where there is the possibility for imperfect interpretation that can be detrimental to the Kingdom of God, then dogmatism and crusading have no place. The risk of division and rancor is too great. Many do not agree on these subjects and they continue to feed the antagonism that has become well established among the people of God. There is no conflict between science and religion nor between evolutionary theory and the profound theology of Genesis. The conflict is between modern science and the literal, pseudoscience of Genesis.

It is hoped that with this very cursory overview of some of the historical factors that have led to and impacted the creationism/evolution conflict the reader can understand how certain beliefs and loyalties have arisen. History provides illumination. It helps in weighing issues and in appreciating the origins of various perspectives and theses.

Additional Reading

Alexander, Paul J. (Ed.). (1963). *The ancient world to 300 A.D.* New York: The Macmillan Co.

Austin, Norman (1990). *Meaning and being in myth.* University Park: Pennsylvania State University Press.

Barbour, Ian (1965). *Issues in science and religion.* Englewood Cliffs, NJ: Prentice-Hall.

Barbour, Ian (1990). *Religion in an age of science.* San Francisco: Harper.

Barbour, Ian (1997). *Religion and science.* San Francisco: Harper.

Barbour, Ian (2000). *When science meets religion,* San Francisco: Harper.

Bates, Marston & Humphrey, Philip, (Eds.). (1956). *The Darwin reader,* New York: Charles Scribner's Sons.

Bender, David L. & Leone, Bruno (Eds.). (1988). *Science and religion: Opposing viewpoints.* St. Paul, MN: Greenhaven Press.

Brooke, John H. (1991). *Science and religion:Some historical perspectives,* Cambridge: Cambridge University Press.

Brown, Robert McAfee (1955). *The Bible speaks to you.* Philadelphia: The Westminster Press.

Childs, Brevard S. (July 1997). Interpreting the Bible amid cultural change. *Theology Today. 54.* (2), 200-211.

Darlington, C. D. (1960). *Darwin's place in history.* Oxford: Basil Blackwell.

Darwin, Charles (1960). *The origin of species by means of natural selection,* Garden City, NY: Doubleday and Co., Inc.

Draper, John W. (1875). *History of the conflict between religion and science.* New York: Appleton and Co.

Dunan, Marcel (Ed.). (1981). *Larousse encyclopedia of ancient and medieval history*, New York: Excalibur Books.

Dupree, A. Hunter (1968). *Asa Gray*, New York: Athenium.

Eiseley, Loren (1961). *Darwin's century: Evolution and the men who discovered it.* Garden City, NY: Doubleday & Co.

Ferris, Timothy (1989). *Coming of age in the Milky Way.* Anchor.

Finocchiaro, Maurice (1989). *The Galileo affair: A documentary history.* Berkeley, CA: University of California Press.

Gilkey, Langdon (1981). *Religion and the scientific future.* Mercer University Press.

Goldstein, Thomas (1980). *Dawn of modern science: From the Arabs to Leonardo da Vinci.* Boston: Houghton Mifflin Co.

Greene, John C. (1959). *The death of Adam.* Ames, IA: Iowa State University.

Greene, John C. (1961). *Darwin and the modern world view.* Baton Rouge: Louisiana State University Press.

Hankins, Thomas L. (1985). *Science and the enlightenment*, New York: Cambridge University Press.

Haught, John F. (1995). *Science and religion: From conflict to conversation.* New York: Paulist Press.

Hawking, Stephen W. (1988). *A brief history of time.* Bantam.

Himmelfarb, Gertrude (1968). *Darwin and the Darwinian revolution.* New York: W. W. Norton.

Hooykaas, R. (1972). *Religion and the rise of modern science.* Grand Rapids, MI: Wm. B. Eerdmans Publ. Co.

Hummel, Charles E. (1984). *The Galileo connection: Resolving conflicts between science and the Bible.* Intervarsity Press.

Irvine, William (1955). *Apes, angels and victorians: The story of Darwin, Huxley, and evolution,* New York: McGraw Hill.

Jaki, Stanley L., (1978). *The road of science and the ways to God.* University of Chicago Press.

Kelsey, Morton T. (1974). *Myth, history and faith: The remythologizing of Christianity.* New York: Paulist Press.

Kuhn, Thomas S. (1970). *The structure of scientific revolutions* (2nd ed.). University of Chicago Press.

Langford, Jerome J. (1971). *Galileo, science and the church.* Ann Arbor, MI: University of Michigan Press.

Lindberg, David and Numbers, Ronald (Eds.). (1986). *God and nature.* University of California Press.

Lindberg, David (Ed.). (1998). *Science and the Middle Ages.* Chicago: University of Chicago Press.

Lindberg, David (1992). *The beginnings of western science.* Chicago: University of Chicago Press.

Magnum, John (Ed.). (1989). *The new faith-science debate.* Augsburg/Fortress Press.

Martin, Daniel W. (Ed.). (1991). *Science and Christian faith: The connection,* Presbyterian Publishing House.

Morris, Henry (1984). *History of modern creationism,* San Diego, CA: Master Book Publ.

Murphy, Nancey (1990). *Theology in the age of scientific reasoning.* Ithaca: Cornell University Press.

Newell, Norman D. (1982). *Creation and evolution: Myth or reality?* New York: Columbia University Press.

Numbers, Ronald L. (1992). *The creationists.* Berkeley: University of California Press.

Peacocke, Arthur (1986). *God and the new biology*. San Francisco: Harper and Row.

Pennock, Robert T. (Ed). (2001). *Intelligent design creationism and its critics: Philosophical, theological and scientific perspectives*. Cambridge, MA: MIT Press.

Polkinghorne, John (1989). *Science and creation: The research for understanding*, Boston: New Science Library-Shambhala.

Polkinghorne, John (2001). *Faith, science and understanding*. New Haven: Yale University Press.

Prigogine, Ilya (1980). *Being to becoming: Time and complexity in the physical sciences*. Freeman.

Richardson, W. Mark & Wildman, Wesley J. (Eds.). (1996). *Religion and science: History, method, dialogue*, New York: Routledge.

Roberts, J. M. (1976). *History of the world*, London: Penguin Books.

Rolston, Holmes III, (1987). *Science and religion:A critical survey*, Random House.

Simpson, C. A. (1952). Genesis. In G. A. Buttrick (Ed.), *The interpreter's Bible* (Vol. 1). (pp. 437-829). New York: Abingdon Press.

Simpson, James (1926). *Landmarks in the struggle between science and religion*, New York: George H. Doran.

Singh, T.D. & Gomatam, Ravi (1987). *Synthesis of science and religion*. San Francisco/Bombay: The Bhaktivedanta Institute.

Trefil, James S. (1983). *The moment of creation: Big Bang physics from before the first Millisecond to the present universe*. Collier Books.

Turner, Frank M. (1974). *Between science and religion: The reaction to scientific naturalism in Late Victorian England*. New Haven: Yale University Press.

Van Doren, Charles (1991). *A history of knowledge: Past, present, and future*. New York: Ballantine Books.

Van Huyssteen, J. Wentzel (1998). *Duet or duel: Theology and science in a postmodern world*, Harrisburg, PA: Trinity Press International.

White, Andrew (1955). *A history of the warfare of science with theology in Christendom* (Vol. I and II). New York: George Braziller.

Whitehead, Alfred North (1925). *Science and the modern world, Lowell Lectures*. New York: The Free Press.

Knowing *about* the Bible

Chapter Six

The Bible contains the mind of God, the state of man, the way of salvation, the doom of sinners, and the happiness of believers. Its doctrines are holy, its precepts are binding, its histories are true, and its decisions are immutable. Read it to be wise, believe it to be safe, and practice it to be holy. It contains light to direct you, food to support you, and comfort to cheer you.

It is the traveler's map, the pilgrim's staff, the pilot's compass, the soldier's sword, and the Christian's charter. Here Paradise is restored, Heaven opened, and the gates of hell disclosed.

Christ is its grand subject, our good the design, and the glory of God its end. It should fill the memory, rule the heart, and guide the feet. Read it slowly, frequently, and prayerfully. It is a mine of wealth, a paradise of glory, and a river of pleasure. It is given you in life, will be opened at the judgment, and be remembered forever. It involves the highest responsibility, will reward the greatest labor, and will condemn all who trifle with its sacred contents.

Author Unknown

Introduction

For the Christian, there are two sources that provide information concerning the origin and history of the universe, of Earth, of life, and of species of plants and animals including humans. One of these sources is the Bible, God's word, and the other is the natural world, God's handiwork. This includes the rocks, fossils, and features of the Earth and moon, the surrounding cosmos and distant galaxies as well as the living forms that are present in the Earth's biosphere (the area where life resides).

A Christian's faith and commitment to the Bible as God's word demands that its witness be investigated, and a Christian's God-given inquiring mind demands the examination of the record in nature, God's work. If God is both the author of the Bible and the creator, then these two sources ought to be synchronous and corroborate one another. If they appear to contradict one another, it follows that one or the other is not being read correctly or perhaps both are being inappropriately interpreted. The perpetual challenge of scientists is to gather accurate data and interpret it correctly. The perpetual challenge of theologians is to interpret the scriptures accurately. There is ample room for both to err. Neither record is easy to read!

The story that is written in the rocks, in the cosmos, on DNA, and in other areas of nature is read and interpreted by scientists in such fields as geology, paleontology, astronomy, physics, molecular biology, genetics, and biogeography. These disciplines flourished during the past century and much information can now be clearly deduced from the data of strata, fossils and rock types, stars, galaxies, space, planets, the biochemistry, genetics, and anatomy of living forms, and the distribution of species. New data often result in a bevy of new questions. A multitude of them remain and it is probable that many of the mysteries in the natural world will never be fully explained.

The other source for information on origins is preserved in the Bible which is diligently read and interpreted, in whole or in part, by Jews, Christians, and a host of other inquirers. Biblical scholars are found in each of these groups. Like the natural record, this one is also difficult to decipher in many places, but the scholarship of the last 150 years has shed much light on scriptural interpretation. It, too, however, will perpetually hold its share of mystery.

It was noted earlier in this book that one of the main reasons why there is a conflict between evolution and creationism is that many Christians do not know how to read their Bibles. They know the Bible. Many have memorized large sections and faithfully follow it as a guide for living but they don't know *about* the Bible. Who wrote it? When? Where? Why? To whom? Under what circumstances? What kind of literature is it? How was it compiled? By whom? Did any of it come from pre-existing oral tradition? How did the original authors think? What were their concerns and what was the nature of their cultures and how were these factors reflected in Scripture? What did terms and images mean to the original authors? How do we make this ancient literature relevant and apply it to our culture and personal lives (Towne, 1995, pp. 67-69)? This chapter attempts to speak to these very significant issues.

The Identity of the Bible

The word "Bible" means "the books" in Greek. The Protestant Bible is a library consisting of 66 books of different literary genres written over a period of more than a thousand years by numerous authors, some known and some unknown. The Catholic Bible includes the Apocrypha, seven additional books considered to be of canonic stature to Catholics. The writers lived in the region presently known as the Middle East. None of them supposed they were writing sacred scripture when they recorded their thoughts and prophesies, chronicled events, wrote letters to friends, penned love songs, proverbs and poems, registered genealogies, related the teachings of Jesus, and catalogued laws. Their writings composed a part of the common literature in the culture of their time.

The contrast between the various authors' purposes, language, vocabulary, literary forms (genres), writing skills, time spans (over a millennium), and cultural settings is clear, yet the Bible possesses a remarkable unity and revelation that supports the universal belief by Christians that it was inspired by God. The agent of this enlightenment is believed to be the Holy Spirit.

The Bible is composed of two testaments or covenants. The first covenant, the Christian's Old Testament with 39 books, was originally written in Hebrew. It covers almost two thousand years of ancient Hebrew history, over dozens of generations, and includes, among other literary forms, law, history, genealogies, records, stories, prophesy, lamentations, songs, proverbs, and poetry. This literature originated as part of an extensive oral history which was influenced by surrounding cultures and spanned hundreds of years. The writings that compose the Hebrew scriptures were eventually chosen from among the common literature and canonized, that is elevated to the status of holy, sacred writings. The canonization process of the Old Testament took hundreds of years and was completed by approximately 100 A.D. This compilation of literature was the official collection of the holy scriptures of the Jews before becoming the first testament of the Christian Bible. It was translated from Hebrew into Greek during the second century B.C. in Alexandria, Egypt, and was available to the early church. Jesus and New Testament writers drew heavily from this covenant literature.

The Hebrews' writings came from an ancient period and represent a combination of historical fact and legend originating within their distinctive, prescientific, patriarchal, nonliterate (oral) culture. A progressive development of the human understanding of God and a succession of levels of God's saving grace and power, of promise and fulfillment, are seen within the Jewish canon.

The New Testament is composed of 27 books including the Gospels, the Acts of the Apostles, letters, and Revelation. After parts of it were preserved orally for many years they began to be written during the latter decades of the 1st Century A.D. Canonization was completed in the 4th Century A.D. It was originally predominantly recorded in Koine, or commonly used Greek, but in subsequent centuries was translated into Latin, Syriac, Coptic, Armenian, and many other languages.

The New Testament covers events from the 1st Century A. D. including the birth, life, teachings, death, and resurrection of Jesus of Nazareth, and the establishment of the Christian church. For Christians, the New Testament expresses the fulfillment of the prophecies and hopes of the Old Testament and is a continuation of God's revelation to humankind. Compared to the Hebrew scriptures, the New Testament is the product of a different time and culture and reflects Roman and Greek influence, which was different from the Hebrew world view. The conscientious reader of these two testaments should be acquainted with the factors that influence the meanings in these distinctive texts.

None of the original manuscripts of the books of the Bible have survived. Most were no doubt written on papyrus, a vegetable medium that is vulnerable to disintegration over time. Ancient copies exist, mostly on parchment (sheep or goat skin) or vellum (fine parchment: kid, lamb, or calf skin).

It is important to remember that the English Bible is a translation, in some settings having come from the Latin, which in turn came from the Greek, which, in the case of the Old Testament, had originated in Hebrew. Most recognize that in each of these steps of translation there is the potential for error. Translation can now come directly from the oldest available copies of Hebrew (Old Testament) or Greek (New Testament), however. In any case, the English Bible does not contain the exact original words of any of the biblical writers, and meaning is always subject to the decisions made by translator scholars. The original texts were not divided into chapters and verses. They were inserted in the 16th century.

The scholarship of the 47 translators who participated in the King James Version, published in 1611, was remarkable. Strict guidelines kept their work nonpartisan and of the highest quality. Since 1611, however, earlier manuscripts have been discovered, such as the great early Greek codices and Hellenistic papyri. Presently, some New Testament manuscript originals date to the 2nd Century A.D. Some of this material consists of mere fragments of papyri, which were preserved in the Egyptian sands. Scholars were given earlier manuscripts of the Old Testament with the amazing discovery in 1948 of the Dead Sea Scrolls. Recent translations rely on the most ancient manuscripts, which are assumed to be most accurate since they are closest in time to the missing original writings. Also, English has evolved in the past 400 years since the King James translation and modern scholarship reflects these changes. Scholars have established criteria to analyze the ancient materials.

In the 19th and 20th Centuries revised versions were produced with thousands of changes. These revisions incorporate data from the most recently found manuscripts and also modernize the material. They include the latest scholarship which contributes to as accurate a presentation of this amazing book as is humanly possible at present. Most would agree that as long as people are involved there is opportunity for error. Translators and the earlier copyists are people and the best of them often disagree. People are not inerrant.

The Bible is a perpetual best seller with perhaps one hundred and fifty billion copies having been printed since Gutenberg invented the printing press in 1453, the Bible being his first project (Boadt, 1984, p. 11). More than one hundred million Bibles, complete or in portions, are produced every year. The Bible has been read by more people than any other book, and has been translated in whole into more than 250 languages and in portions into more than 2,000 languages and dialects. It is available in languages spoken by over 90% of the world's population.

Why is this ancient book, which is difficult to read, overwhelming in length, and written by people who have long disappeared, from cultures that are poorly understood, in such demand? Partly it is because the experiences of the biblical characters parallel the experiences of all humans. More likely it is because the Bible deals with the great questions of life. The questions of people during biblical times were universal questions:

- Where did we come from, and where are we going?
- What does life mean, and what should we do with it?
- What is wrong and what is right?
- Who is God, and where can we find him?
- How can we live and die happily?
- How do humans fit into the cosmos and the web of life? (Towne, 1995, pp. 76-77)

While other great and sacred books have sought to answer the questions of origins, purpose, and destiny many believe the Bible comes closer to revealing the answers than any of the others. It deals with real people: how they thought, blundered, doubted, believed. No one is left out: young, old, rich, poor, faithful, treacherous, innocent, guilty, wise men, fools, tall, short, kings, common folk, the sick, the beautiful and handsome, the strong and weak, deceivers, connivers, prostitutes, victims, enemies, nephews, uncles, lovers, murderers, beggars, friends, parents, siblings, and children (Chase, 1944, p. 5).

People read the Bible because they are looking for God and for meaning. They believe God speaks through its words and that they are inspired, alive, ever relevant, having a divine influence. The Bible is recognized as more than a record. It is a call, an invitation, an urgent message, a guidebook. In spite of its being a book penned, copied and translated by humans with all which that implies, it is believed by millions to be God's revelation.

Most biblical scholars concur that the Bible was not written to be a book of science. To demand accurate, 21st Century science of this book is to embarrass it, some suggest. Furthermore, science changes and would be outdated by the science of the next century. The idea that the sun could "stand still" (Joshua 10:13) implies that it was moving, and that, according to modern science, is most inaccurate. The same verse claims the moon could stop, a phenomenon physics cannot explain. Ecclesiastes 1:15 asserts that the sun rises, sets, and returns to where it arose. If taken literally this is just not true. While some statements are scientifically accurate such as Leviticus 17:11 "The life of the flesh is in the blood," many are not.

On a flat Earth, no distance is farther than the east is from the west ("As far as the east is from the west so far has he removed our transgressions from us" Psalm 103:12). Yet on a spherical Earth the east eventually meets the west! If he had known that the Earth is spherical, the author may have chosen different imagery for this message. When we understand the setting of this statement we grasp its powerful meaning and the lack of scientific precision in no way interferes with its amazing theological message.

The Bible asserts that the Earth was made before the sun and that there were days and light before the sun was formed, claims that are not supported by science. It states that cattle were created by the word of God (Genesis 1:24) yet we know that cattle have been domesticated from wild animals and didn't abruptly begin as "cattle."

A most primitive and inaccurate understanding of genetics is exposed in Genesis 30:31-43 when Jacob took poplar and almond branches, made stripes by peeling them and placed them near the water source where the animals mated. Supposedly, those that bred before these carved branches produced spotted or speckled cattle.

The prescientific world view of the Bible is seen when people seek with their *heart* (Psalm 119:10), evil thoughts proceed from the *heart* (Matthew 15:19), they reason in the *heart* (Mark 2:8), Mary ponders things in her *heart* (Luke 2:19), and they believe in their *heart* (Romans 10:9). It appears that emotions and wisdom reside in the heart. This contradicts modern physiology where it is clear that such activity occurs in the mind and the heart is understood to be a muscle whose function is to pump. Furthermore, the sciences of anthropology and linguistics would disagree with the biblical assertion that the diversity of language originated at a tower named Babel. The Bible simply was not meant to be nor can it assume the identity of a science book. It has more important work to do!

To seeking, sincere Christians scientific inconsistencies do not detract one iota from the Bible's authenticity and power as a book of faith. These statements are understood as the peripheral, cultural, sometimes allegorical thinking of prescientific minds, but many of them are irrelevant to the great questions of faith and purpose. Those who look for theological messages will find them within these references. Scholars affirm that the purpose of the scriptures is to bring God to humankind and humankind to God through a variety of genres originating in that particular place and era of history.

It can be seen that the Old Testament writers powerfully reflected the distinctive cultural thought processes of the Hebrews, all the while paying attention to the great and profound questions of humankind. They wrote poetically and did not give accuracy of detail or numbers priority and were incapable of providing precise, technical data with respect to science. Our thinking has been molded by Greek thought which is logical and concrete, adheres to deductive reasoning, and gives more emphasis to precise numerical and historic accuracy. If we insist on coming to the Hebrew literature with a Greek mindset there is room for misunderstanding and misinterpretation.

The Bible answers the questions "Why?" and "Who?" whereas science seeks to answer the questions "How?" and "When?" The Bible is a book of faith, disclosing truths that only God could reveal about human nature: our purpose and nobility as creatures made in the Creator's image, yet our willful revolt against that Creator. The precepts of the Bible are changeless and timeless and perennially applicable to human lives. In a variety of ways it reveals the character, awesomeness, demands, plan, and love of God. It is a very old book, yet remarkably new. A book of faith and meaning, its sweep is to develop a relationship between the Creator and the created. It was not intended to be a book of science.

Inerrancy, Infallibility and Inspiration

Some Christians claim inerrancy for the Bible. They acknowledge that some parts of the Bible are more important and more valuable than others, however they cannot concede that it contains any errors. They assert that whatever God does is flawless and inerrant. God would not put revelation into something that was imperfect, they claim.

Other Christians cannot subscribe to the assertion of inerrancy. While the Bible is alive, sharper than a two-edged sword, relevant throughout the ages, speaks truth, is a dependable guide in faith and life, and has inspired individuals and nations to justice, charity, and freedom, none of these qualities requires inerrancy. It is the word of God to humankind through humans who are by nature errant. These Christians hold the Bible to be infallible, a term defined in the dictionary as without error, yet their inference is that infallible means that it is a reliable guide in faith and life and holds dependable doctrine. They do not claim that the Bible is always literally accurate in geography, numbers, history, or science or that it has not been impacted by the frailty of its human oral preservers, writers, copiers, and translators.

Since inerrancy means without error, just one error anywhere nullifies this claim. It is not hard to find inconsistencies in the scriptures and several are included here as examples, demonstrating the weak foundation inerrantists have. It is not gratifying to identify errors in the Bible but this reality must be confronted because of the division and confusion that reigns within Christendom over the subject of inerrancy and the ramifications such belief has on the creationism/evolution controversy. The longer Christians refuse to be honest with this book, the longer dissension will flourish within the body of Christ on subjects such as origins.

1. In Matthew 27:5 the means of Judas' death is by suicidal hanging.
   In Acts 1:18 the means of Judas' death is by falling headlong, his body bursting open and his intestines spilling out.

   Some say both happened. He hung himself and in so doing, fell. But what was the cause of his death? Asphyxiation from hanging, or hemorrhage? Matthew says the former, Luke in Acts says the latter. If both explanations contributed to his death, then both authors misstate the truth in not being complete.

2. Matthew 21, Mark 11, and Luke 19 all record Jesus in the temple court area accusing the moneychangers of making it a den of robbers. This event occurred at the end of Jesus' ministry just before he was taken into custody to be crucified.
   John 2, however, records this event as one of the first episodes in Jesus' public ministry.

   Scholars have no problem with this, believing John's account was more theologically founded and differed in purpose from the Synoptic Gospels, which were more historically based. John was not concerned with sequence but with deeper meanings. However, if we hold to literalism there is an inconsistency here.

3. The Genesis 1 account of creation describes God creating with the spoken word. Humans were created last. The Genesis 2 account of creation states that God first formed man from dust and breathed into his nostrils. Plants and animals came next. Woman is made last from the rib of a man. Did God create by the spoken word, ex nihilo (out of nothing) as in Genesis 1, or from dust and a rib (out of something) as in Genesis 2? Which was it? Was man made first or last? It can't be both.

Once again, scholars take these two accounts as separate creation stories from two unique sources living at different time periods. They have no problem with these inconsistencies if they are not read literally. But most inerrantists believe these to be correlating records of an actual creation event. If they are so recognized, there are serious contradictions here.

4. In Matthew 15:38 and Mark 8:9 the authors state that 4,000 men were fed with the five loaves and two fish. In Luke 9:14 and John 6:10 the number is listed as 5,000. Were they two separate events? Probably not. If they were, are 5,000 or 4,000 accurate, literal numbers? Probably not.

5. In John 12 Jesus is reported to be in the home of Lazarus, and the perfume is poured on his feet. Matthew 26 and Mark 14 place Jesus in the home of Simon the Leper and the ointment is poured on his head. Two separate events? Probably not.

6. Leviticus 11:6 includes rabbits as cud-chewing animals. This is incorrect.

7. Leviticus 11:13-19 lists bats with birds. Bats are not birds.

8. Leviticus 11:21-23 suggests that grasshoppers and beetles have just four feet. They have three pairs, or six feet.

9. Matthew 27:9 quotes Zechariah 11:12-13 yet it states that it quotes Jeremiah.

10. In Exodus 9:6 plague destroyed *all* the livestock of the Egyptians. Yet in 9:9 boils come upon the animals throughout Egypt. What animals? Supposedly they all died from plague. Chapter 10 records a hailstorm

killing the Egyptians' animals. Again, what animals? There is confusion here.

11. Genesis 3:14 says that the serpent will eat dust all of its life. Why do many of them have fangs and poison?

12. Two sites are given for the grave of Rachel: Bethlehem in Judah in Genesis 35:19 and at Zelzah in I Samuel 10:2. Which was it? Both?

13. Several references are made in the King James Version to a nonexistent animal, the unicorn (Numbers 23:22, Deuteronomy 33:17, Job 39:9, and Psalm 29:6).

14. In Mark 10:35-37 James and John, the sons of Zebedee, ask Jesus if they might sit on his right and left hand in glory. Matthew's record (20:20-21) states that the mother of Zebedee's sons makes this request of Jesus.

15. Moses' father-in-law is called Jethro (Exodus 3:1, 4:17, 18:1), Reuel (Exodus 2:18), and Hobab (Judges 4:11). Which was it? Did one man have three names? Were there three fathers-in-law? Is it a discrepancy that arose from a long oral tradition?

16. The Gospels give different accounts as to what occurred at Jesus' grave after the resurrection. Matthew 28:6 says an angel of the Lord rolled back the stone and sat on it. Mark 16:4 says the women saw a young man dressed in a white robe sitting on the right side of the tomb. Luke 24:4 says the women saw two men in clothes that gleamed like lightning. John's account (20:1-12) states that Mary Magdalene saw two angels seated in the grave, one at the head and one at the foot.

Some errors exist because down through the centuries numerous scribes of varying expertise have unintentionally transposed or omitted letters or words, repeated, or in some other way miscopied. There is some evidence that they of their own accord purposely added words or phrases in an attempt to clarify or removed what they saw as objectionable. Even after the invention of the printing press and the computer there is opportunity for error. Three examples of scribal errors are:

1. Confusion of similar letters such as a D and R: See Genesis 10:4 and I Chronicles 1:7. The D is used in the King James Version (Dodanim) and the R is used in the New International Version (Rodanim).

2. Transposition of letters: See Psalm 49:11. "Qirbam"= "inward thoughts" is in the King James Version. "Qibram" = "their tombs" is in the New International Version

3. Incorrect separation of words: See Amos 6:12. "bbqrym" = "Will one plow there with oxen?" is in the King James Version. "bbqr ym" = "Do men plow the sea with oxen?" is in the Good News Bible.

Which records are correct? What was the original meaning? What do we do with these little inaccuracies? None of these events or details or particular translations are crucial in any way or detract in the least from the main thrust of the scriptures, which is to establish a covenantal relationship between creature and Creator. None of these inconsistencies is important or fundamental to the main truths of the Bible. They do not bother anyone who looks for deep, spiritual, and profound insights in scripture, but they are there and there are many more examples that should be honestly acknowledged by those who claim inerrancy.

Inerrantists begin with an a priori belief in perfection and will go to extreme means to explain away any possible problems. Nowhere does the Bible itself claim inerrancy. Some maintain the original manuscripts were without error, rather than modern translations, but this thesis cannot be proven or disproven because none of the original manuscripts remain. It can only be stated that evidently it was not God's intention that we in this age should receive a flawless edition if indeed the originals may have been perfect.

The various manuscripts that have been preserved differ among themselves, some in minor and some in major ways, and this requires that some person or committee of scholars must sort out the difference. They must decide, sometimes subjectively, which version will be used in a printing of the Bible, what the original meaning was for various words or phrases, and how best to translate them into the most relevant, modern English. In part this explains the great variety of versions now available, and why more appear every year.

The translation of the Korean Bible came from the Chinese Bible, which is a translation of the King James English, which came from Greek manuscripts of the 10th Century, which are not the earliest, or preferred translations. Would anyone claim that the Korean Bible (or any of the others) is inerrant? Without a single error?

Contemporary Bible translators relate the difficulty of translating for perfect understanding such words as mercy, redeem, eternity, sin, forgiveness, devil, Passover, or even sheep or olive tree into languages and cultures, some of which have no concept or language for those ideas, animals, or plants. Cultures in the far north have never seen a sheep, have no word for it, and cannot relate to a shepherd in the way that biblical authors envisioned. Those in the rain forest cannot identify with desert imagery. In all of this conscientious yet frail human endeavor, however, Christians retain a confidence that the Spirit of truth oversees the process and preserves the integrity of the main messages of God to humankind in the scripture, in spite of its errors.

God in his wisdom and grace honored normal, imperfect human beings to communicate his message. Just as his Spirit inspired them, so it has inspired countless translators down through the centuries who have brought the Bible into hundreds of languages and dialects across the globe. Would these servants claim inerrancy or perfection for their scholarship in translation? In spite of their extensive training and innate intellectual gifts God did not take away their humanity, limitations, and tendency to err. In this way the book is genuine. In its fallibility the book follows natural law yet its eternal and profound wisdom, truth, majesty, cohesiveness, power, universality, and mystery demonstrate its divine Inspirer and Revealer.

While discussing errors in the text in a seminary course in New Testament, my distinguished professor commented that if the scriptures were perfect in every point it would suggest that they were written by impostors who set about to invent a religion. They couldn't, no matter how hard they tried, incorporate the subtle, buried, sporadic and authentic inconsistencies that would have been necessarily a part of ancient writings derived from myriad oral histories over hundreds of years. Their tendency would be to clarify issues, numbers, and events, and they certainly would not include two conflicting creation stories. *In their attempt at perfection their deceptive agenda would shine through.* The errors, he said, provide the very proof of the authenticity of scripture!

It is an ancient book written by at least forty authors, some unknown. It has miraculously persevered in spite of time, being hand written on papyrus that disintegrates, repetitive episodes of being hand copied, valiant attempts to eradicate it, and numerous translators over centuries. Errors would be expected, inevitable. Lack of errors would make it suspect. Its supernatural dimension is its very survival in spite of great odds. It is remarkably cohesive, in spite of hundreds of years of oral transmission and varied authors writing over centuries, representing different regions, cultures, and languages. Its powerful, universal, life changing, ever relevant message also reveals its sacred origin.

If one thinks about it, this pattern is consistent with how God has always worked. God chose to communicate a plan through a sinful nation with its flawed judges, priests, kings, and prophets. God continued this modus operandi through frail disciples, apostles, and a peasant girl who delivered his Son in a manger. Moses (Exodus 4:10) was "not eloquent," was "slow of speech," and was a murderer. Abraham lied. David planned and allowed murder. Noah became drunk. The announcement of his Son's incarnation was made first to shepherds, not kings or rulers! Peter and John were described as uneducated, ordinary, nonprofessionals (Acts 4:13). Members of the Sanhedrin, the Jewish high court, were astonished that men such as these could accomplish such remarkable and courageous feats. Paul had a "thorn in the flesh." Yet God used them all to do his work.

Down through the centuries, God's will was accomplished through the remarkable yet limited memories of those who kept the oral tradition alive, and then through the skills of imperfect authors, scribes, and translators of the sacred texts. Today our Lord is pleased to use very human but gifted artists, musicians, preachers, teachers, pastors, poets, athletes, parents, editors, authors, and theologians. God continues the ancient modus operandi by using committed but sinful modern Christians and the errant church to express love, reveal the good news to the present generation, and complete the mission on Earth. God honors those individuals by using them for heavenly glory and works the divine design through them in spite of their fallibility. In fact, God declares, "My strength is made perfect in your weakness" (I Corinthians 12:9). We constantly behold and humbly participate in this miracle.

Modern Christians who insist on an inerrant Bible are left with a tremendous burden of proof. What is of greater concern is their need for this book to be perfect. This can lead to an unhealthy attitude towards the Bible, one that elevates it beyond what it was meant to be. It ceases to be the mere medium of bringing people to God and God to the people, and becomes an end in itself. It is practically idolized by some. Respect, esteem, and reverence are very different from bibliolatry (worship of the book), yet the line separating these concepts is not always easy to discern. The Bible is a tangible in the Christian's world of faith and it can be insidiously construed beyond its intended purpose. Idols and relics have been required by the religious over the centuries, but Christianity is a religion of faith. Its tangibles include the institution of the holy, catholic (universal) church and its people. Both are imperfect and marred by sin, yet both have endured against extreme odds. They, along with the Bible, are overwhelming evidence for the faith within, but no one is to worship or idolize any of these. Some suggest that the very fact the Bible is errant helps prevent misplaced adoration or veneration.

Most informed Christians believe that the authors of the Bible were not divine amanuenses whose hands were directly guided by God to write a supernatural, word-for-word infallible message of revelation. The writers played a pre-eminent role under divine tutelage and inspiration, but they were confined to their own expression and vocabulary, and bound by their spiritual experience, humanity, and cultural, literary and intellectual parameters. The male-dominated culture depicts woman consistently as inferior. She was created last, as a helpmeet, was outsmarted by a snake, and caused the male to err. It appears to be culturally acceptable in Genesis 19:8 for Lot to give his virgin daughters to his guests to "do what they like with them." Women are generally excluded from genealogies. Is this God speaking or is it the literature of a specific culture? A progressive revelation of moral and spiritual truth can be seen throughout the Bible, but its writers did not transcend the boundaries of mundane culture or normal human capabilities. As in the creation, where God has operated through natural laws, so God's book does not escape the confines of natural law.

The Bible contains, conveys, represents, and is the word of God, God's message to humankind. However, it is not the actual *words* of God. If it were, how can the many examples of trivial data that are included in the Bible, such as lengthy and repetitive details on how to treat mildew, (Leviticus 13:47-59 and 14:33-53) be explained? How can Leviticus 21:16-23 be defended where God supposedly says that people who are crippled, blind, dwarfed, hunchbacked, lame or with sores cannot go near the curtain or approach the altar because they would desecrate the sanctuary? Who was *this* God? Why would the same trivial records be included twice (see Genesis 10 and I Chronicles I)? Why are there three accounts of the original presentation of the Ten Commandments (Exodus 20:2-17; Leviticus 19:1-27; Deuteronomy 5:6-21)? Why would God devote an entire chapter (Genesis 23) to a discussion of the burial of Sarah? Certainly God's words are not those of the Psalmist who in Psalm 137:8-9 rejoiced to think of enemy babies having their heads bashed against a rock!

God's message is shrouded in the language and literature of a far off and alien culture of long ago, but if it is sought it can surely be found. The actual words in the Bible reflect the numerous authors' vocabularies and passions as well as the unique culture from which they arose. Through mystery and marvel God chose to use the human medium and yet wove the divine element throughout the scriptures, inspiring the authors and conveying a wondrous message of love, hope, and forgiveness. This is expressed poignantly in the Presbyterian's 1967 Confession, seen in Appendix E.

The Bible is the church's book, not her Lord. God speaks powerfully through the words of the Bible but they are not without error. Jesus Christ, not the Bible, is the infallible, inerrant Word of God. See John 1:1-5. "In the beginning was the Word and the Word was with God and the Word was God (John 1:1)." Some suggest that Christians' insistence in biblical inerrancy is a product of the subtle, cunning power of evil. The church is warned to be alert to this deceptive, shrewd, crafty power or force in its midst. The doctrine of inerrancy has divided God's people and caused deep dissension within the kingdom. Perhaps the Bible has even displaced some of the glory that is due its Lord as it has been given such reverence.

Martin Luther suggested that the Bible is like a cradle holding the Christ child. The beautiful wood, and exquisite carved design and workmanship must never detract from what it holds inside. It is not an end in itself to be venerated. The Bible is a conduit that leads us to and helps us know God.

The Authors, Origin, and Canonization of the Old Testament

Who were the Hebrews who gave us this great and holy literature? The Old Testament authors' ancestors were semi-nomadic wanderers of the desert Semitic tribes in what is modern Iraq. Sources differ on specific dates, but they invaded the land of the Canaanites, which is modern Palestine, in the first half of the second millennium B.C. under the leadership of the patriarch Abraham. Their precise origin is shrouded in antiquity, but it certainly was not at the dawn of human history. Genealogies that purport to extend to the origins of humanity should not be interpreted in a literal manner, for the data of archeology and anthropology definitely do not support this thesis. There are records of many earlier cultures (Babylonian, Egyptian, Assyrian, Sumerian) in the general area well over a thousand years prior to the organization of the Hebrew people. In addition, there is an abundance of data pertaining to human existence in other geographical areas, far earlier than those identified cultures. The Hebrews arrived comparatively late on the scene, were much smaller in number than the neighboring, established tribes and were less technologically advanced. The story of David and Goliath demonstrates this well.

Famine sent the Hebrews to Egypt where they were enslaved. They eventually re-entered Canaan, the Promised Land, somewhere around the 14th to 12th Centuries B.C. After a period of judgeships, a monarchy was established. In approximately 1,000 B.C., King David ruled, subduing the neighboring tribes and establishing an impressive empire. The nation fell almost as quickly as it had sprung up. It wasn't long after David's son Solomon died that there was an internal, political division and the northern part of the dynasty (Israel) split from the southern part (Judah).

During this historical era the primary questions asked by the ancients were not whether a god or gods existed, but what kind of god it was and what did he (they) require? The gods all had names and the God of the Hebrew people

117

was called YHWH (Yahweh, Jahweh, eventually Jehovah). Throughout the pages of the Old Testament this God is met in the uncountable vicissitudes of life. Yahweh's purposes, omnipotence, demands, character of love, justice, mercy, and compassion, as well as anger and punishments are revealed.

The authors of the Old Testament include prophets such as Daniel, Amos, and Ezekiel, and poets, such as Solomon. However, many of the authors of the Old Testament are not known. For example, the individuals or sources that compiled the Pentateuch (the first five books of the Old Testament) are not known by name, nor, among others, are the authors of the Chronicles, Proverbs, Judges, Ruth, Samuel, Esther, or Job.

After the oral stage of biblical formation, which lasted for hundreds of years, the Hebrew people began to convert their oral history to a written one somewhere between 1,000 and 760 B.C. This record reflects their struggles from within and without and the relationship that their God, Yahweh, played in this drama. The scriptures attest to their curiosity about the mystery of existence as well as to their purpose and meaning as a nation and as individual human beings.

There were no copyright laws and ancient authors felt free to quote anyone at any time. Sometimes they even erroneously but purposely credited esteemed people with authorship, such as Moses and the Pentateuch. Moses' authorship is questioned for many reasons, not the least being the description in Deuteronomy 34:5-12 of Moses' death and burial! Materials were accrued from a variety of sources both within the culture and from the surrounding cultures. (See II Chronicles 25:4 and Nehemiah 13:1) Just as we have novels, legal codes, directories, comics, dictionaries, recipe books, children's books, history books, books of poetry, encyclopedias, and manuals, they had an original national literature including origin tales, annals of the kings, rules of sanitation, oracles, priestly liturgies, popular songs, chronicles, laws, prophesies, and wisdom of the sages. Some of the books that were not included in the canon are mentioned in the Bible, such as the Book of Jashar, the Book of the Covenant, the Records of Nathan, the Records of Gad, and the Records of Solomon. Why they were excluded from the canon of holy scripture is of interest, but there was definitely a careful discrimination by those who made canonical choices.

In approximately 760 B.C. and continuing until about the middle of the 2nd Century B.C., the actual books of the Old Testament were written and edited. The first book to be written was Amos. It was followed by writings of other prophets during the Babylonian captivity, which began in the 6th Century B.C. These materials were not regarded as sacred; in fact the writings of the prophets were usually disregarded. The last books to be put into written form were Daniel, Esther, and the book of Psalms.

The final stage in the formation of the Hebrew scriptures was when parts of the literature within the culture, after many years of use, were recognized by the people as distinctive and holy writings. They were designated as sacred and became part of the canon. The book of Deuteronomy was the first book given this status. By 400 B.C. the other four books that compose the Pentateuch (Genesis, Exodus, Leviticus, and Numbers) were added. This was the Torah, the first five books of the Jewish canon, which eventually became the first five books of Christianity's First or Old Testament.

In addition, many Jewish and Christian scholars theorize that these first five books are a composite work in which several traditions or sources have been blended together by subsequent editors called redactors. This is called the Documentary Hypothesis and it rests on more than two centuries of intensive study. Its thesis is that there are four main literary strands or authorships, which are designated J (Jahweh), E (Elohim), D (Deuteronomic), and P (Priestly). These four sources use different words, for instance J called God Jahweh, while E called God Elohim. Many stories are in doublets, there being two records. There are two creation stories, both distinct, and two flood records, though they are not literally synchronous. There are three accounts of the original giving of the Ten Commandments. Other literary differences suggest that these sources originated at different times, each author or authors reflecting their respective eras. Eventually their writings were woven together until the Pentateuch reached its final form about 400 B.C.

Not all Christians hold to this thesis. Some believe that Moses was the sole author of the Pentateuch for references are made to Moses writing (Deuteronomy 31:9; Exodus 17:14 and 24:4). This is held in spite of the fact that reference to his death is included in it (Deuteronomy 34:5). With careful, scholarly analysis of the Hebrew it can be seen that the original language and word choices within the books are inconsistent and reflect not only different authors, but varying time periods. The presence of duplicate stories also suggests more than one author. Those familiar with the support base of the linguistic scholarship can more readily affirm the multi-author thesis.

Gradually, other books were included. By the time of Christ the canon of the Old Testament was completed, after almost five centuries of development. It is important to appreciate that every part of the Old Testament was originally a part of the normal cultural literature before it received its canonical designation and was recognized as sacred. All of the writers would no doubt be dumbfounded to see how their writings have been preserved and honored and the impact they have had on myriad cultures across the planet for millennia!

Canonization identifies and sanctifies (sets apart) writings that are believed to have the stamp of divine authority. The word "canon" originally meant "reed," which inferred a tool for measuring, a rule, or standard. Most of the literary works that became a part of holy scripture circulated for centuries within the culture and became eligible for canonization as the people recognized their unique qualities of literary beauty, profound religious insight, divine authority or nationalistic appeal. Usually a council of religious leaders gave final canonization status to a written work but it had previously been chosen by the people as well as they witnessed its power in their worship experiences.

There is much uncertainty among scholars as to how and when the literary pieces that compose the Old Testament were chosen for canonization as well as the bases upon which some were excluded. This is referred to as "the problem of the canon." Its distant history contributes to this lack of understanding and mystery.

These writings reflect the culture of the time; the organizers of the canon did not seem bound to compile perfect materials. They included two separate and conflicting creation stories. An anthropomorphic (human form) God was introduced. He could be heard walking in the garden in the cool of the day, planted a garden, talked to a snake, made garments, breathed into the first man's nostrils, needed a day of rest, and made a rainbow to help him remember. As the scriptures are studied, the progressive revelation of this great God unfolds. Over the years his identity and nature are revealed: just, perfect, forgiving, holy, omnipotent, immanent, transcendent, triune, personal, and loving. Eventually God is mightily unveiled as the incarnate and risen Christ, Jesus, who loved, even unto death.

Mythical Literature

Because of the capacity of the human intellect for curiosity, most societies as well as individuals have asked fundamental questions over the millennia: "Where did we come from?" "How did the world begin?" "Why is there death?" "What happens after death?" Phenomena were noted that stimulated further questions: "What makes a rainbow?" "Why is childbirth in humans so difficult?" "Why do we have weeds?" "Why do snakes have no legs?" "What is the origin of evil?" "Why do even the best of us err?" "Where did all of the languages originate?" "How was marriage established?" "How did the animals get their names?" "Why do humans have to work so hard?" "Why do only humans wear clothes?" From the beginning, because of their advanced mental capacity, humans have wondered about the things that no one knew. These questions were asked around the campfires across the millennia and across the globe.

The literature of many cultures reveals attempts to answer these universal questions. The answers vary in detail but are often remarkably similar among diverse primitive societies. For instance, many cultures believe that people and the world exist because they were brought into being by a series of creative acts, usually by supernatural beings or forces. These accounts and explanations are known as origin myths. Myths, in this context, can be defined as primitive science, where attempts are made to explain phenomena that are curious, frightening, puzzling, surprising, or emotionally significant. They attempt to make the unknown knowable. "Mythos" in Greek means "story." It is not equivalent to "untruth."

Until the advent of modern science, myths provided the only answers for the deep questions of those who dared to think. They included mixtures of stories, imagination, dreams, memories, observations, and legend. Gifted story tellers were no doubt a central part of the community and helped establish the tribe's identity, traditions, taboos, ethics, customs, stories, and values. Anthropologists (those who study humans; anthropos = human being) relate that people in various regions and cultures of the present age continue to incorporate myth into the parts of their world that they cannot explain. It gives them a comfort zone and reassurance in the complex and enormous universe in which they live.

Archeologists (those who study artifacts, which are any objects made by humans) have shown that there were creation myths carved in the Egyptian pyramids dated in the 23rd Century B.C. Also, Sumerian clay tablets dating from approximately 2,000 B.C. or earlier relate origin stories that include the creation of humans and the universe, a serpent and paradise myth, and conflict among brothers similar to that of Cain and Abel. One of these pre-Hebraic accounts parallels the Tower of Babel story, and another relates a deluge (flood) event.

Many scholars suggest that the small Jewish community, which had not even assembled until approximately 1,800 B.C. or more recently, borrowed some of these explanatory stories of cosmic and human history from the large, established, and dominant cultures surrounding them. The stories are modified for their own purposes. It is believed that God inspired these modifications, for important, profound, and divine insights are buried in them. Some of the amazing theological truths found in the Genesis 1 and 2 stories of creation are listed in the final section of this chapter.

Origin myths or stories are usually tied in with religious beliefs and the element of explanation gives them some scientific qualities. Science, however, tests explanations and proves or disproves them, whereas myths are accepted with no requirement of verification. Because of this, prescientific origin accounts differ markedly from science. The Genesis accounts,

121

incapable of being tested, differ profoundly from evolutionary theory, which is supported by empirical, inferred and verifiable data.

Mythological thinking has God residing up in Heaven, as those with a flat Earth thesis would imagine. Punishment is down below. "Above in the universe" has lost meaning and cannot be taken literally by modern humans who live on a globe and not on a flat Earth. Australia's "above" is Canada's "below." Mythological thinking allows people to converse with a snake or a donkey and God to come down and somehow physically walk in the garden in the cool of the day. It claims one man could view, name, and apparently remember the names of all the kinds of animals that have ever lived on the Earth. It pictures a female being made from a man's rib!

If all animals were created "in the beginning" as creationists attest, and these stories were literal accounts of actual historic events, that would require the presence of all kinds of frogs, salamanders, tropical lizards and snakes as well as polar bears, grizzly bears, panda bears, koala bears, jaguars, walruses, llamas, kangaroos, orangutans, wolverines, snails, insects, spiders, hippos, rhinos, parasitic worms, musk oxen, eagles, birds of paradise, penguins, parrots, pigeons, peacocks, caribou, and camels to be in that garden and given names by that original man. Would all of the thousands of species of beetles be given names?

In addition, if this is a literal account, there is a microscopic world and an aquatic (fresh water) and marine (salt water) contingent, as well as an extinct flora (plants) and fauna (animals) including all the dinosaurs such as stegosaurs, tyrannosaurs, and brachiosaurs as well as mastodons, and saber tooth tigers that would be present. These "living creatures" would have required names as well. Presumably writing had not been invented so all of this data would have to be remembered by this man. Furthermore, it is not clear how the animals destined for the sea, caves, burrows, air, marshes, veld, islands, rain forest, or arctic could be dispersed from this place. How could an Arctic fox and a rainforest sloth, a penguin and a parrot exist in the same environment? These significant problems lead many to conclude that these are mythical stories, not records of historic events.

Mythological thinking also includes the story of a worldwide flood, where pairs of all living animals somehow migrated back to the Middle East approximately 1,650 years later and in an orderly manner got on board an ark and with eight humans apparently survived in peace for over a year. When the animals disembarked they somehow migrated back to their appropriate habitats. There was no problem explaining how kangaroos got to Australia, orangutans to Southeast Asia, Borneo or Sumatra, polar bears to the far north, or blind cave animals to Kentucky. At that time these regions and animals were unknown to Middle East residents. No explanation is given for what the animals ate upon disembarking on a desolate, sediment laden Earth. The world of the authors of these stories was limited to where they could sail, walk, or ride, and their exposure to animals was confined to that narrow geography and time. Our understanding of the numbers of plants and animals, including extinct forms, and of geological data presents too many unanswerable dilemmas. We are forced away from the literal and universal flood account, to a figurative interpretation. Additional problems with this thesis are included in Chapter Ten.

It is important that one understands that the word myth does not equate with untruth, and those who believe the scriptures are inspired by God must look for the truths that are embedded in the mythological literature. It is the prerogative of the modern Christian to demythologize scripture, that is, to identify the profound truths found therein, remove them from their context in an ancient world view, and see them come alive in a present world of reality and personal experience. For example, God up in heaven can be interpreted as a transcendent God, who is greater than the world, not bound to its limitations. Scholars attempt to interpret prescientific writings in the Bible by looking for deeper, theological meanings and they do not get derailed trying to defend a literalism of these early texts for which there is no rational defense. In plumbing these depths their minds and hearts are opened to powerful truths and insights which were unavailable previously.

Biblical Interpretation

There is a popular misconception that the Bible is an easy book to understand. However, there have been more books written about how to study and interpret the Bible than about all other aspects of the art of reading. Biblical literature composes a variety of genres and literary forms such as history, poetry, law, story, genealogy, song, prophecy, proverb, vision, psalm, letter, allegory, metaphor, and parable. The conscientious student must consider each of these in a different way. Even devout scholars do not all agree on interpretations.

Besides being written thousands of years ago by authors from foreign cultures that are now extinct, the Bible was written in several languages that are not in use today. This prevents the modern reader from being able to know all of the subtleties and intended original meanings. For instance if we referred to someone as being "over the hill" or "out to lunch" we would understand those implications. They should not be read or translated literally. What subtleties are so buried in Hebrew literature? Ideally the Bible should be studied in its original languages but very few are skilled to do that. Also, much biblical writing pertains to the deep spiritual and emotional realms, which are elusive in the best of situations.

It is not surprising that Bible studies are common throughout Christendom, often centering on a particular book or theme. Leaders spend considerable time and effort wrestling with the text and there is not always consensus on the resultant exegesis (explanation). Variety of interpretation of the scriptures has inevitably resulted in the disparity of belief and opinion that prevails in modern Christendom. Nowhere is this seen more readily than in the various interpretations of the first eleven chapters of Genesis. Without doubt, no one has all insight and wisdom so humility, prayer, disciplined study and an open mind are most appropriate qualities for any serious Bible interpreter/scholar/student.

It has been suggested that much of the confusion that has arisen between science and the scriptures with regard to evolution has been generated because neither the science nor the scriptures have been well researched and understood by many who seek to resolve these questions. The issues are quite technical and complex and few moderns have had sophisticated, in-depth training in both science and scriptural interpretation. Furthermore, it is difficult for Christians to rightly discern qualified authorities. There are many voices, some of them very appealing and persuasive. Some capitalize on the ignorance that is quite common in these specialized areas.

Many who are burdened about the conflict between science and the scriptures and the division it engenders within Christendom are pessimistic, doubting that there will ever be consensus or widespread tolerance of opposing views. Christians come to the scriptures with unique experience and acculturation, and long established loyalties and methods of interpretation which many are not willing or able to change. Some assume that their interpretation is the only right one and, failing to employ the qualities of careful and humble thinkers, they are not amenable to even considering new approaches to Bible study. Others come with closely held, preformed beliefs and look for means by which the scriptures might support them. We know that God speaks differently to different people, but we assume God's word is consistent and that, correctly interpreted, consensus might prevail.

Anyone can take stories, events, or a verse and contort meanings or take them out of context and assign a personal interpretation that may be quite seriously in error. This has historically resulted in some unusual and errant beliefs, which were often based on one dominant person's faulty assessment. Some interpret the division of language at the Tower of Babel to mean that God desired a divided and polarized world. Therefore, they are opposed to racial intermarriage or other factors that might lead to unity, a one-world community or one race. Others interpret this story merely as an attempt by the ancients to explain the variety of languages.

Other examples of individuals or groups who have interpreted the scriptures to conform to their personal agendas are Jim Jones in Guyana, and David Koresh of the Branch Davidians in Waco, Texas. The Freemen in various parts of the country, including some who claim Aryan supremacy and a disregard for the law, also have quoted the Bible to justify their agendas.

Cultures and nations have used the Bible to champion slavery, justify racism, subordinate women, and abuse or kill homosexuals. Followers who do not think carefully incorporate these beliefs, thus establishing them further. All conscientious Christians must continually monitor their authorities and preserve their right as careful, autonomous thinkers. The original purpose of a story, event, verse, or section of scripture must be prayerfully and studiously sought and the interpretation kept within those parameters.

In addition, there are Christians who interpret the scriptures so narrowly and literally, or selectively, that they refuse to fellowship with other Christians who do not agree explicitly with their interpretations and resultant theology. This exclusiveness and intolerance is seen by many to be a perversion of the message of the scriptures, which calls for forgiveness, love, patience, unity, and humility. The spirit of the law is superseded by the letter of the law, a practice that Jesus clearly opposed. Jesus' teaching repeatedly stressed forgiveness (the woman caught in adultery, the prodigal son, those who crucified him), tolerance (the love he continually showed in spite of people's misunderstanding and ignorance), inclusiveness (eating with Zaccheus, publicans and sinners, respecting women, inviting a tax collector into his inner group of disciples), love of neighbor in spite of philosophical, gender, or ethnic difference (the Good Samaritan, the woman at the well). He was most frustrated by those who held to the letter of the law such as leaving their sheep in a ditch because it was the Sabbath, or those who were blinded to their own imperfection.

How humans think, believe and interpret their world is based, among other things, on their acculturation, age, genetic endowment including gender, and life experience. It is important to be aware of these factors which carry such profound influence. Christians from certain religious heritages interpret the Bible in a particular manner because they have been so acculturated. Searchers for biblical truth must be cognizant of the factors that have influenced their thinking and exercise autonomy by objectively considering alternative means of interpretation. If necessary, they should be willing to modify or adopt new methods if justified. This openmindedness affords growth and is the result of the application of the principles of careful and prayerful thinking.

A variety of exegetical methods are employed in interpreting scripture. For instance, allegory (symbolic representation) can be used for biblical interpretation, but it has a potential to be dangerous. One might, in the story of the Good Samaritan, equate the Good Samaritan with Jesus, the victim of the robbers as the sinner, the innkeeper as a guardian angel, and the inn as the church. A story originally told to teach about being neighborly develops into unfolding the entire message of salvation. If a person who holds this interpretation is authoritative, many will follow and accept this twist as truth. In this case it is not a damaging misinterpretation, but the potential for falsehood exists when this particular method is regularly employed.

Others read the Bible literally. These interpreters see the six, 24 hour day creation account and the story of a worldwide flood as literal, historical events. They believe that a serpent could speak (snakes have no vocal cords or other anatomical endowment for speech), and that a warrior named Samson could kill 1,000 men with the jawbone of one donkey (Judges 15:15)! What do literalists do with Daniel 4:33 where it states that Nebuchadnezzer grew feathers as eagles, or with Numbers 22:28-30 where a donkey rationally communicates, apparently in Hebrew, to Balaam?

Claiming a blanket literalism of the scriptures denies their rich variety of literary forms. Some portions are to be interpreted figuratively and others, such as Jesus' crucifixion and resurrection, literally. This is the challenge of biblical interpretation, to discern which is which.

One tool that helps determine whether a figurative or literal approach is appropriate is to ask: What makes sense? Common sense asks what the historical or rational base is for various stories, parables, or claims of scripture. If there is corroborating evidence that it occurred, which is the case for the Hebrews' history, Jesus' life, death, and resurrection, and many historic events and places associated with the early Church, then it can be literally accepted. If it is part of a culture's folklore, such as origin myth, or is obviously symbolic, allegorical, or poetic, it is perceived differently.

Interestingly, those who claim biblical literalism do not take the visions of Daniel or the images in Revelation literally. They do not take Jesus' parables literally, for they understand how to read that kind of literature. Parables, by definition, are instructive stories that are not records of historic events. Jesus told stories of a sower, a fig tree, and a lost coin. These stories have profound messages but were not literal happenings. They were a most effective teaching tool for illiterate, common people as he incorporated familiar events, people, plants and animals to help explain the serious insights that were being communicated.

Biblical literalists know that Jesus' statements "I am the door" or "I am the true vine" or his title as "Lamb of God" are not meant to be taken literally. Jesus is not literally a door, a vine or a lamb. They know that when David said, "The Lord is my shepherd," he did not mean that literally. David was not a sheep. He meant "The Lord is to me as a shepherd is to a sheep." Literalists do not interpret "Let the floods clap their hands" (Psalms 98:8) or "at the blast of the breath of his (the Lord's) nostrils" (II Samuel 22:16) literally. How can they be sure that when Jesus said, "If your eye offend you, cut it out" he did not mean it literally? How can they exercise such ease in interpreting these portions nonliterally yet cling tenaciously to a strict literal interpretation of Genesis 1 and 2? Why do they call themselves biblical literalists when in fact they are not consistently literal?

Religious language includes symbolism, imagery, metaphor, and poetic description which, if taken literally, can lose its religious significance. Furthermore, what do literalists do with the descriptions in the Bible of the Earth: flat with a sea under it, stationary? Or the heavens as a tent or upturned bowl? Or a sea being above the sky with windows in the sky through which the rain came down? The concept of being "saved" is beautiful imagery. Literalists allow for figurative interpretation for all of these images yet resist employing it with the creation accounts.

Literalism, as far as the Christian church is concerned, is a comparatively recent development. It may have arisen after the Protestant Reformation when many reformers, in a continual repudiation of the absolute authority of the Pope, turned more and more to a belief in the absolute authority of the scriptures. It put the important discipline of biblical interpretation into the hands of lay people who had access to Bibles and were literate. Many of them, while devout and sincere, were untaught and understood little about how the scriptures originated and should be interpreted. They were unacquainted with the respective cultures and timelines of the various authors, and how to interpret in light of these factors. They didn't know *about* the Bible. Some historians believe literalism was born and flourished as a response to Darwin's theory of evolution. As will be shown later in this chapter, literal interpretations applied to Genesis 1 and 2 present great conflict.

The easiest way to read is to read literally. Children begin with stories and literally believe in talking animals, fairies, ghosts, even engines that can speak! Minds must be taught to look for deeper meanings and wrestle with symbolism, poetry, hidden truths, and imagery. Many have never been trained in this discipline. While some parts of the Bible are very clear and their meanings easy to grasp and can be taken literally (God so loved the world. Jesus wept. He is risen! I will come again!), other parts are extremely complex and their meanings are subtle or illusive. In some areas even devout scholars disagree. There will never be consensus on some sections (note the variety of millennialists: pre, a, post).

In I Thessalonians 4:13-18 the Apostle Paul makes reference to the parousia or promised return of Christ. "We who are alive and remain shall be caught up" (verse 17), he says. It sounded like this event was imminent or surely would occur during their lifetime. In fact, Christians in the early church were puzzled that some had died prior to Christ's promised return. As the years, decades, and centuries passed and this second coming did not occur, Christian doctrine adjusted to this reality. Interpretation was modified. His coming is a promise and will take place but his timing is his own. Light is given and truth revealed over time. A tolerance for new insight and adaptation are required on this exciting journey.

Along with common sense, another set of tools that aids Christians in their search for the deep truths of scripture are commentaries. They provide insight from authors who have given considerable time and thought to the careful study of scripture. Numerous commentaries are available, some authored by highly trained, scholarly contributors. Usually the authors' credentials are included and a serious student will consider this data in any book that might be used authoritatively.

In addition, Bible teachers and pastors, and college and seminary professors can be rich sources of insight. Autonomous thinkers prayerfully choose their authorities and arrive at conclusions that they feel are most reasonable. Always they are open to insight from new authorities and, if necessary, are willing to modify belief.

There will be perpetual challenge for biblical inquirers who sincerely seek to discern which writings represent the spirit, with its symbolism, and deep theological meanings, and those that represent literal statements. Sometimes messages are hidden because the subtleties of the original ancient culture cannot be completely discerned in the present age. Indeed, the Bible is not an easy book to understand!

Christians can gain insight by thinking about the authorities who have taught them biblical interpretation. Upon what basis did they earn that position? Were they chosen for their expertise or did they just happen to be there? Is their scholarship up to date and well balanced? Might new authorities be considered or is that out of the question?

Christians can humbly and courageously come as seekers rather than knowers to God's holy word. They can entertain the idea that there might be another means by which the scripture can be validly regarded. Openmindedness to God's revelation of truth affords new perspectives or affirms present understanding.

Biblical Criticism

In recent centuries, scholars have generated many questions pertaining to the original meanings, identities, and origins of the biblical texts. They wonder about the oral tradition and how stories were passed down for hundreds of years and what happened when they were put into writing. Who were the authors, how did they think, under what circumstances and when did they write? What were the original meanings of particular words, phrases, and passages? How were the historical and cultural settings of the Jewish people reflected in the writings of the Old Testament? What influence did the scribes who hand copied the books for hundreds of years have on the texts and how accurate are the various translations? Biblical scholars and linguists have studied the available manuscripts in depth and compared them with one another. They have attempted to identify and separate subjective opinions of people from an honest assessment of original meanings and purpose. Archeological research has contributed to the clarification of certain questions.

This mode of inquiry into the Bible is called biblical criticism. Its origins trace back to the Renaissance, when people were freed from the weight of long-held ecclesiastical authority and tradition. Previous to this, the Bible was exempt from scholarly critique. Criticism in this context does not have a negative connotation. It means to discern, to evaluate, to understand. It does not mean to criticize. It was inevitable that eventually the Bible would be the object of rational inquiry. The Reformation stimulated more rigorous and objective biblical analysis.

As more was discovered about science in the 19th Century, it became clear that some references to nature in the Bible reflect thinking from a prescientific era. When viewed from a modern scientific perspective they are inaccurate. This stimulated many questions. Biblical criticism helps in correctly interpreting these sections and seeing them in a different light, one that does not depend on literal, scientific accuracy.

Some Christians became defensive and feared that challenging such references might dilute the Bible's authority. They felt that this careful analysis of the scriptures was uncalled for and unnecessary, perhaps even irreverent. However, in an era when all literature is exposed to critique, it is a disservice to the Bible to declare it exempt from scholarly scrutiny. Modern minds do not respect the authority of something that is declared off limits to normal intellectual inquiry and investigation. Criticism is demanded of all important literature if its content is to be grasped, respected, or revered. Articulate thought requires careful discernment. Such analysis should never be misunderstood as disparagement, for it can be the highest form of appreciation: discriminating appreciation. Biblical criticism enables Bible students to not only *know the Bible*, the verses, stories, instruction, promises, warnings, and people, but to *know about the Bible*, the time of its writing, its authors, original languages, intent, cultural settings and meanings. Many feel that unless both of these perspectives are comprehended there is deficiency in understanding.

Biblical criticism is divided into subdisciplines: two major ones are textual (lower) criticism and historical (higher) criticism. Text critics seek to recover as closely as possible the exact original words of the Bible by studying the best and earliest texts available. They are proficient in the original languages of the Bible and employ the science of paleography, which is the classification of ancient manuscripts according to their age in the light of handwriting, alphabets, punctuation, and other factors. Text critics look for the most accurate manuscripts and suggest the translations of various words or verses that they feel most closely follow the original intended meaning.

Errors can be identified that may have crept in during the period when scribes were hand copying (manuscripting) the Bible. Some words or sections were inadvertently omitted or repeated during this time. A famous example of the latter is found in II Kings 18:17 (King James Version) where "and they went up and came" is immediately followed by "when they were come up, they came." Errors also arose because of sloppy handwriting; a scribe might misread a word because just one letter was incorrectly written. For instance, in English the word "hay" could be changed to "hag" if the "y" were not formed clearly. Sometimes scribes included additions to the text. These could have arisen because the book from which the scribe was copying included marginal comments which had been added by an owner. They might be difficult for the scribe to distinguish from the original handwritten text. In other settings scribes purposely added to or modified the text or removed what they interpreted as objectionable, according to their best intentions.

The fruits of the endeavors of text critics are often seen as footnotes in modern Bible translations where the compilers attempt to give insight and convey information that was gathered through literary analysis. Footnoted Bibles are called Annotated Bibles. The notes often provide background information for a passage, interpreting it in light of the original language and explaining the author's intent. Reflecting on data accumulated from the efforts of text critics over many decades, Bible commentaries provide prodigious amounts of information pertaining to word meanings, the background of various portions of scripture, or theological insights.

Up until 1947, the texts used were (a) Hebrew manuscripts going back only to the 9th Century A.D., the Masoretic text, or (b) other Hebrew manuscripts from medieval times, or (c) Greek manuscripts from the 3rd and

4th Centuries onward and (d) other Syriac and Latin versions. In 1947, texts were found at Qumran and other areas surrounding the Dead Sea that go back to 200 to 450 B.C.! These Dead Sea Scrolls have enabled scholars to understand more completely what the original Hebrew scriptures must have been like, for about one hundred of these manuscripts include the entire Old Testament, except the book of Esther.

A second form of criticism is historical, or higher, criticism. This is study concerned with authorship, date of composition, original purpose, style, cultural and historical influences and setting, intended audience, and possible oral antecedents. By placing writings in their original cultural environment scholars can understand more clearly the author's meaning. For instance, a book written during the Babylonian captivity (Daniel) or in the midst of an invasion of Jerusalem (Obadiah) will powerfully reflect these conditions and the content will best be understood when these settings are recognized. Since the Old Testament original languages are no longer used and the writings arose from an oral tradition, historical and textual criticism are disciplines that will remain tentative indefinitely.

Biblical archeology has shed some light on the inquiries generated from biblical criticism. It has shown that when the Hebrews appeared on the world scene there were already advanced civilizations in the ancient Middle East. Apparently there was a lively cultural exchange during that era and Israel's history was intimately linked with the cultures of its contemporaries. These influences are reflected in the biblical writings. For instance, the Babylonian laws of Hammurabi resembled, yet preceded, the laws of Moses.

One of the greatest contributions of biblical criticism is its emphasis on the truth of the progressiveness of revelation. God reveals to people of each age what they are able to understand. A progression of understanding has been seen over the centuries as the Bible is studied. At first, God was perceived anthropomorphically, having very human qualities. He breathed, rested, planted, walked, smelled the sweet savor, could be argued with, and became angry. As time and relationship continued, a clearer, more mature perception of God as spirit was understood. The early Hebrews did not see God as the immanent, transcendent, triune, redeemer, risen God known by Christians today. In the 21st Century God is appreciated as the creator of an infinite (telescope) and intricate (microscope) universe, which could not have been imagined previously. By studying creation, God's power and omniscience are revealed. At no time has this been as exciting as during recent decades. Many Christians are expectant as they contemplate the additional insights and qualities that will be disclosed as relationship with this dynamic God continues.

Critical methods of Bible study enable the student to interpret the writings as accurately as possible. Only then can these precepts, promises, lessons, warnings, encouragements, histories, doctrines, and stories be appropriately applied to an individual's theology and belief system and, hopefully, be authentically expressed in his or her life.

The Universality of Sin

A major concern expressed by creationists is that if the Genesis accounts are not taken literally, if there was no actual Garden of Eden, no Adam and Eve, no talking snake, no "fall," no original sin, then there is no need for a savior and Christ would have died in vain. No fall, they say, no sin. No sin, no need for a savior. Believing this rationale to be accurate, creationists reject anything that negates it. No doubt this belief explains, at least in part, the persistent commitment of creationists to deny evolution no matter what valid scientific data are presented.

The good news is that theology speaks to the reality of sin, the universal presence of evil in people, the need for forgiveness and renewal. Christian theistic evolutionists do not deny that evil is present in each of us and that there is need for a Savior. The evil is not blamed on Adam, however, but on the exercise of free will and the subsequent wrong choices of each of us. We all err and express a sinful nature. God did not create us as perfect robots. We were given free will, which includes the freedom to sin. We don't need an Adam to take the blame. The blame is our own. We need a savior not because "Adam" sinned but because *we* sinned!

That we were born in sin is almost irrelevant. That we sin is universally and painfully evident from childhood. A colleague shared with me his shock when he witnessed his four year old telling a lie. "We did not teach him that! Where did he learn it?" he asked. Evolution in no way negates the reality of sin. In fact, it helps explain it. Our need to survive has made us cruelly competitive, greedy, self-centered, unloving, and deceitful. Our basic drive is to stay alive, at whatever cost to others. Jesus came and turned all that around saying that those who keep their lives will lose them and those who lose their lives for his sake will keep them (Matthew 10:39). This is the only way we conquer our sinful natures, to lose our lives in Christ. Evolution does not lead to a theology devoid of the reality of sin and the need for a savior. If anything, evolutionary thinking sheds light on and confirms this state!

The early Hebrews recognized the universal tendency of humankind to err. They questioned its origin and explained it with a story. They did not have the benefit of long years of profound theological, scientific and psychological thought, the Scriptures, Christ's teachings, and the church to provide a medium for such reflection. A story gave them the explanation they required.

We even wonder about a God who, because two people way back then chose wrong, punishes the millions who come thereafter. A more just and loving God is one who gives free will and judges each of us on the basis of our own error, not victimizes us because of others' sin.

The Two Genesis Creation Accounts

The two amazing stories of creation found in Genesis support each other in some respects, but are actually quite different and conflict in detail and chronology at other points. Their consistency is seen as follows:

1. There is one true and living God; monotheism.
2. This God is the sovereign, authoritative Lord of Creation.
3. This Creator existed prior to and is distinct from the material universe.
4. This Creator is personal and caring.
5. Humankind is the epitome of the creation. (Fritsch, 1959, pp. 20-21, 27)

In other ways, the two accounts of creation found in Genesis 1 and 2 are quite different. This can be seen particularly in the order for the creation of humans. In the first account, man and woman are created on day six, after the animals. The Sabbath is sanctioned as a day of rest. In the second account, strong patriarchal overtones are evident as man is created first and in God's image; then the plants and animals, and woman is created last from the man's rib. It is not clear that she is made in God's image. Man is presented as the crown of creation and all other created beings, including woman, are seen as subservient. There is no reference to specific days or the Sabbath. Assessing these two accounts, a biblical literalist is stymied by the question: Was the man made last or first? Which account is *literally* true?

The first account has a schematic, orderly pattern of six solar days, whereas the second account has no such pattern. The first includes an explanation for the origin of the entire universe while the second focuses on humankind and other life forms and says nothing about cosmogony (the origin of the cosmos or universe). The first presents God as the omnipotent creator by fiat, who speaks "Let there be" and it appears, ex nihilo, out of nothing. The second account, more vivid and physical, depicts an anthropomorphic God who doesn't speak to create but *molds* from the dust, *breathes* life into nostrils, *plants*, *builds*, and *takes* a rib from the man and *closes* his wound. He does not just speak to create. Active verbs are involved.

The differences here are very obvious and it is absolutely impossible to take both of these accounts literally.

Besides the five previously mentioned points, additional profound theological messages found in these two remarkable accounts, as well as in the following chapters in Genesis, are:

1. God is.
2. God is the creator (not the gods as believed by the Hebrews' neighbors).
3. God is omnipotent, sovereign.
4. Creation is good.
5. There is an order in the creation/universe.
6. God is benevolent and wishes to commune with humans (many cultures feared their gods and constantly tried to appease them).
7. Humans were created in God's image; we're self aware and have been given free will.
8. There are rules for living to be followed and penalties if they are broken.
9. The problem of evil is presented.
10. Humans were given the responsibility to till and keep the creation; to be stewards of the environment and created order.
11. Marriage and the seven day week with one day of rest are established and affirmed.
12. Explanations for the great questions of life are offered: Where did we come from? Why are we here? Why do we die? How do we live and die happily? How do we relate to the rest of the creation and to the Creator?

Scholars who have analyzed the original language of these two creation accounts hypothesize that they were written by two authors, two separate creation stories composed at two different times in Jewish history, several hundred years apart. They were both included by an editor(s), or redactor(s), for all to see. The obvious differences between the two accounts not only in sequence of happenings but also of language and structure contribute to the validity of this thesis.

The two sources of the distinctive creation accounts in Genesis are referred to as the Yahwist and the Priestly authors. The Yahwist account, in Genesis 2:4-25, is thought to have been composed earlier, probably ~ 9-10th Centuries B.C. God is referred to as Yahweh (YHWH) or Jehovah. This account is not organized around a seven day week.

The Genesis 1 account, believed to have been written down between 500 and 400 B.C. after a long oral tradition, compares more than coincidentally with a Babylonian creation epic from 2,000 B.C., possibly much earlier, known by its opening words, *Enuma elish,* which translated means "When on high." It was found on clay tablets in the ruins of the library of King Ashurbanipal in the city of Ninevah. This epic relates how the universe was created in several steps, a firmament or hard roof which held up the sky was formed, and finally humans were made and then the creator rested.

Another epic from Babylonian culture known as the *Gilgamesh Epic* was also written about 2,000 B.C. A flood is mentioned and an angered god drowns everything. A man builds a large wooden boat and brings his family and others and a pair of all living things on board. All other terrestrial life dies and when the waters recede, a dove, swallow, and raven are loosed to find land. The parallels between this earlier Babylonian story and the Hebrew Noachian flood story are remarkable. See Appendix H for an excerpt of this record. It appears that the Genesis creation accounts and other recorded events reflect the influence of the dominant, established, surrounding Babylonian culture.

The author of the more recent account, Genesis 1:1-2:3, is known as the Priestly source. Scholars believe this author lived sometime around the 6-5th Centuries B.C. during the period from the fall of Jerusalem and subsequent Hebrew captivity in Babylon. Even though it appears in early chapters this account is believed to be one of the final sections of the Old Testament to have been recorded. Poetically composed, the chronological detail of creation clearly establishes the one God as creator who made the heavenly bodies. The week with a day set aside for rest and worship is included. The Priestly source, who called the creator Elohim, reminded the captive Hebrews that the Babylonian belief in many gods, including sun, moon, and star gods, was false belief. The Hebrew God clearly existed prior to and was creator of the heavenly bodies claimed to be gods by the Babylonians. The Priestly author was making profoundly significant theological statements in his Genesis 1 account!

While the similarities between the Genesis accounts and the Babylonian stories suggest a strong influence on the Hebrews by the surrounding dominant culture, the Hebrews' origin stories are unique in that they depict a pre-existing, sovereign Creator, separate from the creation, who effortlessly created. In addition, these accounts are nonpolitical, non-cultic, and include no ritual drama. In all of these ways the biblical stories of creation are distinctive from those of the neighbors. Scholars believe both of these sources were subsequently edited and combined into their present sequence and mysterious beauty.

In spite of the demonstrated intellectual and spiritual depth of the biblical writers, they did not base their views of creation or other aspects of the universe on empirical, scientific data. They were not aware of the methods of disciplined inquiry or how to design and implement experiment, analyze, and form conclusions. They did not have the advantage of modern scientific explanation since they were restricted in their comprehension of the world by the limitations of sense experience and the minimal tools that were at their disposal. Their thinking and writing were imaginative, poetic, and pictorial, meant to delight and inspire rather than explain. Much of it came out of a long oral history that cannot be historically documented.

If the Genesis stories are not scientifically accurate treatises on cosmology, geology, or biology, then what is their purpose? Their purpose is religious, theological. They exclaim loudly and clearly that the universe, the world, and all that is in it was created by a divine, purposeful, and omnipotent, intelligent Creator, and it was good. They deal with *meaning*.

Often moderns, who have been thoroughly acculturated into a monotheistic setting, totally miss the Genesis message of the one God. We have said, "In God we trust" and "one nation under God" since childhood and have no understanding of the historic setting of polytheism. The Hebrews were making a profound and novel statement: God, not gods. The cosmos and life were not brought into being by many gods as was believed by other cultures at that time. The God of the universe was beginning to be known. "In the beginning, God...." Some Hebrew translations say "In the beginning when God created" or "In the beginning of God's creation." These still affirm a God who always was. This God existed prior to the created order.

Furthermore, the Creator desired relationship with the created, another revolutionary idea. This God was benevolent, quite a contrast to the feared gods of their neighbors. The morality expressed in the Genesis accounts attests further to their religious significance. Their meaning goes much deeper than merely being a record of a temporal, historical happening. This is where we awesomely and humbly recognize the inspiration of these passages. It is gross error to assign and limit these narratives to scientific and historic events. Their meaning spans time into eternity. The great theological messages must be sought in these accounts and it should not be demanded of them what they do not and cannot give: science and history.

Genesis Creation Accounts vs. Modern Science

The Genesis creation accounts do not parallel what has been discovered by science in recent centuries. Some contradictions between modern science and Genesis are:

	Modern Science	**Genesis**
a)	Earth came after the sun	Earth first created heavenly body
b)	Water formed much later	Waters on early Earth
c)	Light on Earth provided by the sun	Light created before the sun was created
d)	Earth's rotation as it moves around the sun makes days	Days occurred before the sun was created
e)	Sun is a star	Sun and stars two separate entities
f)	The cosmos is about 12-14 billion years old	The cosmos is about 6-10,000 years old
g)	The Earth is about 4.5 billion years old	Earth is about 6-10,000 years old
h)	Life has been here about 3.5 billion years	Life here about 6-10,000 years
i)	Spontaneous generation and then descent with modification; microevolution and macroevolution	Spontaneous creation of mature individuals; fixity of species; microevolution
j)	Humans related to other animals	Humans created distinctly
k)	Cattle bred from wild stock; domesticated	Cattle created spontaneously as cattle
l)	Plants came long after there was the sun	Plants created before the sun
m)	First life forms were marine or aquatic unicells	First life forms were land plants

n)	Seed, fruit bearing plants geologically recent	Seed, fruit bearing plants created first
o)	Big bang, expanding universe	Universe created mature
p)	Death precedes humankind on Earth	Humankind's sin the cause of death on Earth
q)	Ecosystems include producers (plants), consumers (herbivores and carnivores which cause death), and decomposers (bacteria, fungi)	The Garden of Eden an operative ecosystem with no death
r)	Different plants and animals over the eons; extinction; evolution	All plant and animal kinds generated at one time; *all* kinds in the Garden of Eden and on the ark
s)	Soil takes thousands of years to form	Soil abruptly formed and in Garden of Eden
t)	Snakes do not have the intelligence that most mammals possess	Snake originally created as the "craftiest" of all wild animals
u)	Snakes evolved to be legless and have no apparatus for speech	Snakes legless as a punishment; they could speak and knew Adam's language
v)	Fertile soil requires organic nutrients from decayed matter	Apparently fertile soil before any death
w)	Man and woman from primate ancestor	Man abruptly created; woman from man's rib

x)	Theses based on supporting data	Theses proclaimed; no supporting data
y)	Theses based on scientific method	Theses based on a prior belief

The biblical creation literature is recognized by many as being composed of prehistoric accounts, reflecting an Eastern culture from which much was borrowed. Most biblical scholars and laypersons educated in biblical exegesis read it in light of its theological significance and not from a historic or scientific perspective. As has often been said, if we want to know as much as we can about *how* and *when* we got here we should ask scientists. If we want to know *why* we are here or *who* was responsible for our being here we should read Genesis and the rest of Holy Scripture. Christians who seek to reach truth in their interpretation of the Genesis creation accounts must humbly acknowledge that there are varying opinions on the subject within Christendom and they should be gracious in discussing differing viewpoints. Above all there should be respect for one another with Christian love and tolerance. Scientific explanations and questions should not be negated unless they have been considered thoroughly. Leaders should be competent in science and theology and present all sides. Christians can enjoy the unity that comes from their agreement of the central doctrines of the faith and exercise grace, tolerance, and inclusiveness towards those with whom they disagree on these peripheral issues.

> This is the bond of perfectness
> the anointing from above,
> and all the law of life and peace
> we find fulfilled in love.

Charles Wesley, ca. 1749

Parts of Chapter Six originated in the author's doctoral dissertation, Towne (1995), pp. 67-118.

Additional Reading

Achtemeier, Paul J. (1999). *Inspiration and authority: Nature and function of Christian Scripture*. Henderickson Publishers.

Alter, Robert (1996). *Genesis: Translation and commentary*. New York: WW Norton & Co.

Anderson, B. W. (1962). Creation. In G. A. Buttrich (Ed.), *The interpreter's dictionary of the Bible: An illustrated encyclopedia* (Vol. 1). (pp. 725-732). New York: Abingdon Press.

Anderson, B. W. (1975). *Understanding the Old Testament* (3rd ed.). Englewood Cliffs, NJ: Prentice-Hall.

Anderson, B. W. (1984). *Creation in the Old Testament*. Philadelphia: Fortress Press.

Anderson, B. W. (1987). *Creation versus chaos*. Philadelphia: Fortress Press.

Asimov, I. (1981). *In the beginning: Science faces God in the book of Genesis*. New York: Crown.

Beare, F. W. (1962). In G. A. Buttrick (Ed.). *The interpreter's dictionary of the Bible: An illustrated encyclopedia* (Vol. 1). (p. 407). New York: Abingdon Press.

Bediako, Gillan (1997). *Primal religion and the Bible*. Sheffield, England: Sheffield Academic Press.

Boadt, L. (1984). *Reading the Old Testament: An introduction*. New York: Paulist Press.

Bobrick, Benson (2001). *Wide as the waters: The story of the English Bible and the revolution it inspired*. New York: Simon & Schuster.

Bowie, W. R. (1934). *The story of the Bible*. New York: Abingdon Press.

Bright, John (1959). *A history of Israel*. Philadelphia: Westminster Press.

Bright, John (1967). *The authority of the Old Testament*. Grand Rapids, MI: Baker Book House.

Brown, Robert M. (1955). *The Bible speaks to you*. Philadelphia: The Westminster Press.

Buttrick G. A. (1952). The study of the Bible. *The interpreter's Bible* (Vol. 4). (pp. 165-171). New York: Abingdon Press.

Chase, M. E. (1944). *The Bible and the common reader*. New York: Macmillan.

Clayton, Philip (1997). *God and contemporary science*. Grand Rapids, MI: Eerdmans

Comfort, P. W. (Ed.). (1992). *The origin of the Bible*. Wheaton, IL: Tyndale House.

Efird, J. M. (1982). *The Old Testament writings: History, literature, and interpretation*. Atlanta: John Knox Press.

Denbeaux, F. J. (1958). *Understanding the Bible*. Philadelphia: Westminster Press.

Finegan, J. (1962). *In the beginning: A journey through Genesis*. New York: Harper & Bros.

Fosdick, H. E. (1958). *The modern use of the Bible*. New York: Macmillan.

Friedman, Richard Elliott (1997). *Who wrote the Bible?* San Francisco: Harper.

Fritsch, C. T. (1959). The book of Genesis. In B. H. Kelly (Ed.), *The layman's Bible commentary* (Vol. 2). Atlanta: John Knox Press.

Gilkey, L. (1959). *Maker of heaven and Earth*. Garden City, New York: Doubleday.

Gomes, Peter J. (1996). *The good book: Reading the Bible with mind and heart*. New York: Avon Books.

Grobel, K. (1962). Biblical criticism. In G. A. Buttrick (Ed.), *The interpreter's dictionary of the Bible:An illustrated encyclopedia* (Vol. 1). (pp. 407-413). New York: Abingdon Press.

Harris, Stephen L. (1992). *Understanding the Bible*. London: Mayfield Publ. Co.

Heidel, Alexander (1942). *The Babylonian Genesis*. Chicago: University of Chicago Press.

Hobbs, Herschel H. (1975). *The origin of all things: Studies in Genesis*. Waco, TX: Word Books.

Holladay, William L. (1989). *Long ago God spoke: How Christians may hear the Old Testament today*. Minneapolis: Fortress Press.

Hughes, Robert B. & Laney, J. Carl (1990). *New Bible companion*. Wheaton, IL: Tyndale House Publ.

Hyers, C. (1984). *The meaning of creation:Genesis and modern science*, Atlanta: John Knox Press.

Klein, William, Blomberg, Craig & Hubbard, Robert (1993). *Introduction to biblical interpretation*. Dallas: Word Publishing.

Koch, K. (1968). *The book of books: The growth of the Bible*. Philadelphia: Westminster Press.

Korsmeyer, Jerry D. (1998). *Evolution and Eden: Balancing original sin and contemporary science*. New York: Paulist Press.

Leeming, David A. (1990). *The world of myth*. New York: Oxford University Press.

MacGregor, Geddes (1968). *A literary history of the Bible: From the Middle Ages to the present day*. New York: Abingdon Press.

Mangum, John M. (Ed.). (1989). *The new faith-science debate*. Minneapolis: Fortress Press.

Martin, Daniel W. (Ed.). (1991). *Science and Christian faith: The connection.* Presbyterian Publishing House.

McKenzie, John L. (1956). *The two-edged sword: An interpretation of the Old Testament,* Milwaukee: The Bruce Publishing Co.

Metzger, Bruce M. (1968). *The text of the New Testament* (2nd ed.). New York: Oxford University Press.

Metzger, Bruce M. & Coogan, Michael D. (Eds.). (1993). *The Oxford companion to the Bible.* New York: Oxford University Press.

Miller, James B. & McCall, Kenneth E. (Eds.). (1990). *The church and contemporary cosmology.* Pittsburgh: Carnegie Mellon University Press.

Mixter, Russell (Ed.). (1959). *Evolution and Christian thought today.* Grand Rapids, MI: Eerdmans.

Moreland, J. P. (Ed.). (1994). *The creation hypothesis: Scientific evidence for an intelligent designer.* Downers Grove, IL: InterVarsity Press.

Muilenburg, James (1952). The history of the religion of Israel. *The Interpreter's Bible* (Vol. 1). (pp. 292-348). New York: Abingdon Press.

Mulder, M. J. (1989). Israel to the time of the Babylonian captivity. In A. S. Van der Woude (Ed.), *The world of the Old Testament, Bible handbook* (Vol. II). Grand Rapids, MI: Eerdmans.

Munger, Scott (1999). *Bible, Babel and babble.* Colorado Springs: International Bible Society.

Neibuhr, R. (1957). The truth in myths. In G. Kennedy (Ed.), *Evolution and religion: The conflict between science and religion in modern America.* Boston: D. C. Heath.

Payne, J. Barton (Ed.). *New perspectives on the Old Testament.* Waco, TX: Word Books.

Polkinghorne, John (2001). *Faith, science and understanding.* New Haven: Yale University Press.

Ramm, Bernard (1956). *The Christian view of science and scripture.* Grand Rapids, MI: Eerdmans.

Rolston, Holmes III (1987). *Science and religion: A critical survey.* Random House.

Russell, Robert, Stoeger, William & Coyne, George (Eds.). (1997). *Physics, philosophy and theology:A common quest for understanding* (3rd ed.). Vatican City State: Vatican Observatory.

Sailhamer, J. H. (1996). *Genesis unbound.* Sisters, OR: Multnomah Books.

Sandars, N. K. (1960). *The epic of Gilgamesh.* New York: Penguin Books.

Sarna, N. M. (1972). *Understanding Genesis.* New York: Schocken Books.

Schmitz-Moormann, Karl (1997). *Theology of creation in an evolutionary world.* Cleveland: Pilgrim Press.

Speiser, E. A. (1964). *The Anchor Bible: Genesis.* Garden City, NY: Doubleday & Co., Inc.

Steck, Odil Hannes (1998). *Old Testament exegesis.* Atlanta: Scholars Press.

Stott, J. R. W. (1972). *Understanding the Bible.* Minneapolis: World Wide Publications.

Swaim, J. C. (1953). *Right and wrong ways to use the Bible.* Philadelphia: Westminster Press.

Towne, Margaret G. (1995). *The influence of critical thinking on Christians' belief and belief change with reference to the polarities of creationism and organic evolution.* Doctoral dissertation, Montana State University.

Weber, Otto (1959). *Ground plan of the Bible* (Harold Knight, Trans.). Philadelphia: The Westminster Press.

Wegner, Paul D. (1999). *The journey from text to translations: The origin and development of the Bible.* Grand Rapids, MI: Baker Books.

Wells, Albert N. (1946). *The Christian message in a scientific age.* Richmond, VA: John Knox Press.

Zornberg, Avivah Gottlieb (1995). *Genesis: The beginning of desire.* Philadelphia: The Jewish Publication Society.

Evolutionary Theory

Chapter Seven

*Nothing in life is to be feared, it is only to be understood.
Now is the time to understand more, so that we may fear
less.*
                    Marie Curie

The truth shall make you free.
                    Gospel of John 8:32

Introduction

Since the middle of the 19th Century when Charles Darwin published *On
the Origin of Species,* evolutionary theory has been at the center of
controversy. Even the word evolution is filled with emotional and sensitive
religious baggage for some. When I was a guide in a paleontology museum
while in college, the instructions for one tour, a group of 4th graders from a
private school, said "Do the Hall of Evolution but do not mention the word
evolution."

Many people have rejected evolution because they perceive it to be a
threat to their religious convictions. This threat has motivated them to launch
various crusades to eliminate evolution from the culture and replace it with
a model that is consistent with their religious beliefs. At the turn of the 21st
Century many states were considering eliminating evolution or adding
alternative beliefs to their public school curricula. As discussed in Chapter
Five, in August 1999, the Board of Education in the state of Kansas,
dominated by the apparently fearful religious, succeeded in eliminating
evolutionary understanding as well as Big Bang cosmology from state science
exams. The following year voters replaced board members who voted to
remove these subjects from the exams and in 2001 the new board restored the
Theory of Evolution and Big Bang cosmology to state school standards.

In the 1920s, Tennessee enacted the Butler Act which outlawed instruction
in evolutionary theory in the public schools. Arkansas, Mississippi, and
Oklahoma had similar prohibitions. A substitute teacher, John Scopes,
challenged the law in Tennessee and the resulting trial in 1925 in Dayton,
Tennessee delivered the conflict into the courtroom, and to radios and
newspapers across the nation. Various interpretations and apprehensions

146

regarding this theory were exposed and the ignorance surrounding the subject became painfully evident.

The Butler Act was not repealed until 1967 and its impact on the subversion of education in the field of evolutionary theory over those decades in Tennessee can never be measured. In 1968, the Supreme Court of the United States declared any law banning the teaching of evolutionary theory in the public schools to be unconstitutional. In spite of that ruling, a thick shroud of ignorance about evolution continues to envelop most Americans. While teaching evolutionary theory is legal, many public school science teachers avoid the subject because of the potential for conflict and even harassment by parents as well as school board members and community and religious leaders. Some are silent for fear of losing their jobs. One confided that it is usually at the end of the text and she conveniently runs out of time before getting to those chapters.

In recent decades much has been heard in some religious circles about the apparent weakness of evolutionary data. An aggressive movement against this theory has migrated into the political arena and from there it has rippled into the educational and legal worlds. Since evolutionary theory has survived for almost 150 years, withstanding rigorous peer review within the scientific community and severe attack from without, it is important to ascertain just what basis there is for its tenacity. Furthermore, why is fear associated with this discipline? Is it justified?

Evolutionary theory encompasses many areas of science and is a very technical and complex discipline. It is understandable, therefore, that many citizens are not well informed or do not understand the evidence that justifies its perseverance as a well-founded scientific theory. Most people deny its validity because the authorities they have chosen deny it. They have not arrived at their opinions as a result of autonomous, conscientious, and thorough study. This becomes apparent when inconsistencies, omissions, errors, and misinterpretations are regularly expressed by lay people as well as by those who lead and assume the position of authority in the war against the theory. The latter often generate and propagate the error, knowingly or unknowingly.

Since evolutionary theory is not taught in detail in most public K-12 school settings, it isn't until college that most students are confronted in depth with its supporting data. High school biology teachers who cover this may have, at the most, only a few weeks to cover its many dimensions such as its historical background, thesis, support base, and areas needing further research. Since it is interdisciplinary, competencies in biology (including genetics, embryology, biogeography, physiology and anatomy), chemistry, geology, and paleontology are required in order to comprehend its theses.

Those who major in business, the arts, engineering, mathematics, languages, medicine, law, religion, the humanities, or even the physical sciences may never get adequate grounding in this field which unites all of life, yet has become so suspect and divisive within the religious culture.

The reality is that many college graduates and most who have not gone on to college have never been thoroughly and objectively exposed to this theory's supporting data. They often naively fall prey to pseudoauthorities. As a result, inaccurate, deceptive, or incomplete statements continually appear in the anti-evolutionary literature, at creationist workshops, lectures, seminars and debates, on TV, or are shockingly revealed when conversing with individuals holding creationist views. Rampant ignorance regarding this significant theory of modern science abounds. I experienced this firsthand during research on a doctoral dissertation on Christians' belief positions regarding creationism and evolution.

No one should accept evolutionary theory on faith or regard scientists as omniscient authorities. Just because a lot of people, including those who are very educated, believe a particular hypothesis does not automatically make it true. Seekers should assess authorities, reserve judgment, and critically, openmindedly, honestly, and relentlessly examine the supporting data for this thesis just as with any other body of knowledge. They should be informed of evolution's limitations and unanswered questions, many of which are presented in the following chapter. They should always remember that science is a search for truth and the journey never ends. Science is tentative.

Some of the confusion that surrounds origins and evolution results from the lack of consistency and precision in the terminology commonly associated with these two disciplines. It is difficult for a serious inquirer to fully grasp the fundamentals, let alone the subtleties associated with these various areas of inquiry, when terms are not defined cogently and consistently. This occurs because many nonspecialists, those not trained in theology or science, frequently write about these subjects. They are not familiar with the standard, often technical definitions that are used by professionals in these specialized fields. Some scientists and many devout Christians who are unsophisticated in biblical exegesis write on these issues, as do representatives from the religious community who falsely assume authority in science. Valid authorities should have seriously studied both theology and science at the graduate level at accredited institutions.

Before launching into the support for evolutionary theory, the following important section seeks to clarify the definitions of some key terms which are regularly associated with discussion on creationism and evolution.

Definitions

Science

Science is that reasoned discipline that studies the material universe. It is guided by natural, dependable law and its claims are testable by empirical (observational or experimental; can be demonstrated) or inferential (based on circumstantial evidence) means. It attempts to rationally explain and give grounds for its assertions. Scientists seek to acquire and then systematically organize knowledge about the universe and its parts. Science is sometimes described as a way of understanding or knowing. One of its main objectives is to generate novel ideas, possible explanations, or hypotheses (educated guesses) about an unknown and then seek to prove or disprove them.

The statements and assertions of science are tentative and open to continual refinement. New information and fresh insights that might alter prior conclusions are regularly considered. Science changes. There is no absolute truth in science and there is always the possibility that future evidence will cause former conclusions to be modified or discarded. It is not an embarrassment in science to admit error. It means truth is approached more fully. Scientists should be applauded for correcting error rather than be derided for erring in the first place. All new phenomena or new ways of thinking or interpreting data are vulnerable to initial misinterpretation or misunderstanding. One of my mentors, an expert in dinosaur behavior, humbly stated, "Being the first in this field means that I know the least. I am pleased to be corrected by a colleague or student for then we have moved toward truth."

Scientists, like most other people, sometimes resist change or reject new perspectives. For a variety of reasons it was decades before Barbara McClintock's research with transposons (jumping genes), Alfred Wegener's continental drift thesis, or Gregor Mendel's research with pea inheritance were recognized as being valid and significant. Scientists are human, subject to the limitations of that condition. In spite of that, we are overwhelmed at the amazing data that scientists have provided. The data answer our questions and facilitate subsequent technological development which provides a longer and better quality of life for all.

Science is characterized by objectivity, where precedence is given to verifiable (provable, demonstrable) facts. The critique and input of colleagues helps scientists achieve and preserve this objectivity. Vigorous and healthy science invites peer review, which contributes to correcting error and refining thought although it may take time. The critique of colleagues is a significant activity in science, for it exposes all data to independent review and challenge and sometimes generates lively controversy. Nonscientists often misinterpret this haggling as weakness. On the contrary, it is science at work and it indicates normalcy and health. It is an important means of separating wheat (truth) from chaff (error). There are numerous professional journals, seminars, and conferences that inform the scientific community of new hypotheses or data and provide a forum for questions, alternative interpretation, clarification, and critique as well as stimulate further study. Scientists in the same discipline regularly keep in touch informally and personally. Computer technology has opened up a variety of new opportunities for speedy and efficient data and idea exchange. On-line discussion groups provide forums for interchange and reassessment. The popular media regularly report new ideas from science to the masses. Science is not a secret.

This rigorous and lively activity is one of the reasons why evolutionary theory has become so entrenched in modern scholarly thinking. It has stood the onslaught of constant peer and outside review for over a century! It is very important that the nonscientist understand that the bantering that goes on among evolutionary scientists is normal to the practice of science.

Scientists employ the scientific method in their search for knowledge. They begin with a problem and develop a hypothesis, which is an informed guess. Their subsequent research seeks to prove or disprove this hypothesis. Experiments are designed using controls which eliminate variables and enable the researcher to identify specific factors that impact the data. Data from those experiments are collected and interpreted and then conclusions are drawn based upon the data. Repeated experiments support or invalidate conclusions.

Peers across the globe and down through the years critique experimental design, methods, interpretations, and conclusions, often quite vigorously. Along with providing support for a thesis, it is appropriate for scientists to expose areas that need to be further assessed, and to point out the questions and puzzles that remain. This encourages more research and is being honest with the data. Some believe textbooks dealing with evolution could more conscientiously include these insights and outline the enigmas which persist.

Those who study the literature in the creationism/evolution controversy look almost in vain for a forum of challenge for creationist assertions. Their videos, pamphlets, books, children's books, periodicals, and seminars give one perspective, and avoid the problems. There is little peer review in print and rarely opportunity for public questions at seminars. Letters to the editor in popular creationist publications tend to be complimentary, not critical, and are generally unsigned. It's a quiet world. Why?

A milieu that generates no interaction among those of opposite persuasion or where no differing opinion or perspective is entertained, where peers do not demand accountability or empirical evidence, and colleagues' errors tend to be ignored or overlooked for whatever reasons, where weaknesses are not promptly exposed and admitted, and where there is no forum for alternative hypotheses cannot be practicing science. Science is based on sensate, demonstrated evidence, not cherished but unsubstantiated belief.

Science is falsifiable, which means it is capable of being tested and disproven. Scientists not only seek evidence to verify or prove a theory, but just as vigorously they seek evidence to refute it. When serious attempts are made to disprove a theory and they do not succeed, validity for that theory is strengthened. The real test of proposed truth or hypothesis is finding and exposing its weaknesses and flaws. This is the healthy skepticism associated with critical thinking applied to the scientific method. Creationists could employ this in the following way: instead of looking for data that prove the Earth is young, look for data that disprove that idea. Try to disprove a thesis. If one fails in valid and persistent attempts to disprove a hypothesis, that strengthens it. If one refuses to attempt falsification the thesis remains weak and is not respected within the scientific community.

Assertions that cannot be disproved, such as beliefs in devils, angels, miracles, or supernatural events, do not come under the realm of science. A miraculous, spoken creation that spontaneously appeared out of nothing in a mature state cannot be proven or disproved. It is accepted by faith and is not science. There is no room within the domain of science for authority beyond that which can be proven or demonstrated within the laws of nature. Reason alone is the scientist's means of reaching an understanding of the universe. Natural laws are dependable and a knowledge of them enables scientists to infer events or predict outcomes.

Scientific conclusions ideally are supported by observed data but sometimes they are based on inferred data or circumstantial evidence that cannot be empirically demonstrated or repeated. Similar conclusions are common in law enforcement. When there are no witnesses to a murder, for example, but the circumstantial evidence becomes overwhelming, a jury can conclude beyond reasonable doubt that a particular person is guilty.

A grizzly bear can be strongly suspected in the death of a rancher's calf even though no one saw it kill because wildlife biologists are keenly aware of the telltale signs of grizzly activity and can quite accurately discern the different methods which grizzlies, coyotes, mountain lions, or wolves use to kill their prey. Footprints or DNA assessment of tissue or fur can give corroborating evidence. Just because no one witnessed the kill doesn't mean there are no means to assess quite conclusively what occurred. Conclusions here are based on strong inferential, not experimental, data.

Arriving home one day, I found a note of greeting on the inside garage door in the handwriting of our daughter. Away at college, she was not in the habit of coming home unexpectedly but that note was compelling evidence and I immediately inferred that she had indeed been home. Later, I found an empty soda can by the kitchen sink. Yes, I thought, she *was* here. That evening her laundry bag was discovered in the laundry room. All this circumstantial evidence convinced me that she had paid us a visit. No one saw her but the evidence was quite overwhelming. There is always the slight chance that she didn't drop in and that it was someone else who had the key, wrote the note, left the can and laundry bag, but that was extremely unlikely.

Folded strata exposed on a mountain gives inference that they were at one time horizontal and something caused the upheaval that resulted in angular or vertical layers. No one was there to witness it, but a story with a support base can be extrapolated to suggest what happened. There is no doubt that clues in the present give insight into the past.

This inferential means of gathering information and forming conclusions based on appropriate study, clear reasoning, and corroborating evidence is regularly employed in the exercise of science and is considered a valid means of gaining evidence in evolutionary science and cosmology, in genetics, law, chemistry, medicine, astronomy, and many other disciplines. Molecular change resulting in mutations, atomic structure, virus replication, bacteria traveling to bronchioles in the lungs, dinosaur migrations, or changes in gazelle populations over the millennia may not be observed or repeated yet confirmation can be made regarding all of these from an inferred perspective. No one witnessed the Big Bang, the origin of life, or geological or evolutionary events in the far distant past. The evidence from fossils, astronomy, radiometric dating, DNA, species distribution, comparative anatomy, mathematics, physics, geological features, and even behavior, tells a story that becomes quite compelling. Rational minds find it appropriate to draw conclusions based on that large volume of inferred data. As with all conclusions in science, though, they remain tentative and may eventually be disproved or modified as new data or more accurate interpretations of old data arrive.

It must be clearly understood that conclusions based on a preponderance of supporting evidence arriving from inferred sources can be quite convincing and valid. At a recent conference a leading creationist explained that "Neither creationism nor evolution qualifies as a scientific theory. There were no human witnesses. Science is the study of observable events." This definition rejects all inferred data as being valid. For example, consider teeth marks of a *T. rex* on a *Triceratops* pelvis. Can science not study them and formulate hypotheses? A Concorde crashed in France in July 2000. No one saw what started the engine fire. Scientists weighed the data objectively, considered all possibilities, and concluded that the engine was hit with tire fragments, probably generated by a piece of metal on the runway. This thesis may be altered in the future if more data arrive. Science is always tentative but deductions from the evidence provided can be quite valid.

Creationist literature often suggests that if no one was there to witness an event or if it is unrepeatable then it cannot be known what really happened. "Were you there?" they exuberantly ask at seminars, suggesting that if you weren't present at creation then you cannot know what happened. This is an unfair tactic, ignoring the validity of inferential science. It either betrays an ignorance of science or is an attempt to capitalize on laypersons' naiveté of valid scientific methodology.

Theory

In science, a theory is a detailed description of some aspect of the workings of the universe. It is the result of critical reasoning gained from repeated observations, experiments, and inferences by researchers in a variety of settings over months, years, decades. A theory is a unifying system of ideas or statements that have internal coherence. It synthesizes and explains phenomena from a variety of disciplines. This leads to further hypotheses, and applications. There will be a history that records any modifications, disproved hypotheses, dead ends, enigmas, or anomalies. One scientist's theory must withstand the rigorous and persistent peer review of fellow scientists and other critics. Darwin's theory continues to experience this before our eyes.

Scientists begin their search for knowledge by forming hypotheses, commonly referred to as "educated guesses." An informed researcher may develop a hypothesis and then design experiments to prove or disprove the idea. Many proven hypotheses contribute to the formation of a theory.

Theories are often stepping stones in the search for truth and are always open to revision. They are constantly vulnerable to attack, which either fortifies them or leads to their demise. A good scientific theory should explain and organize unrelated facts, suggest experiments, and predict their outcomes. The results may substantiate the theory or lead to its downfall. Theories must be testable, and vulnerable to challenge and falsification (being disproved).

The support for some theories is so strong that the likelihood of their being disproved is very remote. Ignorance is exposed when one suggests that a scientific theory is "only a theory," implying that it is not grounded in strong supporting data. Scientists define theory differently than the general population, which often assumes that a theory is a new and untested idea or has minimal or weak support. Nonspecialists who assert "It's only a theory" when attacking the evolutionary position expose their amateur status. This statement is misleading for theory in science represents a solid, though always tentative, grounding. Evolutionary theory has been modified and expanded over the decades as new information has been received, but its tenets of change over time are well supported and remain difficult to disprove. It is called a synthetic theory because it unites many widely disparate disciplines from cosmology to geology to genetics to biochemistry.

Other scientific theories besides Evolutionary Theory include the Germ Theory of Disease (micro-organisms are responsible for many diseases), the Cell Theory (living things are composed of subunits called cells), Atomic Theory (explanation of the structure and function of atoms, which compose matter), Quantum Theory (provides a basis for analyzing matter, motion, and radiation), and Einstein's Theory of Relativity (matter and energy are interchangeable and space and time are a continuum). It is apparent that these theories represent profound truths and carry much weight. They do not represent loosely tentative, weak, or uncertain assertions.

Darwin resisted using the term theory in reference to his hypotheses. He referred to his ideas as "principles" or "explanations" and was candidly open about the tentativeness of his ideas and honest as to what had not been proven and the remaining enigmas.

Species

Biologists classify organisms into groups and assign scientific names in a process called taxonomy or systematics. Taxonomy facilitates study of the organisms and provides an understanding of their interrelationships. Taxonomists begin by separating living things into major categories called kingdoms. These are then subdivided into phyla and phyla into subphyla or classes. Further divisions include orders, families, genera, and species. Larger categories such as plants, animals, fungi, or bacteria are fairly easy to differentiate. Organisms in different kingdoms, such as plants and animals, are not closely related and have distinctive morphology (form or structure), behavior, ancestry, physiology (function), or means of obtaining energy. They are easily categorized and described.

A species, however, is a very narrow category. It is difficult to define because every imaginable gradation exists. A variety of characteristics are used to distinguish organisms from each other at this level. For instance, in bacteria, which do not sexually reproduce, morphology, motility, type of respiration, response to various staining methods, and the ability to form spores help separate them from each other.

The main criterion that taxonomists use to assign two sexually reproducing organisms to the same species is their ability to interbreed, either actually or potentially. Actually means that organisms indeed successfully interbreed. Potentially means that if these organisms were in contact they could successfully interbreed. An animal in North America might potentially be able to breed with one from Europe but never be given the opportunity. Likewise organisms on opposite sides of a river, mountain, or even a freeway may be physiologically able to breed but geographically isolated.

Reproductive isolation, then, is the main means by which taxonomists distinguish separate species. It is assumed that when two organisms are able to produce fertile young, they must be closely related anatomically (they are able to mate), physiologically and chemically (fertilization and fetal growth are able to occur), temporally (they mature sexually at the same time), and behaviorally (sexual attraction exists), as well as share a similar geographical environment. They are considered to be the same species. A horse bred with a donkey yields a mule, yet the mule is sterile or nonviable. This demonstrates how tricky it is to define a species. These two animals are very close in that they successfully bear young. Yet their young are not able to reproduce, so the horse and donkey are separate species.

Usually the species definition includes breeding "in the wild," for some animals such as the lion and tiger will breed in captivity and produce "ligers" or "tigrons" but they have never been known to do so in a natural or wild setting. A dog and red fox can conceive, yet their embryos die. This is a clear species separation of closely related organisms.

Another phenomenon that demonstrates why species are not easy to define is the condition where a female of one kind (A) will successfully mate with the male of another kind (B) and produce viable offspring, yet the male of (A) and the female of (B) will not successfully breed. Are A and B the same species??? Researchers were interested in finding out if snails in the USA were the same species as similar snails found in Egypt. They attempted to breed them. Interestingly, they were successful in getting the males of one group to breed with the females of the other group but could not accomplish the opposite. Were they the same species?

Can a Chihuahua breed with a Great Dane? They are anatomically isolated in that they could not successfully copulate and technically they could be considered different species by the interbreeding definition, yet artificial insemination of the female Great Dane would no doubt result in the production of viable offspring. This is also where the clarifying concept "in the wild" would apply. They could not breed in the wild or without technological intervention. If reproductive viability is the present definition of species, obviously this criterion cannot be assigned to extinct animals and plants where only limited morphology, biogeography, age, and a few other factors are known. Other characteristics that can make a species distinct include its particular genetic endowment, including its coloration, anatomy, physiology, and behavior, as well as the habitat in which it finds itself, including its predators, food demands, and competition.

Chance plays a role in species distribution as rivers take new channels, Earth movements occur, a volcano erupts, a new predator or infectious microbe appears, food sources disappear, or the climate changes. Some species are lucky. They just happen to have what is needed to survive in the modified environment, or their members could either move to more ideal settings or adapt to the change. Others can't adapt for innumerable reasons and succumb, becoming extinct. Nature selects for the more adaptable and against those that are less fit at a particular time and place. It is significant to note that nature doesn't whimsically select. Natural selection is not random. There are precise factors that allow some organisms to prevail while others do not.

One could say that luck, or chance, does play a role, however. Species have become extinct because they happened to be in the wrong place at the wrong time. A volcano destroyed an isolated population, resulting in its extinction. When humans decided to use exotic feathers in hats, or tusks as aphrodisiacs, the source animals fell prey. Human activity in establishing cities, overhunting, spraying insecticide, building nuclear reactors, mining, waging war, contaminating rivers, logging, putting in fences or removing habitats in a multitude of other ways have caused many species to suffer serious decline through no fault of their own.

Boundaries between populations are often hard to discern, so additional categories beyond the species level such as varieties and subspecies are designated to help classify and order the living world. A variety of opinion exists among experts as some differences are quite subtle within these categories, especially in the case of fossils, where data are limited. Nature is not bound by human classification dictates and the delineations can be illusive.

The definition of a species is a significant subject in the creationism/evolution forum. Creationists hold that pairs of all "kinds" of terrestrial animals, all modern groups as well as those extinct, were aboard Noah's ark. If "kinds" were similar to species there was just not enough room for that many animals to fit, given the biblical dimensions for the ark. It is estimated that there are approximately 20 million species of animals alive today, and scientists suggest there could be hundreds of millions of extinct species. Not all of these would be terrestrial animals which would have been on the ark, but the numbers needing to be represented would be overwhelming.

Creationists respond that the Bible refers to "kinds" being in the ark and that such kinds do not equate to the modern definition of species. If they do not, then biologists are stymied as to how the enormous variety of present day reproductively isolated species (370,000 beetles, 165,000 moths and butterflies, 4,400 mammals) could have arisen in the 4,500 years since the flood. Mighty fast change over time! Revolution! Even today scientists have not identified all living species. Creationists cannot give a clear definition as to what exactly "kinds" are. They are variously and tentatively described as groups on the genus or family level perhaps. Yet creationists must limit humans to the species level for they dare not lump them with other hominid "kinds." This is one of the glaring weaknesses of the creationist model.

Generally, creationists hold to a "fixity of species" concept whereby only microevolution, to which they do not give clearly defined parameters, occurs. If a worldwide flood took place and pairs of all "kinds" of animals could fit on the ark, including the known numerous and large dinosaurs (and more being discovered every year) as well as all other extinct and living species, then obviously there has been quite a bit of descent with modification since the flood era to account for the vast numbers and variety of living species presently in the world. Ironically, that is exactly what evolution is: descent with modification.

Some creationists allow for much microevolution but insist there is no additional genetic information, just modified information. They deny increasing complexity but must acknowledge the change that has occurred.

Evolution

Evolution is a process that results in changes in a population over time, due to changing genes and allele frequencies in genes, which can in turn be passed on to further generations. Alleles are different forms of a particular gene that result in variations in a population in such characteristics as hair or eye color or blood type. The gene pertains to hair color but the specific message or allele may be any of a variety of different colors. One allele may be selected for in a particular environment or obtain dominance by genetic drift, and subsequent generations will have more of the character that it represents. Others can be selected against and disappear from a population. Humans living near the Equator tend to have dark skin and hair as this gives them adaptive advantage in that sunny milieu. Fair skinned people would be at a disadvantage, would be selected against, and indeed originally thrived only in northern climates. It is important to note that evolution does not occur in individuals but in populations.

Many people in science study contemporary life forms. For example, physicians learn about human immunities, biochemistry, organs and systems and veterinarians learn about cattle or dog anatomy and physiology. Those in agriculture or horticulture are interested in plants. High school biology students dissect a grasshopper or fetal pig. All of this study seeks to answer the question: "What are they like now?" Evolution, on the other hand, is the means by which biology is studied historically. Evolutionists are interested in the *history* of human immunology, biochemistry, organs and systems, the *history* of cattle or dogs. They seek to understand the *history* of grains, pine trees, flowering plants, their origins and changes over time; the *origins* of grasshoppers and pigs and all the *interrelationships* involved over time. They seek to answer questions such as "How did these structures, processes, or individuals get to be the way they are now?" "Who are they related to and what was their journey to this point?" "What is their story historically?"

Evolution holds that similar organisms have a common inheritance. Generally, the greater similarity between two groups of organisms, the closer in time they separated from an ancestral group. Each species proceeded from another species that predated it; this occurred only once in a single geographical setting. A single step can take tens of thousands of years or occur more quickly depending on many factors, some known and some unknown. Extinction occurs because new, more fit forms evolve and displace those less well adapted, or the environment changes to something unsuitable for a previously fit species. An earlier species can persist beyond a more recently evolved species if it happens to be better adapted. That is why we have some "living fossils" today such as the coelacanth fishes, and the tuatara which have outlived some of their evolutionary descendants. It is believed that the Earth is old enough for inherited change among organisms to have occurred and some of the mechanisms that explain these changes have been identified.

Early scientists noted that each generation of plants and animals produces an overabundance of offspring and only a few survive to adulthood. This leads to intraspecies competition for food, mates, territory, and shelter. The individuals in a population, including the siblings in a particular family, litter, pod, herd, or brood (or spores from a specific fern or seeds from a conifer or flowering plant) show genetic variability. It follows that some of these variations may prove advantageous in a particular environment and bestow a better chance for survival on that organism. Different traits may be chosen under different environmental situations. These adaptive or more favorable traits persist as individuals possessing them live to reproduce and pass them on to the next generation. Over time the population will change as nature selects the various genetic characteristics that are most beneficial. In the process some traits will be eliminated. Eventually, enough changes can accumulate to establish a new species.

The processes of natural selection occur when individuals that are most adapted to a particular environment survive and reproduce, resulting in a predominance of those fit genes in the population. A corresponding elimination or decrease of those individuals whose genes are not as fit contributes to the changes observed in populations over time. An example of this is the large ears seen in rabbits on the desert. The greater surface area allows more dissipation of body heat, an advantage in a hot climate. Those with this quality are selected for. Small eared rabbits in this climate do not survive. Smaller ears on rabbits in colder climates help them conserve heat. In this setting those with this quality proliferate. Large ears disappear from the population. This is natural selection at work. Those with the advantageous characteristics prevail and the population is modified over time.

Inherited changes might be expressed in the structure (anatomy), function (physiology), biochemistry, or behavior of living organisms. They can be the result of underlying genetic changes called mutations. Mutations are alterations in the structure of DNA (deoxyribonucleic acid, molecules found in the cell nucleus that carry the recipe for life) such as recombinations, migrations, additions, duplications, and deletions of subunits of genetic material. Environmental conditions such as radiation or some chemicals have been shown to trigger such changes. No doubt other factors not yet identified also operate.

Another factor that influences animal population change is a dynamic referred to as nonrandom mating. Factors other than chance, such as appearance, scent, or behavior, influence the mating behavior of organisms. This results in the dominance of certain characteristics and the elimination of others. Individuals with a preferred quality will be chosen as mates more often than if purely random mating behavior were operating.

In addition, the founder effect is a phenomenon seen in small populations that have become isolated from a larger population. Change occurs as some genes, which may not have been selected for in a large population where there were other competing genes, become established in a small population. In time they can give rise to new species if the new organisms, having changed over long periods in isolation, are not able to breed with members of the original population.

Evolution, change over time, has been demonstrated through artificial selection when humans choose specific qualities and selectively breed plants such as corn, wheat, tomatoes, strawberries, apple trees, and rosebushes, or animals such as lab mice, pigeons, rabbits, cats, cattle, horses, and dogs. When nature does the selecting it takes longer for observed change but the same processes are operating.

When the AIDS virus was first identified in humans in the early 1980s, everyone wondered about its origin. How long had it been in humans, unknown to us? Presumably it had been someplace else prior to invading humans and evolved to the point that it could cross into the human species. Scientists find that the virus continues to change, so that a vaccine that might be developed today may not be effective tomorrow. We have been cognizant of this phenomenon with cold and flu viruses for many years. It results in our requiring a new flu shot each year as the antibodies derived from one year's vaccination are ineffective with the mutated viral strains that appear the next year. This is change seen within a species over time, or microevolution. These changes, when compounded, can eventually lead to the formation of new species, or macroevolution. All of these changes demonstrate descent with modification: evolution.

In the far distant past, North America and South America were separated. Marine organisms were similar in the common ocean between these two continents. Then, approximately 3 million years ago, these two continents joined. This separated the organisms in the west (Pacific populations) from those in the Caribbean region. Over time distinct species evolved in these separated environments. Although related, gastropods (snails), bivalves (clams), corals, and echinoderms (sand dollars and sea urchins) became distinctive in the two areas. The origin of species. Macroevolution.

The rate of evolution varies. It can be comparatively quick in organisms with short lifespans such as bacteria, which can divide in minutes or hours. Animals requiring many years to reach reproductive maturity and having few offspring, such as large mammals, may not undergo visible change for hundreds of thousands of years or even more. Creationists often mention that macroevolution, large change, has never been observed. It is generally preposterous to demand that it be demonstrated in a lab or a lifetime. Some species are extremely well adapted, such as the aforementioned coelacanth fish, various insects, crocodiles, horseshoe crabs, or opossums, and remain unchanged for millions of years. Organisms that have undergone macroevolution have experienced a summation of many microevolutionary events. These events take enormous periods of time and are often hidden within the biochemistry of the body. Therefore, this process of reproductive isolation that results in new species cannot readily be observed. This contributes to the difficulty scientists have in empirically demonstrating evolution and gives much fuel to critics who regularly demand visible, temporal examples.

While many of the mechanisms that result in change over time have been identified, biologists confess to not being aware of all of the factors that explain the changes which have occurred. The vast majority of scientists assert unequivocally that evolution *has* taken place because the observed data are overwhelming, yet at the same time they acknowledge that they are not yet able to demonstrate or explain all of its mechanisms. Much as creationists wish the latter would negate or detract from the former, it does not. Rationality and honesty require us to admit that modification events have taken place. That we cannot explain all of the causes doesn't negate the reality of their occurrence. In August 1996, a passenger airplane to Europe went down near Long Island. Four years later a cause was finally identified. Our inability for 4 years to explain its cause, however, did not shed doubt on its reality. In like manner, presumably in time more of the mechanisms for evolution will eventually become clear.

There is still much that is not known about how genes affect phenotype (how an organism or structure looks) or how they work. Some very exciting research in new disciplines called bioinformatics (finding hidden answers in the genome, understanding the functions of genes) and proteomics (cataloging and understanding the body's protein activity to make sense of the genetic code through an understanding of proteins and the mutations that affect them) will no doubt give some light in the years to come. There is optimism that these two disciplines will fill in huge knowledge gaps that exist in the areas of genetic function and evolution.

Evolutionary belief does not speak to purpose, such as why the universe or humans were created. Science does not deny purpose nor can it explain it. That is outside of its boundaries. Evolution says nothing about God. Evolution, being science, cannot prove or disprove a supernatural creator. It only deals with change over time and, if presented appropriately, allows the seeker freedom to assign cause from a religious perspective or deny cause and claim atheism. It is unfair and misleading to suggest that evolution negates belief in a creator God. Most evolutionists affirm God as creator, operating through natural laws over millions of years giving being to a universe capable of developing within intended, designed laws. Evolutionary theory does disagree with the creation stories in Genesis, if taken literally. As has been pointed out, these stories even disagree with each other, if taken literally.

It is very important to clarify that evolution does not speak to the origin of life. Many authors combine these two subjects, adding much to the confusion surrounding evolution and creationism. How life arose is one area of inquiry. That living things have changed is another very distinct phenomenon. Even though some fascinating experiments have shown that parts of protein molecules can self-assemble, and recent data give hints that may explain why some proteins are "righthanded," there is not at present as much foundation for theses on the origin of life as there is on evolution, change through time. Many people are evolutionists because they respect the substantiating data for change over time but frankly do not have enough evidence to form opinions on life's origins. This is where they must reserve judgment, possibly indefinitely, until more data arrive.

It is therefore imperative that those who write on these subjects distinguish between evolutionary theory and the origins of life or the universe and not lump them together. The latter two have different support bases and are distinct areas of research with their own scientific specialists, history, and foundational theory. They should be considered entirely separately from the former, which has a remarkably strong and distinctive supporting data base. Individuals expose their confusion on the issues when they insist on combining these diverse subjects. It is irrelevant and downright deceptive to argue against evolutionary theory by pointing out problems in the biochemistry of the origin of life or in cosmology. Those who study these issues must always remember that evolution pertains to change over time, descent with modification, and it must honestly be asked: Did or did not that occur? If it did, then evolution must be acknowledged. It is that simple. Just because the origin of life cannot be demonstrated at the molecular level does not negate evolution, which has been strongly inferred at the molecular, cellular, systemic, species, genus levels and beyond.

Evolutionary theory, including macroevolution, is one of the most unifying theories in science, involving and being supported by many diverse disciplines such as geology, biology (physiology, behavioral science, parasitology, systematics, embryology, anatomy, genetics), psychology, biogeography, cosmology, biochemistry, and anthropology. It has withstood rigorous peer review for well over a century and the supporting evidence continues to accumulate from these many and varied disciplines. Even though questions of mechanism remain, this substantial body of data contributes to a certainty beyond a reasonable doubt and leads scientists and other informed and fairminded inquirers to declare evolution, change over time, as fact.

Microevolution and Macroevolution

Authors who write on evolution and creationism distinguish between microevolution and macroevolution. Evolutionists and most creationists accept the former, which is the change among offspring that comes from the genetic variability occurring within species. This explains such phenomena as the diversity of breeds observed among dogs, the changes in kidney physiology as mice adapt to drier environments, or the ability of fawns to be camouflaged in the woods or the Arctic fox in the snow. The modifications noted in some disease-causing microbes, which have led to their being resistant to antibiotics, or insects that have become unresponsive to insecticides are also examples.

Macroevolution, promulgated by evolutionists and rejected by creationists, claims that cumulative changes over time in one species can result in the formation of a new species that can eventually lead to newer, unique organisms that can be classified as new genera. This can continue until the new forms are distinct enough from the parent stock to be put into a separate family.

The lines between two species become muddied, however, for as has been previously discussed, it is not easy to define a species. If species is defined as an interbreeding population in the wild which produces viable (fertile) offspring, macroevolution can definitely be demonstrated as new populations have formed which are reproductively isolated from original populations, geographically, physiologically, or anatomically. The resulting populations either cannot interbreed with the original parent stock, or if they do interbreed, do not produce viable offspring. This process has been documented many times among animals that have been isolated on islands. A physical barrier, such as occurs between neighboring caves may separate populations from each other as well as from the parent stock above the ground. Other isolating mechanisms are mountain ranges, new river channels, lava flows, highways, railroads, cities, and clearcuts.

Darwin noted this phenomenon with finches and tortoises on the Galapagos Islands. Both became distinctive on each island. They apparently could not interbreed with the original parent stock on mainland Ecuador or other isolated populations throughout the islands.

A newly established species may dominate the habitat and perhaps separate further into different niches. The new but related species are termed allopatric (different places) species. This is an example of divergent evolution. With time the new groups vary, and eventually, with nature selecting different genes in each unique habitat, their offspring will look, behave, or be physiologically distinct from each other as well as from the parent stock. If they could not interbreed, according to the generally accepted definition of a species, this would indeed be the origin of a new species.

Paleontologists have found that when the inland sea returned to the Rocky Mountain front it reduced dinosaur habitat, displacing them from the plains and forcing them into higher terrain and mountain valleys where they became isolated from each other. Over time the geographical isolation resulted in reproductive isolation. The distinctive environmental stresses in these new habitats stimulated adaptive change and diversity among these separated populations. The fossil record reveals the variations that occurred subsequent to sea level rise, and then the changes that followed millions of years later when the sea receded and animals were again able to return to the plains.

This slow descent with modification can take millions of years and is understandably hard to envision. It is practically impossible to demonstrate through laboratory experiments. It can be noted in closely related living groups, however. Consider all the different owls, hawks, cats (lynx, mountain lion, cougar), mice, frogs, snails, or butterflies. Descent with modification has occurred and resulted in a marvelous variety of species, each adapted to a special environment. Paleontologists have shown such a variety in the fossil record, there being remarkable transitional fossil records on a variety of plants and animals. These data are presented in Chapter Nine.

Punctuated Equilibrium

Darwin, as well as most evolutionists of the late 19th and early 20th Centuries, assumed that fossil evidence for evolutionary theory would eventually arrive and support his theses. The evidence anticipated would include intergrading transitional fossils which would provide a sequential record of the changes that would have occurred in organisms over time. As it turns out, the fossil record reveals a variety of scenarios, including:

a) gradual change over the millennia with many transitionals
b) gradual change, gaps in the record, then continued progression of change
c) stasis, where an organism appears stable for some time and then undergoes a period of rapid change, as seen in the Lake Turkana snails found in Kenya
d) stasis, whereby an organism remains unchanged indefinitely, as in the coelacanth fishes
e) appearance of new types, such as occurred in mammals; new groups arose from an original group
f) abrupt (relatively speaking) extinction, as with dinosaurs

While gradual changes as in (a) have indeed been demonstrated by the fossil record (horses, camels, sea urchins, trilobites, rhinoceri, some mollusks, ceratopsian or horned dinosaurs) there are many fossil series with missing intermediates, often referred to as gaps in the fossil record. This can be explained by the fact that fossilization is extremely rare, occurring under very specific circumstances. Most animals and plants that have ever lived have left no fossil trace. In the long descent with modification these gaps are not at all surprising. In fact, they would be predicted. Also, many early fossils were no doubt formed but later were destroyed or displaced by Earth movements, heat, pressure, weathering, erosion, volcanoes, or floods. Even now, dinosaur bones recently exposed would eventually be lost if they were not collected and protected. The farther back the organisms lived, or the more delicate the tissue, the more chance that fossilized remains have been destroyed. The chances are slim for those with delicate tissues to ever have become fossilized.

Of course evolutionary scientists wish there were more complete intermediate series and fewer gaps such as at (a) above. At this point, when hundreds of thousands of fossils have been found, it appears that many hoped for series may never become available, although intermediates that close gaps are periodically discovered. This will continue.

The conditions of (b), (c), and (d) are partially explained by the Punctuated-Equilibrium thesis, proposed in the early 1970s. While gradual change over time occurs, this thesis suggests an additional scenario. Two stages occur: rapid change or a punctuated phase, and an equilibrium or more static phase where minimal or no change occurs. These time periods are relative. Rapid change geologically may take millions of years. This hypothesis holds that the rarity of intermediate fossils can be partially explained by the fact that intermediate forms existed for such a comparatively short time that there would be few opportunities for fossilization. If a species were to form or change in several thousands of years, a moment in geologic time, there would be few intermediates, no matter what fossilization processes were operating.

These punctuated eras would result in a sparse fossil record, especially if the short time was during a period that was not conducive to fossilization (no volcanic activity, sedimentation, or other means of preserving). If the changes occurred in an isolated population in a small geographical area, perhaps triggered by a local environmental change where the chances for the fossils being found are even more remote than normal, few fossils would be expected.

The fossils of trilobites seem to support the punctuated equilibrium thesis, as their records reveal short bursts of evolutionary change followed by long periods of stasis. Genetic stasis may be the consequence of environmental stasis, and the change phase may be triggered by a corresponding shift of environmental stimuli. Classical Darwinism predicts that organisms change in response to environmental stress, and population genetics research has lent credibility to this thesis.

The gradualistic approach to evolution, that is slow change over a long time, is not supported universally by the fossil record, although it is borne out with respect to some species. It is definitely seen that organisms such as some insects, snails, crocodiles, and clams do not change over the millennia. The lamp shell *Lingula,* a brachiopod genus, has remained unchanged for more than 450 million years! The tuatara *Sphenodon,* a reptile from New Zealand, seems to have hit stasis for almost 200 million years, and the Gingko tree for 220 million years!

On the other hand, dinosaur extinction occurred comparatively quickly: a punctuation. At the beginning of the Paleocene Epoch nine families of mammals have been identified. By the Middle Eocene, fifteen million years later, there were 74 families of mammals. This was an explosion, a period of great adaptive radiation. A punctuation.

The punctuated equilibrium thesis is being discussed, assessed, challenged, and defended as part of the ongoing peer review of paleontology. It will be interesting to see if over the decades it is confirmed by further research and discovery or if it is eventually falsified. No doubt both models, gradualism and punctuated equilibrium, occur. In that case, the real question will center on their relative frequency.

Evolutionary Naturalism/Materialism

Evolutionary naturalism, sometimes termed evolutionary materialism, is the belief that the universe and life forms on the Earth arose through purposeless, random, unsupervised, natural processes without a designer, strictly by chance. Proponents of this ideology do not acknowledge a creator God. They believe that the origins and operations of all of the universe as well as of the cell can be explained entirely through rational and naturalistic means with no First Cause. This is an atheistic position where no God, either as Creator, Designer, Original Freer, or Sustainer is acknowledged.

It is significant to note that rejecting a creator God is a chosen philosophy and is not grounded in science. No one can scientifically disprove the existence of a God who was involved with the ordering of the universe or of life. This philosophical position is as completely outside the realm of science as is creationism. The creator God of theistic evolutionists is also accepted by faith. Belief systems based on faith assumptions may be valid, but they are not founded on empirical data. Just as it is inappropriate for creationists or theistic evolutionists to demand that their beliefs be included in the public school biology class because these are belief positions that are grounded in faith, so also the assertion that life arose randomly apart from a creator God is equally inappropriate to the science classroom. Supernaturalism, whether present or absent, is not a part of science.

In various polls, approximately 8-9% of Americans are found to hold the position of evolutionary naturalism even though close to half of Americans claim to believe in evolution. Evolutionists are sometimes depicted in the literature or by the media as being evolutionary naturalists/materialists and this is simply not true. Only a small minority of evolutionists fall into this category. Suggesting that evolutionary theory eliminates a God who has ordained societal and personal rules, who requires order and responsibility, and who cares about us is a serious and deceptive misrepresentation. While some evolutionists indeed negate a creator God, the data show that the vast majority of Americans who hold to evolutionary theory believe that there was somehow a creator, designer God involved in the origins of life and the universe and who permits the progression and modification of life through natural law down through the millennia. These North Americans acknowledge a God who demands personal and social order, self-discipline, and accountability with its appropriate rewards or punishments. This is the position of theistic evolution.

Furthermore, evolutionary naturalists, in spite of the fact that they do not accept a divine Creator are, like theists, upstanding citizens, scholars, and good neighbors. It is unfair to suggest a correlation between their belief and societal ills. If beliefs in evolutionary naturalism have been perverted by a few to justify immoral behavior they must be held accountable for such misinterpretation and misbehavior. However a people may have construed the meaning of evolutionary theory, their behavior cannot be used as evidence against its basic scientific validity. It is incumbent upon all those in the natural sciences to accurately and comprehensively interpret the theory of evolution from a scientific and not a philosophical perspective so that such inappropriate assumptions and their potential resultant destructive actions can be averted. There is no doubt that teacher training is essential.

Creationists blame prostitution, divorce, child and spousal abuse, slavery, racism, pornography, and a host of other societal ills on evolutionary theory. It is far too simplistic to make such sweeping generalizations. For one thing, these societal ills or ones similar to them have occurred throughout the centuries and across the cultures, long before Darwin and his theory appeared. Many were present during biblical times. The Bible is full of incidents of societal ills: murder, greed, deception, extramarital sex, slavery, lying. Murder was even validated in the name of religion! What caused the terrible behavior that supposedly triggered the destructive flood of Noah? Not evolution!

Theologians explain most of these behaviors as being the result of freedom of choice, which has been innately present in humans from their beginning. Blaming immoral behavior on evolutionary theory is misplaced blame. Removing evolutionary theory from the culture will not eliminate such activities or mindsets. Christians affirm Christ, not creationism dogma, and it is Christ, not creationism, who revolutionizes personal action and thought and calls us to holy living!

Basis for Evolutionary Theory

Paleontological/Geological Evidence

Paleontology is the study of fossils and ancient life ("paleo" = old and "logos" = study). Paleontologists find records of organisms of distant eras written in the rocks. Their challenge is to interpret what they find and draw conclusions from the data. Geology is the discipline that explores the Earth ("geo" = Earth). Geologists analyze rocks, their composition, age, formations, and fossils. They attempt to understand the Earth's structure and history by reading and interpreting this evidence. No one witnessed the events that occurred when the Earth was younger, so inferences must be made. A generous body of evidence in both paleontology and geology provides substantial basis for conclusions. New data are continually added. Through scientific peer review these conclusions are perpetually challenged. Over the years, some have been rejected and others continue to be questioned. Those which remain have withstood rigorous challenge.

Fossils

Fossils are defined as any recognizable remains of life or direct evidence of animal or plant existence greater than 10,000 years old. They provide the majority of the clues and data upon which paleontologists formulate their hypotheses. The term fossil comes from Latin, *fossa*, meaning "hole." It originally denoted something that was dug up. Fossils can take the form of impressions in rock, such as feathers or shells, or give evidence of animal activity, such as feeding burrows, footprints, or walking trails. They can be bone, teeth, claws, bony plates, scales, spikes, shells, seeds, spores, capsules, petrified fecal matter (coprolites), gizzard stones (gastroliths), chalky ear stones (otoliths), even preserved nests and eggs. Although rare, even some petrified viscera (soft organs), stomach contents, and skin impressions have been found. In addition to preservation in sedimentary rock, bygone life forms have been preserved in tar, peat, coal, volcanic ash, oil, lava, and amber (petrified tree sap). Some have been frozen in ice or mummified in dry, desert sand. Fossils can be as enormous as the 54 ton *Brachiosaurus* dinosaur or as small as a single celled organism that requires a microscope to detect.

As far back as the ancient Greeks, people recognized that many fossil remains represent organisms that were quite distinct from existing species. Aristotle reasoned that change over extended time had probably occurred. The Greeks were puzzled by finding fossils such as seashells on mountaintops! Fossils give a tremendous insight into life in the past. Unfortunately only a fraction of the organisms that ever lived are represented in the fossil record because conditions have to be ideal for preservation. Also, fossils are usually incomplete records, providing only skeletal remains, teeth, or partial imprints such as the leaf or seed of a plant but no stalk or trunk.

Initial fossilization is rare. For the fossil to be preserved over the ages is even rarer. An articulated skeleton (all the bones in place) is rarer still. Some fossils dissolve, others can be distorted by high temperatures and pressures or chemically altered when exposed through weathering. Such exposure makes them vulnerable to disintegration or displacement. Only a few are preserved and fewer still are found. Sea urchins, starfish, crabs, bryozoans (colonial, marine, sessile "moss animals" whose fossil forms have massive skeletons), fish and other organisms have hard skeletons but they are held together by soft tissues. When the latter decay, the hard parts become dispersed, making it difficult to locate and reconstruct them. Some structures, such as the bones of a mackerel or the shell of the crab, decay quickly even in anoxic (without oxygen) conditions because of their high organic content.

For fossils to be formed, certain conditions must be present. The remains must be quickly covered by volcanic ash, lava, sand, or other sediment. They are then preserved as the surrounding matrix hardens to rock. Eventually the rock becomes folded and/or eroded, exposing the fossils on the surface. Sometimes fossils are exposed in quarries, mines, and in blasted roadcuts, railroad tunnels, or even in plowed fields. Some have been found when people excavate for a backyard swimming pool!

When they die, animals are usually immediately eaten or scavenged and their bones dispersed and destroyed. Plants decay before being preserved if they are on the surface. Only a few plants and animals fossilize. They have to be buried quickly and deep enough so that they are protected from scavengers and won't be quickly exhumed. The most likely setting is in a shallow sea (continental shelf). This is one reason why most fossils are of marine origin. They have quick burial with storms and a modestly decent chance at avoiding exhumation. There are also large numbers and a great variety of marine organisms and that also accounts for their large fossil numbers.

Most fossils are found in sedimentary rocks. These rocks were originally composed of mud, silt, sand, or pebbles, small parts that came from other rocks, which were subsequently worn by weather or water action. Wind can blow sand, forming layers on land, or cause erosion, which results in layers in valleys. Often running water deposits these sediments in lakebeds or oceans as mud or sand. At the same time, organisms in the lake or ocean die and their bodies fall and join the sediment at the bottom. The bodies of dead organisms from a distance can be swept into this material as well. Additional sediments accumulate over the millennia, some slowly, the result of gradual processes that are not ideal for fossil preservation. Some accumulate quickly, the result of catastrophic events that are conducive to fossil formation. Volcanic material and masses of plants from swamps, which turn to coal, also contribute to sedimentation. Layered sediments exert pressure on the preserved materials below. Chemical action over time metamorphoses the materials into rock. These processes are operating today but are usually very slow and therefore extremely hard to see or demonstrate. On limey seafloors, such as in the area of the Bahamas, sediment can lithify (turn to rock) comparatively quickly, in a matter of years. This activity has resulted in rocks with visible strata that often contain a variety of fossils.

The ideal setting for fossil formation is rapid burial without oxygen, which can happen when remains are quickly covered by mud, lava, sand, or ash. The dead organisms may have undergone no change or may have experienced mineral replacement in the vacancies in bone that were left when soft tissues decayed. This process can take place more quickly if mineralized water is available. It occurs minimally if an animal dies in a dry area. Therefore, the extent of mineralization does not equate with the age of the fossil. The scarcity of original skeletal material increases with the age of the fossils. When mineralized water permeates the remains they can become infused with a variety of materials such as metal ions, lime, or silica.

Because fossils are so ancient, many of them, even though they may have been well preserved originally, have been subsequently disturbed by various Earth movements which have crushed, distorted, or scattered remains. In addition, the rocks they are in may experience erosion, which can expose them to the elements and cause damage or even destruction. Our discovering them means we were there at the point between their being exposed and being destroyed.

Generally the deepest layers of sedimentary rock are considered the oldest (Law of Superposition) unless Earth movements such as overthrusting or folding have occurred. Overthrusting is when layers on the bottom are contorted and tilted by severe geologic events and end up on the top, or when older layers glide over younger layers as a result of Earth movements. The well- known Lewis overthrust can be seen in the Rocky Mountains of Glacier National Park. Folding occurs when Earth movements cause layers to bend and fold, sometimes so severely that older layers end up on top of younger layers.

Over a quarter of a million species of organisms have been identified through fossils. This presents an amazing story since most of them are extinct. Without doubt, this representative group reflects millions of other forms, extinct, not preserved, and therefore unknown. Because fossilization is so rare, we will never become acquainted with unnumbered missing life forms. This void partially accounts for the lack of transitional fossils, the gaps in the fossil record that are often mentioned by creationists.

Fossils have been known for thousands of years but only in recent centuries have hunters diligently sought them. Thomas Jefferson (1743-1826) discovered the extinct, clawed, giant sloth, *Megalonix jeffersoni,* in western Virginia in 1796. Many of the fossils paleontologists and museums possess have been discovered in recent decades. There is optimism that additional finds will contribute to greater insight into life in the past and help close some gaps. New discoveries are revealed regularly. Recently, a dinosaur find in the Cedar Mountain Formation of Utah was announced. It closes a gap of 70 million years between the Late Jurassic era, 145 million years ago, and the Late Cretaceous, 75 million years ago. Included in this find were the oldest marsupials and Gila monster in the world and the first, and therefore oldest, North American snake. In Jamaica a 50 million year old pig-sized mammal that lived in the sea but could walk on land, *Pezosiren portelli,* was discovered in 2001. The Struniiformes, a fleshy finned fish from the Devonian, was found recently. One can only guess how many others were not preserved or, if so, have not yet been found. Paleontologists are limited by the data in hand and meanwhile they persistently search for fossils that can potentially fill existent gaps, occasionally making significant and exciting discoveries. What will be in the news next?

Microfossils, the remains of microscopic organisms from Precambrian times, have contributed important information in recent years. New technology will enable further discovery and examination of these significant forms, which provide insight into very ancient life.

Nonevolutionists continually speak and write about the gaps in the fossil record as though they negate evolution. Gaps certainly contribute to many questions and account for some of the uncertainties but their presence does not destroy evolutionary theory. In fact, evolutionary theory and what we assume about the Earth's geological history predict the gaps. Creationism, holding to a geologically recent worldwide flood, would predict few missing species as there would have been no weathering and eroding of lower strata since there were no dry periods and immediate sedimentation in the water would have preserved, somewhere, practically all organisms as they died. Why wouldn't the Struniiformes have been found long ago if flood sediment had faithfully preserved most of its specimens? Scientists have supporting data in spite of the gaps to substantiate evolutionary hypotheses. Fortunately, though more rarely, some lineages are actually quite complete despite all of the biases of the fossil record.

The incompleteness and therefore bias of the fossil record is explained, at least in part, by the following factors:

1. Soft bodied forms, such as worms and jellyfish, are not preserved easily. Burial must come quickly after death or soft bodied animals decay or are scavenged

2. Smaller, delicate land animals such as insects are not as readily preserved as larger ones; their fragile bodies are destroyed if not buried quickly.

3. Bones can become dispersed or disintegrate by heat and weathering if they are not promptly buried. Scavenging is a major cause for displaced and destroyed bones.

4. Millions of years of Earth movements, erosion, and tremendous pressures leading to deformation subsequent to their preservation have destroyed fossils.

5. If the original populations were relatively small in number, such as with early hominids, there will inevitably be fewer corresponding fossils. Today, for instance, more raccoons would probably be fossilized, all things being equal, than wolverines.

6. Some environments are more conducive to fossilization than others. Three fourths of the Earth's surface is covered with ocean. This is where sand and mud are deposited, and many animals residing there have hard parts, so it is an environment conducive to preservation. It is important to note that most of the ocean, except for continental shelves, gets recycled through subduction with plate tectonics, thus destroying fossils.

7. Many fossils are hidden in inaccessible areas, far below the land surface or deep in ocean or lake sediments. Comparatively few fossils have been retrieved from the sediments composing the lake or ocean floor, and below, primarily because of the technical challenges. Recent attempts using specialized equipment have begun. Most fossils that have been collected feature organisms that lived on land or in shallow seas which have through uplift become part of the continents.

8. Animals and plants from upland regions or mountaintops receive no protective eroding sediments to cover them and therefore they are exposed and destroyed without the possibility of being buried and preserved. As a result, whole groups will never be known. Sedimentation occurs in lowland areas so dwellers there have more potential for preservation.

9. Known fossils have predominantly come from the Northern Hemisphere simply because historically most fossil hunters have inhabited, studied, and searched in these regions. This is changing as fossil seekers branch out to more remote areas and local folk across the globe are trained and search in their respective geographic environs.

The examination of a fossil gives one kind of information. Other data come from the successions of organisms in the strata and a comparison of their relative positions and respective anatomies, as well as the kind of rock in which they were formed. These data provide information about transitions and relate a story of change over time. Radioactive decay rates make it possible to estimate the age of the fossils and their associated rocks, which further illuminate events in the past. Geologists' research methods and conclusions are obviously valid for they routinely analyze rocks and fossils to facilitate the search for oil and other resources. Those who deny the data of geology with respect to evolutionary theory must explain why these same methods and data are so useful, practical, and accurate when applied to petroleum science.

It is apparent in the comparative study of sedimentary rocks that some layers have been eroded before they had a chance to harden or be covered by another layer. They are forever gone! Also, it is possible that conditions were not conducive for millions of years for any strata to be deposited. The rocks so exposed can be eroded over time and they, too, are gone. This leads to inevitable gaps in the fossil record where unconformities (missing layers) occur, sometimes representing millions of years. The record of life during that period is forever lost. At times geologists can identify missing layers in one formation by paralleling it with corresponding intact strata in nearby formations. Radiometric dating applied to igneous rock such as lava flows sometimes contributes clues to the extent of the missing layers.

If a body of water or just its periphery temporarily evaporates, the footprints, burrows, or trails of animals can be preserved as they walked or crawled in mud. If the mud hardens and is eventually covered by additional layers of sediment the imprints will be preserved. Mudcracks or wave action can also be found on rock. Some sedimentary rocks are thousands of feet thick, their numerous strata containing these remarkable records of the past. Geologists and paleontologists attempt to decipher and interpret this fascinating history.

Within the Colorado Plateau, which encompasses a major portion of Utah, Arizona, and parts of Western Colorado and New Mexico including the Four Corners region, there are predominantly horizontal, undisturbed strata forming an extensive, intact record from Pennsylvanian to Tertiary periods. At least thirteen different levels have revealed fossil trackways of land vertebrates. These footprints are not uniform. Lower strata generally have four and five toed amphibians and reptiles, while three toed dinosaur prints are found on more recent layers. Progressively younger rocks have new and varied dinosaur prints. These sequences present support for a descent with modification thesis. Also, these tracks are not only made by running animals but also those at a relaxed pace. The fine grained sediments dictate preservation under noncatastrophic conditions.

These varied, progressive, and extensive trackways negate the creationist thesis that fossilizations all occurred about four to five thousand years ago at Noah's flood and that practically all the sedimentary rocks were laid down during that time as well. Creationists suggest that animals fleeing the floodwaters made these footprints or tsunamis exposed land for animals to walk on during the year of the flood. However, tracks are made on land or in shallow mud. Layers of sediment representing thirteen episodes of alternating flood and dry land or mud do not support a year long, continual flood hypothesis. Some suggest that the data of the Colorado Plateau alone are enough to discredit once and for all the worldwide flood thesis.

In addition, sedimentary Badlands in South Dakota reveal rain prints and mudcracks, records of exposure to air during various periods in their history. This also destroys the view that a universal flood was the primary factor in sedimentary deposition.

Animals without hard parts are not preserved as often as those that have bones, carapaces, shells, scales, chitinous exoskeletons, or teeth. Even with organisms that are more readily fossilized, their internal organs or skin are usually not preserved, so fossils give important but limited information. The lack of data on delicate invertebrates such as sea anemones or jellyfish presents a major void in the world of paleontology, as is the lack of internal body systems information for vertebrates.

Many fossils can provide information on muscle attachments on bones and bone proportions, often giving clues as to running or walking capabilities. Muscle marks on jawbones betray bite pressures. Sometimes blood vessels, nerves and some organs, such as the brain, leave telltale clues on bones, supplying insights. Whole systems, however, such as the digestive, respiratory, nervous, endocrine, reproductive, circulatory, and urinary are usually absent.

Missing also is behavior information, coloration, and qualities such as warm-bloodedness. However, some hypotheses with supporting data in these areas are being pursued. The histology (tissue study) of dinosaur bone has given clues to growth rates and has suggested that some might possibly have been warmblooded. If so, some behaviors can be hypothesized. Dinosaur nesting sites in Montana give evidence for communal nesting behavior. Tiny embryos in dinosaur eggs imply the need for maternal behavior upon birth. Skull anatomy provides information on the size of the olfactory (sense of smell) and sight nerves, which gives clues about sensory endowment which can infer hunting and eating behavior. Teeth give information about diet. Numbers of similar fossils at one site can hint at possible herding behavior. Prey preserved inside a predator or teeth marks from a predator or scavenger on bone yield behavioral data. Bone diseases or healing scars are sometimes preserved.

Occasionally soft body parts are preserved, such as in the Burgess Shale in British Columbia, where many marine invertebrates were buried in mudflows. Also, mammoths frozen in permafrost have soft parts preserved, or insects enclosed in amber (petrified resin). Other animals, such as the saber tooth tiger, have been found in tar or peat bogs where quick mineralization resulted in preserved body parts.

In the late 1980s, the first dinosaur ever found in Italy, a baby, was found. A new species, this remarkable fossil of *Scipionyx samniticus* contained significant amounts of intestine and liver, as well as the muscles and cartilage that once surrounded its windpipe. This soft anatomy had never been seen in any previous dinosaur find and it provided insight into the relationship this animal might have had to either lizards or birds (Dal Sasso & Signore, 1998, p. 383-7).

A common area of disagreement between creationists and evolutionists centers on the rate of sedimentation and fossil formation. Creationists claim catastrophism, where short-lived calamities such as a year-long, worldwide flood caused rapid change. As a result, almost all of the sedimentary rocks are believed to have been formed in a comparatively short time conforming to their 6-10,000 year old Earth model. Evolutionists recognize that quick and violent events such as floods, earthquakes, meteor impacts, or volcanic eruptions do occur and cause sudden, often catastrophic change which contributes to the extinction of species, a thesis called neo-catastrophism. They also hold, however, that there are uniform forces operating, such as weathering, erosion, and glaciation that take much longer and exert their subtle influence over very long periods of time. While rapid events obviously transpire, evolutionists contend that change occurs irregularly, opportunistically, and predominantly through slow processes.

The fossil record reveals a succession of related organisms with generally simpler forms appearing earlier in the record. Vascular plants, for instance, which are more complex, appear more recently than the simpler non-vascular plants. Plants with net veined, alternate leaves are more recent than parallel veined or whorled leafed species. Bilaterally symmetrical flowers such as orchids are more recent than radially symmetrical ones such as tulips. More recent also are fused leaves or flower parts such as are found in daffodils or orchids. All of these data support the evolutionary paradigm. Evolution predicts this orderly succession. A catastrophic deluge predicts mixing of species. The former is universally found in the fossil record. Creationists are left with a huge burden to explain this remarkable, orderly, consistent record.

Geological Column

Geologists look at time in two ways: relatively and absolutely. Relative time refers to time sequences or events in relationship to each other. Lower strata are generally older than upper strata (Law of Superposition). How much older may not be known. The geological column was first described in the 18th and early 19th Centuries, prior to Darwin. Early paleontologists noted that rock strata in one area had patterns that were similar to strata in other areas, even other continents. Particular kinds of fossils were found together, and this was consistent worldwide. It was deduced that those rocks having similar fossils were generally the same age. The sedimentary rocks containing these identified fossils could be matched and compared in relative age to other strata with their distinctive fossils.

There are clues in the rocks that can be deciphered to give information on ancient climates, continental movement, volcanism, and ice ages. These data and the fossils enabled geologists to design a column with various identified layers that could be positioned in relationship to each other. Predictably, the column is rarely complete at one spot because of weathering, erosion, Earth movements, floods, or other local influences. This results in gaps in the record where these unconformities (missing sections) occur, sometimes representing millions of years. Such gaps vary and are expected as geological history is not uniform across a continent or throughout the world. For instance, volcanic activity in a localized area can add layers that would not be present in parallel strata in distant areas.

It is possible to piece together missing strata by comparing rocks in other formations and distinguishing sequential records. Strata missing in one area are present in another so the relative and corresponding layers can be named

176

and identified everywhere. The book can be read even though pages are missing because other books exist that include those pages. If strata ABCDG can be identified in one area (site 1) and BCDEFG at another (site 2) then it can be assumed that E and F were eroded from or never deposited at site 1 and A was eroded or never deposited at site 2.

The strata that compose the geological column vary in thickness from paper thin to many meters thick. They are distinguished by the various types of parent materials of which they are made, the environmental conditions under which these materials were deposited, and the way the particles were transported. If fossils are present, they also contribute significant information about the time in the geological past in which the sedimentation occurred.

Some identified rock layers in the geological column are named after regions in which they were first recognized. The Cambrian name originated from Cambria, the ancient Roman name for Wales, where rocks of this age were first identified. Ancient rocks in Devon, England inspired the term Devonian. The younger chalk cliffs at Dover, England gave the Cretaceous Period its name, cretaceous being from the Greek word for chalk. Ordovician rocks, on the other hand, were named for the Ordovices, a prehistoric Welsh tribe that once inhabited the area where rocks of that age occurred. The Silurian period was named for the Silures, a tribe from the southern part of Wales.

The histories of each region of the Earth are varied, since they have had distinctive climates, sedimentary influences, plate tectonic activity, volcanism, flora and fauna, and erosion records. Much of the history is recorded in the geological column. While in some areas large sections of the column are amazingly complete, it is not surprising that in other regions the record is incomplete. A region that had been a streambed will show different sedimentation than one on the plains. Their resulting records will not be identical. Neither would they be the same if one area was layered with lava or volcanic ash or if one suffered severe erosion and lost some or extensive layers. One region might have experienced an overthrust and another have been exposed to the rampage of a retreating glacier. We do not expect the column to be regularly intact but it can be correlated and deduced.

If all the sedimentary layers on the Earth's surface were deposited during a year long catastrophic deluge only a few thousand years ago one would predict that there would be few unconformities present. Furthermore, strata on the entire planet would show more correlation, for more homogenous sedimentary events would have occurred. Yet heterogeneity is what is generally found. In addition, the layers certainly would not contain land animal footprints and burrows, or mudcracks, or raindrop impressions, all of which are formed on dry or moist land at many different levels. Yet they do, which is exactly what the uniformitarian thesis predicts. Layers were deposited, animals roamed or dug burrows, rock formation occurred, a sea or river returned, more layers were deposited, some were eroded, others remained and solidified, and new layers were formed perhaps by volcanic activity, more animal footprints, shells or bones, and on and on. That is precisely what is observed in the geological column.

A biblical scale flood would also predictably leave heterogeneity of fossils, a mixture of plants and animals throughout the column. As rampaging currents occurred, various individual animals and plants would irregularly die and eventually fall to the bottom. Humans could be at lower layers. A veritable mixture would be predicted throughout the strata. What is found are simpler organisms sorted on the lower layers and more advanced organisms as the strata progress to the top. There is no mixing of more recent, complex organisms with those long extinct unless older fossils are found in river gravel when they were transported and displaced by river action. Nothing is out of place that cannot be explained.

Besides relative time, geologists are also able to assess rock in absolute time, which measures the ages of rock in actual years. This value is determined in a variety of ways. Strata can be dated by analyzing radioactive isotopes that may be present. This technology was perfected during the 20th Century. Certain elements such as uranium, argon, carbon, and potassium occur in more than one form, variations called isotopes. Isotopes of a particular element have more or fewer than the normal number of neutrons in their atoms and therefore have a different atomic weight and unique properties. If an isotope is unstable it can break down over time, a process called radioactive decay. This results in it becoming another isotope or even another element. The original element, such as uranium, is called the parent element, and the subsequent element formed as a result of the parent element breakdown is the daughter element. Lead is the daughter of uranium.

The time it takes for a particular parent isotope to decay to a daughter isotope can be measured. This breakdown process results in radioactive rays and heat being released. This rate of decay can be calculated and the age of a rock determined, a process called radiometric dating. Geologists measure what is called the half-life, which is the time required for half of the parent to decay into the daughter. The half life of uranium-238 (U-238) is 4,510 million years. If a rock were to contain the same amount of U-238 as daughter Pb-206 (Pb is the symbol for lead), then it would be 4,510 million years old.

There are refined techniques and equipment which measure a variety of radioactive elements and the values gained can be compared so that a date assigned to a rock is based on more than one calculation or parent/daughter activity. Accuracy to the nearest million years can be obtained. Problems with this technology occur when rocks have been reheated or buried within the Earth, thus skewing values. Also, some rocks have no radioactive elements to be measured! Radiometric dating has correlated with sea floor spreading measurements and coral reef building, confirming its accuracy. The data indicate that the Earth is in fact four to five billion years old.

Radiometric dating and fossil age designations together help scientists assign dates to rocks. The former process has been used to date the islands of Hawaii, which were formed from volcanoes coming up from the sea floor. The oldest and most northern island is Kauai, 5.6 million years old. The islands successively become younger heading southeast, toward the island of Hawaii. Hawaii is the most southern and youngest, at one million years of age. The extreme age assigned to rocks, some to 3,900 million years, supports the evolutionary thesis, for long time periods are required for the slow changes of evolution to occur.

Another time measurement of radiometric dating, or "rock-clock," employs a technique called fission-track dating. It is known that the mineral zircon contains uranium atoms that emit particles that leave tracks in a crystal. More tracks mean a longer time. By determining the number of tracks, one can calculate the time since the formation of the crystal.

The orderly and even predictable position of fossils in the geological column is the major justification which paleontologists give for their adherence to evolutionary theory. This column generally reveals simpler organisms such as smaller, extinct, marine invertebrates at the bottom and a progression to more complex organisms such as large, terrestrial vertebrates toward the top. Paleontologists assume that sedimentary layers that are the deepest are also the oldest. Therefore the geological column presents a record from ancient to recent and its fossils reveal the progression of change over time. These powerful data cannot be understated. Anyone who seeks to disprove evolutionary theory must address these data, which most scientists perceive as indisputable evidence for an old Earth and change over time.

Those who seek to discredit the validity of evolutionary theory attempt to explain away this record by suggesting that those organisms hydrodynamically settled out in that order during a worldwide flood, with the lightest organisms sinking first, followed by heavier and heavier organisms and finally the vertebrates at the top which supposedly could have sustained themselves the longest in such a flood. However the geological column does not support this explanation. Heavy invertebrates such as large trilobites are found beneath smaller, lighter species, and there is regular discontinuity in the column according to heavy/light organisms.

If this explanation were correct then similar weighted vertebrates should be found in similar strata. Sharks, alligators, and tuna, for instance, should be found together or in same age strata throughout the world. However the column reveals that the cartilaginous shark is consistently found lower (therefore it lived earlier) than the alligator or teleost (bony) tuna. Smaller mammals appear toward the top, above larger reptiles and fish.

In some instances the progressive changes that have occurred between animal or plant groups are clearly revealed in the strata. These intermediate forms present powerful evidence for evolution, which is descent with modification. Furthermore, there are no incidents where a fossil is inappropriately placed; there are no mammals prior to reptiles or flowering plants before cone bearers or extinct nonvascular plants. Only in overthrusts where rock is folded on itself are more recent strata beneath older strata and more recent organisms found below more ancient forms. This predictable sequencing is among the strongest support for evolutionary theory.

The Geological Column is included in Appendix D.

Varves

Varves are annual strata of sediment usually composed of two laminae, or delicate layers, one dark and one light. They are formed under water in response to seasonal changes where different materials precipitate out at varying temperatures. Algae and other flourishing life in the summer contribute richer organic material, so particles settling at that time would differ from those deposited in the winter. One light layer of fine sediment and a darker layer of coarser sediment represents a year's accumulation of silt and mud deposits. This delicate stratification process is still occurring and its resultant layers can be observed at the bottom of glacier fed lakes.

Varves record a period of time in the past. There are approximately twenty million varves in the Green River Formation of Wyoming. Since freshwater fish fossils are often found amid varves, their deposition in a lake is confirmed. Varves have an average thickness of about 0.015 centimeter. They support the ancient Earth thesis and their existence is hard for worldwide flood proponents to explain. How could millions of delicate, consistent, dual layers have been formed during a single year of catastrophic deluge?

Biochemistry/DNA/Genetics Evidence

The discipline of biochemistry, which studies the chemistry that pertains to living things (bio=life), has flourished since the middle of the 20th Century. Biochemists have recognized a fundamental unity at the molecular level in living organisms, both plant and animal. Life forms carry genetic information on the molecule deoxyribonucleic acid (DNA), the "blueprint" or "recipe for life." Ribonucleic acid (RNA), another significant molecule of life, functions in protein synthesis. Proteins, meaning "of prime importance," are composed of subunits called amino acids. Even though there is a potential for a great variety of amino acids in living organisms, only about twenty are found, albeit in varied percentages and in an infinite number of sequences resulting in an infinite number of proteins. It has been noted that cells across the living world, from bacteria to human muscle cells, incorporate identical or similar enzymes (proteins that facilitate rate change of chemical reactions, usually speeding them up) and share common metabolic pathways (chemical reaction sequences). The relatedness of all living things is quite apparent on the molecular level.

Biochemical affinities across species are also seen with respect to antibodies. They are proteins produced by the immune system in response to a stimulus called an antigen. It has been known for many years that the antibodies milkmaids manufactured in response to cowpox had a protective value for them against smallpox. This also affirms the relatedness of organisms.

A comparison of the genomes (DNA composing a particular organism's genetic code) of various species reveals how closely related they are. The greater the variation, the less related they are. It is possible to chart the history of relationships among organisms. Humans and chimpanzees, for example, share 98% of their genes, suggesting that they are closely related and they or their relatives veered from a common ancestor in the comparatively recent geological past. There is such a genetic likeness between humans and baboons that there have been organ transplants between these two species. The fact that the AIDS virus was originally infective for apes and then jumped to humans shows the relatedness of humans and apes, even if the virus mutated prior to its human habitation.

In recent decades, protein sequencing has provided additional data that enable scientists to estimate genetic change and species relationships. In the 1960s it was observed that the numbers of amino acid differences in a particular protein in any two given species was almost proportional to the time of their divergence from a common ancestor. It has been found that the rate of evolution of proteins and DNA sequences can provide a molecular clock of evolution. This information not only provides insight into relationships, but can reconstruct the timing of various mutational events.

Assume that an ancestral organism in a particular population had a protein recipe of A B C D E B G, these letters representing the amino acids that compose proteins. Subsequently a mutation occurred so that an offspring had the recipe A B C D F B G. If this modified protein could still function, the mutation being inconsequential, it would not be selected against and would remain in the gene pool (the total genetic endowment of a population) of that population. If it gave an adaptive edge, it would in time be selected for through natural selection and become prevalent in that population. Over the generations it might undergo an additional mutation having the recipe A B C D F C G. Subsequent species arising from this mutated branch would continue to possess this new recipe. Molecular biologists predict that such "mistakes" would be present in related species since they would have picked this recipe up from a common ancestor. Species less related would share fewer of these unique modifications. This has indeed been demonstrated.

The amino acid sequences of a protein named cytochrome C are well understood. It is known that this protein is a slowly evolving molecule. Relationships between various species can be constructed on the basis of the number of amino acid differences in their cytochrome C proteins. Such research shows, for instance, that chickens are more closely related to penguins than to ducks or pigeons.

Proteins that evolve more rapidly are studied in closely related species. Other molecular biology procedures such as DNA sequencing, DNA hybridization, and gel electrophoresis also give information on the genetic changes (evolution) of species. Not surprisingly, these data from molecular biology correlate with the geological data on changes observed in fossils over time! Over and over during the 20th Century, as new data accumulated from many areas, evolution was affirmed and strengthened. It has a tremendous and varied support base. It is not "just a theory."

In 1953, the anatomy (structure, or what it looks like) of DNA was revealed and ever since its physiology (function, or how it works) has been probed. Little by little, secrets of life have been disclosed. In the 19th Century, when Darwin observed differences in the finches of the Galapagos Islands and in the pigeons that were artificially bred in England, he could not account for these variations. Much of the explanation is now available on the molecular level with an understanding of DNA. It can be demonstrated that rearrangements of the subunits (nucleotides) that compose DNA can result in observable change such as flower color, fungus or drought resistance in a plant, ear size in a mammal, or beak morphology in a bird. Darwin hypothesized that, just as breeders selected preferred characteristics, perhaps nature did the same. Natural selection!

There are four kinds of nucleotides in DNA. Hundreds of them occur in precise order to make up genes which are segments of the DNA molecule. There are hundreds of genes, each composed of the four nucleotides, in the DNA molecule. Along with varying the sequence of the nucleotides, rearrangements, omissions or additions of gene components can also result in changes known as mutations (muta=change). Diseases such as sickle cell anemia, hemophilia, cystic fibrosis, and muscular dystrophy and variations in eye or skin color, height, musical ability, kidney chemistry, hearing acuity or other physical, psychological, and personality characteristics have been explained by alterations in DNA. The changes that have occurred in DNA across the living world result in modifications of gene pools and account for the marvelous variety observed within species, including humans. These changes result in microevolution, and eventually, as numerous microevolutionary changes accumulate, macroevolution.

It has been clearly demonstrated that many mutations are detrimental and can even lead to death, while others appear to have no effect. However, some provide an adaptive advantage. The sciences of biochemistry and genetics provide explanations for mutations. It has been shown in the laboratory that radiation or certain chemicals from the environment can impact the DNA in plants or fruit flies or mice, resulting in offspring that have new characteristics. These changes also occur naturally, and over the years breeders or researchers have selectively bred for desired qualities that have spontaneously appeared in individuals or populations. Modified DNA in the sex cells carries the genetic recipe (genotype), which is expressed as physical characteristics which are seen (phenotype). In plants, for instance, new varieties that will be cold, drought or disease resistant, larger or sweeter express desired phenotypes. Now that mutations and genetic codes are better understood, scientists can manipulate in the laboratory what nature takes thousands or millions of years to accomplish by natural selection.

Some genetic messages give the organism greater adaptability to a particular environment, which enables it to live longer and produce more offspring. A prairie dog may receive genetic messages from one or both parents which give it extraordinary sight. If this enables the prairie dog to see its enemies sooner and seek shelter, it will live longer and therefore produce more offspring than its peers. Some of these offspring will inherit this advantageous quality. Over time the prairie dog village to which they belong may contain more and more offspring with this capability, as nature selects for this desired phenotype. This was Darwin's explanation for the changes observed in populations. Such qualities as a more camouflaged color, a smaller or larger sized beak, resistance to a parasite, a keener sense of smell, drought adapted kidneys, greater speed, better maternal care, behavior or appearance which attracts mates, or some other capability that provides that organism with an adaptive edge will be selected for over time and will ultimately be reflected in the population.

Individuals don't evolve. Populations do. An individual is bound by its unique genetic endowment. A population is fluid and can evolve over time as the characteristics that give an adaptive advantage are chosen, or selected for. Those that are less adaptive, having deleterious mutations, are eliminated. If the environment changes quickly, it is possible that no members of a population can adapt quickly enough. If the population cannot move to a more suitable setting, it will become extinct. When populations are challenged, individuals generally have three options: (a) move to a better setting, (b) adapt to the new environment, (c) die.

A sexually reproducing organism receives half of its DNA from its mother in an egg and the other half from its father in a sperm. No two eggs or sperm are alike so all offspring will be unique except in the case of identical twins where the fertilized egg has split and develops into identical offspring. Populations are in turn composed of many individuals, each distinctive. This can be observed in a pod of whales or seals, a pack of wolves, a herd of elk, a covey of partridges, a desert of cacti, or a community of humans. It is not so obvious in mosquitoes, swallows, trout, or lilac bushes, but if the genetic endowments of each of these were analyzed, variations would be demonstrated. Over time nature selects for those qualities that give the best advantage in a particular environment.

The gene pool of a population can be modified over time in a variety of ways. DNA can mutate, as just discussed, introducing new characteristics that result in new phenotypic (observable) variabilities. Sometimes within a population there are more than two messages (alleles) for any one characteristic. An individual gets one of these messages (a) from its mother and perhaps a different one (b) from its father, resulting in a particular phenotype or visible expression. But some characteristics have more than two such possibilities. Another individual may get a (c) message from its father instead of a (b) and express a different phenotype. This multiple allele condition contributes to great variety in a population. Combinations of AA, AB, BB, AC, CC, or CB all lead to variations. Some may be more adaptive than others. Population geneticists can calculate gene or allele frequencies within a population, and they can analyze their change over time as natural selection operates. This multiple allelic phenomenon is seen in eye color or in human blood types, where combinations of A, B, and O messages can be inherited resulting in AA, AO, AB, BB, BO, or OO. New members may join the population and introduce new alleles or mutated DNA.

Some variation in a population may be non-genetic. A fetus may have excellent genetic endowment but have been malnourished or malformed because of its gestation (embryonic) environment. A fetal alcohol syndrome baby may not live to reproductive age because of the influence its fetal environment had on its development. Even though it may have had an outstanding genetic endowment, it will not be realized. An individual may show variation because of non-genetic factors such as communicable disease or accident, or life choices such as overeating. While natural selection will act on the phenotypic (what is seen) manifestations of these individuals for the short term, its action on the genotype (the genetic message) is what affects population change for the long term.

Mutations introduce new genetic messages into a population. A gene may be quite rare, yet because of its advantage become quite common over time. Conversely nonadaptive genes either will not be established, or will be eliminated eventually. Population gene pools vary if immigrants join the population or if individuals emigrate from the population. This has been seen in the Hawaiian Islands over the centuries, where humans arrived from varying islands and continents, intermarried, and produced a unique gene pool.

Probably ancestral giraffes had short necks. No doubt there was some variation within the population due to several genes or multiple alleles of one gene, which resulted in certain neck length phenotypes. If the food supply was limited, those individuals with the genetic combination leading to longer necks would have had an advantage and would have survived, leaving offspring with their genetics. This would result in a change in the gene pool over time, as the longer necked giraffes were favored. Competition for food in higher branches would result in a selective advantage for those with longer necks. Continuance of this trend would result in the long necked characteristic that now prevails.

Environmental dynamics are constantly in flux. Weather and geological factors such as floods, earthquakes, or even slow continental drifting cause change, as do newly arrived predators, changes in the food supply or disease threatening organisms. Over the millions of years of life it is estimated that 99% of the species that have ever existed have become extinct because they weren't able to adapt to environmental change fast enough. For long term survival, organisms must not only be well adapted to their immediate environment, but be able to deal with changes that inevitably will occur. Since environmental change can come quickly and genetic change generally comes slowly and is unpredictable, it is entirely possible that stressed populations would not be able to adapt quickly enough to the new conditions. Extinction would be inevitable.

Many members of a population will succumb to the stress of change but sometimes, because of the variability in the gene pool, some fit individuals will survive. Among those who do survive, fixity of species is generally not the rule unless environments have been stressless and unchanging or unless that organism is extremely well adapted to a variety of circumstances. An example of such an animal is the opossum. It is a prehistoric animal, an early mammal that has survived over millions of years. Its scaly tail reveals its relationship to reptiles and its marsupium (abdominal sac) is a primitive mammalian characteristic. It obviously has adapted well to have survived so long and under so many circumstances. Many of us have witnessed its adaptability in city neighborhoods and its versatility of diet! So many other animals have been displaced by humans but it tenaciously survives. However, before our eyes we also observe the extinction of many plants and animals because of environmental stresses such as habitat decimation, insecticides, and various other kinds of pollution.

In recent decades, strains of insects, rodents, and microbes have arisen that are, respectively, unresponsive to the insecticides, toxin poisons, or antibiotics, which at one time controlled them. Chloroquine, once a cheap anti-malarial drug, is now ineffective among resistant strains of malaria on many continents. The resistance apparently has occurred independently in each area. This is evolution at work.

Patients often pick up very infectious and antibiotic resistant micro-organisms in hospital settings. Infections contracted in hospitals are called nosocomial infections. After being exposed to antibiotics in hospitals over the years, resistant bacteria have survived in these environments and have become established. Hospital patients are often in a weakened state, and their immune systems are less capable of fending off these new, resistant villains. As a result, a patient can go to the hospital with a non-life threatening illness and die of a resistant infection contracted at the hospital. Evolution is change in a population over time, which is exactly what is occurring in this instance. New genetic configurations that happen to bestow resistance to antibiotics in these populations of microbes would obviously be selected.

Gregor Mendel, an Austrian monk, was discovering some basic principles of heredity at the same time that Darwin was researching evolution in England. Unfortunately, the significance of Mendel's data was not recognized until the beginning of the 20th Century. Modern genetics has contributed tremendous credibility to Darwinian evolution by explaining on the molecular level the changes that are observed in the organism. The Modern Synthesis, first propounded in the late 1930s, was the marriage of Darwinian evolution with Mendelian genetics.

Genetics also explains why some characteristics are more common in a population than others. In humans, dark hair is more prevalent than blonde hair, the dark hair gene being dominant over the blonde hair gene. Mendel noted that some characteristics in garden pea plants were masked by more dominant ones but he did not know why. Some characteristics occur in grandparents and grandchildren but are not observable in the parents of those grandchildren. The characteristics seem to skip a generation. They were present, we now understand, but were not expressed, and we can now explain why. For every characteristic, two genetic messages are given to a child, one from the father and one from the mother. Some genes are recessive and they will be hidden if the other message is dominant. Recessive genes will be expressed if there are two copies of them, one from the sperm and one from the egg. Recessive characteristics lurk in the genome, sometimes being masked for generations if they are rare. Eventually if they are matched with another identical recessive then that characteristic will suddenly be expressed in a child. This is seen in cystic fibrosis. The gene is recessive and fairly rare. Healthy people will carry it unknowingly. Two such people can produce a child with this genetic disease which was unknown in either heritage.

As yet we do not know how the complex DNA molecule arose. Reasonable hypotheses are suggested based on a variety of disciplines such as molecular biology, genetics, and information theory. Some hypotheses can be tested in the lab or simulated on the computer. No doubt insight will come from ongoing origin of life research. Those who hold that an intelligent designer spontaneously created the DNA molecule would not pursue research in this area. They already claim to know what happened. Intelligent design belief may in the future discourage scientific research which could give insight to complex molecular formation. Science is based on dependable laws which can be known. This would include an understanding of the origin of complex molecules and metabolic pathways.

To fully grasp the scientific underpinnings of evolutionary theory, biochemistry, mathematics, and genetics should be studied in addition to geology and paleontology. Many questions related to Darwinian evolution are resolved when these disciplines are understood. These are technical fields requiring years of training, and few people have had even a superficial exposure to all of them. Many who reject evolutionary theory are quite unacquainted with its base and frankly cannot give a fair justification for its apparent untenability. Unfortunately even some who assume and are granted authority in this controversy are ignorant of these technical disciplines and are clearly unqualified to be given authoritative status.

Biogeography/Adaptive Radiation Evidence

Biogeography is the study of the distribution of plants and animals throughout the world. Until the 15th Century, Europeans had a limited grasp of the Earth's expanse. Then, global explorers to the continents of Asia, Africa, and the New World, and to islands across the oceans, brought back

187

samples of exotic plants and animals and described many more. How did organisms get to islands and why do some species in the New World resemble species on the African veld? Why are some species exclusively found on one remote island? Why do islands sometimes have great species diversity? Why do others, as expansive as continental habitats, have minimal diversity? How is it that skeletons of the same dinosaurs are found on several continents?

For hundreds of millions of years the Earth has had a history of continental migration, called continental drift or plate tectonics. The Earth's crust rests on plates that undergo slow, but measurable, movement. This activity generates earthquakes and volcanoes along the margins of the plates which we witness at the present time. Current maps showing volcanoes and earthquakes reveal activity at continental margins, for example, California and Japanese earthquakes and the Mt. St. Helens volcano. Movement in the past resulted in mountain building, climactic changes, and sea level modifications explaining why marine fossils are found inland or on mountaintops and why tropical plant fossils are found in nontropical settings such as coal in the Antarctic which contains fossil remains of organisms from the tropics.

Continental drift explains why the eastern coast of South America and the western coast of Africa seem to fit geographically and why rock formations and fossils in both regions correlate. Both also bear evidence of glaciation, which suggests that these two land masses were at one time connected.

Furthermore, the drifting of continents also explains the biogeographical distribution of many species such as the seed fern *Glossopteris,* and extinct, terrestrial animals such as the mammal-like reptile *Lystrosaurus,* or the lizard-like *Mesosaurus,* which have been found in South America, Southern Africa, India and Australia. In 1997, a fairly complete skeleton of a big-bodied, long-necked dinosaur of Cretaceous age, *Titanosaurus,* was found on Madagascar. It had previously been found in Africa, India, Europe, and both North and South America. These data suggest that the continents were once joined together in an enormous land mass, called Pangaea, when these organisms lived about 260 million years ago. Geological strata around the world support this unicontinent thesis as formations on different continents, thousands of miles distant, match each other in content, size, and age.

Biogeography gives clues to the Earth's as well as an organism's history. It explains why rocks in the Sahara Desert have marks of glacial movement. It negates the claim that a worldwide flood escorted these exotics to new places or was responsible for quick Earth movement. Creationists are challenged to explain geographical distribution from their model's perspective. How did species originally disperse to the various continents and islands from the Garden of Eden or from Mt. Ararat after they disembarked from Noah's ark? Are there data to support these claims?

Creationists postulate that the Earth was one landmass at creation and through the period of the flood. Organisms dispersed from the Garden of Eden throughout the huge continent and died during the flood. The surviving pairs from the ark redistributed after the flood. Creationists claim a rapid continental movement just 4,500 years ago (the approximate time they give since Noah's flood) has resulted in the present continental geography and biogeography of the globe, a thesis with no scientific support. On the other hand, much data substantiate a slow (millimeters or centimeters per year) movement causing continental separation over millions of years. Such movement continues to this day and can be measured.

The Earth's crust is made of approximately twenty tectonic plates. They continually pick up molten volcanic rock which originates in the deep layers of the Earth and is pushed up through rifts in the ocean floor. As the rock cools, metallic particles align themselves with the magnetic poles. Since the Earth's magnetic poles change direction over the millennia, a record is preserved over time which can be read in the varying magnetic directions in the rocks. This provides a history of movements and timing. Such varied data would not have accumulated if the continents had separated only 4,500 years ago after the Noachian flood.

Pangaea extended from pole to pole with an immense ocean covering the rest of the globe. This supercontinent broke up over 100 million years ago. As its smaller fragments drifted apart (Laurasia toward the north and Gondwanaland toward the south), they took with them whatever organisms happened to be on them and whatever fossils had been preserved to that point. Each subunit arrived at a different latitude and longitude where distinctive climactic factors and unique selection mechanisms operated. The movement of continents over millions of years influenced climate, species distribution and extinction, and geographical features such as mountain formation. Organisms adapted to these new environments or, if unable to adapt, became extinct. Over millions of years species underwent natural selection with genetic divergence. As a result, few of the populations that ultimately developed resembled the parent population from Pangaea or each other, although they had many characteristics in common.

Geographical dispersion reflects the fact that only those plants and animals whose ancestors colonized a certain region can be found in that region. Giraffes, hyenas, lions, hippopotami, and monkeys without prehensile tails (adapted for wrapping around an object) are found in Africa. They are not found in other regions that may be suitable for their survival because they had no ancestors present in those areas. South America has tapirs, llamas, jaguars, and monkeys with large prehensile tails. Geographical distribution is dictated by the animals which have developed from ancestors which were isolated on a particular land mass, or who happened to float, swim, or be carried there.

Biologists note that on the comparatively small land mass of the Hawaiian Islands there exist over a thousand species of snails and other terrestrial mollusks that occur no place else on Earth. How can this remarkable diversity on this small land mass be explained? Were they all spontaneously created in the Garden of Eden and in turn represented on the ark? How did they get from Mt. Ararat to volcanic islands in the Pacific and nowhere else? Might they have arisen from one or more common ancestors that happened to be carried to these fairly recently formed islands by fowl, wind, or floating debris?

Snails that arrived by chance at these uninhabited islands would have found a plethora of empty niches in which to settle. There would have been few predators or competitors over the millennia in that remote landscape. They and other mollusks would have rapidly, geologically speaking, diversified into the various habitats and become distinctive, separate species, another example of adaptive radiation.

Evolutionary theory explains why oceanic islands only have animals that have been able to cross great ocean expanses. Frogs, toads, and newts were originally missing, as they die upon exposure to salt water. Large mammals can't get across the water. What would creationism predict for these habitats? If the continents were united after the flood and then split, why wouldn't some large mammals or frogs have ended up inhabiting islands?

Why are there woodpeckers with the apparatus for climbing and drilling into wood found on the treeless pampas of Argentina? These birds forage on the ground for food. The evolution model explains that they happened to arrive at this site and adapted to the treeless environment.

Australia, South America, and Antarctica were one land mass which subsequently split. Since Australia was isolated, there was little opportunity for placental mammals (the young develop within the mother's uterus) to become colonized as they evolved after its isolation. The few placentals there, some bats and rodents, must have come from Southeast Asia comparatively recently. Before the division of the continents, marsupials (animals having no placenta; they bear immature young which complete their development in a pouch on the mother's abdomen) probably dispersed to pre-Australia from the region that became South America, via pre-Antarctica. They were free in that isolated environment for 50 million years to change into the exotic life forms they eventually became. The marsupials in Australia are interrelated and rarely found any place else on Earth. This unique distribution was accomplished because ancestral marsupials were stranded on the island continent of Australia. Having minimal or no placental competition, they flourished. They radiated to numerous niches and there is a tremendous variety: anteater, bandicoot, mouse, wombat, koala, flying phalanger, Tasmanian wolf, native cat, kangaroo, wallaby, and mole, all marsupials. Furthermore, there are records of more than 50 species which have gone extinct. Evolution accounts for this biodiversity.

Recently, one extinct placental from 55 million years ago was identified in New South Wales in Australia, so the marsupials were apparently not totally alone in the past. However, with minimal competition they flourished, adaptively radiating. Marsupials on other continents had to compete with placental mammals and never achieved such diversity or numbers. The opossum was unique in having adapted very well.

Darwin saw that tortoises and finches varied in the Galapagos from island to island. He reasoned that they all were related having come from the same stock on the Ecuadorian mainland, yet they had changed as they were isolated on their respective islands. Over time, various characteristics were selected on each of the islands and the tortoises and finches modified substantially such that they could not breed with members on other islands or with ancestors on the mainland. This is another example of speciation and the phenomenon called divergent evolution or adaptive radiation.

Darwin noticed that regions that had similar climates, such as parts of North and South America and Africa, had distinctive plants and animals, yet the various organisms shared many similarities. It appeared as they had been patterned or selected by their parallel environmental stresses and characteristics. In other words, instead of grazing animals such as the gazelle, zebra, or antelope happening to migrate after the flood to their respective continents, it appeared that they all had individually arisen from their particular ancestors, nature having selected for properties consistent with the grassland environment that was their home. Grazing animals in North America resemble grazers in Africa, even though they had very different lineages. They exhibit similar herd behavior for protection, have large molars for chewing grasses, and hoofed toes and elongated legs for fast running. They became quite similar as they adjusted to similar environments, even though they were not closely related from an ancestral or genetic perspective. This phenomenon is called parallel evolution. These organisms have many characteristics in common yet have derived them from distinctive lines of inheritance being quite unrelated genetically.

Parallel evolution is also seen in the cacti and euphorbs, both fleshy plants with thick, spiny, leafless green stems adapted for storing water. At first glance they appear to be closely related. Yet their flowers are extremely dissimilar and their respective spines and storage tissues have different origins, which points to very different heritages. The reason the vegetative parts appear so similar is that they have independently adapted through selection to harsh desert environments on two different continents.

The close resemblance of several marsupials from Australia with placental mammals on the other continents is another example of parallel evolution. Selection for survival in similar habitats in different places led to similar adaptations; parallel evolution. The placental wolf, ocelot, and groundhog parallel the marsupial Tasmanian wolf, native cat, and wombat. Although coming from separate lineages, these animals have qualities in common that have been naturally selected over millions of years in environments which shared close resemblance.

If environments are comparable it would be predicted that their respective fauna and flora might have characteristics in common, even though their ancestral origins were dissimilar. The particular composition of populations and the appearance of animals and plants in habitats around the world reflect their distinctive genetic endowments, their competition, and the unique adaptation to environmental stresses which they have experienced.

Biological Evidence

Comparative Anatomy/Homology

Comparative anatomists have noted that while there is great diversity within the vertebrates, from fish to amphibians, reptiles, birds, and mammals, they nevertheless all share some interesting characteristics in common. For example, forelimb bone arrangements of birds and mammals are very similar even though they live in varied habitats, and their respective limbs have unique functions and appearance. The wing of a bat, eagle, or hummingbird, the flipper of a seal or whale, the foreleg of a giraffe, gopher, or elephant, or the arm of a sloth or chimpanzee, as well as forelimbs of many extinct vertebrates, all have similar internal anatomy. They have comparable bones arranged in the same pattern. Limb functions are unique, varying from swimming, to flying, digging, running, climbing, and grasping, but the limb anatomies have a lot in common.

This phenomenon is called homology, meaning similarity. Evolutionary theory explains these homologous structures by suggesting that these birds and mammals came from similar lineages. Divergent evolution has occurred as these animals radiated to myriad habitats and adapted to corresponding environmental demands. All the while, nature selected for those changes that best contributed to this adaptation. Even after millions of years there remain certain anatomical and physiological homologies that they share, which attest to some type of relationship. Some are more closely related than others, suggesting a more recent divergence from common stock. Others share less anatomy in common and represent much earlier divergence. Animals that are most similar, such as elk and caribou diverged comparatively recently from a common ancestor. More dissimilar animals such as cats, wolves, and rodents had much earlier common ancestry.

Another example of homology is that all mammals, from the giraffe to the mastodon, to a platypus or shrew, have seven cervical (neck) vertebrae no matter how distinctive they have become. Also, all vertebrates from fish to mammals have a double-lobed brain. These homologous consistencies would be predicted if there were relatedness through common ancestry.

Homology is also seen on the cellular and molecular levels. Humans have cellular structures and chemistry that parallel many other species: a double layered cell membrane, similar cell organelles, identical cellular respiration metabolic pathways including enzymes and ATP functions (energy conversion), and other similar or even identical biochemical pathways. DNA is the universal carrier of the genetic code of each species of living organisms except for some viruses which use RNA for that purpose.

Comparing the anatomy of animals that occur early in the fossil record with those that appear later also affirms this relatedness. Consider the annelids, the 9,000 species of segmented worms, including the common earthworm. They were established in number and variety in Cambrian formations. Concurrent with these organisms are found primitive and varied arthropods such as trilobites, and some similar to brine shrimp, as well as a segmented, worm-like species with feet, *Oncophoran*. This organism, which is still living, appears to be an intermediate between the annelids (segmented worms) and the arthropods (jointed foot). It looks like a worm but has feet like an arthropod. Arthropods retain the segmented body, but the body is shortened, with fewer, more specialized segments. The basic segmented pattern is remarkably evident in arthropod immature stages such as the caterpillar, however. It can also be seen in the adult musculature and nervous system. As would be predicted from evolutionary theory, complex arthropods, such as arachnids (spiders), crustaceans (crabs, lobsters), and insects, appear later in the fossil record.

Many examples of comparative anatomy which show transitions and relationship can be noted: lunged fish arriving prior to air-breathing amphibians, larval amphibians (tadpoles) resembling fish, jawless vertebrates prior to those with jaws, scales on birds' legs resembling their reptilian ancestors, or the scaly tail of one of the early prehistoric, yet nonextinct mammals, the opossum. Pelvic bones and leg appendages on some snakes and whales hint to past relationship with ambulatory reptiles and mammals respectively.

The evolution of the mammalian jaw is a classic example of transitions. The jaw joint is between the quadrate bone in the skull and the articular bone in the lower jaw in reptiles. In mammals, it is between the squamosal (skull) and dentary (jaw) bones. The whole transition between reptiles and mammals can be seen in the fossil record where in-between stages are noted in reptiles such as the Permian *Dimetrodon* (reptile), and *Thrinaxodon,* a Triassic mammal-like reptile, and one of the first mammals, *Morganucodon* (early Jurassic). The fate of the bones and the transitional progress of this joint can be clearly demonstrated through comparative anatomy.

There are many transitional fossils that demonstrate the evolution of the horse. Small, four-toed woodland *Hydracotheriu,* which had teeth for eating berries and buds, can be traced through larger organisms such as *Mesohippus* and *Merychippus* and *Pliohippus* to *Equus,* grazing animals with teeth specialized for eating grass and single-toed feet capable of great speed. The extensive fossil record of horses does not show a single line of descent. Evolution is more complex, with branching lines of descent rather than a unilinear history. A great variety of anatomical and physiological variations going off in many directions occur over time. The horse fossil series represents individuals from many parts of this branching tree, yet gives an overall progression of evolution over time.

Comparative Embryology

Comparative embryology also supports evolutionary theory as it shows patterns of relationship. Great similarity of structure and function can be seen in various stages of all vertebrate embryos. They all contain gill slits and tails as embryos, even though these structures are not necessarily retained after birth. Animals most closely related have similar embryological development persisting almost to birth. Those less alike share stages early in embryonic life and diverge as time and development continues.

Barnacles, which attach to rock, ships, or other animals, do not appear to be very similar to freely moving crustaceans such as shrimp or lobsters. However the barnacle larval stage is remarkably similar to the larvae of these other crustaceans, suggesting some relationship. Embryology, not anatomy or behavior, is the link in this case.

Although rare, human babies have been born with clefts from gill slits in the neck region or tiny tails. The very presence of these nonfunctional structures, which usually disappear prior to birth, trigger questions such as: If this species was uniquely designed and abruptly appeared, then why would these useless structures be present in the embryonic life and then disappear? Evolutionary theory explains their presence. They are left over remnants from a past where they have been selected against in ancestors which inhabited environments where other characteristics were more advantageous.

A comparative embryological progression is the blind sack that branches from the developing pharynx in vertebrates. In fish it either disappears or gives rise to the air bladder, which is used for buoyancy. It is the origin of lungs in other groups. This related development in embryological stages lends credibility to evolutionary theory, which predicts this kind of progression.

Vestigial Structures

Vestigial comes from the Latin "vestigium" meaning "footsteps" or "tracks." Comparative anatomists have identified rudimentary organs, vestigial structures, which seem to have degenerated and have either minimal or no known use. They give insights into an organism's ancestry and are not always easy to explain. Previously useful, they are no longer necessary and are apparently left over from a more fully developed, functioning organ in the past. Providing more support for the evolutionary thesis, they are in the process of being selected against, becoming smaller or being modified in other ways, and they are generally less functional.

Rudimentary pelvic bones and reduced hind limbs remain on some whales and snakes, sometimes even being visible on the outside. Reduced eye stalks persist in blind, cave-dwelling crustaceans. Some moles have vestigial, nonfunctioning eyes. The spines of cacti are vestigial leaves with a new function. Some remnant structures retain a minimal function and yet some seem to have lost their functions altogether. In cave dwelling salamanders the young stages have eyes, which are lost as the animal matures (Brandon, 1971). Paleontologists suggest that the tiny, muscle-bound arms of *Tyrannosaurus rex* are vestigial. They didn't meet and had minimal movement, appearing quite nonfunctional. It is theorized that if *T. rex* hadn't gone extinct it may well have lost its arms completely in time.

In humans, external ear and scalp muscles are rudimentary and generally nonfunctional although some individuals still have control over them and can move their ears or scalp! They show a relationship to many other mammals where these muscles function in moving the ears for better hearing. Inflection of the foot in human infants, a mechanism for grasping, degenerates in adults but is a characteristic of other primates. It enables them to grasp tree limbs as they climb or as their infants hold on to their mothers.

Other rudimentary structures in humans include reduced tail bones, remnants of tail muscles, sparse and practically nonfunctional body hair, wisdom teeth, nipples in males, and the appendix of the cecum. The cecum is a blind pouch in the region where the small intestine joins the large intestine and the vermiform appendix is a small, wormlike ("vermin"= worm) structure attached to it. While appearing to be quite functionless in the human, this organ is a vestige of a fully developed organ found in rabbits and other herbivores, where the enlarged cecum and appendix store cellulose from plant materials for bacterial digestion. Most plant eating animals (including termites which eat wood) cannot digest cellulose and depend upon bacteria or some other symbiont (an organism living with it; "sym"= together, "bio"= life) for this function. The appendix is a site for such digestion in plant-eating animals. Its vestigial nature is clearly demonstrated when it is not missed after surgical removal in humans!

Vestigial structures are noted in the water fern, *Marsilea*. Quite obviously it was once adapted to land. Like whales, it has returned to an aquatic existence, yet it retains telltale traces of its evolutionary past. It still has a water-resistant cuticle, now quite superfluous, and a complex internal transport system which is not required of aquatic species. It also has openings (stomata) needed by terrestrial forms for the exchange of oxygen and carbon dioxide gases. Evolution explains the existence of these useless stomates.

Vestiges, being superfluous and nonfunctional, are fully understood as a result of evolutionary change. Why do flightless beetles have useless wings buried beneath fused wing covers? Why do bird embryos have the ability to grow teeth under precise conditions in the laboratory? All of this is quite puzzling in an abrupt creation by design model.

Bizarre Structures

Unique or bizarre body parts of animals and plants also support evolutionary theory. One such structure is the thumb of the giant panda. Pandas have six digits rather than five. Their forepaws are bear-like with five toes, and one of their wrist bones, the sesamoid, has evolved into an extra digit, a useful but inelegant thumb for grasping bamboo stalks and leaves. This evolutionary adaptation is an imperfect structure yet fulfills its function adequately. It is surmised that the panda originally had just the five toes that evolved into a paw. The adaptation of the wrist bone as a thumb is a secondary specialization quite consistent with the evolutionary paradigm.

Enormous Number of Species

Both Darwin and Wallace had reservations about the concept of special creation and the fixity of species as they traveled through the tropics where species diversity is almost limitless. Biologists do not know how many species of animals and plants are present on the Earth today, let alone how many have existed in the past. It is estimated that there are over 2 million known species of living things today, from amoebas and armadillos to zinnias and zebras, and that there remain three to five times that many still undiscovered (Schopf, p. 145). It is thought that there were far beyond 100 million species in the past, 99% of all of them being extinct. Even though that may be the case, there are more species living today than at any previous time. For example, there are at least 370,000 species of beetles alone. Their order, Coleoptera, is the largest order in the Animal Kingdom. They are extremely varied in habitat, food, behavior, and appearance. Some are a fraction of a millimeter in size and others are almost 200 mm (eight inches) long. The evolutionary paradigm explains the remarkable divergence of this group as it radiated and successfully adapted to innumerable niches.

Biologists in the 19th Century came to doubt special creation because they were becoming aware of the tremendous variety of species and habitats across the globe. They found untenable the thesis that pairs of all land animals could fit on an ark or be represented in a Garden named Eden and be given names by one person. Scientists continue to discover, classify, and name undescribed, unnamed species. Paleontologists regularly unearth previously unknown extinct species. The end is nowhere in sight.

It has also been noted that organisms are not as distinctive as was originally thought. It is often hard to distinguish a "kind" or even a "species." Gradations can be observed in both plants and animals, evidence that modifications have taken place over millions of years as a result of adaptation to various environments. This, too, supports evolutionary theory.

Adaptations

Populations undergo gradual changes over time as a response to particular environmental demands. Mimicry in behavior or appearance, unique behaviors and anatomy such as the peacock's feather display or the opossum playing "dead," coloration either for sexual attraction (male cardinal) or for camouflage (female cardinal), secretions for sexual attraction (porcupine) or defense (skunk), verbal (elk) or nonverbal communications can be explained through evolutionary theory. So can coevolution such as the anatomy of some flowers being particularly adapted to the insects which pollinate them. Psychologists parallel the human smile with a similar expression in other primates. It communicates non-aggression and a position of subordination. The thousands of beetle species previously mentioned demonstrate adaptive capability. The many larval stages of insects are an elaborate adaptation whereby the young or intermediates do not need to compete with the adults for the same food supply.

Archaea

The Archaea are very primitive bacteria living in protected hydrothermal vents on the ocean floor. The mineral-rich waters support anaerobic (without oxygen), methane-producing bacteria also. These ancient appearing organisms have primitive means of synthesizing life molecules from sulfur and hydrogen sulfide at hot springs around deep ocean trenches and may well have persisted unchanged through the eons. Biologists wonder if they might be descendants of the earliest known cells. However, some specialists recently have suggested that earliest life may have originated in an aquatic environment.

The Archean period is the earliest of Earth's history. Comprising 43% of Earth's existence, it composed the first 2,000 million years of its 4.5 billion year history. During most of that period the continents were devoid of life, which is hypothesized to have arisen in the seas. Less is heard today about the "organic soup" and more attention is given to deep hydrothermal vents as the site of life's beginning. Microfossils and stromatolites (structures produced to this day by mats of blue-green algae) represent this period. The Archean period ended when oxygen became prevalent in the atmosphere about 2,500 million years ago. Paleontologists note that organisms similar to those from the Archean period exist today in oxygen-free environments on the sea floor, in marshes and even in human intestines.

Additional Reading

Alters, Brian J. & Alters, Sandra M. (2001). *Defending evolution in the classroom.* Sudbury, MA: Jones and Bartlett Publishers.

Appleman, Philip (Ed.). (2001). *Darwin.* New York: W.W. Norton

Ayala, Francisco, J. (Ed.). (1976). *Molecular evolution.*

Ayala, Francisco J. & Valentine, James W. (1979). *Evolving: The theory and processes of organic evolution.*

Ayala, Francisco J. (1982). *Population and evolutionary genetics: A primer.*

Barrow, John & Tipler, Frank (1986). *Anthropic cosmological principle.* Oxford University Press.

Bell, G. (1997). *Selection: The mechanism of evolution.* New York: Chapman and Hall.

Benton, Michael (1986). *The story of life on Earth.* New York: Warwick Press.

Berra, Timothy (1990). *Evolution and the myth of creationism.* Stanford: Stanford University Press.

Beus, Stanley S. & Morales, Michael (1990). *Grand Canyon geology.* New York: Oxford University Press.

Bodmer, Walter & Cavalli-Sforza, L. L. (1976). *Genetics, evolution, and man,* New York: W. H. Freeman and Co.

Bonner, John Tyler (1988). *The evolution of complexity by means of natural selection.* Princeton, NJ: Princeton University Press.

Bowler, P. J. (1989). *Evolution: The history of an idea.* Revised edition. Berkeley: University of California Press.

Bowler, P. J. (2001). *Reconciling science and religion.* Chicago: University of Chicago Press.

Brandon, R. A. (1971). North American troglobitic salamanders: Some aspects of modification in cave habitats with special reference to *Gyrinophilus paleucus*. *National Speleological Society Bulletin, 33*, 1-21.

Busbey, A. B. III, Coenraads, R. R., Willis, P. & Roots, D. (1996). *The Nature Company Guides: Rocks and fossils*. San Francisco: Time/Life Books.

Carroll, Robert L. (1988). *Vertebrate paleontology and evolution*. New York: W. H. Freeman & Co.

Carroll, Robert L. (1997). *Patterns and processes of vertebrate evolution*. New York: Cambridge University Press.

Cole-Turner, Ron (1993). *New Genesis: Theology and the genetic revolution*. Louisville: Westminster/John Knox Press.

Dal Sasso, Christiano & Signore, Marco (1998, March 26). Exceptional soft-tissue preservation in a theropod dinosaur from Italy, *Nature, 392*, pp. 383-387.

Dawkins, Richard (1976). *The selfish gene*. London: Oxford University Press.

Dawkins, Richard (1995). *River out of Eden: A Darwinian view of life*. New York: Basic Books.

de Camp, L. S. (1988). *The great monkey trial*. New York: Doubleday.

Dickerson, Richard & Geis, Irving (1976). *Chemistry, matter and the universe*, Menlo Park, CA: W. A. Benjamin, Inc.

Dobzhansky, Theodosius (1937, reprinted 1982). *Genetics and the origin of species*.

Edwards, Denis (1999). *The God of evolution: A Trinitarian theology*. Mahwah, NJ: Paulist Press.

Eldredge, Niles (1985). *Time frames: The rethinking of Darwinian evolution and the theory of punctuated equilibria*.

Eldredge, Niles (1985). *Unfinished synthesis: Biological hierarchies and modern evolutionary thought*. New York: Oxford University Press.

Eldredge, Niles (1999). *The pattern of evolution*. New York: W. H. Freeman Press.

Eldredge, Niles (2001). *The triumph of evolution and the failure of creationism*.

Ellegard, Alvar (1990). *Darwin and the general reader*. Chicago: University of Chicago Press.

Ford, Adam (1999). *Faith and science*. Epworth Press.

Fortey, Richard (1997). *Life: A natural history of the first four billion years of life on Earth*. New York: Vintage Books.

Freeman, Scott & Herron, Jon (1998). *Evolutionary analysis*. Upper Saddle River, NJ: Prentice Hall.

Futuyma, Douglas (1983). *Science on trial: The case for evolution*. New York: Pantheon Books.

Gillespie, J. H. (1991). *The causes of molecular evolution*. New York: Oxford University Press.

Godfrey, Laurie (Ed.). (1983). *Scientists confront creatinism*. New York: W.W. Norton.

Godfrey, Stephen J. (1989-90). Tetrapod fossil footprints, polonium halos, and the Colorado Plateau. *Creation/Evolution* (Vol. XXVI). pp. 8-17.

Gould, Stephen Jay & Eldredge, Niles (1977). Punctuated equilibria: The tempo and mode of evolution reconsidered. *Paleobiology, 3*, 115-151.

Gould, Stephen Jay & Eldredge, Niles (1993). Punctuated equilibrium comes of age. *Nature, 336*, 223-227.

Gould, Stephen Jay (1980). *The panda's thumb: More reflections in natural history*, New York: W. W. Norton.

Gould, Stephen Jay (1984). Evolution as fact and theory. In *Science and creationism*, A. Montagu (Ed.). New York: Oxford University Press.

Gould, Stephen Jay (1985). *The flamingo's smile: Reflections in natural history*. New York: Norton.

Gould, Stephen Jay (1989). *Wonderful life: The Burgess shale and the nature of history*. New York: W. W. Norton.

Gould, Stephen Jay (Ed.). (1992). *The book of life: An illustrated history of the evolution of life on Earth*. New York: W. W. Norton.

Gould, Stephen Jay (2002). *The structure of evolutionary theory*. Boston: Harvard University Press.

Grafen, A. (Ed.). (1989). *Evolution and its implications*. Oxford: Oxford University Press.

Gregersen, Niels & van Huyssteen, Wentzel (1998). *Rethinking theology and science*. Grand Rapids, MI: Eerdmans.

Halvorson, H. O. & Van Holde, K. E. (Eds.). (1980). *The origin of life and evolution*. New York: Alan R. Liss.

Hartmann, William K. & Miller, Ron (1991). *The history of Earth*. New York: Workman Publ.

Hoagland, Mahlon & Dodson, Bert (1995). *The way life works*. New York: Time Books, Random House.

Horner, John R. (1997). *Dinosaur lives: Unearthing an evolutionary saga*. New York: HarperCollins.

Hotton, Nicholas III (1968). *The evidence of evolution*. The Smithsonian Library. New York: American Heritage Publishing Co., Inc.

Huxley, Julian (1974). *Evolution: The modern synthesis*. (3rd ed.).

Judson, Horace (1979). *The eighth day of creation: Makers of the revolution in biology*. New York: Simon and Schuster.

Korsmeyer, Jerry D. (1998). *Evolution and Eden: Balancing original sin and contemporary science*. Mahwah, NJ: Paulist Press.

Kuhn, Thomas S. (1996). *The structure of scientific revolutions* (3rd ed.). Chicago: University of Chicago Press.

Marshall, Charles R. & Schopf, J. William (Eds.). (1996). *Evolution and the molecular revolution*. Sudbury, MA: Jones and Bartlett, Publ.

Matt, Daniel (1996). *God and the big bang*. Woodstock, VT: Jewish Lights Publishers.

Mayr, Ernst (1963). *Animal species and evolution*. Cambridge: Harvard University Press.

Mayr, Ernst (1982). *The growth of biological thought: Diversity, evolution, and inheritance*. Cambridge: Harvard University Press.

Mayr, Ernst (1991). *One long argument: Charles Darwin and the genesis of modern evolutionary Thought*. Cambridge: Harvard University Press.

Mayr, Ernst & Provine, W. B. (Eds.). (1980). *The evolutionary synthesis*. Cambridge, MA: Harvard University Press.

McMullin, Ernan, (Ed.). (1985). *Evolution and creation*. Notre Dame, IN: University of Notre Dame Press.

McNamara, K. (Ed.). (1990). *Macroevolutionary trends*. Tucson: University of Arizona Press.

Miller, Kenneth R. (1999). *Finding Darwin's God: A scientist's search for common ground between God and evolution*. New York: HarperCollins.

Miller, J. & Van Loon, B. (1982). *Darwin for beginners*. New York: Pantheon Books.

Miller, James B. (Ed.). (2001). *An evolving dialogue: Theological and scientific perspectives on evolution*. Trinity Press International.

Minkoff, Eli C. (1983). *Evolutionary biology*. Reading, MA: Addison Wesley.

Montagu, Ashley (Ed.). (1984). *Science and creationism.* New York: Oxford University Press.

Morris, Simon Conway (1998). *The crucible of creation: The Burgess shale and the rise of animals.* New York: Oxford University Press.

National Academy of Sciences (1998). *Teaching about evolution and the nature of science.* Washington, DC: National Academy Press.

Nelkin, D. (1982). *The creation controversy: Science or scripture in the schools?* New York: W. W. Norton.

Newman, James R. (Ed.). (1955). *What is science?* New York: Washington Square Press.

Oparin, A. I. (1964). *Life: Its nature, origin, and development.* New York: Columbia University Press.

Pannenberg, Wolfhart (1993). *Toward a theology of nature.* Louisville: Westminster/John Knox Press.

Peacocke, Arthur (1979). *Creation and the world of science.* Oxford University Press.

Peacocke, Arthur (1986). *God and the new biology.* Harper and Row.

Pennock, Robert T. (Ed.). (2001). *Intelligent design creationism and its critics: Philosophical, theological and scientific.* Cambridge, MA: MIT Press.

Peters, Ted (Ed.). (1989). *Cosmos as creation.* Abingdon Press.

Polkinghorne, John (1998). *Science and theology.* Minneapolis: SPCK/Fortress Press.

Quammen, David (1997). *The song of the dodo: Island biogeography in an age of extinction,* New York: Simon and Schuster.

Ramm, Bernard (1954). *The Christian view of science and scripture.* Grand Rapids, MI: Eerdmans.

Ratzsch, Del (1996). *The battle of beginnings: Why neither side is winning the creation-evolution debate.* Downers Grove, IL: InterVarsity Press.

Richards, Robert J. (1992). *The meaning of evolution: The morphological construction and ideological reconstruction of Darwin's theory.* Chicago: University of Chicago Press.

Ridley, Mark (Ed.). (1997). *Evolution.* New York: Oxford University Press.

Rolston, Holmes (1987). *Science and religion: A critical survey.* Random House.

Rolston, Holmes (1995). *Biology, ethics and the origins of life.* Boston: Jones & Bartlett Publishers.

Rudwick, Martin J. S. (1985). *The meaning of fossils.* Chicago: University of Chicago Press.

Ruse, Michael (1996). *Monad to man: The concept of progress in evolutionary biology.* Cambridge, MA: Harvard University Press.

Ruse, Michael (1998). *Taking Darwin seriously.* Amherst, NY: Prometheus Books.

Ruse, Michael (2001). *Can a Darwinian be a Christian?* New York: Cambridge University Press.

Ruse, Michael (2001). *The evolutuion wars: A guide to the debates.* New Brunswick: Rutgers University Press.

Ryan, William & Pitman, Walker (1998). *Noah's flood.* New York: Simon and Schuster.

Schmitz-Moormann, Karl (1997). *Theology of creation in an evolutionary world.* Cleveland, OH: Pilgrim Press.

Schopf, J. William (1999). *Cradle of life: The discovery of Earth's earliest fossils.* Princeton, NJ: Princeton University Press.

Simpson, George Gaylord (1944). *Tempo and mode in evolution.* New York: Columbia University Press.

Simpson, George Gaylord (1967, reissued 1971). *The meaning of evolution: A study of the history of life and of its significance for man* (2nd revised ed.).

Stebbins, G. Ledyard (1974). *Flowering plants: Evolution above the species level.*

Stebbins, G. Ledyard (1982). *Darwin and DNA: Molecules to humanity.* Freeman Press.

Strickberger, Monroe W. (1996). *Evolution* (2nd ed.). Sudbury, MA: Jones and Bartlett, Publ.

Swinburne, Richard (1986). *The evolution of the soul.* Oxford: Clarendon Press.

Taylor, Paul D. (1990). *Fossil.* Eyewitness Books, New York: Alfred Knopf.

Teilhard de Chardin, Pierre (1969). *Christianity and evolution.* Harvest/HBJ Books.

Thomson, Keith (1991). *Living fossil: The story of the coelacanth.* New York: W. W. Norton & Co.

Towne, Margaret G. (1995). *The influence of critical thinking on Christians' belief and belief change with reference to the polarities of creationism and organic evolution.* Doctoral thesis: Montana State University.

Untermann, G. E. & Untermann, B. R. (1969). *Grand Canyon geology.* New York: Oxford University Press.

Van Till, Howard J. et al. (1988). *Science held hostage.* Downers Grove, IL: InterVarsity Press.

Van Till, Howard J. et al. (1990). *Portraits of creation.* Grand Rapids, MI: Eerdmans Press.

Volpe, E. Peter (1985). *Understanding evolution.* Dubuque, IA: Wm. C. Brown Publ. Co.

Ward, Keith (1996). *God, chance and necessity.* Oxford: Oneworld.

White, Michael (1978). *Modes of speciation.*

Wilson, David B. (Ed.). (1983). *Did the devil make Darwin do it?* Iowa State University Press.

Wilson, E. O. (1992). *The diversity of life.* New York: W. W. Norton.

Weiner, Jonathan (1994). *The beak of the finch: A story of evolution in our time.* New York: Knopf.

Woodmorappe, John (1981). The essential nonexistence of the evolutionary uniformitarian geologic column: A quantitative assessment. *Creation Research Society Quarterly, 18* (1), 46-71.

Questions Relating to Origins/Evolution

Chapter Eight

Now we see but a poor reflection; then we shall see face to face. Now I know in part; then I shall know fully.
I Corinthians 13:12

Evolutionary theory, which supports the thesis that living things change over time, is a distinct area of inquiry, not related to cosmology (the origins, processes and structure of the universe), or abiogenesis (the origin of life). However, it is not uncommon to see these three subjects intertwined. Much of the conflict surrounding the theory of evolution has been generated by this confusion. Some suggest that evolution could not be true because of unexplained questions pertaining to the other two disciplines. Evolution stands on its own. How life originated is one thing. How it changed is another. Evolution refers to change. While the thesis of this book centers on evolutionary theory, this particular chapter will include, among other things, discussion on the origin of the universe and of life in an attempt to explain how their scientific support base is irrelevant to that of evolutionary theory. Some of the unanswered questions that surround all of these subjects will be presented in this chapter. Good thinkers are fair and honest and should be as quick to expose weaknesses and enigmas as they are at heralding strengths. The reader can judge whether these problems, weighed in light of the supporting data, negate the concept of slow change over time.

Origin/Future of the Universe

Unanswered Questions:

What existed prior to the Big Bang?
What event(s) triggered the Big Bang? The sudden decompression of matter from a single point of infinite density? When was it, exactly?
How exactly did the cosmic bodies emerge and change?
What were all the mechanisms that were (are) at work?
How did electrons and nucleons emerge?

What is the future of the universe? Will it expand forever or will it contract and collapse into the infinite density from which it came? Or will it experience some unknown destiny?

Origin of Life

Questions:

What *is* life?

Where did life arise? Did it arise more than once? Could it arise today either naturally or in the laboratory? Is there primordial significance to the anoxic, thermophilic (heat loving), methane-producing bacteria found inhabiting deep sea volcanic vents on the ocean floor? Might these be descendants of the first living cells? Is their means of chemosynthesis (making molecules), the most primitive among organisms, similar to how first cells chemosynthesized?

Did life arrive on a meteor from elsewhere in the universe (Panspermia)? How did it occur there?

How did life arise from nonlife? From an organic soup? From clay? From crystals? In hydrothermal vents? In a reducing (oxygen-free) atmosphere? In an aquatic environment?

How did complex molecules such as proteins, RNA, and DNA develop?

Exactly when did life arise? How, specifically, did the interdependent relationship between DNA, RNA, and proteins get started? Is this irreducible complexity (the interacting parts of a basic function whereby the loss of any one part results in the system's failure)?

Is there extra-terrestrial life? Is there extra-terrestrial intelligence? Are we alone?

Evolution/Geology

Questions:

What are all the mechanisms that result in change over time? How do messages on the DNA molecule get altered? Is evolution small, steady DNA change, large change, or both?

What are the main factors that precipitate evolutionary change in populations? Is it competition with other plants and animals, or changes in the physical or chemical environment? What might these factors in the physical and chemical environments be?

What is the role of "jumping genes"?

How do various proteins become modified?

What is the origin of the algae? What are the evolutionary relationships between algal groups? Why are some more closely related to fungi and protozoa than to other algae?

How did human speech originate? Why are there no primitive languages in existence? How did complex language evolve?

How can we account for the awesome human mind? How could such complexity have evolved, step by step?

Why do humans have mental qualities such as intelligence for music, art, beauty, or mathematics, which are not needed for survival? Why would those capabilities have evolved? Do the chromosomal recipes for these characteristics tag on to the genes of qualities necessary for survival?

Did vertebrates originate from tadpole-like chordates?

What caused the mass extinctions in the past, including dinosaur extinction? An asteroid? Climate change? Forest environments replaced by grasslands? Something else?

What explains the Cambrian explosion? Was it indeed an "explosion"?

What was the origin of fishes, of lagomorphs (rabbits, hares, picas), of bats, and turtles?

What were the intermediates and time sequences between the fishes Placoderms (first jawed fish with paired fins) and Chondrichthyes (cartilaginous fish)? Placoderms and Osteichthyes (bony fish)?

What is the relationship between the sturgeon and paddlefish, both very old?

What were the first tetrapods (four footed animals) like?

Where and how did they invade land? Did it happen more than once?

How did the long neck of the giraffe evolve in tandem with its need for high blood pressure, fast heartbeat, and blood pressure reduction when it stoops to drink?

Why are polar bears white? They have no need for camouflage as they have no enemies. Does it relate to their being able to sneak up on their prey unnoticed?

Why have no new phyla appeared?

How did the mechanism evolve to turn animals such as the ptarmigan brown in summer and white in winter?

How are once useful organs, such as the eye of a burrower, lost?

The earliest fish as well as the trilobite had quite a sophisticated eye. What is the estimated number of mutations necessary to bring about this structure?

What factors accounted for the glacial and interglacial periods?

What comes first, behavior change or structural change? Either?

How is the evolution of behavior explained?

What is the origin of sexual reproduction? Whence came maleness and femaleness?

Did doubling (progress to multicellularity) occur by the ingestion of one cell by another as is observed in some microbes?

Why, when, and how did some land animals revert to the sea?

How is the stability of species such as crocodilians (pretty much the same for 200 million years except for growing smaller), and the reptile tuatara *Sphenodon punctatus*, sturgeon, some insects, the brachiopod lamp-shell *Lingula* (unchanged 450 million years) and coelacanths explained? Why did crocodilians (alligators and crocodiles) and turtles survive the mass extinction at the end of the Cretaceous Period 65 million years ago when most reptiles went extinct?

What accounts for periods of apparent acceleration of evolutionary change and then unpredictable periods of extinction? What accounts for punctuated equilibrium?

How important is genetic drift compared to natural selection in evolution?

Can there be major mutations rather than just slight DNA alterations?

Why are there so few transitional forms between phyla?

What caused the horses, camels, and rhinoceri to go extinct in North America during the Pleistocene?

How are all the primate fossils to be accurately classified?

It must be noted that there are hypotheses for many of these questions with some impressive supporting data. It would not be surprising, by the time this book is read, that some of these questions will be resolved, at least in part. Science marches on.

While this list looks imposing, the number of unanswered questions scientists could entertain is infinite. This list is a mere beginning. Ichthyologists (those who study fish) ask questions pertaining to their field, some included here. Every discipline, from entomology (study of insects) to ornithology (birds), herpetology (reptiles), malacology (mollusks—snails, clams, octopi) to neurophysiology, genetics, geology, and anthropology (humans) has particular questions. Scientists who do research in geology, astronomy, evolution, biochemistry, and paleontology have extensive lists of unknowns which they seek to understand. One can only imagine how much will be added to our knowledge base by the end of the present century. But by then there will be new questions.....

If this book were written a few decades ago the list of unknowns would be different. Many questions from that period have been resolved. Darwin, more than a century ago, spoke of missing pages in the record in nature, even missing chapters! He had numerous questions, especially those pertaining to genetics and molecular biology. Many puzzles of his era were answered during the last century. Present enigmas are being researched and various hypotheses leading to the resolution of some are being tested. Almost every day newspapers and journals supply answers to former questions, correct inaccuracy, or relay information in areas about which we previously didn't even know enough to ask.

While some questions are solved, at the same time, new data are discovered continually and they usually present a whole new menu of dilemmas. They in turn stimulate research. For instance, finding a new dinosaur is exciting and informative but it leads to a whole bevy of questions: When did it live? Who was it related to and who were its ancestors? What was its behavior? What did it eat? Who were its enemies? Did it migrate, herd, or have maternal behavior? Did it lay eggs? Was it warm blooded? Why did this one die? Why did its species go extinct? How extensive was its territory?

There will *always* be unknowns, for the more we learn the more we find to question. Since records have been forever lost due to such forces as erosion and volcanism as well as violent Earth movements, there will always be unanswered questions surrounding evolution and paleontology. Destroyed records can never be read. Soft tissues are rarely preserved. Many events left no records.

Evolutionists regret this data void and creationists often capitalize on the gaps in the fossil record or all these present mysteries. If this line of defense gives creationists a security it will be forever in their service. If in their teaching of the lay masses only the problems of evolutionary theory are introduced then there is deception and serious bias. Rather than dwelling on and even reveling in what is absent, those challenging evolutionary theory might concentrate on the mass of supporting data that are available, and seek to experimentally negate or falsify them. This is a much more demanding activity requiring qualified scientists doing sophisticated research, much time and funding, and is precisely the role of peer review. It would be welcomed.

In past centuries when questions arose and there was no scientific evidence to explain them, a "god of the gaps" mentality was employed. If an unexplainable conundrum presented itself, then a miracle would fill the gap and be the explanation. What was not humanly understood was resolved by putting God into that intellectual gap. What occurs however is that, little by little, the enigmas are explained and the gaps become filled and the God of miracles is forced to retreat. Rational explanations are formulated, proven, and subsequently fill the gaps.

Many people still comfortably explain any mysteries of life with a "god of the gaps." If cellular metabolic pathways or bacterial flagella physiology seem too complex, "irreducible complexity" is claimed and God or an intelligent designer is called in to explain. People who accept this explanation would see no need for, nor be curious about, rational answers. Others reserve judgment, live with ambiguity, work for reasonable and logical resolution, and claim honestly that as yet the answers are not available. Further, they have some conviction that with perseverance at least some of these questions may one day be resolved, and on this rests the vitality and future of scientific inquiry. Indeed, while new questions continually arise, others are regularly answered.

As has been stated throughout this book, unanswered questions relating to the origin of the universe or the origin of life do not impact the discipline of evolutionary theory. Therefore such problems cannot detract from the validity of evolutionary change over time.

It behooves evolutionists to delineate the areas in their field for which answers have not yet come. Then those who are interested can carefully assess and decide if they are significant enough, in light of all the supporting evidence, to seriously question this theory. Not clarifying the problems also disserves upcoming scientists, for they do not become informed of the significant areas which need inquiry.

Creationism
and the Evolutionary Response

Chapter Nine

*If man wishes to know anything about Creation (the time
of Creation, the duration of Creation, the order of
Creation, the methods of Creation, or anything else), his
sole source of true information is that of divine
revelation.. . . Therefore, we are completely limited to
what God has seen fit to tell us, and this information is
His written Word. This is our textbook on the science of
Creation!*

Henry Morris, Studies in the Bible and Science

Creationism/Creation Science Defined

Most Christians would identify themselves as creationists in that they
believe a transcendent, omniscient, designer God was the creator of the
universe and of life. This is a church doctrine and is supported by many
scriptures, as seen in Appendix A. Technically and literally the term
"creationist" could include anyone who believes that God is the creator. It can
be argued that theistic evolutionists are creationists since they affirm God as
creator.

As is popularly defined in the culture at present and used in this book,
however, a creationist holds the belief *that* God is the designer, but also
includes the *how* and *when* of creation. A literal interpretation of the biblical
creation texts is claimed. God created in six, twenty-four hour solar days, ex
nihilo (out of nothing), by fiat (suddenly by authoritative decree), as is
literally recorded in Genesis Chapter 1 of the Bible. This belief asserts that
the universe and humans were created within 144 hours of each other. Many
creationists believe this occurred as recently as 6,000 - 10,000 years ago.
They maintain that each type or "kind" of organism and plant, those living
today as well as all that are extinct, were created separately and abruptly.
They were all present (at least the terrestrial ones) in the Garden of Eden,
someplace in the present Middle East. All the land animals which have ever
lived were represented on Noah's ark.

Creationists affirm fixity of species, which means that species do not change into new species. They allow that species are capable of much variation, however, as is seen with dogs, cattle, Galapagos tortoises, sparrows, bears, snakes, owls, people, roses, apples or corn. Changes leading to variation are termed microevolution (small change over time), a concept that they support.

Creationists believe that God brought the universe and life into being with a spoken word (Genesis 1), miraculously, using unknown mechanisms that are not operative today. Therefore, they cannot be studied, demonstrated, or refuted. This belief must be accepted by faith. While it may indeed be true, it is not a scientific truth. Science is based on rational law, where beliefs are subject to analysis and can be either demonstrated empirically or be falsified (disproved).

The introduction to this chapter quotes a creationist asserting that the Bible is the sole source of information on origins. Since the 1960s, however, creationists have introduced the terms "scientific creationism" and "creation science" suggesting that their claims can be demonstrated scientifically as well.

While this chapter presents creationist belief generally, it must be noted that there is great disparity of belief across the creationist spectrum. Some, for instance, hold to an old Earth thesis, believing the creation events took place literally and miraculously as in Genesis but much farther back in history than 10,000 years. Others include the concept of progressive creation over the centuries or millennia, suggesting that creation did not occur during just one week. Specific creative acts are believed to have punctuated normal developmental processes that were following natural laws. Those holding this position would assert that one of these manifestations of divine power occurred when humankind was created, an act referred to as special creation, where the creator chose to intervene in the natural developmental sequence. The "Cambrian Explosion" or the organization of the first cells are also given as examples of the creator's abrupt intervention.

Some creationists believe in a "Gap Theory." Two creations occurred, separated by a gap in time. The first creation occurred millions of years ago (Genesis 1:1) and the second was the more recent event (6,000 - 10,000 years ago) as recorded in Genesis 1:2 - 2:3. The extinction of dinosaurs is believed to have taken place in the gap after the first creation.

Others hold to the "Day-Age Theory" whereby each of the six days recorded in Genesis 1 represents a long period of geologic time, thousands or even millions of years. In support of their position "day-agers" often point to Psalm 90:4, "For a thousand years in your sight are like a day...."

There are additional beliefs, including various modifications of the above theses. Recently, a position called "Intelligent Design" (ID) has been offered (see Chapter Five). It holds that there is irreducible complexity at the cellular level and that an intelligent designer (God?) had to have spontaneously and supernaturally created these complex molecules, structures, and metabolic pathways to form the first life. Life did not and could not evolve on its own, step by step, through naturalistic, evolutionary mechanisms. This reflects a belief that if something is not yet explained or if it appears at present to be too improbable or too complex to imagine, then supernatural creation, intelligent design, must be operating. Being unexplained is somehow equated with being unexplainable. This is similar to the intervening creator referred to previously. It is also a throwback to an old idea referred to as a "god of the gaps." When something could not be explained, God filled the gap with a miracle. History has shown that this god is forced to recede over the decades as natural answers are provided which fill in the gaps. Intelligent design enthusiasts predict that they can eventually demonstrate their thesis scientifically. Since supernatural miracle is outside of science, that is a remarkable claim. It must be noted that many who believe in intelligent design hold to evolutionary belief. Intelligent design applies to certain complexities including the origin of life, but evolution over long periods is acknowledged by many.

Creationists see truth as something already possessed, while scientists see truth as something to be pursued. Creationists don't begin with a question such as "How did we get here?" They begin with an answer from scripture. Their research consists of conforming data to the answer. What appears to falsify their belief is ignored. For example, with respect to belief in a global flood some 4,500 years ago, not a single human artifact such as a plow, spear, jewel, coin, or building fragment, and not a single human or goat skeleton or olive tree fossil has been found in lower geological strata. Such remains would be predicted in deeper strata if such a flood inundated and deposited sediment on all the cities and countrysides of the ancient Earth. This omission is ignored. Many more of these dilemmas are presented in the questions in Chapter Ten.

Scientists, on the other hand, begin with a question, which leads to a hypothesis. Their research includes attempts to support as well as to falsify or disprove. They are obliged and free to go wherever the data lead. They assume that enigmas or complexities can eventually be explained through dependable, natural laws. Theistic scientists affirm God as the creator designer of these remarkable laws. Naturalism in no way denies an original Creator. It reflects the Creator's omnipotence, genius, order, freeing design, providential and empowering love, and dependability. No magician or miracle waving wand is involved; nothing capricious, irrational.

Creationists live with certainty. Scientists live with uncertainty and in anticipation of answers ultimately supplied, even though this may not occur during their lifetimes. Creationism and science can be seen as separate ways of thinking. Some would say they are in separate worlds.

Most creationism includes the belief that the supernatural creation accounts in Genesis Chapters 1 and 2, the flood narratives in Genesis 6-9, and the origin of languages at the Tower of Babel in Genesis 11 are actual explanations of historical events and must be interpreted in a literal manner. There was a real Garden of Eden with two people, Adam and Eve, the first humans, who were created as adults with the appearance of age, the female from the male's rib. In that garden was a serpent with feet. It could speak their language and even outwitted Eve! All of the animals were created herbivores (only ate plants) and the original creation had no death. Representatives of all beasts and birds that have ever existed were present, were named by Adam, and they subsequently dispersed throughout the world into their various niches from that garden. With the exception of the flood and the origin of languages, these creationist beliefs cannot be supported, demonstrated, authenticated, or falsified by the methods of science. They are belief positions, explanatory stories.

When Genesis is interpreted literally, God, who is *spirit*, planted a garden, could be heard walking in the garden, formed living things from dust, took a rib and made a woman, closed a wound, breathed into nostrils to begin life, and needed to rest on the seventh day. Furthermore, the omniscient God of the universe requires a rainbow to help him remember the covenant he had made (Genesis 9:14-16). As can be seen, literalism delivers readers of the biblical record into some difficulties. How can a spirit plant, walk, form, breathe, get tired? How can an all knowing God forget? Did God speak (Genesis 1) or form from dust and take a rib (Genesis 2)? Were humans made last (Genesis 1) or was the male made first and the female last (Genesis 2)?

Creationists identify themselves as catastrophists, asserting that the geological formations, mountain ranges, positions of the continents, and major extinctions occurred quickly and are all the result of the catastrophic flood. They believe that God miraculously brought pairs of all animal kinds from all over the world to the Middle East and kept them and eight people alive on an ark for about a year. Just as there are two distinctive creation stories, there are two flood accounts that relate different numbers. One, in Genesis 6:19-20, says of every living creature a male and female will be aboard the ark. In Genesis 7:2-3, a second account, God asks Noah to take seven of every kind of clean animal and every kind of bird and two of every unclean animal aboard the ark. The extra clean animals would be ceremonially sacrificed (Genesis 8:20) or eaten (Genesis 9:3).

The flood thesis holds that only one pair of each animal kind survived. Animals living today are believed to be descendants from those pairs. Nothing is said in Genesis about plants on board the ark except what was brought for food. The present varied human gene pool supposedly can be traced back to this family of eight, five of whom were closely related.

At the end of the flood, approximately 4,500 years ago, the continents are believed to have quickly separated, having moved apart at miles per hour. The animal pairs and plants were somehow miraculously dispersed to ideal environments throughout the world from Mt. Ararat, in present day Turkey: polar bears to the Arctic north, kangaroos to Australia, some blind cave animals to Kentucky, *Tyrannosaurus rex* to Montana, Bengal tigers to India, jaguars to South America, wolverines to North America, mammoths to Siberia, etc. Creationists claim that an ice age after the flood enabled people and animals to walk from continent to continent, the water being confined as ice in the poles. There is no mention of the devastating marine extinctions this must have caused, yet marine life today is unbelievably diverse. How did they all survive the widespread diminishing of their ocean habitat? How plant life became re-established is also of interest. The sedimentation attributed to the flood would have buried all plants. The Earth would have been desolate. Seeds do not readily survive for months in water.

Creationists believe that all kinds of dinosaurs, saber tooth tigers, mastodons, Irish elk and all other extinct species were present in the Garden of Eden and represented on the ark and that they have undergone extinction only within the past several thousand years since the Noachian flood. Obviously, humans are believed to have lived concurrently with dinosaurs. Support for this thesis include dragon-like cave drawings and the mention of dragons in the Bible. Some suggest that dinosaurs may still be alive in Africa or in Loch Ness in Scotland.

The young Earth hypothesis (6,000 – 10,000 years old) is based on a careful study by James Ussher (1581-1656), Archbishop of Armagh in Ireland, of genealogies recorded in the Old Testament. The assumption is made that these records are historically accurate and complete, even though they were part of an oral history for hundreds of years over dozens of generations. Indeed, creationists would assign the oral history to over 2,700 years, the supposed time from creation to when this material was recorded. Presumably (and luckily), someone in Noah's family would have learned and memorized all the genealogies up to that period (1,650 years) and passed them along verbally after the flood until they were finally written down hundreds of years later. Since Noah's family is believed to have dispersed to populate the Earth after the flood these records would no doubt be most difficult to maintain orally.

Creationist belief requires *everything* in the Bible, including genealogies, numbers, sequences, historic references, names, ages and places to be not only theologically and culturally significant, but literally and factually accurate as well. The assumption is that a group of nomadic people, small in number, preliterate and prescientific, kept precise dates, names, numbers, and details as we are accustomed to do in our culture. A further assumption is that they thought just as we moderns in a Western culture think, that they were exactly like us in dealing with or responding to stories and events. Such an a priori stand compels the believer to make the data conform to these tenets, by hook or by crook. No attempt is made to consider their unique cultural setting and life situation and how these factors might have influenced their thinking and writing. What previous cultures impacted their thinking and how did it differ from our 21st Century mindset? Is there room for poetry, metaphor, story? Is literalism the *only* way to go? Is there a freedom to even imagine another means of interpretation?

Theistic evolutionists insist that the writings of Genesis have much more significance than being mere science or history. They have greater work to do. They contain powerful *theological* messages. They bridge God to humankind and humankind to God!

Creationists believe that the original creation was designed to have no death. All animals living in the Garden of Eden, including those we classify as carnivores (meat eaters), were created to be vegetarian. Death arrived when Adam and Eve sinned. Without death, Adam and Eve, Cain, Joshua, Saul, David, Ruth, Rachel, Lot and his wife, Jonah, Mary, Judas, Peter, Paul, St. Augustine, Martin Luther, the Cro-Magnons and Neanderthals and all other people who have ever lived as well as all the animals, including all kinds of dinosaurs, would be with us to this day. There would have been no extinctions, no plagues, no infant death, no childbirth death, no killer tornados, volcanoes, floods, comets or lightning. How humans would have clothed, warmed or fed themselves in cold climates without animal skins and meat is a dilemma. In addition, we must question a design that leads to an overpopulated planet or a non-functioning food web. What organic material would enrich soil to support more vegetation for all of these vegetarians?

It seems obvious that many of the plants or their tissues would have died, as they were eaten in that early environment, but their life is apparently not defined by the creationists in the same way as animal life. Physiologists know that throughout the body, cells have varying life expectancies, some living for hours, days, weeks, etc. Cells that line the digestive tract constantly die, as do hair cells. Ten million red blood cells die every second in humans. Skin cells continually are shed (origin of dandruff!). Soon after birth placental tissue dies. In wounds, tissue has died. Healing is the replacement of this tissue. Presumably Adam's wound caused by the rib removal would have resulted in dead tissue. Did this kind of death not count, or were these processes not occurring then? Was it God's original plan that no eggs or sperm would ever die? Why are so many of these sex cells made?

Creationists Morris and Morris have this explanation for the death of plants:

> Plant life, of course, is not conscious life, but only very complex replicating chemicals. The eating of fruits and herbs was not considered "death" of the plant materials since they had no created "life" (in the sense of consciousness) anyhow. (1996a, p. 21)

Where would carnivorous plants such as the Venus flytrap fit? Did they become carnivorous after the fall? The Bible does not state anywhere that plant materials were not considered "life." What is creationists' definition of life? Could organisms that have no apparent consciousness such as earthworms, jellyfish, bacteria and *Amoebae,* corals, snails, starfish, clams, mosquitoes and butterflies undergo "death?" Are they alive? Where does "consciousness" begin? Are fish conscious? This is an example of the creationists' need to manufacture an explanation to stay within a prior belief model. Does anyone see an oak or cherry tree or a rosebush or climbing ivy as being merely "complex replicating chemicals," not "life?" Ironically, microbiologists note that on a cellular level, the similarity of many metabolic pathways in both plants and animals is quite remarkable.

There is no explanation of how a food web would work in the Garden of Eden, or anywhere in the world, if everything alive only ate plants and there was no death. The plants would be extinguished eventually, as the garden became overrun with animals, which would apparently continue to reproduce but never die. Picture all of the offspring of every organism living. All frog eggs laid become frogs, all escargot becoming snails, all chicken eggs becoming chickens to lay even more eggs. The Earth is a limited entity. How could a no death plan have succeeded? Rationality demands that animals would eventually die of starvation as their numbers increased unless continuous miracles were invoked. Were reproduction and the need for food not included in the original plan? Is that how it could work? Did reproduction and hunger come as a result of the fall? Furthermore, if everyone descended from Adam and Eve, from whence did the incest taboo arise?

These beliefs are based on a literal interpretation of religious writings, claimed to be inerrant, which came from the ancient oral history of a preliterate, prescientific culture that yearned for explanation just as we do today. It must always be noted that as long as miracle is involved, a thesis is not science and it should not masquerade as science. It might indeed be true, as Christians believe Jesus' resurrection was, but it is not science.

There is no explanation as to how the soil originated which supported the garden. Soil comes from rock, a process requiring many, many years, and the soil that supports life contains organic nutrients (carbon based materials from previously living organisms which have decomposed). What was the origin of the organic material that would have been in the Garden of Eden soil? If in the original design there was to be no death, where over the eons would nutrient-rich soil, which originates from decomposed living material, originate? In nature, death leads to life. Decomposed plants and animals give nutrients to support new life.

Creationists hold that the early Earth was covered by a vapor layer. It supposedly afforded a uniform climate and protection from cosmic radiation, resulting in very long human life. The land was irrigated by water from under the ground. There was no rain until the flood. There is as yet no scientific support for any of these beliefs. No human skeletons or other anthropological or archeological evidence have been found to support the thesis that humans lived for centuries. Methuselah reportedly lived almost a millennium (Genesis 5:27). Furthermore, geologists find very old rocks with raindrop impressions. How did these imprints form during a deluge, or prior to the deluge, if it had not rained previous to that time?

The museum of the Institute for Creation Research, in El Cajon, California gives insight into creationist belief. It asserts that there was just one ice age, after the flood, and that cave men were weak, degenerate descendants of folk who migrated away from the Tower of Babel. Under stress on the ark, animals went into a state of hibernation or aestivation and therefore required minimal food and no exercise. The museum claims that in the face of danger, predators and prey mingle together and enter a torpid (death-like) state. No scientific support is provided for any of these statements. They appear to be invented to help explain why carnivores didn't eat their prey on the ark, why the animals required minimal food on the ark, why space wasn't required for large animals to exercise for a whole year, and why there would have been manageable wastes generated.

The depth of a fossil, its rock type, its radiometric date, or the kind of fossil it is must not be used to establish the age of a fossil, the display at the museum warns, as only the Bible is a valid source for dating. Data gathered from scientific inquiry are totally rejected if they do not support creationist theses no matter how compelling the evidence or how rigorous the peer review. It is puzzling how the term "creation science" can be supported if so much science is not considered valid. Authority is wholly derived from an ancient, prescientific, religious literature. The Bible is seen as a dependable geology, anthropology, paleontology, biology, genetics, biochemistry, physics and astronomy text. This thinking distinguishes creationism from science, creationists from theistic evolutionists, and creationists from most biblical scholars.

Some Christians hold to creationist belief not because they have been convinced of its legitimacy, but rather because they believe evolutionary theory has minimal support. The assumption is that any conflict or disagreement among evolutionists infers weakness and this automatically lends credibility to creationist claims. Yet conflict is the nature of science. Without it, science would be unproductive. Conflict is the means by which inaccurate conclusions or faulty research designs are challenged. Furthermore, no matter how much disagreement there is within the scientific community that is totally irrelevant to creationist credibility. Any thesis must have its own supporting grounds and does not gain points by its opponent's weakness. One of the main lines of defense used by creationists is to dwell on evolutionary enigmas. They conclude by default that this leaves creationism as the only alternative. Not true. It, like evolution, must stand on its own.

Creationists regularly define evolution as a failed idea about an unobserved fact. As long as no one saw it, it cannot be valid, they say, not acknowledging the vast amount of inferred data that is routinely incorporated into scientific research and upon which much of science operates. Furthermore, evolutionary theory is grounded on far more than inferential data, as was noted in Chapter Seven. There is much that can be seen and demonstrated.

Scientists challenge "creation scientists" to apply the principle of falsification to their beliefs, as scientists continually apply it to their respective hypotheses. Can belief in a 6,000 year old Earth be disproven? Instead of assuming the truth of a worldwide flood, should they not attempt its falsification? Is there global geological support for this thesis? How did representatives of all "kinds" get to the site of the ark? How did they survive upon disembarking on a desolate Earth? Could one man build a boat that big without a single nail to last a whole year in a catastrophic flood?

Can the thesis that sedimentary layers, in some places miles high, were all deposited in one year during a global flood be disproven? Since sediments that compose sedimentary rock have been weathered from igneous, metamorphic, and pre-existing sedimentary rock, can creationists demonstrate how sediments thick enough to form mile high formations could have weathered and formed in a mere 1,650 years from creation to the time of the flood? Can it be explained why in some formations, sediments were layered horizontally, then cross bedded (tilted by Earth movements), then weathered flat, then topped with many horizontal strata? How could these elaborate formations be made during just one year? How can fossil ripple marks, raindrops, mudcracks, animal burrows, and footprints, which are found in middle sedimentary layers, be explained if all the layers were supposedly deposited during a continuous flood, under water?

A creationist with a PhD in science was asked at a seminar how a series of dinosaur footprint fossils on different layers could have formed during a flood. He said that the footprints were formed when dry land was temporarily exposed by tsunamis, which occurred in the raging flood and gave opportunity for animals to walk about. The dinosaurs just happened to be swimming in the vicinity when a particular area of dry land appeared and they walked on it. Then they, or others, were in the same general area after sedimentary layers were deposited and when subsequent tsunamis apparently exposed dry land again, they walked on it. How these footprints were not quickly erased when the swirling waters returned is not explained. Furthermore, the footprints are evolutionarily progressive. This is remarkable support for an old Earth, evolutionary hypothesis. How did dinosaurs survive month upon month of swimming or floating, or being swirled about by tsunamis? That would require a lot of energy. Where did they get their food?

If in seeking to disprove a global deluge the data supporting it become more extensive, then the thesis is strengthened as truth is born. If, on the other hand, the data are found to negate this hypothesis, then it must be recognized as false and discarded, the sooner the better. If no attempt is made to falsify or disprove, science is not operating. Creationist belief is based on a literal reading of Genesis, incorporating miracle and supernatural intervention. There is no scientific authentication. Many explanations are submitted, but they are not accompanied by evidence or peer reviewed support. This is why scientists reject this dogma as inappropriate in a science classroom and consider "creation science" to be pseudoscience, as is astrology.

Can it be disproved that all the plants and animals composing all fossils lived contemporaneously? Can the thesis that hydraulic sorting caused perfect fossil sequencing be falsified? Why are human and dinosaur bones, trilobites, brachiopod and cephalopod shells, cartilaginous and bony fishes, or various corals found in the order that would be predicted by evolutionary theory?

Can a once-for-all creation in six solar days be proven through science? Is there scientific support for the thesis that dinosaurs lived at the same time as Adam and Noah, or any human? Are there any data to support fast continental drift and mountain uplifting immediately after or during the flood, or that rainbows did not occur before the flood 4,500 years ago? Can peer-reviewed linguistic analysis support languages having arisen spontaneously, unrelatedly, concurrently, and diversely at the Babel dispersion? Are creation scientists intent on exposing their theses to rigorous scientific analysis?

Creationists publish many books, videos, pamphlets and newsletters aimed at all age levels. They travel around the country and across the globe giving seminars, lectures, and debates. There are radio and television ministries, websites, numerous organizations (see Appendix G), some offering college courses and degrees. Through these various media they disseminate their thesis that a six day creation by fiat (immediately), ex nihilo (out of nothing), occurred some 6,000 to 10,000 years ago. The lay masses have little opportunity to hear or critique alternate theses. Organizations and churches which sponsor these seminars do not bring in theistic evolutionists to give a different perspective. Critical thinkers should demand familiarity with all sides.

This chapter outlines further factors associated with creationist belief, including their challenge to evolutionary theory. Theistic evolutionist responses to these assertions are provided.

Scriptural Authority

(Creationist Perspective) Without doubt the main foundation for creationism comes from a literal reading of the Bible, especially the first eleven chapters of Genesis. Appendix A lists many additional sources in scripture where God is affirmed as Creator. The Bible is God's inspired and inerrant Word and whatever it says about anything, whether it be numbers, geography, names, plants, animals, genealogies, dates or stories is truth, meaning literal truth.

(Theistic Evolutionist Perspective) The Old Testament is a remarkable compilation of a culture's literature over many centuries. The Bible's authority is acknowledged and it is believed to be infallible (dependable in faith and life) and inspired by God. Just as any culture today produces a panorama of writings, such as poetry, stories, ledgers, law codes, novels, how-to manuals, letters, telephone directories, nursery rhymes, and joke, history, art, science, or recipe books, the Hebrew people also produced a variety of literature. Some of the literary genres of the Bible are psalm, poetry, history, lamentations, genealogy, prophesy, letters, proverbs, laws, stories and songs, including love songs. Each should be read in a way that is appropriate to its particular literary style. History is read literally, as is law. Prophesy and poetry, with symbolism and colorful imagery, are read

figuratively. Parables are not read as historic truth. Other stories, such as that of a man claiming that the moon (which moves) stopped and the sun (which doesn't move) stood still about a full day (Joshua 10:13) are read figuratively. The record of a man who boasted of killing a thousand men with one donkey's jawbone (Judges 15:16) is not read literally! Love songs are read figuratively. "His arms are rods of gold set with chrysolite" (Song of Solomon 5:14) is not to be read literally.

Much of the Old Testament was for hundreds of years an oral history of nomadic, prescientific people. It was recorded thousands of years ago by cultures which thought very differently than the scientifically informed and oriented 21st Century mind. These factors do not seem to be relevant and are not considered by literalists.

Some cultures are not as precise and do not require accurate numbers, especially preliterate societies. The Hebrews were poetic and wrote with beautiful imagery. The Bible is one of the most magnificent works of literature ever written. The Hebrew mindset was not like that of the more rational Greeks from which Western culture arose. This is why modern critics insist on an understanding of the original culture and setting of biblical authors in attempting to accurately interpret scripture. It is as crucial to know *about* the Bible as it is to know the Bible. This is why those in authority in the creationism and evolution controversy should have extensive training in theology and biblical criticism (see Chapter Six) as well as in science. The lack of such training is glaring to many who sorrow over this division.

The challenge to the seeker of biblical truth is to identify the setting in which the author wrote, become acquainted with the cultural, political, and geographical environments, and understand as much about the language as possible. This is not easy to accomplish, as the cultures of the Hebrew Old Testament and the Greek New Testament are foreign to moderns in both time and setting. The original languages are not spoken today, so there is great potential for subtleties of language to be overlooked or misunderstood. The student of the Bible needs spiritual and academic insight, common sense, an open mind, critical thinking skills, and input from a variety of scholars to help him or her rightly interpret this word of truth.

Presently, most biblical scholars interpret Genesis 1 and 2 figuratively. Their rationale was outlined in Chapter Six. One of the reasons for this conclusion is common sense. The fields of paleontology, biblical archeology, geology, astronomy, biogeography, ecology, botany, zoology and genetics just do not support a literal interpretation of Genesis 1 and 2. Instead, these two remarkable chapters are seen to communicate powerful theological messages which are lost if a literal historical or scientific message is sought. Finally, if read literally, these two stories contradict each other in both the means and sequence of creation. That alone negates the authenticity of the literal translation paradigm.

Archeologists and historians have found creation and flood stories with similarities to those in Genesis in cultures that preceded the Israelites by hundreds of years (see Appendix H). These remarkable commonalities lead to the conclusion that the Hebrews adapted their stories from pre-existing legends found within neighboring cultures. Creationists are challenged to falsify this hypothesis if they do not agree with it.

Scientists have serious trouble with a discipline that operates from preformed tenets and then calls itself science. Conclusions based on sacred scriptures are formed before research is commenced. It would seem that divine revelation and supernatural intervention have provided all answers beforehand and inquiry is therefore superfluous. Falsification is rarely attempted, no doubt because it cannot be accomplished. In addition, there is no motivation to challenge these sacred and established beliefs.

It seems that the main challenge for creationists is to manipulate and conform what appears in the natural world into this prepackaged, ancient, prescientific, theological and magnificently poetic compendium of writings. This is the antithesis of science which begins with the unknown rather than the known, encourages questions and doubts, entertains alternative hypotheses, goes wherever the data lead, and attempts to falsify all conclusions. Over all, modern scientists have no fear that any discoveries will in any way threaten the overarching power and glory of the creator God.

God created us and blessed us with remarkable minds and has placed us in a time and culture where we have access to a spectacular array of technology and accumulated information, including the blessings of modern biblical and archeological scholarship. It doesn't seem consistent with God's order and dependability that we should ignore the minds we were given and deny the scientific reality that is before us. To some, to do so is not only irrational and unscholarly, but dishonest. It dishonors the Lord who has blessed us with amazing, questioning, seeking minds and commanded us to ask, seek, and knock (Matthew 7:7-8).

Christians of creationist belief cannot comprehend Genesis 1 and 2 as story, poetry, legend, myth, or symbolic and profound theological record. This arbitrary decision by their leadership to not even consider an alternative means of interpretation in spite of the voluminous scientific data and scholarly biblical exegesis (interpretation) which negate it is puzzling to those who attempt to understand their position especially when a literal interpretation finds the Genesis 1 record inconsistent with the Genesis 2 record. Some would suggest this is not being honest to Genesis and that it reflects a lack of scholarly theological training.

As long as the scriptures are seen as being without error, and that they must be literally interpreted, creationists are bound to their six day, young Earth position *no matter what evidence is presented by science or the world of the senses.* The majority of Christians who are trained in careful thinking, and especially those in biology or geology, reject this thesis. Unfortunately, many non-Christians reject Christianity along with the creationist claims. They are not attracted to a religion that requires the negation of the rational, thinking, remarkable mind that God has created.

It doesn't bother creationists that light or days came before the sun, or that the Earth preceded the Sun, moon and stars, or that the Sun, moon and stars are lumped together as similar entities (the Sun is a star, the moon is not). They have no problem with representatives of all of creation, plant and animal, fungi, viruses, bacteria, parasitic worms and insects having been present together in a Garden called Eden, or that in one Genesis account (Genesis 1) mankind is created last and in another Genesis account (Genesis 2) man is created first and woman last. In one account humans are created by the spoken word and in the other they were formed from dust and a rib. A woman came from a man's tissue (a bone!) but apparently had her own unique genetics (?). Presumably they were not twins.

They are not troubled by a snake which could speak and reason, or by God who is spirit, breathing life into the man, removing a rib and closing up the opening, making sounds while walking in the garden, conversing with Adam and Eve, or fashioning garments of skin. They do not question that Adam could have named the multitudes of "kinds" and kept it all straight. Did he know how to write and keep records?

Theistic evolutionists also deeply respect the authenticity of the scriptures and hold to their authority as inspired by God. They, however, perceive passages in the Old Testament in the prescientific, preliterate, Hebraic context in which they were written and recognize that the data presented in Genesis 1 and 2 were not meant to be science or history. More importantly, they were intended to be profoundly theological. In this light no conflict is seen between the ancient writings of scripture and the modern breakthroughs of science.

Evolution Negates Jesus' Sacrificial Death

(Creationist Perspective) Evolution means that we got here by chance, that there was no plan or purpose. It denies God's existence and creative power. It is atheistic naturalism, a philosophical, not a scientific position. Since the sin of Adam and Eve is not acknowledged it makes the crucifixion and resurrection of Jesus the Savior unnecessary. No Adam and Eve, no sin. No sin, no fall. It follows that there is no need for a Savior. Evolutionary

belief is very dangerous, for from its perspective Jesus' death was in vain. The Christian faith finds its center in Christ's death and resurrection and making them irrelevant undermines the whole foundation of Christianity!

(Theistic Evolutionist Perspective) There was no literal Adam and Eve. Therefore, there was no Adam and Eve sin. But *there surely is sin*, committed by each one of us. We are *all* guilty before God, not because of someone else's error. We are guilty before God because of *our* error. God gave us free will. From childhood we, just like the mythological characters Adam and Eve, have willed and continue to will to err. Indeed, *all* have sinned and come short (Romans 3:23). Humans have loved darkness rather than light (John 3:19). They have all gone astray (Isaiah 53:6). The need for Jesus' death and victorious resurrection, for redemption and perpetual forgiveness, is candidly and humbly acknowledged by Christian theistic evolutionists. The sacrificial death of Jesus as an atonement for sin is recognized as necessary and thankfully claimed. It is indeed the foundation of our faith.

The Christian community does not need to fear that evolutionary belief renders Jesus' death unnecessary or that it can say anything about sin. This is a totally inaccurate understanding of what evolutionary theory means from a scientific perspective. It means change over time. It says nothing about purpose, sin, a creator or a savior. It is not philosophy or religion. Science cannot speak to the need for a Savior or negate the fact that there is sin. Science cannot prove there is no God or no meaning or purpose. It has no such power! In fact, the science of psychology affirms the human tendency to selfishly choose, to egocentrically perceive the world, even from childhood. We escape this bondage through religion, which most humans recognize as a basic need. God our Creator blessed us with free will. Unfortunately, we all at times will to sin. This loving God provided us escape with the sacrificial death of the only begotten atoner, Jesus. We are not guilty because two people erred thousands of years ago. We are guilty because *we* err today.

Worldwide Deluge: Noah's Flood

(Creationist Perspective) The sedimentary layers, which can be commonly observed in exposed rock formations throughout the Earth, were laid down during the year of the Noachian flood and since. Lighter animals sorted out and fell to the bottom first and their fossils can be found in the lowest layers. Then, slightly heavier bodied animals fell and can be seen in the next lowest layers. The fossils can be explained by this hydraulic sorting, so that unicellular organisms are at the bottom, multicellular organisms such as hydra or jellyfish might be next, heavier animals next, etc. It is not

surprising to find the vertebrates toward the topmost layers and the humans quite near the very top. They could have run to higher ground during the flood or found refuge and would reasonably have been the last to have succumbed to the torrents. Therefore it would be predicted that they would be in the topmost layers.

It is also believed that the mountains buckled and formed mainly during or soon after the flood so there didn't have to be as much water as might be imagined, looking at the Earth's topography today. The continents split and rose during the last six months of the flood. The worldwide flood during the time of Noah, some 1,650 years after creation, in ~2,350 B.C., gives a comprehensive explanation for the present paleontology and geology of the Earth.

(Theistic Evolutionist Perspective) Most people imagining a worldwide, catastrophic deluge that covered all mountaintops and killed all terrestrial animals and plants (possibly some spores or seeds could survive) as well as some fresh water and marine organisms which were unable to adapt to the shocking osmotic changes in the water (too salty for some and too dilute for others) would envision carcasses falling and trees being uprooted. They would all be strewn about the globe by currents and then buried in sediments in a haphazard manner. There would be evidence of this universal catastrophe throughout the geological strata and in ice cores around the world.

Remarkably, the fossil record does not reveal such activity. Plants and animals are consistently sorted phylogenetically (according to anatomical and physiological relationship) into strata. Bones are not found in bottom strata, and invertebrate (those without bones) extinct forms are not found at the top. There is a chronological orderliness in the record. Some organisms appear and then disappear totally. In fact, this would be predicted by the evolutionary model. A deluge model with upwelling water from the depths of the Earth and tsunamis would predict mixing and variability of fossils throughout the strata. Yet no trilobite appears with bones of any animal. Extinct Placoderm fishes (jawed, many armored with bony plates) are not found with modern fishes or birds. Dinosaurs are not found with primates. If all of these animals lived and died contemporaneously, there should be a mixing of their remains, someplace, somewhere in the fossil record.

Creationists believe a hydrodynamic sorting occurred: drowned bodies of small, dense, more streamlined or spherical animals fell out first and were buried. Yet the fossil record neatly differentiates into perfect layers ammonite (a mollusk) fossils, which are all the same size but have progressively modified shell design (as a result of evolution, evolutionists claim). It has been documented that trilobite species that were closely related and similar in weight and body design have been preserved in perfect sequence, not together. The more ancient forms were deeper and the more evolved forms were progressively preserved in order, toward higher layers. How could this be explained with the creationist model? How could animals of the same size and weight not be treated similarly by the floodwaters and mixed? Yet they were not buried concurrently.

Creationists explain that vertebrates are in the topmost sedimentary layers because they could run to higher ground and therefore would be overcome by rising waters last, a phenomenon called differential mobility. Not *one* old, lumbering *Tyrannasaurus rex*, or pregnant mammoth, or disoriented cow, or fenced in pig, or goat tethered to a stake in a Mesopotamian village, or frail, newborn lamb, or elderly, arthritic Neanderthal was drowned out of sequence? Not *one* vertebrate got caught in a coulie, valley, marsh or mudhole and was buried out of sequence? Not *one* found itself on flat land such as desert, plains, pampas, or prairie where there was no high ground to which it could run? Not *one* mole, prairie dog or gopher was drowned underground early? Not one! Alas, even today with modern technology and means of heroic rescue, strong, young people and other fast running vertebrates regularly die in floods that are just local. A global deluge would be more catastrophic and all animals would be more prone to become victims at any time.

Humans supposedly could run to high ground and be preserved last, but a clay vessel would be left to be buried. It seems reasonable that some pottery, parts of houses, sculptures, jewelry, tools, plows, sandals, weapons, or other artifacts would be buried quickly during the first days of the flood. Yet no human related items have ever been found except in the surface layers where they are expected by the evolutionary thesis. These data are astounding!

Why aren't flying reptiles found on the same strata as birds? If they lived contemporaneously why would they not be found together in the fossil record as the creationist model would predict? Wouldn't the model also predict that some sea turtles would perish and fall into early layers during a deluge? Yet they all appear in more recent, uppermost layers. Evolutionists believe that anatomical and physiological data point to sea turtles having evolved from land turtles. Their position in more recent strata is exactly what would be expected.

The position of plants in the geological record is remarkable also. The creationist model assumes that all plants and animals lived at the same time. Huge tree ferns were contemporaneous with daffodils and mulberries. Brachiosaurs lived at the same time as coyotes and penguins. This thesis would predict that the willow would be buried with ancient amphibians. Yet that is not what the fossil record reveals. Ancient amphibians are consistently in much lower strata than the willow or magnolia. Tree ferns are found much lower than flowering plants. Vascular plants (those with vessels containing sap) are not found in lower layers. A progression is seen in the fossil book. Primitive, less complex plants (those without vascularity or cones, fruits, nuts, seeds or flowers) occur in lower, older strata. Grass, wheat, flax, and barley, all more recent, do not occur in lower layers which would be expected if sediment from a flood fell and buried the fields of biblical times. Plants with more advanced morphology are observed in upper layers, including most species occurring at present. This orderly sorting would not be expected from a year-long catastrophic deluge. What is more, parallel-veined leaves occur lower and thus earlier than net-veined leaves. Cones came before flowers, opposite leaves before alternate leaves. Faithfully.

The catastrophic model of a worldwide deluge contrasts with the concept of uniformitarianism which holds that many of the geological features of the Earth at present have been formed by slow processes occurring over millions of years, which were then interspersed with catastrophic events. These would include steady, time consuming phenomena such as erosion, soil formation, sedimentary deposition, glaciation impacts (boulder displacement, lake carving, moraine deposition), continental drift, weathering resulting from repeated freezing and thawing, and the varied effects of subtle climate changes such as sea level rise and fall. Indeed, catastrophic events such as tornadoes, mudslides, volcanoes, avalanches, tsunamis, earthquakes, asteroid or meteorite collisions, floods, wind and hail storms or other local or widespread devastations are also occurring presently. Both quick (catastrophic) as well as time consuming (uniformitarian) processes are and have been at work and impact the geological formations and present geography of the Earth. Uniformitarianism is not supported in creationist literature. It requires too much time.

Frankly, there is just no evidence in the Earth's geological record for a worldwide flood. Floods and tsunamis definitely have occurred in many parts of the world over the eons and these localized episodes have left their records and fossils and in recent (comparatively speaking) millennia have generated many stories and remembrances among numerous cultures of the world. The devastating floods in South Dakota, South Carolina, Vietnam, Cambodia, Laos, England, India and Mozambique surrounding the turn of the 21st Century have no doubt left their stories. Past local flood catastrophes have left their mark in the geological record as well. The rocks on Earth contain a record and it must be read carefully and honestly. The record reveals that floods occurred at many different times and in different localities. It does not support the thesis that these flood episodes were contemporary and worldwide.

Why is the city of Ur in Mesopotamia seen to have been occupied without interruption from at least 4,000 BC to 400 BC? In antiquity, the Euphrates River flowed near the city walls. There is evidence of a local flood. However, Eridu, just seven miles from Ur, has no flood evidence. There are no signs of Ur being permanently inundated by a flood with no continuing habitation. Archeology attests to people having lived there right through the period when supposedly a worldwide flood buried everything and everyone. How is this explained? Have attempts been made to falsify this account?

Remarkably, the fossil record across the Earth follows and supports the evolutionary paradigm. There are places where more recently evolved species appear below older species in geological strata. Either a folding of the strata has occurred, where older layers end up on top of younger layers, or older layers are pushed by Earth movements and override younger strata, a phenomenon called overthrusting. The folding is clearly the explanation as plant and animal fossils, footprints and raindrop craters are found upsidedown on rocks, on the bottom of the rock layer rather than on the top. It is a dilemma for creationists with a recent flood thesis to explain footprint, raindrop, and mudcrack prints found in geological strata. These formed on dry or lightly moist land, not under a catastrophic flood setting.

Erosion can expose fossils for subsequent displacement by water, wind, gravity, or even animals from their original sites to bizarre situations. However, the record can be read and events inferred, based on rational explanations.

It is clear that if the worldwide flood is historic then many miracles must have occurred.

1. Gathering and fitting representatives of all of the species (or kinds) of terrestrial animals that have ever lived on to the ark.
2. Animals from cold areas (penguin and Arctic fox) being able to survive with animals from hot climates (anaconda and tree sloth).
3. Feeding animals for a year, disposing of wastes, and having them disperse after the flood across the desolate globe to appropriate habitats.
4. Carnivores not eating the herbivores.
5. Animals going into hibernation or torpor so they didn't need much food, wouldn't be tempted to prey on others, wouldn't reproduce, generate wastes or need large areas for exercise.
6. Eight humans, and all other animal pairs housing all the parasites of that species, some deadly, including worms, insects, bacteria, fungi, viruses, protozoa, and not getting sick or dying.
7. Fresh water animals not dying from the saltier water; marine organisms not dying from the dilution.

8. Noah possessing shipbuilding skills. An amateur made an enormous vessel of wood and pitch, which was tossed about in a catastrophic flood for a whole year and it didn't leak.
9. Orderly phylogenetic sorting of fossils.
10. The tremendous diversity within and between species in the few thousand years since the flood, including the great variations among humans, all coming from just eight people, five of whom were closely related. One hundred and nineteen thousand, five hundred species of flies! Four thousand species of aphids!

When something is hard to explain, the creationist modus operandi is to invent a miraculous explanation. A prior assumption compels the believer to make the data conform to this tenet no matter what. In contrast, valid science confronts a problem with no previous expectations and is obliged and free to go wherever the data lead. Science cannot manufacture explanations without providing supporting proof. It can propose hypotheses but attempts must be made to prove or disprove them. If over time and valiant attempts at proof they cannot be substantiated, they do not survive.

Supernatural intervention (miracle) is not part of science. If "creation science" allows for miracle, it is not science. Science explains natural phenomena using rational, dependable, predictable, orderly laws and procedures. The theistic evolutionist credits God with this remarkable design of dependable law.

Flood Stories from Around the World?

(Creationist Perspective) Dozens of stories and legends having flood themes have accumulated from a variety of cultures including some in the South Sea Islands, India, China, Burma, Greece, Wales, Australia, Tierra del Fuego, Alaska, and North, South and Central America. These diverse flood legends lend great support to the thesis of a worldwide deluge.

(Theistic Evolutionist Perspective) There are geological and archeological data and cultural stories throughout the world that reflect the occurrence of floods at various times and places in the past. This is not surprising, as flooding is common in many localities as is witnessed in our present era. However, there is no *global* evidence of a flood of the epic proportions of that described by the creationists, where the whole surface of the Earth was submerged at one time for months.

While there are numerous flood legends in many cultures across the globe, it is significant to note which areas *do not* have flood stories. They are not found in Egypt (a culture with extensive writing, yet no flood records) or the rest of the continent of Africa, and they are rare in Europe. None come from East, Central, and Northern Asia. These regions are not as flood prone; it is not surprising that flood legends are nonexistent there. Could it be that many cultures have flood stories because (a) floods have been common in many places on this Earth over the centuries and it is not surprising that particularly catastrophic ones would have been remembered, or (b) the flood story of the Hebrew people has been dispersed to the uttermost regions of the globe by Christian missionaries or other visitors and the oral traditions of many people could have incorporated these remarkable details into their own flood stories? It is suggested that this is exactly what the Hebrews did in including ancient Babylonian stories of a flood into their literature. Flood stories from the Middle East region such as the Gilgamesh Epic (2,700 – 2,600 B.C.) predate the history or written records of the Hebrews who first appeared from a nomadic existence ~1,900 B.C. The Hebrew account has many similarities including the release of birds at the end and it appears they adapted aspects of the earlier story to their own (See Appendix H). If a worldwide flood had occurred, the legends should be universal and not correlate so directly with the climactic realities of particular regions and their flooding histories.

What is not clear is this: if all of the people of the world were drowned by the flood except the eight on the ark, then all of the regions around the world that have flood tales would have had to become secondarily populated by descendants of the flood survivors within the last 4,500 years or so. How these four pair and their offspring could emigrate throughout the world across vast ocean expanses to remote islands and continents and establish cultures and diverse languages in that time is not explained. It is especially problematic when one reads the Bible (Genesis 10) and notes where the descendants of Noah's family settled. It does not appear that they dispersed to all regions of the world, i.e. Australia, North America, China. If they subsequently migrated to exotic continents after 2,500 BC it must be noted that there are voluminous data that attest to many peoples having been there prior to that date. For instance, impressive archeological data show that Native Americans had been established and perpetually lived in North and South America thousands of years prior to that, and at no time were they decimated by a global flood.

Presently some thirty subgroups of *Homo sapiens sapiens* have been identified based on genetic variations. How the distinctive and diverse human genetic characteristics of hair (color, texture, distribution on the body, curl), eyes (color, shape, focus and color capability), skin color and texture, height (neck, torso, femur, lower leg bones), blood type, numerous body and facial features, as well as many talents and immune and physiological disparities got established in such a short time in Japan, Borneo, Greenland, India,

Nigeria, Finland, New Zealand, or Brazil from just eight individuals, five directly related, is not explained. The magnitude of human genetic diversity was marvelously displayed during recent Olympic Games!

Was it luck that fair skinned descendants of Noah settled in northern European habitats where there was minimal sun and dark skinned migrants happened to go to equatorial regions? How fortunate that tall settlers happened to go to hot climates where evaporation would help them adapt and stockier folk settled in colder climates where heat would be conserved! Noah's three sons were from the same genetic heritage and had limited genetic variability. The genetics of their three wives must have been remarkably diverse to have such variety result in the human gene pool in just a few thousand years! If so, how did those three women gain such genetic diversity just 1,650 years after Adam and Eve?

The evolutionary model explains the dispersal of humans and their adaptive characteristics to various climates and continents throughout the globe. Dark skin and tall, lean bodies were selected for in tropical regions, while shorter and stockier body anatomy proved advantageous in cold climates. Fair skin was selected for in less sunny northern climates. Ultraviolet light through the pale skin enabled Vitamin D to be synthesized more easily than through a more pigmented skin, preventing rickets. The science of genetics holds that these adaptations occurred over tens of thousands of years, nature subsequently selecting the fittest.

Archeological Evidence for Noah's Flood

(Creationist Perspective) Data gleaned from archeological sites in the Middle East attest to a flood event. After many searches it even appears that the ark has been located! This supports the Noachian worldwide deluge thesis.

(Theistic Evolutionist Perspective) It is true that some excavations in the Middle East (Ur, Kish, and Suruppak) have yielded evidence of floods. The flood remains at Kish are less than ten inches thick, and at Suruppak about fifteen feet, and at Ur about eleven feet. These various events are dated at different times, however, so do not relate to a single event. Eridu, just seven miles from Ur, has produced no flood evidence (McDonald, 1988, pp. 14-20).

There is no doubt that some regions have experienced serious local floods, but these cannot support the claim of a single, worldwide event lasting a year. Furthermore, the floods identified by archeologists record evidence of survivors and artifacts, and building remains show a continuity of culture. The biblical account, having only eight survivors, is not supported by archeological evidence.

If the whole world was covered by raging floodwaters for months, artifacts from antidiluvian (pre-flood) civilizations should be found erratically buried in many layers of sedimentary rocks, especially the lower ones. The creationist position would predict this. Metals, pottery, precious stones, tablets, jewelry, implements of agriculture, spears and other equipment for hunting or war, even bodies of people, cattle, or sheep would presumably have been buried in low sedimentary layers throughout the globe. The Bible speaks of cities having been established as far back as during Cain's life. Where would all of these remnants of human culture have been buried? Interestingly, human artifacts are found in the topmost layers, supporting the prediction of evolutionary theory which holds that humans are relatively recent on the extensive biological/geological scene. Neither archeology nor anthropology support a flood submerging the whole surface of the Earth for months.

The claim that Noah's ark has been found is not verified. Some previous claims have been debunked. Exploratory trips to find the ark have been attempted, are recorded on videos, much discussed, and even seen on television specials, but there is *no* scientific evidence which supports these wishful assertions.

It is of great interest that scientists have recently found significant evidence for a devastating flood in the Black Sea region, which occurred approximately 7,600 years ago. The Black Sea was formed when the Mediterranean Sea burst through the Bosporus valley, flowed into a freshwater lake and covered beaches, rushed up rivers, destroyed life and forced those who survived to flee. Data reveal that this human dispersion spread west to Europe, south to the Persian Gulf and East to Central Asia. Many wonder if this catastrophic event was the one from which the flood stories arose in numerous oral cultures.

New Testament Writers Believed in a Literal Adam

(Creationist Perspective) The apostle Paul makes the following references in the New Testament to Adam: Romans 5:12-14, I Corinthians 15:22, 44-49, Colossians 1:20, and I Timothy 2:13-14. This proves that Adam was indeed a historic person who was in the Garden of Eden and who sinned by eating the forbidden fruit. In addition, Jesus makes reference to creation in Matthew 19:3-6 and Mark 10:6, quoting directly from Genesis 1:27 and 2:24. If Paul and Jesus believed Genesis literally, so ought we.

(Theistic Evolutionist Perspective) Jesus became human. He took upon himself the form of a servant and was made in the likeness of men (Philippians 2:7). What does that *mean?* He was born of a woman. He

237

hungered, wept, slept, became angry, questioned, loved, was subject to temptation, celebrated weddings, needed friends, needed to pray, bled, died. Many believe he not only was confined to human flesh and blood but also to human understanding and was limited to the knowledge available to the culture in which he was born and raised. He knew no science, no technology, no geography, no art, no music beyond what they knew. He was reared in a devout Jewish family which studied and memorized the Old Testament texts and interpreted them differently than do modern rationalists. In becoming a frail human he was limited to all that that encompasses.

Krister Stendahl, Bishop Emeritus of Sweden and Professor Emeritus at Harvard Divinity School, when asked about this by the author explained that being confined to the human mental capacity was, in Bishop Stendahl's exact words, "Christ's ultimate condescension." Jesus was bound not only by the physical but by the mental restrictions of the human condition. Embracing this limitation was part of his deep love and humiliation for humankind. He did not understand all things. Even on the cross he asked "Why?"

Of course New Testament writers, including the Apostle Paul, had the same limitations. They did not grasp all doctrine and theology. Indeed, parts of Paul's theology poignantly reflect the mores of his time. That culture did not have all truth. People living in the first century did not have the benefit of scientific, cultural, historic, theological, linguistic or psychological information that has accrued for twenty centuries. A literal interpretation of the Old Testament served them well. They were used mightily by God just as people today with limited understanding are used for God's glory. That does not mean that the faith did not or does not encompass deep mysteries.

In Mark 4:31 while speaking to the crowd, Jesus said that the mustard seed was "less than all the seeds that be in the Earth" (King James Version). Matthew 13:32 says that it is "the least of all seeds" (KJV). We now realize that the statement, literally, is not accurate. There are many seeds that are smaller than the mustard seed. Taken literally, this statement is not true, even though it was spoken by Jesus! It is not a big deal. We understand his message which came through very clearly. We must assess very carefully how we come to the scriptures and always remember their original setting. We must try to understand the thinking of the people who lived at that time. Jesus was a man of his time. So were all of the New Testament authors. We believe God inspired their writings, but they were not edited for ultimate scientific and theological clarity. Much of the vast disparity of belief in modern Christendom bears this out. Interestingly, translators of the New International Version have rendered Mark 4:31 thus: "It is like a mustard seed which is the smallest seed you plant in the ground." There is room in this translation for smaller seeds across the globe.

The thinking that flourished after the Reformation, Enlightenment and Scientific Revolution, as well as the knowledge explosion of the 20th Century have expanded our worldview and helped us interpret scripture more accurately. Advances in theological understanding have immeasurably contributed to these changes. Over the centuries God has progressively revealed the truth. We humbly look for guidance to seek to know the will and understand the ways and the word of God. No one knows what insight will be given in the future that will shed new light and require modification of some present assertions.

Complex Structures/Uselessness of Intermediates

(Creationist Perspective) It cannot be conceived that complex structures such as the flagellum of the bacterium, the eye or brain, the secretory apparatus of the bombardier beetle, or the intricate steps of blood clotting could possibly have arrived on this Earth in any manner other than through the abrupt and supernatural action of an omnipotent Creator. How could such elaborate structures with so many interdependent parts, step by step, have evolved? What good is a partially functional eye or a half-formed wing? The intergrading structures demanded by evolution would be nonfunctional. Just as a watch infers a watchmaker so the eye must have an eyemaker, an intelligent designer.

The woodpecker is also an example of the intricacy of interdependent structures. This bird pounds at wood with great force. Impacting at this speed and strength requires a reinforced skull, elaborate neck muscles, and an almost unbreakable beak. One adaptation without the others would not work. These complex structures, which are mutually dependent and are all needed for the organism's survival, could not possibly have evolved in such a parallel and cooperative manner in the same organism.

(Theistic Evolutionist Perspective) Creationists ask: "If the eye evolved, what good was 25% of sight?" "If wings evolved, what good was a half formed wing?" Early eyes may have been mere light receptors, as are seen presently in many organisms. This is a useful adaptation in some settings. An eye that senses light and shadow is better than no light sensor. The absence of a light sensor would deprive the organism of any visual information about the environment. Ten per cent of sight can be just what is needed.

Some unicellular organisms (*Amoeba*) appear to have general light sensitivity which results in either positive phototrophism (movement toward the light) or negative phototrophism (movement away from the light). Others (*Euglena*) have a light sensitive eyespot, a specialized organelle. There is a wide variety of photoreceptive organs within the Animal Kingdom; some are one celled and others are multicellular.

Biologists study the origin of light sensitive tissue in multicellular organisms embryologically and have identified separate origins of this tissue. Some come from skin tissue and some from deeper organs. Across the Animal Kingdom light sensitive tissue is seen to have arisen independently, not once but numerous times. This variety is expressed in instances of partial sight, which contribute adequately to a particular organism's survival. The photoreceptors in starfish are different from those in a flatworm. Some are specialized to perceive various light intensities only, while others can detect the direction of the light source. Eyes have many variations as well, there being inverse and everse retinas, convex lenses or concave reflectors.

Some multicellular animals such as earthworms have photoreceptive cells scattered in various regions of their bodies to help them in orientation. Gradual steps from a light sensitive spot to an eye with a complex lens and retina can be seen in various species of living snails. Hagfishes, which are very primitive chordates, and the lungfish are practically blind yet both are well endowed with other senses such as smell, taste, touch, or sensitivity to water turbulence. The rhinoceros also has weak eyesight, depending on other capabilities for survival. Many organisms survive with less than perfect optical endowment.

There is great variety of visual perception, and correspondingly, many structural themes across the Animal Kingdom. Twenty-five per cent eyesight, whatever that means, or 50%, is just fine if it meets that organism's needs. The suggestion that transitional eyesight is nonadaptive or nonexistent is just not valid. Not all require the complex eye of the human for survival. Indeed, some, such as nocturnal animals, have specialized ability to see at night far beyond the capability of humans. The soaring eagle is able to spot a camouflaged gopher far below, a remarkable adaptation for its particular needs. Not every organism needs three dimensional, twenty/twenty, multicolor, binocular, night vision. There is a diverse spectrum of sight capability and each species obviously has what is required for its success in its particular environment. Species that did not have the sight capability required for their survival are extinct.

Creationists maintain that the eye is perfect as a result of the eyemaker. Evolutionists hold that while the eye is awesome, it is in the process of evolving. Most human eyes, even of young adults, require corrective lenses. Therefore most people do not have perfect eyesight. The size of the eyeball is either too long or too short. The light waves sent from the lens, which is supposed to focus them on the retina, either fall short of the retina, resulting in nearsightedness, or focus behind the retina, resulting in farsightedness. The

240

lens is not in tune with the shape of the eyeball and perfect sight is not realized unless modern optics provides appropriate lens technology. Another common imperfection is astigmatism, a defect in the curvature of the cornea or lens. The practically universal imperfection of the human eye is easily explained by the evolutionary model yet difficult to justify if it is a result of direct and intelligent design.

What good are wings that are half formed? This question assumes wings were always used for flight. All birds have feathers but not all birds fly. Consider the penguin, emu, rhea or ostrich. Original wings may have been used to help balance swift running birds, which is how ostriches employ them today. As the birds ran along the ground and stretched out their forelimbs for balance, the rudimentary feathers could have given greater surface area for balance or enhanced lift in leaping for insects or extra speed that helped them avoid predators. Early feathers may have had a heat regulating function, or may have been used in display as with peacocks, or for gliding, or for some other use as yet undetermined. Evolutionists hold that the evolution of birds is distinct from the evolution of flight even though they are related. It is believed that feathers were present before flight evolved and were originally used for other purposes. It is within the realm of possibility that a variety of complex structures served a different purpose as they were developing than they serve once they have achieved complexity.

The steps required for blood to clot are many and complex. Cellular physiologists have identified many of these steps in various animals. The progression can be demonstrated from simple to more complex animals.

The half inch long bombardier beetle is famous in creationist circles. It is capable of combining enzymes with two materials (hydroquinone and hydrogen peroxide) which are manufactured in glands in the beetle's posterior. This results in benzoquinone, a noxious gas that explodes from the beetle's body at a boiling 112 degrees. The fluid is pumped through rotating nozzles which can be precisely aimed at an enemy such as another insect or a frog. Creationists wonder how this organism could have evolved the remarkable capability of manufacturing these secretions, and the elaborate apparatus to fire them. Scientists have suggested reasonable steps by which this admittedly complex system could have evolved. The carabid beetles have poison glands that are less complex than the brachynids, which include the bombardier beetles. It is reasonable to suggest that the carabid apparatus was a precursor to that of the more advanced brachynid.

It is known that quinines are produced by epidermal cells in arthropods for tanning the cuticle. They could be used in defense as they happen to be distasteful. If over time invaginations in the surface formed to house these secretions, with accompanying muscles the secretions could be expelled as a further defense. Ants have similar structures. Over time these structures could become more elaborate. Also, as predators become resistant to quinines, hydroquinones may have developed. Various chemicals have been noted in insects. Hydrogen peroxide, which is generated through cellular metabolism, could mix with the hydroquinones. The sequences for more complexity can continue. It is important to note that structures for one purpose can be used for another purpose down the line. While no one can say for sure which steps actually occurred, some of these intermediates can be observed in living organisms today and could have been similarly operative as the beetles evolved. Among the beetles a variety of mechanisms are seen for firing the defensive spray. Lots of possibilities appear to have developed over time to enable these insects to adapt.

The bombardier beetle isn't the only organism capable of producing toxic chemicals. None of the beetle's chemicals are unique to it. Other insects can spray benzoquinone but lack the elaborate aiming mechanism. The bombardier beetle has perfected the defense, an example of a remarkable evolutionary process.

Furthermore, if animals were created to be vegetarian (creationists claim there was no death until Adam and Eve sinned) then what was the purpose of the bombardier beetle's defense? In a vegetarian ecosystem who was there to fear, to defend oneself against? Why would a creator give it this apparatus if there were no predators? In addition, the woodpecker has structural adaptations to help it find and eat insects. Why would it need them in a vegetarian world? Were these two organisms different before Adam and Eve sinned? Were they created after the fall, one as a carnivore and the other to defend itself against carnivores? Evolution explains these adaptations but creationism is stymied to explain them in a vegetarian world.

Reasoning that if something cannot be imagined then it must not have happened is a weak base for any thesis. It is as though nature is limited to whatever we in our finite, contemporary condition are able to conceive as possible or probable. Also, it is always difficult to appreciate the expanse of time available for such change. Scientists admit that there are mechanisms operative that are not yet understood. For most of us the known is more comfortable than what is unknown. This can tempt some to reach for irrational explanations to relieve themselves of this state of suspended understanding. Ancient cultures manufactured explanatory myths to accomplish this. Claiming the miraculous supernatural wand can be another means of resolving this uncertainty.

If someone had told Lewis and Clark that one day unmanned intercontinental ballistic missiles, which could travel around the world and pinpoint buildings in target cities in another hemisphere, would be buried in silos on the prairies of Montana near where they journeyed, or that one day a man would walk on the moon, they would have laughed at these incredible ideas. They could not have imagined such bizarre ideas. Yet those things evolved, step by step, by microevolution (slow change over time). Complex weaponry such as these missiles evolved over thousands of years, step by step, from handmade spears. While intelligence was behind this progression, genetic change and then natural selection, not mere chance, and other processes were behind evolution to trigger and facilitate change over time.

The remarkable, sequential evolution of the bombardier beetle's apparatus in no way detracts from the awe surrounding God's creative activity. It expands our understanding of what such activity might be and frees the creator God to accomplish the work in a variety of ways. This creator is not limited to a spoken word envisioned by the prescientific Hebrews. Science exists to unlock these mysteries, little by little. Those who hold to a creator God revel in the new insights and their awe for God is expanded as the creative methods are revealed. They regard God as the creator who works through or gives freedom to designed natural laws which, little by little, are comprehended by mortals.

Polonium Halos

(Creationist Perspective) In recent years data has been published on halos, microscopic spheres that have formed in rocks as a result of the decay of certain atoms. Polonium halos from the isotope Po-218 (Po is the chemical symbol for the element polonium) can be found in granite in Ontario. They result from the decay of polonium 210 atoms. Because Po-218 has a half-life of only three minutes and becomes extinct within a few hours it has been claimed that these halos prove an abrupt creation, that the halos formed within days of creation while the primordial Earth rocks were solidifying by the word of the Creator. This supports the young Earth thesis.

Polonium halos have been found in samples of coalified wood from three geological periods within the Colorado Plateau. It is suggested that these halos formed as a result of infiltration and subsequent decay of a one-time-only exposure to radioactive uranium. Therefore the vast depth of sedimentary rock composing the Colorado Plateau was probably formed within a period of months, such as during Noah's flood, and did not require millions of years as geologists claim.

(Theistic Evolutionist Perspective) Interestingly, the granite from Ontario with Po-218 halos has been shown to be intrusive, meaning it was forced into already formed sedimentary rock. Therefore it is younger than the rock it intrudes. The intruded, older rock is composed of sediment that came from

even earlier rocks. Thus the younger, intrusive rock could not be the molten material of the forming Earth. This disproves the claim that these halos give evidence for a young Earth and an abrupt petrification of original rock from a primordial creation. It was a major error that it wasn't noted that the halos were in intrusive rock. Peer review has falsified these claims.

The trees from the Colorado Plateau were no doubt uprooted by local floods at three different periods, millions of years apart, and deposited in stream channels. The sands surrounding them and their position indicate that the logs were carried in a rapid flow of water. That does not prove a global flood, however. Scientists point out that the layers of rock between these three episodes include wind blown sand dune layers, marine beds, non-marine strata, and gypsum beds that require arid climates. Much environmental diversity is represented, requiring long periods of time. How could such distinctive strata requiring such varied settings be deposited during a one year flood episode? Furthermore, if these logs were laid down within the last 4,500 years, their carbon 14 age should be within this range. All of these wood pieces have lost their C14 components, which indicates that they are at least 50,000 years old.

Scientists assert that the polonium halos in samples of coalified wood found in three geological periods (Triassic, Jurassic, and Tertiary of the Eocene) in sedimentary rock in the Colorado Plateau were from three different events, millions of years apart. This would disprove their having originated simultaneously within the last several thousand years.

Polystrate Trees

(Creationist Perspective) Polystrate trees are upright tree fossils found in a variety of sites such as in Nova Scotia, Alaska, and Yellowstone National Park. The trees were buried by many sedimentary depositions (poly = many, strate = strata, layers). It is believed that these sediments were laid down by Noah's flood. They were all buried simultaneously.

It is of interest that trees killed by the Mt. St. Helens volcano on 18 May 1980 in the state of Washington have subsequently moved and are being buried in the vicinity. This supports the hypothesis that the tree fossils at Yellowstone were formed during one quick event such as the Noachian flood rather than over millions of years. Trees positioned in an upright state in Spirit Lake, which is at the base of Mt. St. Helens, are being buried at different depths because they sink at different rates. Early ones are lower and subsequent sedimentation has established them. Then other trees sink and are buried at higher levels. These trees mimic the twenty seven layers of fossil trees at Yellowstone. These observations prove that the trees were not buried at twenty seven different periods of time over millions of years, but were formed during the one year long worldwide deluge.

(Theistic Evolutionist Perspective) Polystrate fossils, a term seen in creationist literature, refers to fossils such as trees which intersect several strata. Upright, giant lycopsid trees, several meters tall, were described in Pennsylvanian coal deposits in Nova Scotia in the middle of the 19th Century. A river flood delivered sediment within a forest, leaving taller trees above the ground. Subsequently, another flood washed through the area and deposited an additional layer on these exposed trunks. This occurred several times within a few years until the trees were completely covered or rotted.

Eventually, another forest could have become established on the sediments. In time, it too could be buried by sediment-laden water. The record would show this series of events. Since these trees had roots and rootlets preserved in the rock it is clear to geologists that the trees were buried in place. Some of these stumps contained fossils of small reptiles inside of them (Dawson, 1868)! Other polystrate fossils have been discovered in Ontario, in the Yahtse River area of Alaska, and at Specimen Ridge in Yellowstone National Park.

It is possible that vertical trees that have been transported into Spirit Lake or to rivers in the vicinity of Mt. St. Helens will also eventually fossilize. However, geologists distinguish between trees that have been buried in situ (in place) such as at Yellowstone and those that have been transported and then buried, such as at Mt. St. Helens. The roots appear very different in the surrounding rock matrix. Those buried in place have their more delicate root endings intact while those that have been transported do not have these structures.

It is quite clear that the trees in Yellowstone were preserved over many thousands of years. Forests in situ were repeatedly formed on top of forests in situ. Flood waters apparently buried the trees with a rapid rate of sedimentation. Later, water with much sediment contributed additional deposits. If the waters flowed gently enough, the trees remained upright. When the floods subsided, in time new forests grew on the buried forests and, over long periods, additional floods surrounded them and the process was repeated. Each time the forests were buried and destroyed, within about two hundred years new forests became established on top of them. This happened at least twenty seven times as that many distinct layers of petrified trees have been identified. The depth of these buried trees totals 1,200 feet. It is estimated that approximately 20,000 years of alternating volcanism, stream activity, and quiet growth was required to form all of these layers.

Geological assessments in the surrounding regions testify that the flooding that caused the trees' burial was definitely localized. The suggestion that this was the result of a global event of a single year has no foundation. These polystrate trees do not give evidence for a young Earth.

The petrified forests in Yellowstone were showered with ash and debris coming from volcanic activity. With the earthquakes and boiling cauldrons in the region today, it is predicted that such volcanism may well return in the future. They also were buried by conglomerates (rounded pebbles that are laid down by stream deposits). Breccias, which are angled, not rounded, pebbles were deposited by mudflows or landslides, and they also surround some of the fossil trees.

The transported, vertical, submerged trees at Mt. St. Helens have been partially buried by sediment. The trees are buried at different depths, depending upon when they sank. Creationists note that the burial at these different depths is happening quickly, not slowly as is theorized at Yellowstone. Being in position to be fossilized and actual fossilization are two different states. Presumably, fossilization of these trees will take a very long time. Even if it occurred comparatively quickly at Mt. St. Helens, that would not disprove the fact that this process took much longer in other areas, especially if the data indicate that it occurred at twenty seven different times! It must be emphasized that the processes, sediments, and matrices, as well as the positions of the tree trunks are definitely distinctive at these varying settings, leading to disparate explanations. The record will show one event at Mt. St. Helens and reveal twenty seven events in Yellowstone.

It would also be predicted that polystrate tree fossils would be very common around the world if they formed in a global flood. This is not what is observed.

Catastrophism at Mt. St. Helens

(Creationist Perspective) The historic catastrophic volcanism which took place in 1980 at Mt. St. Helens and the witness given firsthand to the profound and devastating influence it had can be extrapolated to and shed light on the profound and devastating influence the Noachian flood had in the year of its occurrence. The Mt. St. Helens volcanic explosion was an event within historical times, a before and an after that was witnessed and can be studied by moderns and paralleled to the catastrophic flood. Groups go to the vicinity of the volcano and study the changes that have occurred and present this data in support of a young Earth thesis. For instance, there are areas around Mt. St. Helens where multi-layered sediments can be observed. If these distinct layers were formed in a period of hours or days, then it is reasonable to assume that the high walls of the Grand Canyon, made of many

layers of sedimentary rock, could certainly have been laid down in the year long flood.

There are carved river channels that were cut during and after the event at Mt. St. Helens. They can be compared to the channel of the Colorado River. It is reasonable to suggest that the Grand Canyon was not eroded over millions of years, as geologists maintain, but was catastrophically cut during the year of the flood or soon after. It didn't take a lot of time, just a lot of water!

(Theistic Evolutionist Perspective) The processes that occurred as a result of the Mt. St. Helens volcano cannot be paralleled with the formation of the Grand Canyon. The sedimentary layers deposited as a result of this recent catastrophe are distinct from those at the Grand Canyon. When the layers are accurately analyzed, the data destroy the thesis that both of these sites were formed in a similar manner in a comparatively short period of time.

Creationists claim that since layered sediments totaling almost thirty feet in thickness were deposited within hours in the vicinity of Mt. St. Helens that the layers of the Grand Canyon could certainly have been deposited within a whole year, during or soon after the Noachian flood. What is not understood, apparently, is that if sedimentary layers were indeed deposited in a short period of time, whether in hours, or a year, the organic matter in the various layers would be identical in age and much of it in composition as well. There might be pollen grains in lower levels that could also be found in upper levels. Perhaps an insect, squirrel, owl, spore, piece of bark, pine cone or leaf was caught in one layer. Identical specimens could and would be found in other layers. Animals and plants would not sort out perfectly, though it is possible that one species could be found in just one layer. This evidence would demonstrate that sedimentation occurred comparatively quickly, as there would be material of an identical nature and age in many layers. Geologists in the future would read these sediments and conclude that they were formed during the same time period.

Creationists suggest that the swollen Toutle River, near Mt. St. Helens, which carved through soil and made the equivalent of a "mini Grand Canyon" in a matter of hours or days models what occurred during the formation of the Grand Canyon. Paleontologists can demonstrate from several perspectives, however, that the strata surrounding the Grand Canyon as well as the canyon itself were formed over an extensive period. Radiometric dating, an analysis of fossils and intrusive rock, and unconformities (identification of missing and therefore eroded layers), all provide support for the thesis that millions of years were involved. The Grand Canyon's history differs significantly from that of the recent formations seen near Mt. St. Helens, which were laid down and carved quickly.

A geologist studying fossils at the Grand Canyon finds distinct specimens in the layers, progressing from extinct invertebrates at the bottom to more modern forms at the top. An evolutionary story can be read. If dated, the fossils would register older values at the bottom and progress to more recent values toward the top. It is a geological and evolutionary record that obviously developed over millions of years. The sedimentary layers are not only distinct from each other but have distinctive fossils. The earlier rocks with their fossils are overlaid by more recent strata with their respective organisms demonstrating the Law of Superposition. The layers are not homogeneous in organic content as are those at Mt. St. Helens where the strata were formed within hours, days, or weeks of each other.

The suggestion that these two sites were formed similarly cannot be substantiated. Careful scrutiny of their ages, their fossils, and their formational history reveals their distinctiveness. This must be considered in their interpretation.

It is not clear how creationists account for the layers of the Grand Canyon forming and solidifying within one year and then being inundated by a huge torrent of water that cut the canyon so cleanly. Freshly deposited layers do not harden so quickly and therefore would have eroded and dispersed if they were assaulted by so much water power such a short time after being formed. Sediment becoming rock, petrified, takes hundreds, thousands, millions of years. Also, intrusive layers exist and were weathered, possible only over long periods. This is impossible to explain with the flood model.

Coal Produced Quickly?

(Creationist Perspective) Creationist videos show samples of coal that have been artificially made in ovens in a very short time. This proves that belief in coal being millions of years in the making, contributing to support for an old Earth, is unfounded. Also, coal could have come from floating, vegetative, matted debris, which would have been generated at the time of the flood. Matted vegetable material in Spirit Lake at Mt. St. Helens or in other places in the world substantiates this hypothesis.

(Theistic Evolutionist Perspective) Geologists hold that coal has been formed from ancient plant material over long periods of time under great pressure and other specific circumstances. At times in the past, the sea has flooded across huge land masses, or rivers have swollen and created massive floodplains. These events have resulted in trees falling and log jams forming, including the accumulation of plant material such as sap (which becomes amber), spores, pollen, leaves, and cuticle (the waxy surface on certain species' leaves). If this organic material was buried before it decomposed,

and was overlain by thick sediments of mud or silt and pressed for long periods of time, sometimes even millions of years, coal formed.

Before becoming coal, this mass is called peat. It can be seen today in bogs and swamps. Coal comes in a variety of forms, such as lignite, bituminous or anthracite. They have different histories and ages, depending on how much decay occurred before the organic material was buried and how much heat and pressure were generated over the years. In a video there is no way to assess the composition of the block. Just because it *looks* like coal doesn't mean it *is* coal.

If the sea withdraws or the river returns to its banks or reroutes and dry land returns, plant life can become re-established. This cycle can be repeated over and over. In the geological record many coal swamp cycles have been preserved on top of each other with soil horizons, some very delicate, between them. Sometimes they are filled with plant roots or the polystrate trees previously discussed. This is a record that required a long period of time to form. The fact that trees were preserved in the soil speaks to the fact that coal can be formed near the surface and at times at faster rates. Some coal layers have preserved dinosaur footprints. This indicates that waters that triggered the peat formation receded and dry land returned for footprints to be formed. The delicate strata between organic layers are hard to explain if one believes that a swirling deluge was responsible for these layers.

Coal deposits have distinctive parameters, such as river channels flowing through. The multiple layers of coal, some containing footprints, and the delineated seams, as well as the superficial formation of coal would be hard to explain from a flood model where all coal is supposed to have been formed in a short time.

At Spirit Lake at the base of Mt. St. Helens creationists point to mats of bark that float and eventually sink. It is suggested that this mass could eventually become coal in a short period of time, giving support for a young Earth. Time will tell. Wishful thinking fills a great chasm between an idea and demonstrated proof. Even if rapid coal formation does occur, it does not negate the fact that most coal was formed over long periods of time. One cannot extrapolate and infer that *all* coal formed in geologically short periods.

Dinosaurs Contemporary with Humans

(Creationist Perspective) Tracks found in the Paluxy River area in Glen Rose, Texas, represent contemporaneous human and dinosaur footprints. Since humans and dinosaurs were in the Garden of Eden together, and on the ark, it would be predicted that their tracks would be found together. In addition, human and dinosaur bones have been found together, although

rarely. References to Leviathan (Job 3:8, 41:1; Psalm 74:14, 104:26; Isaiah 27:1) and Behemoth (Job 40:15-24, Psalm 50:10) in the scripture are proof that humans have seen dinosaurs. Furthermore, the Anasazi Indians of the American Southwest left pictographs on rocks of monsters resembling dinosaurs.

(Theistic Evolutionist Perspective) Paleontologists assert that the last of the dinosaurs went extinct some 65 million years ago. Anthropologists tell us that bipedal (two-footed) hominids arrived on the scene some 6-10 million years ago. Therefore, we would not expect to find any rocks of the same age containing both dinosaur and hominid fossils. They, according to modern science, were far from being contemporary. If anyone could conclusively prove that fossil footprints or any other kind of evidence showed that dinosaurs and humans lived at the same time that would surely impact many tenets of evolutionary science.

Considerable research has been conducted by geologists in the Paluxy River region. They have ascertained that the supposed human footprints were not human. Careful analysis would have established this long ago, but creationists clung to this thesis without critique for many years. During the 1980s creationist leadership acknowledged that the Glen Rose footprints were not of contemporaneous dinosaurs and humans. Many have removed the literature and videos that promulgated this error. Yet not everyone is aware of this retraction. It is not uncommon to hear individuals, including those giving independent seminars, refer to the tracks as being supportive data for a young Earth. I heard an itinerant creationist speaker make these claims in 1998 in Montana. In 2000, in Pennsylvania, a representative from a creationist organization inferred at a seminar that the tracks were authentic.

A literal interpretation of Genesis requires that humans lived at the same time as dinosaurs. They would have been together in the Garden of Eden where dinosaurs would have been named by Adam, as well as together on the ark. Since some dinosaurs were enormous and their variety is impressive, it is questionable as to how pairs representing all of them could fit on the ark. Creationists have explained that they must have come on board as juveniles or possibly in egg form, even though the Genesis accounts infer to most readers that mating pairs, i.e. adults, were aboard. Furthermore, gender couldn't be determined in eggs.

Creationists believe that dinosaurs lived after the flood and then went extinct within the last 4,000 years or so. With the vast climate change after the flood, including an ice age (the only one, they believe), it is suggested that these animals could not adapt. What was God's plan in protecting all of them on the ark and then having them meet their demise so soon?

250

Biblical support for the human/dinosaur thesis is claimed because of references to Leviathan in Job, Psalms, and Isaiah. Leviathan, meaning "coiled one," also known as Rahab, was the name of a primeval, marine dragon monster from Canaanite mythological literature which supposedly was killed by Baal (Hughes and Laney, 1990, p. 223). A prototype of it appears in the Canaanite texts from Ras Shamra-Ugarit (14th Century B.C.) (Interpreter's Dictionary of the Bible, 1962, p. 116). The Psalmist (74:14) refers to its multiple heads. Isaiah (27:1) describes it as a gliding, coiling serpent. Leviathan is found in older, nonbiblical literature and was borrowed by the biblical writers. Untamable by man, this helped them describe the power of God who was able to subdue it. In apocalyptic literature (II Esdras 6:52 and II Baruch 29:3-8) Leviathan is destined to become free from his bonds at the end of this era, only to fall in defeat a second time. This marine creature may have been initially inspired by a crocodile.

Behemoth, an enormous and strong animal in Job 40:15-24, is identified as a dinosaur by creationists especially since it has a huge tail. The word actually is the plural form of the Hebrew word for beast. Scholars wonder what this animal might be: elephant, hippopotamus, or rhinoceros (Hughes & Laney, 1990, p. 228). They maintain that these mythical motifs helped the Jewish people express in a most impressive and metaphorical manner the nature and activity of God. Assigning dinosaurs to these references is interpretation that scholars and scientists find hard to affirm. Does the Bible's reference to unicorns (Numbers 23:22, Deuteronomy 33:17, Job 39:9, Isaiah 34:7) mean that they literally existed? How literally do we read these passages?

Creationists suggest that animals from various cultures, such as the Loch Ness monster or the Thunderbird of Native American origin, may have been dragons (Morris and Morris, 1996, pp. 120-123). They claim that monster drawings on rocks by Indians in the American Southwest support human/dinosaur interaction. However, the artist could have had very small animals in mind or could have pictured mythological beasts. It would be hard to prove that they were identical to any known dinosaur. Native American pictographs also depict images in the sky. Does that support extra terrestrials having arrived? One must be very careful interpreting the artwork of unknown artists from a very different culture and time. Artwork is regularly nonliteral. We do not conclude that there was a sphinx just because the Egyptians fashioned that image.

Reference is made by creationists to dinosaurs possibly living presently in Africa. Supposedly their researchers saw these animals but had damaged cameras and could not get evidence. They explain that "mythological embellishments" may explain why dragons sometimes have two heads or

251

breathe fire. Might such an explanation be given for a talking snake or donkey or the colorful Genesis stories? Could they be mythological also? Why not?

A creationist video shown at a seminar in late 2000 claimed human and dinosaur bones have been found together, although rarely. When I contacted the creationist organization that produced the video to inquire as to *where* these two sets of bones were found together, I was told that human bones had been found in a copper mine in Utah at stratigraphic levels that have yielded dinosaur bones, far below what would be expected for human bones. However, there were no dinosaur bones with them. The human bones could have been moved to this site by water, Earth movements, or some other mechanism, including animals or people. This support base which was used to make generalized statements about humans and dinosaurs is shockingly invalid and deceptive. After some communication, the creationists stated that they would "re-evaluate the video for possible editing." One wonders how many thousands of viewers have been misled. It is remarkable that no one caught this serious error earlier. Anyone faintly familiar with these issues would question this assertion. Christian laity and many pastors unquestioningly trust whatever creationist organizations claim. Peer review should be operative everywhere.

There is absolutely no scientific evidence that supports the thesis that humans and dinosaurs lived contemporaneously. If they had, it would be predicted that human bones or artifacts would be found in layers which date to the time of the dinosaurs or in sediments with dinosaur bones or teeth with no possible indication that they had subsequently been displaced to those strata by Earth or water movement or even human interference. No such combinations have been found anywhere. The young Earth model predicts that human bones and dinosaur bones would have similar dating values. They are most dissimilar, tens of millions of years apart. Creationists must deny the validity of these dating values to maintain their young Earth thesis even though several methods are used and the dates concur.

Mutations are Usually Detrimental

(Creationist Perspective) Mutations are mistakes in the genetic code and they are harmful, even lethal. They cannot be the change agent required by evolution which requires things to progress to something better or more complex.

(Theistic Evolutionist Perspective) The word "mutation" comes from the word root "muta" meaning change. Genetic mutations are modifications of nucleotide bases that compose genes which occur in chromosomes. Genes are

small units of DNA and nucleotide bases are subunits of genes. New information can be added, original information can be changed, repeated, or deleted, or genetic material can migrate to new sites on chromosomes. Mutations could also result from the addition, duplication or deletion of larger segments of chromosomes, or movements and recombinations of segments. All of these changes can result in new recipes which can lead to new characteristics, some of which can be observed and some which confer no phenotypic (observed) change.

It is true that changes in the genetic recipe of a parent's sperm or egg can pass on new information that results in offspring which are less well adapted. Some changes have no effect on the offspring, while other chromosomal modifications result in detrimental qualities. Mutations can lead to death, either of the sperm or egg or of the fertilized egg, embryo, fetus, infant, child or adult. Obviously, if the parents are alive and reproducing they have successfully adapted, but change in their sex cells presents the risk of passing less adapted qualities on to the offspring. In humans, mutations have led to cystic fibrosis, muscular dystrophy, albinism, and hemophilia. Some genetic changes are so serious that the fetus does not live long enough to be born. Evolutionists admit that changes in the genetic message are generally not beneficial. Organisms are eliminated as nature selects those that are better adapted.

There are some changes, however, that result in beneficial qualities, giving that organism an adaptive edge. A wheat plant mutated such that its offspring could thrive in a drier climate. Or it may have mutated so that its offspring were dwarfed and did not blow over on the windy plains as easily as taller siblings. Some time a Galapagos finch hatched and had a beak that could crack nuts that no other birds could crack. Some time an antelope was born with the ability to run faster, giving it an edge over its more vulnerable siblings.

If it has longer legs, slightly keener eyesight, a color that confers camouflage, a kidney that requires less fluid in a dry climate, or if it secretes a chemical that is injurious to predators, that organism may be able to succeed in niches where its brothers and sisters cannot survive. It thrives and subsequently passes its advantageous genetic endowment to its offspring.

It is known that the red blood cell mutation that causes sickle cell anemia, which would be considered detrimental to many people, has been beneficial to those who live in the region of Africa where malaria is common. The heterozygous form (a message for that trait received from just one parent) protects from the malarial parasite. The genetic changes we see before our eyes in bacteria which give them antibiotic resistance are surely beneficial to those bacteria!

One cannot generalize that all mutations are injurious. It is those few that are not which, over long periods, exert their influence on populations and cause change over time. The combined effects of several mutations can eventually cause enough change to result in new species. Creationists affirm microevolution, change within species. Apparently they see how these changes can be beneficial and lead to great variation within a species. How can they affirm beneficial microevolutionary mutation and yet claim that mutations are detrimental?

Lack of Change/Punctuated Equilibrium

(Creationist Perspective) Algae, ferns, cockroaches, horseshoe crabs, crocodiles, and crossopterygian fishes have changed minimally or not at all over the millennia. This stasis is difficult to reconcile with evolution, whose very meaning is change. Therefore, these species support the creationist paradigm. Punctuated equilibrium is the evolutionists' desperate effort to explain both these long periods when no apparent change occurred and the gaps in the fossil record. They expect to save the theory of evolution. It is a manufactured idea which covers up a serious weakness in the evolutionary model.

(Theistic Evolutionist Perspective) The thesis discussed in Chapter Seven that organisms go through spurts of change over a relatively short period of time geologically (it still could be thousands or millions of years) and then experience stasis or very little change for millions of years gives an alternate paradigm to the gradualistic model of slow change over time that had been the classic understanding of evolution for so long. Punctuated equilibrium ("punk eke" for short) images a stairstep design where an organism experiences relatively fast change and then undergoes little or no change for long periods.

It has indeed been noted that many organisms have experienced long periods of stasis where it appears that little or no change has occurred. The record reveals that certain insects such as those in amber, ferns, horseshoe crabs, the tuatara reptile which still lives but whose fossils go back to dinosaur times, gingko trees, and crocodiles hit an evolutionary plateau for millions of years. No change. No evolution. They obviously were very well adapted to have survived without change for such long periods, possibly even in a variety of environmental settings. Scientists are not aware of all of the mechanisms that run evolution. The explanations for these periods of equilibrium are not all understood. It could be that they had few competitors or predators and a stable environment and stasis was just fine, most adaptive.

Possibly the changes that did occur were detrimental and were eliminated, nature selecting for the status quo.

Punk eke is a working hypothesis which has been analyzed and critiqued by scientists over the past several decades. Eventually, if it is seen to have a weak support base, it will not stand. It was not a defensive move among evolutionists to keep evolutionary theory alive by justifying gaps in the fossil record. It attempts to explain the rarity of transitional forms as well as their absence. If change occurred rather abruptly, followed by further abrupt change, it follows that the chances for the fossilization of these intermediates would be less as there were fewer of them in a limited period of time and possibly a limited geographic area. Thus the gaps. In no way does it suggest that transitionals never existed. As always, *any* fossilization is rare. That, combined with comparatively few individuals in a limited time period and place could lead to missing intermediates. It explains the geological record by suggesting that speciation appears to occur relatively quickly at times and more slowly or gradually in other settings, and even is absent for long periods in some species. Researchers have found ample examples of intermediate forms, and believe that punctuated equilibrium does not apply to all species at all times.

In science, a hypothesis is presented with supporting rationale. Over the years data are gathered that either support or negate (falsify) it. Science changes as new data arrive. Evolution as presented by Charles Darwin has been modified into "neo-Darwinism" as 20th Century science shed light on this subject. Change will no doubt be seen in the future as additional insight is gathered. "Punk eke" has been rigorously peer reviewed for several decades and will continue to be discussed and challenged. Support will be maintained, increased, or eroded. That is science at work. It is a fascinating drama to watch!

The Second Law of Thermodynamics Negates Evolutionary Theory

(Creationist Perspective) This law states that entropy (randomness and disorder) increases over time. Order constantly trends to disorder in a closed system where no new energy is being provided. We see that trees rot and raccoons get old, die, and disintegrate, tires blow, mountains are eroded, potholes form, rooms become messy, the environment gets polluted and the universe loses heat. Things don't get better or more organized, they get worse as they head toward chaos. Energy is continually being lost and ultimately the end of life, the Earth, and the universe will be chaos. Since evolution requires change resulting in more order and complexity, this contradicts the Second

Law of Thermodynamics and could not possibly happen. A movement downhill also can be seen in moral, cultural and language degradation.

(Theistic Evolutionist Perspective) While entropy is indeed increasing in some parts of our world it is quite obvious that the opposite is also occurring. Babies develop from a unicellular, fertilized egg, children grow and mature, pollywogs become frogs, caterpillars metamorphose to butterflies, plants grow, flowers bloom, fruits ripen, cars are assembled, a cake is baked, a block of granite becomes a piece of sculpture. There are definitely trends towards more complexity, size, beauty and order. What forces enable this and might these trends towards complexity be operating in evolutionary change as well?

The Second Law of Thermodynamics states that entropy increases *in an isolated system*, a closed system, one into which no energy is being added. In other words, when new energy sources are not being introduced, as in an isolated, closed system, energy is continually being lost, often in the form of heat, and entropy or chaos increases.

There is a major misunderstanding with creationists' interpretation of this law. Evolving entities are not in an isolated system! The Earth is not a closed or isolated system. It is part of a huge solar system where the Sun radiates light energy continually toward the Earth. This increases the disorder in the solar system as a whole, but allows for an increase in order on the Earth. Eventually, in the far distant future, the Sun will run down because of this tendency to lose energy. At the moment, however, the energy directed at the Earth enables its small part of the solar system to increase in order.

Evolution does not contradict any law of physics, including the Second Law of Thermodynamics. Evolution can proceed uphill from simple to complex as long as the Sun faithfully provides an uninterrupted and adequate flow of energy to the Earth. This is exactly what occurs. Solar (light) energy is converted to chemical bond energy by plants in the remarkable process of photosynthesis. Animals then eat plants and receive the chemical bond energy, mainly in starch, which in digestion is broken down to sugar, which is used to do work. As work is accomplished on the assembly line or while cleaning a room, energy is continually being lost as heat. It is faithfully being renewed through sunshine, photosynthesis, and eating! Just as people correct disorder by expending energy to paint houses, clean dishes, sweep the porch, tidy the den, and repair the bumper, so energy enters the Earth to enable work to be accomplished and order to be restored.

When energy is available, order comes from disorder such as in the formation of sand dunes or snowdrifts by the wind, or ripples carved at the water's edge, or snowflake development, or flowers that bloom in a garden. Cars at the assembly plant take shape and are driven away at the end of the line because energy was contributed and work could therefore be accomplished. The gasoline originally came from plant material, which had been formed because of sunshine.

Order from disorder is ubiquitous in nature, or in the kitchen, garden, womb, laboratory, art studio, or automobile assembly line as long as an appropriate source of energy is present. As long as the sun shines the Second Law is not contradicted in evolution. Few people remember the Second Law of Thermodynamics from physics class. Creationists can capitalize on this, making technical claims that most laypeople are not equipped to deny.

Catastrophism Rather than Uniformitarianism

(Creationist Perspective) The changes that formed or subsequently modified the geological as well as the biological features of the Earth were caused by short term catastrophes particularly during the Noachian deluge. Giant bone beds and the multitudinous strata of mountains or cliffs are evidence of a catastrophic flood, which happened in just one year, approximately 4,500 years ago. Other factors which contributed to change would be volcanoes, earthquakes, sandstorms, mudslides and hurricanes. Some can be seen before our eyes!

(Theistic Evolutionist Perspective) Uniformitarianism holds that many changes in the crust of the Earth have occurred slowly over millions of years, at rates similar to those presently observed, and by events that are similar to those currently operating, such as weathering, erosion, continental drift, and glacial carving. Actually, *both* catastrophism as well as uniformitarianism have operated in the Earth's past and both are operating today.

If the deaths of animals in giant bone beds were caused by a global catastrophic flood, one would expect to find a variety of bones in the beds, washed in from hither and yon. However, bone beds usually include just a few species. For example, the Agate Springs Bone Bed in Nebraska is composed primarily of extinct rhinoceri. Geologists explain their deaths as the result of a river flood that overtook a herd during the Miocene. Such localized episodes occur today when herds cross rivers and are overcome by raging waters. The May 1986 National Geographic describes a "horned avalanche" of wildebeests migrating across a river in the Serengeti with hundreds drowning, especially the young. A local flood also explains the mass of dinosaur bones found at Dinosaur National Park in Utah.

If sedimentary rock formations were formed from one catastrophic event they would show a certain similarity of composition, fossils and dating. However, sedimentary layers in an area are varied in composition, some being of limestone, or sandstone, shale, volcanic ash, lava or mudstone. In addition, they have variable ages. Presumably the layers originated at different time periods from separate events. They show a progression of fossils. The telltale signs of erosion can be seen and some strata reveal mudcracks, raindrop marks, animal burrows, footprints, or sand dunes, all formed on dry or moist land to give evidence that they were at one time exposed. These data point to longer periods with gradual processes punctuated by catastrophic events. Sometimes an abrupt, catastrophic, igneous intrusion, lava flow, local flood, or Earth movement is detected, interspersed in the gradualistic, uniform record.

Uniform events are the slow changes brought about by erosion, wave action, freezing and thawing, weathering, continental migration, coral formation, gravitational influences, volcanism which builds islands, cave formation or the grinding of glacier movement. Soil and smooth, rounded boulder, rock and pebble formation result from long periods of such activity, as does mountain uplift, mountain erosion, glacial moraines, or carving of water basins such as of the Great Lakes. Uniformitarianism essentially states that what is happening today happened in the distant past; the present is the key to the past.

Imperfect Geological Column

(Creationist Perspective) Nowhere on the planet does the geological column occur intact.

(Theistic Evolutionist Perspective) The Earth has had a checkered past. A variety of catastrophic episodes as well as long periods of uniformitarian activity have occurred across the globe. Events such as volcanoes and floods are local or regional, so the strata in the geological column reflect these variations. Layers deposited in one area may not be deposited in another. In turn, a layer can be eroded or completely destroyed in one region and be protected by a new layer in another. Geologists have to decipher this puzzling record across the planet. In many places, numerous strata are intact and extrapolations can be made. Radiometric dating and index fossils have also enabled geologists to read the record in the rocks and match specific layers with others. In any case, the erratic history of the Earth with varied uniformitarian as well as catastrophic activity would predict the irregular geological column that is seen.

While the column is incomplete in many places, its various eras are well represented in some regions, such as the Cambrian to Tertiary records in Iran, Indonesia, Australia, Canada, Mexico, Alaska, and North Dakota! Granted, every era is far from complete in these areas but they are at least all represented. Where the column is not complete the strata can often be correlated with comparative work to give a composite picture. Formations with parts missing are not a threat to evolutionary theory, in fact, they are predicted. It is of interest that the geological column was first recognized by creationists, decades before Darwin.

Dating Methods

(Creationist Perspective) A literal interpretation of Genesis demands a young Earth. Scientists' data that negate this thesis are questionable. For instance, a creationist video featured dated rock samples collected from the base of a volcano in Hawaii, which had erupted during recent times. Lo and behold, the rocks that were spewed from the volcano at the same time, when analyzed, showed various dates. This is vivid proof that science's dating methods are not reliable. The dates were an embarrassment to scientists who would have predicted that the volcanic rocks that erupted together would all be of the same age.

Also, there are various factors that can distort radiometric dating values. Elements might have entered or exited the rock after it was formed. No one would have known and this would interfere with the ratios that are used to determine age. Since no one was there to measure or observe, how can the original composition of the rock be assured? Furthermore, how can anyone guarantee that decay rates have been constant over the centuries?

(Theistic Evolutionist Perspective) The disparate dates of the rocks from the volcano in Hawaii can be explained. It must be understood that the volcanic mountain that spewed the rocks had been built up over the ages from many eruptions. The earliest one, far back in time, emitted lava of a certain age. The next eruption sent hot lava up through a vent, scraping rocks from the previous eruption and sending everything out to the surface. These rocks would be of two different ages. Over time, the volcano would become larger as each layer of lava piled on top of previous layers. After many eruptions the vent would travel through numerous rock layers of varied ages. Hot lava from the most recent eruption would scrape samples of all of these previous layers and deliver them to the surface. It is reasonable and predictable to find rocks of different ages on the surface after an eruption. The inaccurate and misleading claims expressed in the creationist video reveal a serious lack of scientific expertise which may not be recognized by nonscientists.

In another video, a creationist with a doctorate claimed that when geologists or paleontologists send materials to the lab for dating, they are required to supply an approximate age of the rock or fossil. The suggestion was that the lab dates just concur with the researcher's guess. Paleontologists relate, however, that if the researcher has an idea of the approximate age of the materials, he or she can include that on the form. An approximate date can save a lot of time and money, for the dating procedures can be concentrated in a generally known age range. Different tests are formed on different aged materials. If no clue is given as to date, myriad tests are required. If the researcher has no idea as to the approximate age, the lab will need to perform more tests, which cost time and money.

The creationist in this case made it appear that the scientific community does not have accurate means to date rocks and fossils and that they deceive by agreeing to agree on dates. Many would no doubt believe this credentialed Christian. This deception or fallacious reasoning can garner disrespect among scientists for the researcher and the faith he represents.

Carbon 14 dating can be used for fairly recent (50,000 years or less) fossils such as woolly mammoths or rhinos, charred wood, bone, or some human artifacts at archeological sites. This form of dating measures the proportion of a rare, radioactive isotope of the element carbon which is found in all living things. Normal carbon is C-12. This isotope is C-14, a carbon atom with two extra neutrons. It is maintained at a steady level in the Earth's atmosphere. Living organisms contain known, constant levels. When they die, however, C-14 decays into nitrogen at a known rate. Therefore, the amount of C-14 that remains in an animal or plant, bone or wood, can be used to calculate the approximate date of death. Other dating methods such as Uranium/Lead (discussed in Chapter Seven), Potassium/Argon, and Rubidium/Strontium are used when the age of the material exceeds 50,000 years. Values from these several methods are consistent, giving support for their accuracy.

Creationists reject the data that support an old Earth. Yet how is it explained that the calculated dates from radiometric dating, position of strata in the geological column, tree rings, ice cores, sea corals, continental movement, and even supernovas, confirm each other? These values are derived from many fields such as zoology, botany, chemistry, physics, geology, and astronomy. Isn't it more than coincidental that these various sources produce similar results? Furthermore, it is incumbent upon those with creationist belief to demonstrate scientifically *why* they find this data scientifically undependable. Rejection is based solely on the necessity to hold to a young Earth because of the literal records in scripture.

Buttercup-Eating Mammoths

(Creationist Perspective) Mammoths preserved in ice have been thawed, and buttercups can be identified in their digestive tracts. This must be proof of a very quick freeze, the only ice age, which occurred after Noah's flood.

The subtropical climate that could support buttercups was drastically modified to an arctic environment as a result of the flood and ice which quickly froze the mammoths.

(Theistic Evolutionist Perspective) Mammoths in Siberia, found with plants in their stomachs, had thick fur. They did not live in a mild climate. The plants that were identified were arctic species such as tundra grasses and conifers. The animals' bodies were partly decomposed. The soil surrounding them was putrid, signifying a much slower decomposition process than the quick freezing the creationists claim. Cold Siberian rivers could wash carcasses during the spring thaw.

Also, frozen mammoths are quite rare and only they and woolly rhinoceri have been found. If the Noachian flood and subsequent ice age had caused these deaths, it would be predicted that many other species of animals would have been frozen as well. These various animals date from 11,450 to 30,000 years ago, long before the supposed date of Noah's flood (approximately 4,500 years ago, according to creationists).

The Earth is Young

(Creationist Perspective) Since no one could observe something like uranium decay in rocks, it must be rejected as it can't be scientifically verified. Past processes operated at rates different from today's rates so they cannot be studied (rejection of uniformitarianism). God created an appearance of age (Omphalos Argument): the Earth appears old, just as he created Adam, a grown man, who was just minutes in age. The presence of fossils might be explained by the fact that God put them there as fossils, and they had no other history. Also, if the Earth were old there should be much more helium (He) in the atmosphere, as it is constantly being generated by radioactive decay. Unlike hydrogen, it is too heavy to escape from the atmosphere and should have accumulated. In addition, metals in the oceans should be in a greater concentration if the Earth is old.

(Theistic Evolutionist Perspective) Limestone caves such as Carlsbad Caverns in New Mexico or Mammoth Cave in Kentucky provide evidence that disproves a young Earth. The caves are etched out of the rock by a weak acid, specifically carbonic acid, which forms when carbon dioxide combines with water. Carving is a very slow process and can only occur after the rock has been formed by sediments, which in turn originated from much older rocks.

After the cave is carved, stalactites and stalagmites form, so four processes occur. First is the formation of sediment from primordial Earth rock. Then the events that contribute to stratification and solidification occur. Third comes the slow carving of the cave, and finally, the development of unique sculpted formations. All take extremely long periods of time. Carlsbad Caverns is over a thousand feet below the surface and includes space large enough for over a dozen football fields. Scientists estimate it has taken 60 million years to develop this extraordinary formation.

Other data supporting an old Earth come from ice core dating analyses including pH balances, evidence of volcanic eruptions, dating of gaseous inclusions, and comparisons with other ice cores. All these data point to the formation of the ice approximately 150,000 years ago. Ice cores can include records of past events, yet none show evidence of the catastrophic Noachian deluge. Scientists suggest that such a flood would have floated polar ice caps off of their beds. There is no evidence for such an event. Varves, discussed in Chapter Seven, also disprove a young Earth model.

Other evidence for a universe much older than the creationists' 6-10,000 year model comes from astronomy. A supernova explosion occurs when stars at a certain mass explode. Their matter is violently dispersed. This has been observed. What had been a normal star tends to brighten for weeks or months and then fades into faintness. A cloud of expanding gas surrounds it. The velocity of the gas can be calculated as it expands outwardly and the time of the explosion can be extrapolated. Astronomers were able to measure the dispersed gas from a supernova explosion and calculations suggest that it occurred 60,000 years ago.

Astronomers measure how far stars are from the Earth. When their light is seen through the telescope one is aware that it left its source five or ten or however many millions of light years ago, and has just arrived at Earth. Creationists, believing the universe could not be that old, say that God created light en route from stars millions of light years away, giving the appearance of age. The light could not have possibly come from those stars because of the time limitations imposed by the scriptures. *Everything* is adapted and construed to conform to the dogma of a literal interpretation of scripture. None of these omphalos beliefs/miracles is capable of being scientifically proven or disproved.

Creationists also claim that if the Earth and the solar system were as old as evolutionists and astronomers insist there should be a thick layer of dust on the moon, hundreds of feet or more, that accumulated over millions of years. Measurements of the rate of cosmic dust falling on the Earth at Mauna Loa in Hawaii were taken. Extrapolation back in time led to the hypothesis that a thick layer would be present on the moon if the solar system were old.

However, a thin layer, approximately two and a half inches thick, was actually found on the moon. Creationists claim this as evidence of a young Earth.

It has been shown that the Mauna Loa data were faulty, contaminated by materials other than cosmic dust. Satellites in space can now measure space dust directly. Scientists have found that moon rocks are eroded, not by normal weathering processes, which do not occur there, but by the constant bombardment of interplanetary dust grains called micrometeoroids. The rate of such erosion is 1-3 billionths of a meter per year. As small particles are broken off, they in turn are hit and become smaller. Scientists conclude that an extremely long period of time was necessary for the moon's surface to become as eroded as it is. It is not a "young moon." Moon rocks have been dated at 3.5+ billion years, while some of the soil is 4.6 billion years old.

The recent data predicted that there would be less than one foot of dust on the moon, which is exactly what was found. These values are correspondingly supported by values of dust levels found on Earth. Many creationists have acknowledged these data, yet some of their literature and itinerant speakers still present this "problem" as support for a recent universe.

Many meteorites have landed on the Earth and have been dated by several methods. All values agree that they are approximately 4.5 billion years old. The oldest rocks on Earth so far date to 4.03 billion years.

Creationists' assertion that there is not enough helium in the atmosphere for an old Earth is not valid. While helium is constantly being added to the atmosphere, it is also escaping by polar winds. It has also escaped during the Earth's magnetic field reversals.

It has been shown that oceanic metals such as aluminum, iron, lead, nickel, and copper remain in equilibrium in the ocean. The rate of their entrance has been shown to equal the rate of their exit, so the particular concentrations of these metals do not lend support to a young Earth thesis.

All of these factors negate a young Earth unless proponents hold to an appearance of age designed by a miracle working Creator. The Earth would *appear* old yet not *be* old. Yet miracles are outside of science. To some, this argument presents a God who creates whimsically and inconsistently, a magician, certainly not in accordance with dependable laws.

The appearance of age is called the "Omphalos Argument" ("omphalos" means navel in Greek). It relates to the puzzler question, "Since Adam was spontaneously created as an adult, did he have a navel?" Creationists would say yes, that God created him with the appearance of age and normalcy. Applying this reasoning to the creation of the Earth results in a planet with the appearance of age, with massive, stratified formations, carved lakes, round boulders and pebbles, sand, soil and silt, ancient-appearing corals, enormous chalk cliffs, fossils, expansive caves, coal and oil deposits, worn down mountains, migrating continents, and large river deltas. All of these normally take long periods of time to form. If the universe or Earth appear old, creationists say, it is not because they *are* old.

Thousands of Scientists Endorse Creationism

(Creationist Perspective) Thousands of scientists affirm the position of the young Earth, six-day creation, Noah Flood paradigm.

(Theistic Evolutionist Perspective) Few practicing biologists (geneticists, embryologists, anatomists, physiologists, ornithologists, mammalogists, etc.), geologists, or paleontologists would question that life *has* evolved. Disagreement among them centers on the *how* of evolution. All of the mechanisms are still a matter of discussion. Creationists' claim that thousands of scientists with post-graduate degrees have forsaken the evolutionary model and embraced creationism (Morris and Morris, 1996, p. 9) is difficult to believe or prove. Some mathematicians, engineers, chemists, and physicists may disclaim evolution. However, few biologists, geologists, or paleontologists, those who study the subject in minute detail, do. Creationists infer that scientists have weighed the data openmindedly on all sides and have chosen creationism apart from their religious persuasions. Where are the lists? Can there be creationists who are not religious? Can creationism be arrived at by scientific means alone? Then there should be young Earth atheists. Are there any?

Scientists who are engineers, medical doctors, dentists, architects, optometrists, nutritionists, psychologists, pharmacists, veterinarians, or information technologists are generally no more competent in their training to judge evolutionary theory than are artists, linguists, musicians, lawyers, writers, economists, philosophers, theologians, or any number of people with respectable, prestigious, post-graduate degrees in the humanities. The vast majority of educated people, even those in science, have never had a course in evolution. Just as a biologist would not be qualified to design a bridge, or a dentist to remove an appendix, many scientists are laypersons when it comes to evolutionary theory. It would be of interest if creationists could show that respectable numbers of biologists, geologists, or paleontologists, all of whom have seen the data firsthand in their training, have moved from the evolutionary paradigm. Sweeping statements about the converted evolutionists must be verified with data and how they were collected.

One biologist, a college professor with degrees from esteemed universities, admits to having moved from an evolutionary perspective to a creationist perspective even though he saw all the data supporting evolution.

His change occurred because he became involved with a Christian community which interpreted Genesis literally. As a committed Christian, he felt he *must* support the scriptures. He moved, against rationality, to the creationist position. This is an example where a person, although highly trained in science, was not informed in biblical criticism and appropriate hermeneutics (interpretation) and felt compelled to support a prescientific perspective out of loyalty to the Bible. If Christians are informed *about* the Bible, such intellectual conflict between science and faith need not occur.

It is of interest that the majority of the leadership in creationist organizations have never been to seminary and have no formal training or credentials in theology and biblical interpretation. While many have advanced degrees in science, they have not been exposed to varying perspectives of biblical interpretation and understood their support bases. They are not experts in theology and biblical interpretation. They have been indoctrinated into one position and have accepted it without being in a scholarly environment which might have enabled them to consider other possibilities. Yet they assume a position of authority as biblical interpreters as they regularly quote and exegete (interpret) the scriptures. Laypersons, no doubt impressed with the scientific credentials, never question their lack of authority in hermeneutics. I asked one itinerant biologist, a delightful man who presented a program on creationism, where he had received his biblical training. "In my local church!" he enthusiastically replied. The thought that he should have more formal training with the scriptures seemed novel to him. Whether he realized it or not, the laity to whom he spoke recognized him as an expert in two disciplines: biology *and* hermeneutics.

As can be seen from the many subjects discussed in this book, evolution is a very complex science requiring expertise in the specific fields of zoology, botany, geology, paleontology, anthropology, cosmology, astronomy, genetics, and biochemistry. Persons trained in other technical fields are not familiar with all of the supporting data of evolution and must lean on authorities. Sometimes these authorities are pastors or religious leaders, many of whom are not skilled in science and have not personally assessed the pertinent data. Unfortunately, too, some pastors are not acquainted with the discipline of biblical criticism that allows and incorporates rationalistic biblical interpretation. Scientists or pastors who hold to a young Earth creationist model are challenged to honestly grapple with the questions in Chapter Ten.

Lack of Transitional Forms/Incomplete Fossil Record

(Creationist Perspective) There is a serious lack of transitional forms in the fossil record. If indeed slow change occurred in plants and animals over time then examples of these progressions should be revealed in the record. This is exactly what Charles Darwin predicted when he presented his evolutionary thesis. He assumed that in the decades following, paleontologists would find evidence of a transitional nature that would support the theory of descent with modification.

Transitions have not been found in the fossil record or in living forms and this void discounts evolutionary theory. One creationist, a teacher, expressed it this way: "There is no half this and half that anywhere. No swoose, half swan, half goose." Another, a PhD, said, "No 'dat,' half dog, half cat."

(Theistic Evolutionist Perspective) Everyone acknowledges that gaps exist in the fossil record, however there are not as many gaps today as there were yesterday. The record is quite complete in some areas.

Creationists assume that the lack of transitions in the fossil record lends credibility to their theory of special creation, where it is postulated that organisms appeared abruptly. They ask, "Where are there organisms that are half this and half that?" The suggestion is that there should be organisms in the fossil record or still alive which are half and half, or three fourths one thing and one fourth another. This reveals a severe lack of understanding of evolution. Evolutionary changes come slowly. There are hundreds of organs, tissues and physiological processes in the body that have the potential to change, all at different rates and times. On the other hand some do not change at all. Many of the changes occurred at the molecular level or in soft tissues, organs or systems that could not be preserved and subsequently observed in the fossil record. The suggestion that in evolution the whole animal changes into something slightly modified, and then that whole animal changes again, and this repeats until half of the original organism remains and half of something new appears supports the thesis that few are knowledgeable about how evolution operates and therefore cannot judge it fairly.

There are many transitions, many examples mentioned in this book, but they aren't as creationists visualize them because each part of an organism changes at its own rate. There is rarely a perfect one half/one half animal, for that suggests that all ten organ systems, including dozens of bones and skeletal muscles, evolve at the same rate. They do not. If only one gene mutates, only one part is affected. Organism A will become Organism B by having a modified kidney. It would still be the same species but a change has occurred. That kidney may not change for hundreds of generations. At some time a population of Organism B may have a change in the jaw, or claw, or intestine, and become Organism C. If they could still viably reproduce with each other they would still be in the same species. Meanwhile, a separate population of Organism A may undergo a change in nostrils, or may have a modification in lung anatomy or reproductive behavior and become Organism D. With this scenario we have Organism A becoming B which became C and Organism A also becoming Organism D while some representatives of A may persist, basically unchanged. Some changes (mutations) are beneficial and those members survive. Other changes are not adaptive and those members die. Instead of a straight line there is branching with some dead ends and lost parts. The progression goes on and on over time; modifications occurring, with characteristics being selected for or against. The organisms are related and similar in many areas but are distinctive in other areas. If the changes become significant enough, new species evolve. If the population of Organism B goes extinct and no individuals become fossilized, a gap occurs. Even if the organism were fossilized, its soft tissue modification may not be revealed.

Transitional organisms may have changes in, among other things, structures, biochemical pathways, secreted chemicals, or even behavior. The population endures changes of various subunits over time rather than sequential changes of the whole animal body which would require synchronized mutations. Animals do not progress in a straight line from one major group such as the fishes to the amphibians with intermediates which are half and half, all systems modifying in an organized way. There is no animal halfway between a wolf and a Pekingese, even though we know the latter came from the former. The journey from the wolf is complex and circuitous and not all body parts were selected at the same time. Those who demand orderly transitions of whole organisms, half and half, misunderstand how evolutionary change occurs.

The Ordovician Period saw the earliest vertebrates, the jawless fishes. Hagfishes are living examples of this primitive group. They lack paired fins and scales and have no cerebrum or cerebellum, no jaws or stomach, are almost blind, and are hermaphroditic (both sexes) at first but can change sex. They have a partial cranium (skull) but no vertebrae, and are cartilaginous, not bony. Predictably, hagfishes appeared early in the fossil record as did the Agnaths, jawless lampreys. These are primitive vertebrates, definitely transitional, as the more advanced vertebrates developed specialized and refined structures such as bone, vertebrae, separate sexes, jaws, eyes, etc.

Eocene lake deposits in Wyoming have produced remarkable sequences of the evolution of amphibians from fishes. The development of whales from land mammals can be demonstrated as well. In neither is there the one fourth, three fourth or one half, one half condition of all body parts required by creationists.

Archeopteryx is a classic example of an organism that has characteristics from two distinct groups. Dated 150 million years ago and first discovered in the 1860s in Germany, this fossil shows reptilian and avian (bird) qualities. The seven specimens now extant reveal lizard-like teeth and other reptilian characteristics such as claws on their wings and heavy bones (not hollow as in present day birds), and a rudimentary breast bone. There is no keel on the breast bone for attachment of power flight muscles, as is seen in contemporary flying birds. Yet this animal had wings and feathers, distinctively birdlike! Furthermore, the age of its fossils coincides with the age when such a transition would be predicted.

Recent findings have given new insights into bird evolution. Fossils from France, Spain, China, and Mongolia shed light on this significant transition. In 1996, paleontologists discovered three chicken-sized dinosaur fossils in Liaoning Province in China. They appear to have proto-feathers. *Sinosauropteryx prima*, dated at 120 million years ago, appears to have structures resembling the simple feathers called plumules on modern birds (Discover, May 1998, p. 19). Parts of the world that were not previously explored by paleontologists are presently yielding exciting data. More is anticipated as the search continues across the planet.

One of the significant sources of transitional fossils is in the Karroo Basin near the southern tip of Africa. It consists of vast numbers of mammal-like reptiles including *Lystrosaurus*. Vestigial structures give significant transitional data. Paleontologists deign it a mammal if the lower jaw has only one bone (the dentary), while multiple bones designate a reptile. These animals, the synapsids (reptiles) and their offshoots, the therapsids (mammals), show a transition in jaw bones of reptiles which become modified to be the malleus and incus (inner ear bones) of mammals.

Other step by step transitions can be seen between the great white shark and the butterfly ray and between lizards and snakes. An orderly sequence of the evolution of the ceratopsians (horned dinosaurs) can be demonstrated (Edwards, 1982, pp. 2-7). Brachiopod successions are also documented in the fossil record (Zeigler, 1966, pp. 523-543 and Johnson, 1979, pp. 549-567). Onychophorans have characteristics of both annelids (worms) and arthropods (jointed footed animals). Some of their Annelid qualities include a tough cuticle coat in the absence of a mineralized body wall, little cephalization, and unjointed appendages. Arthropod characteristics include having antennae, molting (shedding their cuticle), and having reproductive organs similar in shape and size to arthropods.

Transitions occurred in humans and human-like creatures. Some can be documented. Our fully rotating shoulders came much earlier than the pelvis, legs, and feet designed for walking. Even more recently came the expansion in skull size and reduction in jaw size. This alteration left too many teeth, including the nonfunctional wisdom teeth which sometimes do not even erupt. These transitions took over four million years. They come parts at a time. Everything does not change in sync.

Troglobites are organisms that live either partially or completely in caves. They include such animals as salamanders, crayfish, fish, and various insects. Before there were caves, these animals lived above the ground. As the cave habitat became available they moved into it. Over the years many have either lost their eyes completely, have tiny spots where their eyes used to be, or have eyes that are covered with skin. Some have eyes in their embryonic stages but not as adults.

These animals are in transitional states between being sighted, having nonfunctional eyes, or being eyeless. Eyes that don't work or eyes in embryos that are absent in adults present a quandary to the creationist, however. If specifically designed, why are eyes present when none are needed or functional? Transitionalism is in action in troglobites as they progress from the ancestral state on the surface to specialized cave forms which can be very different.

Adaptive radiation occurred after species above the ground moved into this new underground ecological niche. If caves are isolated from each other, the particular organisms that have invaded each restricted environment become distinctive over time (founder effect). Many cannot breed with ancestors above the ground or with neighbors in the cave next door. This is macroevolution, the origin of species.

Australian lungfish are transitional. They respire via gills when water is plentiful and highly oxygenated, yet they can use lungs and breathe air if water levels decrease and the water is oxygen depleted. During the Devonian Period, a time of floods and droughts, some fleshy finned fish could move about both on land and in water. This ability to leave the water and invade the land, albeit lumbering in a clumsy manner, enabled them to reach an additional food supply of land plants and insects which had evolved prior to this time. They were also able to move to a new pond if the one they inhabited dried up. Some eels living today can also do this.

Monotremes such as the duck-billed platypus and spiny anteater are mammals that lay eggs! They are warm blooded, have hair, and have modified sweat glands which secrete milk (platypus) or mammary glands (anteater), all mammalian characteristics. Yet they have retained the reptilian characteristic of egg laying. Their eggs resemble reptilian eggs, having large yolks and rubbery shells. These animals have other reptilian characteristics, including a cloaca. This is a collecting area for the digestive, reproductive, and urinary systems, and there is a single opening to the outside. More advanced mammals have specialized openings for these specialized systems. Furthermore, in the platypus the penis is used solely as a reproductive organ and does not function in urination as it does in other mammals. The platypus also has pectoral girdle skeletal features similar to extinct mammal-like reptiles. Many would call this a transitional form.

The Monotremes are found native to Australia, where they had little or no competition from placental (give live birth) mammals. Marsupials, such as the koalas, kangaroos, and opossums, which are born in an immature state and must crawl into a pouch in the mother's abdomen where they attach to nipples and complete their gestation, are found mainly in Australia. These are early mammals. If they had had to compete with the more adapted placental mammals they may not have survived. It was to their advantage to be isolated from competition on the island continent. Placentals dominate. They have radiated into a multitude of habitats, from the sea (whales and porpoises), to air (bats). They occupy practically every niche available on land, from the coldest Arctic to the dry desert, rain forest, plains, mountains, caves, and burrows. The opossum, an early mammal with a scaly tail similar to a reptile, has successfully adapted to a placentally dominated environment as we all know. Possums eat anything, including human garbage, and live everywhere, including in human neighborhoods. They are *very* adaptable and have survived remarkably.

There are organisms living today that exhibit characteristics somewhere between two groups and show relationship with both groups. Opossums are one example, having scaly, prehensile tails and fur, a mix of characteristics from reptiles and mammals. Lungfish have lungs, yet they are fish. Amphibians are partly aquatic, similar to fish, yet partly terrestrial, similar to reptiles and mammals. Tadpoles have gills yet adult frogs have lungs. Birds have scales on their legs and claws at the ends of their toes, a reminder of their reptilian ancestry yet they are warm blooded.

In the late Devonian Period four footed animals (tetrapods) appeared. They retained gills and a tail fin, remnants of their heritage from the fishes, yet they had feet. Two species from Greenland, *Ichthyostega* and *Acanthostega*, are examples of these early Amphibians.

Transitions of the various body systems throughout the vertebrates are studied in comparative anatomy, a subject discussed in Chapter Seven. For instance, the kidney's development, or the heart, or various blood vessels, or bones such as vertebrae, jaw or arm bones, or the notochord, can be compared. It is of interest, for instance, that fish have a two chambered heart and appear earlier in the fossil record than amphibians, which have a three chambered heart. Reptiles, which appear next in the record, have a three and a half chambered heart, and birds and mammals, most recent, have a four chambered heart. These demonstrate transitions.

There are fossils that have characteristics shared by several distinctive groups. *Seymouria* had teeth like early amphibians and a postcranial skeleton, more reptilian. It could raise itself off the ground, a reptilian characteristic. The Condylarthra, an extinct order of hoofed mammals, gave rise to more advanced ungulates, which are plant eating, hoofed animals. They appear to be intermediate between the more modern grazers and the more primitive insectivores (shrews, moles, hedgehogs). Lancelets appear between invertebrates and vertebrates with very simple chordate characteristics. Since they were soft bodied, there are few fossils that give steps between invertebrates and vertebrates, however.

Much information is available to demonstrate that features of *Homo habilis* and *Homo erectus* are intermediate between the much earlier *Australopithecus afarensis* or the advanced *Homo sapiens* (Neanderthal) and *Homo sapiens sapiens* (Cro-Magnon). *Proconsul africanus* had a skull that resembled monkeys more than apes yet had chimpanzee-like teeth. They were similar to monkeys but have been called "dental apes."

The record *is* biased. Some species are more likely to be fossilized than others. Mollusks with their shells will fossilize more readily than tiny insects or other delicate invertebrates such as *Hydra* or sea anemones. Terrestrial vertebrates are more common in the fossil record than birds. Marine organisms are preserved more readily because they have sediment to protect them. Land animals whose dead bodies will rot, be moved, scavenged, blown away, or disintegrate will not be preserved unless some catastrophic event, such as a volcano with ash or lava or a flood with silt or a sandstorm with sand, covers them quickly and protects them. There *will* be intermediates missing. That is predicted.

Little by little, transitional fossils are discovered and fill some of the gaps in the fossil record. One of the most recent is a new species of Cretaceous dinosaur from Patagonia, the seven foot long carnivore *Unenlagia comahuensis*. It did not fly, but its forelimbs were held in a winglike manner making it the most birdlike dinosaur known. Its pelvis and long, powerful hind limbs resemble the much earlier (150 million years ago) *Archaeopteryx*, the earliest bird.

In 1996, the fossil remains of a jumping frog were discovered from the early Jurassic (~190 million years ago) Kayenta Formation of Arizona. Named *Prosalirus bitus*, this organism exhibits primitive characters of early amphibians yet it has skeletal features that indicate an ability to jump.

271

Scientists have assigned this organism to the Anura, which includes frogs and toads, and at present it is considered the oldest member of the family. Having characters of more primitive as well as more advanced groups qualifies this organism as a transitional.

A fossil of a 95 million year old, three foot long water snake found on the marine rocks on the Jordan River's West Bank has inch long rear legs. They were functionally useless but distinctive full limbs from the hip to the two toes. This vestige gives remarkable intermediate evidence of the trend from legs to leglessness in snakes. Such leg remnants have also been found in whales, giving poignant support for the thesis that whales originated on land. Other transitionals showing relatively gradual change with time are the camel, horse, rhinoceros and hominid. The horse is discussed in Chapter Seven.

The fossil record reveals transitional fossils in land plants. Those in lower strata which are early plants such as the Psilophytes of 438-360 million years ago (mya) had scale-like leaves or none at all and no roots. The pre-ferns of 380-280 mya had leaves but some were scale-like. They reproduced by spores and had wood that was similar to the gymnosperms of today. Ferns and seed ferns came next and then the cone-bearing gymnosperms. Finally, the flowering plants appeared. This progression is clear in the record and supports an evolutionary thesis. It would seem that the creationist model would result in a mixing of plant types if they all had lived at the same time and were killed and displaced by swirling catastrophic flood waters.

Mathematical Impossibilities

(Creationist Perspective) The vast numbers of gene modifications that must have taken place from earliest life to arrive at the complexity of humans, especially their brains, could not have occurred even in the time evolutionists allow for such development. Since life is so extremely complex it is beyond the realm of rationality and the laws of probability that it could have arisen from nonlife no matter how much time has been provided. The chances for a protein composed of 100 subunits (amino acids) in the appropriate sequential order to be synthesized and functional is beyond mathematical probability in the time allowed. There are potentially twenty different amino acids which would have to be in proper sequence in a protein of 100 amino acids. There are 10 to the 130th power potential variations. It is far beyond probability for a functional protein to self-assemble. This leaves no recourse but to assume there was an intelligent designer.

(Theistic Evolutionist Perspective) It has been demonstrated that a protein can be functional without having to have a perfect amino acid sequence.

Biochemists have found, for instance, that when hemoglobin is compared across the species only seven out of a total of 140 sites always have the same amino acid (Perutz, 1968). The chance for the seven to be in the right places is reduced to one in a bit more than a billion. If only one sequence formed each second, any place on Earth, a functional protein could form in 32 years. With the millions and millions of years available and the enormous size of the oceans these probabilities become reasonable (Freske, 1981, pp. 13-14). It is presumed that millions of such building blocks were formed and available for appropriate bonding with other potential building blocks. The scenario would have occurred over millions of years with utterly billions of submolecular possibilities.

Scientific data show that modern proteins have developed from ancestral proteins. All the specialized proteins were not required to have assembled at one time. Proteins functioned even though they were not as perfect as they are at present. It has been demonstrated in the laboratory that some sequences of nucleotides can spontaneously generate in small chains and, in addition, they have the capability to reproduce.

All admit that there is much to be learned about how complex organic molecules formed, but research on these questions is being accomplished even as we write. Because we cannot explain all of the mechanisms today doesn't preclude our gaining more insight tomorrow. It was just as hard for our ancestors to visualize a heavy vehicle that could become airborne or a man one day walking on the moon. Just a few decades ago experts stated that the common person would have no need for a home computer. That our minds cannot grasp the reality of molecular synthesis at present does not mean that it did not occur naturally or will not one day be explained. Inserting divine intervention whenever something is not yet explained is the "god of the gaps" again. We have seen this god retreat in the past as explanations eventually arrived.

Living with uncertainty is a quality of a critical thinker. Dependable law from the Creator well may provide explanation one day. Or it may be that we will never fully understand all of the mechanisms. To be sure, scientists will keep patiently and painstakingly trying! When these complexities are explained as being the work of an intelligent designer and not scientifically demonstrable research can be discouraged for it is presumed that the answers are in place.

Speaking of mathematical impossibilities, what are the chances that the only eight good people living on the Earth during Noah's time, out of the thousands of inhabitants, were all from the same family? And everyone in the family made it. Whew! That's quite a coincidence! Not *one* other good person????

No Macroevolution

(Creationist Perspective) Microevolution, small change that is seen in the varieties of horses, dogs or apple trees, is affirmed. But where have large changes occurred whereby populations visibly undergo modification from one species to another? Evolutionists are challenged to demonstrate these changes in the field, in a laboratory or in a lifetime. Macroevolution did not occur and therefore it cannot be demonstrated.

(Theistic Evolutionist Perspective) A creationist was once heard saying: "Show me one clear example of macroevolution, and I will believe in evolution." Microevolution is conceded, as all of the different kinds of dogs, cats, cattle, horses, grapes, roses, butterflies, frogs, snakes, hawks, beetles or mice are observed. These data cannot be denied. Yet macroevolution is just cumulative microevolution. The same factors that contribute to microevolution, change within the species, cumulatively cause enough change that living things become reproductively isolated and new species are formed. This is macroevolution.

Creationists are not all agreed on their definitions of microevolution and macroevolution. Some would not agree that new species originate and they are fuzzy on their definition of species as well as of the biblical "kinds." Others freely admit the origin of new species but define that as microevolution. Creationists do have a conundrum. If "kinds" are genera, or families, then large groups of organisms are lumped together as a "kind." Yet they can't lump primates at the genera or family levels, for that does not give *Homo sapiens sapiens* distinctiveness. Humans *cannot* be lumped with other primates. They *must* be a "species-kind" yet others must be "genus or family-kinds" or there would be a problem of space on the ark. It's very hard to define kind.

New species can definitely be demonstrated, as adaptive radiation has occurred. Creationists have to acknowledge that all of the different species in the world today as well as the extinct ones could not have fit on the ark. All of the species of kangaroos in Australia alone (living and extinct) would have begun to crowd the ark. Speciation, to many scientists, *is* macroevolution. It can be demonstrated to have occurred in isolated populations, which migrated from parent groups. Over time populations have modified such that they cannot successfully reproduce with each other or with the parent group. Cave animals provide one example of this. Many insects look alike, yet are distinct species and cannot interbreed.

Admittedly, it is not easy to demonstrate macroevolution in the laboratory or even in a lifetime, although microbiologists have seen new bacterial strains arise in laboratory settings. Part of the reason we must have flu shots every year is that new viral strains have evolved and must be combated. Creationists call this microevolution. Macroevolution's *results* can be observed as distinctive species are seen, yet its *process* often takes long periods. Evolution, even punctuated evolution, by definition, takes place over long periods of time. Inferred data to support it come from genetic analysis as well as biogeography, fossil evidence and comparative anatomy. Genetic analysis shows 18 of 23 pairs of chromosomes that are nearly identical to their counterparts in gorillas and chimpanzees. The other five pair differ at inverted and translocated regions. The duplications on a gibbon chromosome (#19) correspond to human chromosomes #2 and #17. The relationships, the variations, tell a story that can be inferred. Evolution is change over long periods of time through many small modifications which cannot always be observed in a lifetime, a laboratory, or in the fossil record. How do creationists handle inferred data? Is it ignored?

Evolution is to Blame for the Ecological Crisis

(Creationist Perspective) Since evolutionists do not believe in the Genesis creation accounts, they do not embrace the responsibility of being stewards of God's creation as outlined in that book. Therefore, they give license to destroying the beauty of the Earth. Since no one brought us here, no one designed us, then no one demands environmental stewardship or accountability.

(Theistic Evolutionist Perspective) In reality, most evolutionists are theists so it is faulty reasoning for creationists to blame evolution for the negation of a God who requires morality and environmental sensitivity. In addition, morality is not dependent upon what one believes about the age of the Earth, how long it took for us to get here, or whether there was a worldwide flood. One's morality is based upon many factors and beliefs, which may or may not include a righteous God who demands responsible living. It cannot be generalized that atheists are immoral or irresponsible towards the environment.

Ironically, rather than evolution being blamed for environmental degradation, Christians have sometimes been accused of contributing to such abuse because of a misinterpretation of Genesis 1:26 or Psalm 8, where humankind was given license to rule, subdue, or have dominion over all other creatures. There doesn't seem to be much emphasis within the creationist movement regarding the prevention of habitat destruction that leads to the extinction of species, even though Genesis clearly tells the humans to till (use) and to *keep* (preserve). We've done a lot of tilling but not very much keeping.

A theology that holds that this Earth will pass away and that the parousia (return of Jesus Christ) is near can contribute to less concern for preserving the Earth for generations to come. When humankind is perceived as the center and epitome of creation, rather than as an integrated part of it, the result can be an attitude of use and abuse that is detrimental to the natural order. The scriptures challenge Christians to be stewards for the created order (Genesis 1:26, 2:15 and Leviticus 25:4-5). This responsibility can be ignored or overlooked when belief in an imminent end of the world is held.

Little is said in churches about the population explosion and its impact upon the environment. How does the caring Christian respond to this reality? Some might suggest that there is some truth to the saying "It is no longer fruitful to multiply!" (See Genesis 1:28) It is clear that both evolutionists and creationists have contributed to environmental misuse. It must also be said that many in both arenas have seriously taken the charge to keep God's handiwork and are conscientiously involved in its renewal and preservation.

Evolution is the Source of Societal Problems and Atheism

(Creationist Perspective) Evolutionary theory is responsible for numerous social phenomena such as humanism, communism, pornography, chauvinism, euthanasia, racism, beastiality, promiscuity, abortion, scientism, slavery, child and spousal abuse, animism, divorce, infanticide, atheism, liberalism and many more. Belief in evolutionary theory denies a just and holy God who calls people to righteous living. Therefore humans are free to do whatever they wish and these behaviors are the inevitable result.

(Theistic Evolutionist Perspective) The long list of societal ills that creationists claim are caused by evolutionary theory arouses emotions in people who think uncritically. They reason that if the results of evolutionary theory are all of these evils then, without doubt, evolution must be rejected. This argument bypasses whether evolutionary theory is valid by arguing against its supposed consequences. Many people fall for this reasoning.

Do creationists maintain that all of the societal phenomena they list are new, and have developed since the mid 19th Century when Darwin published his *Origin of Species*? Were they nonexistent prior to 1859? These isms and sins go back as far as humankind's existence on this Earth. They would not disappear if evolutionary theory were declared untrue by all of science. In fact, these behaviors and beliefs are expressed today across the globe by humans who have absolutely no understanding whatsoever as to the tenets of evolutionary theory. Ironically, the scriptures record many of these ills during biblical times: killing of innocents, worship of idols of all kinds, disrespect for women or people of other tribes, sexual abuse, slavery, ethnic cleansing, genocide. The evil world of Noah's era was not caused by evolutionary belief! Furthermore, evolution has been minimally taught in the last century across America. Few Americans are acquainted with its theses. How could it be blamed for all of these ills when very few really know the science of evolution?

If one throws out evolutionary theory because some have misinterpreted it and evil has resulted, then to be consistent, any number of technologies or beliefs would need to be discarded. Since computers carry pornography, then they must be rejected. Any idea or machine can be perverted, but that does not establish that the original thought or machine was less than truthful or useful. Many beneficial technologies, such as the telephone or automobile, have been converted to agents of crime. Advertising in itself is innocuous, yet it can lead to greed, discontent, covetousness, waste and overconsumption. Should it be totally discontinued or outlawed? Dynamite, which was originally designed to help in road building and subsequently became an instrument of death, has been used for purposes far afield from the original intention.

This is where critical thinking must be employed. If evolutionary theory is invalid, it must be proven so. It cannot be eliminated because of some misapplied use or misunderstood application. This would be equivalent to throwing out religion or the Bible because some people have misinterpreted their tenets and in their name have killed, enslaved, excluded, or discriminated. Many suggest that the evils we see in society derive from the selfish and cruel choices we make which come as a result of free will. Sin we call it. It has been with humans from the beginning and won't be eradicated if evolution were to be disproved. Christians believe it can only be conquered through Christ's atoning death at the cross.

Cambrian Explosion Explained by Special Creation

(Creationist Perspective) All of the major invertebrate phyla have been found in Cambrian rocks and there are no records of evolutionary ancestors. The sudden explosive appearance of varying life forms in early strata is what would be expected if a supernatural Creator, intelligent Designer, abruptly created these organisms. That is exactly what the geological data appear to demonstrate.

(Theistic Evolutionist Perspective) The farther one goes back in geological history, the harder it is to find evidence for life. Rocks are not eternal. The earlier they were formed, the less chance they remain. Some on ocean floors are destroyed over time by continental movements, plate

tectonics. As continents and ocean basins collide often the continents override the ocean sediments, forcing them down where they are destroyed by the Earth's heat. They may in the future erupt back to the surface as lavas but they are changed and any fossils they may have housed are long gone. In addition, older rocks are covered with newer strata. Pressure and heat result in change in rocks and any fossils they housed are changed or destroyed as well. Reality is such that records of first and early life are for the most part *gone*! That does not mean that they never existed.

All admit that evidence of the Earth's earliest life is rare. The older the remains sought, the fewer the chances of finding anything. Exacerbating the situation is the reality that Precambrian life forms (prior to 570 million years ago) were delicate, most lacking hard parts, so many never fossilized to begin with. However, in recent decades some exciting new findings have been discovered; there is optimism for continued insight into life's earliest existence on this planet.

The Gunflint Formation, which occurs on the United States/Canadian border between Minnesota and Ontario and dates back over two billion years, has yielded remarkable data on early life. With state-of-the-art technology, including use of the electron microscope, fossil remains of cells have been detected in these ancient rocks as well as from rock in the Simpson Desert, deep in the Australian outback. These fossils are varied. The cells have filamentous and spherical shapes and occur in clusters or colonies. The Bitter Springs region of central Australia has yielded a variety of filamentous and spheroid microfossils.

Since the 1960s, much has been learned about Precambrian life. Several species of cyanobacterium-like filamentous fossils as old as 3.5 billion years have been found in the Early Archean Apex Basalt of northwestern Western Australia. These fossils date back to more than three quarters of the age of the Earth. Their discovery is exciting, as it reveals that life was apparently flourishing only a few hundred million years after the Earth first became hospitable to life. The science of geochronology specializes in determining the age of early rocks.

Many scientists are now concentrating on this ancient era, and new species are regularly being identified. Because scientists must err on the side of being accurate, they can only accept fossils that have reached a fairly complex level of development. Obviously, unicellular (one celled) life existed prior to the existence of multicellular or colonial forms, but microscopic, simple organisms are most difficult to identify in these ancient rock formations.

Besides Australia and North America, discoveries are coming from many areas including Brazil, China, England, France, India, South Africa, Israel, and Russia. More than 95% of the scientists (paleobiologists: those who study ancient life) who have ever researched Precambrian life are living today. They concentrate on the chemical environment of the early Earth and how life evolved, in addition to searching for and identifying fossils. Much has been learned in the past twenty years and new insights and data are expected in the months and years ahead. It's a very exciting area of research. One thing becomes clear: The "Cambrian Explosion" was not quite as explosive as was once thought.

Esteemed Scientists and the Founding Fathers Were Creationists

(Creationist Perspective) The fact that famous scientists in the past, many of whom were Christians, as well as the devout founding fathers of the United States of America were creationist gives credibility to this paradigm. If so many brilliant and devout scientists and statesmen, including Newton and Kepler, Washington and Jefferson, believed in creationism it must have some validity.

(Theistic Evolutionist Perspective) It is true that esteemed scientists from the past such as Newton, Boyle, Priestly, Morse, Galileo, Maxwell, Kepler, Pasteur, and Pascal affirmed a six day creation by fiat, ex nihilo. It is said that Robert Boyle and Joseph Priestley saw science as a religious vocation. Respected men of deep religious commitment who were distinguished leaders in early America were creationist as well.

However, all of these men lived before evolutionary theory became an option so there was no choice for these traditionalists to be anything but creationist. *Everyone* in western culture at that time who was not atheist assumed a biblical literalism and held to creationist belief. This was prior to the discipline of biblical criticism. Data supporting evolutionary theory were not available either. In addition, these men lived during a period when religious authority was strong and there were few opportunities to diverge from the dominant thought of the church.

While the scientists mentioned above made great contributions to science, they did not have all knowledge. Einstein came along and modified Newton's laws. These scientists were limited not only in their religious perceptions, but also by what was known in science at that time. Science, technology, and religious understanding have progressed beyond what they could have imagined. We will never know how these men would have responded had they seen the impressive data supporting evolution that has accumulated in the past century! None of them owned VCR's, drove Oldsmobiles, or understood evolutionary theory and a scholarly biblical exegesis. That doesn't mean they wouldn't have purchased, driven or affirmed them if they'd had the chance!

Evolutionists' Past Errors

(Creationist Perspective) There are several well-known examples of errors that evolutionists have made in the past and therefore everyone should be wary of their claims. The Piltdown man and Nebraska man are prime examples of evolutionists' attempt to jump at data to substantiate their thesis without using scientific rigor. If they did it in the past how do we know they are not doing it in the present?

(Theistic Evolutionist Perspective) Scientists are human. Humans err. Science exists to reveal truth, but in the process falsehood sometimes prevails. Hopefully it is recognized, admitted, and corrected, the sooner the better. The Piltdown hoax reflected a gross error on the part of the scientific community. It wasn't exposed for over forty years! In 1912, fragments of a cranium, jawbone, and other bones were purportedly found in a gravel formation on Piltdown Common near Lewes, Sussex, England. These bones were claimed to represent a "missing link" between the apes and humans. Not until 1953 was the cranium identified as that of a modern human, no more than 50,000 years old, and the jaw and teeth were recognized to have come from an orangutan. The bones had been deliberately stained and the teeth filed and then planted at the site.

The perpetrator(s) of this hoax remains a mystery. The scientific community uncritically jumped to judgment but finds some comfort that it was science's self-correcting properties which eventually led to the exposure of this fraud and admission of the error. This episode points out the frailty of scientists who desperately wanted to believe what these bones were claimed to represent. Their bias and uncritical questioning of the data for so long is disappointing and embarrassing. Peer review took decades to do its work.

In 1922, evolutionists claimed that a tooth that had been found in Nebraska gave evidence of an intermediate between apes and humans. They were dead wrong! About five years later it was shown that this tooth from so-called "Nebraska Man" was from an extinct peccary!

Another example of science correcting itself was when *Ramapithecus* was heralded as the ancestor of man-like creatures. Some upper jaw fragments from India were interpreted to be from a forerunner of man. For over two decades the proponents of this theory were not adequately challenged. Finally, in the 1980s, this hypothesis was destroyed by a researcher in molecular chemistry who demonstrated that *Ramapithecus* was far too old to be related to hominids. Further study within the scientific community affirmed this thesis and the idea that *Ramapithecus* was an early man-like creature has been negated. This is science at work.

Science is accomplished by people who, though trained in its methods, sometimes prejudge or develop conscious or unconscious agendas that they hope will be affirmed. Some are not careful in gathering and interpreting data, and other scientists fail by not carefully assessing their colleagues' work and offering critical peer review. Creationists point out that while scientists presently claim the universe to be approximately 13.7 billion years old that it wasn't long ago that they told us it was 14 - 20 billion years old. The suggestion is that scientists are always changing their numbers and conclusions. Yet scientists are the first to acknowledge that the search for knowledge leads to additional information, which can modify previous assertions. The very nature of science is to disprove and correct. Science is tentative. The journey for truth will *never* end!

Scientists recognize that theses they presently hold may be disproved, yet they point out that evolutionary theory has stood for almost 150 years and has been seriously challenged from within and from without. Although it has been modified as new insights are revealed, its main thesis of change over time is continually supported rather than weakened as more data accumulate from a variety of disciplines. Whether they were made innocently or purposely, one hopes the errors of the past will encourage researchers to be more rigorous in identifying and correcting sloppy science. It is unfair, however, to suggest that just because there have been errors in the past that everything scientists have concluded relating to evolutionary theory must be suspect.

Creationists, also being human, have made serious errors which they have been forced to admit. These errors include claiming for years that human footprints occurred contemporaneously with dinosaur footprints in the Paluxy River area in Texas. After many years, creationists had to acknowledge they were wrong about the Lewis Overthrust in Glacier National Park, where older fossils were found in layers above younger fossils. Geologists hypothesized and proved, even to openminded creationists, that the Precambrian limestones slid along on top of much younger shales as a result of continental movement. Creationists had claimed previously that these fossils, apparently in the wrong order, would disprove evolution. Not so.

Everyone makes mistakes. Evolutionists and creationists must both be intent on attempting to falsify whatever they propound. That will facilitate progress in the search for truth.

No Support for Life's Origins

(Creationist Perspective) Evolutionists cannot demonstrate where or how life originated. There is a huge void in their literature when it comes to how life began, abiogenesis (bio = life; genesis = beginning), and this seriously weakens evolution's credibility. In fact, it supports the design hypothesis: an omnipotent Creator abruptly created life.

(Theistic Evolutionist Perspective) Scientists are very candid in admitting that little is known about abiogenesis. Much of it is profound mystery. Some are pessimistic that we will ever know exactly how life originated on the Earth. Even if someone produced life in a laboratory tomorrow, we could not be sure that the method was the exact way life originally began. Is there more than one road to "life?"

As always, however, scientists *want to know*. Some things have been learned about the early Earth's chemical composition and what is necessary for molecules to form. Hypotheses have been suggested. Did life begin as an information-containing clay mineral material that eventually developed into DNA based life? Might organic molecules have generated at deep-sea volcanic vents? Was there an "organic soup?" Was it a thick or thin soup?

Interestingly, meteorites have been found to contain amino acids, the building blocks of proteins. Through the space program we have learned of many nonbiologic organic (carbon based) compounds from the hydrogen-rich clouds around Jupiter and Saturn and in comets. It is apparent that organic compounds, those necessary for life, exist in many regions of the cosmos. More than eighty five different kinds have been identified.

How these simple compounds became the complex molecules such as carbohydrates (sugars and starches), fats, proteins, and nucleic acids remains a mystery, though some things are known about energy requirements, sources, and some intermediate sequences. The challenges of how metabolic pathways developed and the ability of cells to replicate (divide) remain. Many scientists are working on these questions and much has been published in the last decade that sheds light on the subject.

We do know that millions of years were required for the development of life, bit by bit. This isn't the first time science has confronted mystery. The drama unfolds.....The book is nowhere near being closed. It must always be remembered that just because we don't understand everything at present doesn't mean that we can't understand it in the future. The reality is also that we, indeed, may never know how life arose on this planet but to claim an intelligent designer in the face of such mystery will discourage the pursuit of a scientific explanation.

It is very important to point out that how life arose is a distinctive area of science studied by biochemists, molecular biologists, geneticists and others. Evolution, change over time, is a different discipline and is studied by biologists, geologists, paleontologists, chemists and biogeographers. Lumping these two distinctive areas together can confuse issues. We may not know how life arrived, but there are abundant data supporting its change over time.

Evolution is the Antithesis of a Loving God

(Creationist Perspective) Evolution, with its pain, cruelty, death, competition, extinction, and waste does not reflect the loving and orderly nature of God who declared his creation "Good." The evolutionary paradigm is contrary to God's spirit of grace, compassion, and love. God created only vegetarians in the perfect world before sin. Death was not part of that plan at all.

(Theistic Evolutionist Response) The following questions are asked:

1. Why would God have allowed a worldwide flood to destroy the good creation, to kill billions of organisms and thousands of people, including innocent children? Was this fair and loving and consistent with God's character?

2. Why would this same God encourage the Israelites to kill whole groups of people? With respect to Jericho, Joshua 6:21 states "They devoted the city to the Lord and destroyed with the sword every living thing in it, men and women, young and old, cattle, sheep, and donkeys." Joshua 10:29-30 relates that "Joshua and all Israel with him moved on from Makkedah to Libnah and attacked it. The Lord also gave that city and its king into Israel's hand. The city and everyone in it Joshua put to the sword. He left no survivors there." In the following verses they moved on to Lachish, Eglon, Hebron, and Debir and left no survivors there either. All who breathed, presumably including innocent children, were destroyed throughout the whole region.

3. Why were animals given sharp teeth, camouflage, speed, stealth, venom, nocturnal adaptation and night vision, and poisonous chemicals to be squirted if there was to be no death?

4. Why is there such an overabundance of reproductive capability if there was to be no death? Millions of insect eggs, acorns, frog eggs, sperm, caviar, pollen grains; each bird pair with many eggs, turtles laying dozens of eggs, dogs giving birth to a dozen puppies. The Earth could not

support this exponential growth. Death is inevitable. Nature selects the fittest.

5. How can a food web operate with no death?
6. How can soil be productive with no organic nutrients, which come from other living forms that have died?

Was all of this design?

Only God Knows the Mystery of Creation

(Creationist Perspective) Since science is experimental observation, no one can know what happened on the Earth before there were people to witness and record it. God used processes that are not now operating, so there is no way we can know the mechanisms of his creation or how long it took. We read his word of truth, the Bible, to know what happened. Only God was there and he told us in Genesis what occurred. We can't prove it, demonstrate it, or falsify it. It must be taken on faith.

(Theistic Evolutionist Perspective) Over the centuries, God has been pleased to reveal some of creation's secrets. Modern genetics and biochemistry have given us profound insight into how we are made, including an understanding of the anatomy and physiology of the DNA molecule. Geology with its fossils and records in the strata has given us data that tell quite a story about the past. Science operates on inference as well as observation and experimentation and while there are many unanswered questions about our origins, we have indeed learned a lot in the past century. Some suggest that through science God has given us one of his greatest gifts, the gift of understanding ourselves, our beginnings, and our relationship to the created order. Many Christians who are scientists are awed at this knowledge and can only thank and honor the One who created and sustains it all. Meanwhile we also are thankful for the scriptures which give us purpose, hope, guidance, inspiration and encouragement.

Evolutionists are Secular Humanists

(Creationist Perspective) Evolutionists are secular humanists.

(Theistic Evolutionist Perspective) It is not uncommon for creationists to refer in their literature to anyone who believes in evolution as a secular humanist whether he or she is an evolutionary naturalist, atheist who does not affirm a creator God, or a theistic evolutionist, theologian, or pastor, who is convinced that there is a creator God. The inference is that evolutionists are non-religious, atheistic people. The two belief positions, evolution and

humanism, are held in tandem. Humanism is not defined but is perceived as being contrary to a Christian belief position.

The term "humanism" came from the Latin "humanitas" and it denoted scholarship in the classics: grammar, poetry, rhetoric, history, and philosophy, leading to an educational and political ideal. This term was first used by 19th Century scholars in Germany, who described the Renaissance emphasis on classical studies. It described the striving for virtue, including understanding, kindness, compassion, and mercy, as well as judgment, eloquence, and love of honor. Actions as well as contemplation were sought.

While modern humanistic thought continues to emphasize the importance of personal worth and significance, there are some who include a nontheistic dimension to this philosophy. That is not true of all contemporary humanists. They should not be universally judged as atheistic. In fact, some describe Christianity as humanistic. It has been demonstrated through God's creating humankind in his image and in Christ's sacrificial death that the individual is of utmost value. Indeed, the gospel asserts the preciousness and uniqueness of each soul. Jesus relates the story of the shepherd who was willing to risk his life for one lost sheep (Luke 15:4-8). Terminology should be defined. Sweeping name calling is generally nonproductive, not honorable, and a sure sign of a weak defense.

The word secular, of course, rings bells for the Christian. This is the antithesis of sacred. To call someone secular indicts his or her spirituality and faith commitment. Judgmentalism rears its ugly head. When creationists call other Christians names, they are not honoring their Lord.

Humankind: The Epitome of Creation

(Creationist Perspective) Humans are the epitome of creation. All creatures and nature revolve around them. They were given dominion over all of nature, created in the image of God with an immortal soul. They could not possibly have arisen from prehumans and share a common ancestry with primates such as apes.

(Theistic Evolutionist Perspective) Many people in the 19th Century were shocked at the idea that humankind may have risen from lower animals. Theologically, they had always seen *Homo sapiens sapiens* as the culmination and crown of the creation, made in God's image, given dominion over all other life forms. We were special. It was for us that Jesus died. We, alone, have a soul and immortality. We are set apart and could not possibly have had relationship to the beasts of the field.

This mindset, of course, had to be modified. Many see that self-image as a prideful one and appreciate that evolution requires a humility of us that does not come easily. Evolution does not negate the theology that humans are very special to God. It was in human form that God sent the Christ. Indeed, it was for humans that Jesus suffered and provided a deliverance. It is through humans that God is pleased to do his work on this Earth. Their hands and feet are used for divine purpose. They were given the responsibility to till and keep God's creation. It was to humans that God gave minds which are able to contemplate the Creator and the Creator's marvelous handiwork. God's plan is to spend eternity with humans.

Evolution declares that humans are part of the created order, that we have much in common with other species and we are all interdependent. It explains our differences as well as our similarities and presents an order for which the Creator can be praised. Environmental issues that impact this thinking are myriad, and to many, the sooner we see ourselves as part of the created order rather than lord over it, the better for every one and every thing.

Genesis 2:7 declares that man came from the dust of the ground. Is that any more earthshaking than belief in evolution's slow change over time? Dust, a rib, or primate ancestor....does it make any difference? Is pride the reason that this thesis is so difficult to accept?

Jesus, Lord of the universe, had humble beginnings in a manger, born of a species called human. We, too, had humble beginnings.

> It is high time that we grew up and left the Garden. We are indeed Eden's children, yet it is time to place Genesis alongside the geocentric myth in the basket of stories that once, in a world of intellectual naivete, made helpful sense. As we walk through the gates, aware of the dazzling richness of the genuine biological world, there might even be a smile on the Creator's face— that at long last His creatures have learned enough to understand His world as it truly is.
>
> Kenneth R. Miller, in *Finding Darwin's God*, p. 56

Additional Reading

Alters, Brian J. & Alters, Sandra M. (2001). *Defending evolution in the classroom: A guide to the creation/evolution controversy.* Sudbury, MA: Jones and Bartlett Publishers.

Aneshansley, Daniel J. & Eisner, T. (1969). Biochemistry at 100 C: Explosive secretory discharge of bombardier beetles (*Brachinus*). *Science, 165*, 61-63.

Alexander, Shana (1986). The Serengetti: The glory of life. *National Geographic, 169* (5).

Anderson, Bernhard W. (Ed.). (1984). *Creation in the Old Testament.* Philadelphia: Fortress Press.

Anderson, Bernhard W. (1987). *Creation versus chaos.* Philadelphia: Fortress Press.

Barbour, Ian G (1966).*Issues in science and religion.* Englewood Cliffs, NJ: Prentice-Hall.

Behe, Michael (1996). *Darwin's black box: The biochemical challenge to evolution.* New York: The Free Press.

Benton, Michael (1986). *The story of life on Earth.* New York: Warwick Press.

"Book of the Year (1996): Life Sciences:PALEONTOLOGY" Britannica Online.<http://www.eb.com:180/cgi-bin/g?DocF=boy/96/JO2875.html>

Brooke, John H. (1991). *Science and religion: Some historical perspectives,* Cambridge: Cambridge University Press.

Brush, Stephen (1982). Finding the age of the Earth by physics or by faith? *Journal of Geological Education, 30*, 34-58.

Chittick, Donald E. (1978). *The controversy: Roots of the creation-evolution conflict.* Portland, OR: Multnomah Press.

Coffin, Harold (1983). *Origin by design.* Washington, DC: Review and Herald Publ. Assoc.

Colbert, E. H. (1965). *The age of reptiles.* New York: W. W. Norton.

Conkin, Paul L. (1998). *When all the gods trembled: Darwinism, Scopes, and American intellectuals.* New York: Rowman and Littlefield Publishers.

Criswell, W. A. (1957). *Did man just happen?* Grand Rapids, MI: Zondervan Publ. House.

Davis, Jimmy H. & Poe, Harry L. (2002). *Designer universe: Intelligent design and the existence of God.* Nashville: Broadman & Holman Publishers.

Dawloms. Richard (1995). *River out of Eden: A Darwinian view of life (on DNA).* New York: Basic Books.

Dawson, J. W. (1868). *Acadian geology: The geological structure, organic remains, and mineral resources of Nova Scotia, New Brunswick and Prince Edward Island.* (2nd ed.). London: MacMillan and Co.

Dean, Jeffrey, et al. (1990). Defensive spray of the bombardier beetle: A biological pulse jet. *Science, 248,* 1219-1221.

DeCamp, L. S. (1988). *The great monkey trial.* New York: Doubleday.

Dembski, William A. (Ed.). (1999). *Mere creation: Science, faith and intelligent design.* Downer's Grove, IL: InterVarsity Press.

Dembski, William A. (1999). *Intelligent design: The bridge between science and theology.* Downer's Grove, IL: InterVarsity Press.

Denton, Michael (1986). *Evolution: A theory in crisis.* Bethesda, MD: Adler & Adler, Publ.

Dettner, Konrad (1987). Chemosystematics and evolution of beetle chemical defenses. *Annual Review of Entomology, 32,* 17-48.

Dorf, Erling (1980). Petrified forests of Yellowstone. *The National Park Handbook Series, 108.* Washington, DC: U.S. Gvmt. Printing Office.

Draper, John William (1898). *History of the conflict between religion and science*. New York: D. Appleton and Co.

Dundes, Alan (Ed.). (1988). *The flood myth*. Berkeley, CA: University of California Press.

Edwards, Denis (1999). *The God of evolution*. New York: Paulist Press.

Edwards, Frederick (1982). The dilemma of the horned dinosaurs. *Creation/Evolution, IX*, 2-7.

Eisner, Thomas, et al. (1977). Chemistry of defensive secretions of bombardier beetles (*Brachinini, Metrinini, Ozaenini, Paussini). Journal of Insect Physiology, 23*, 1382-1386.

Eldredge, Niles (1982). *The monkey business: A scientists looks at creationism*. New York: Washington Square Press.

Eldredge, Niles (2000). *The pattern of evolution*. New York: W. H. Freeman and Co.

Fishes: THE PRIMITIVE FISHES (LIVING REPRESENTATIVES): The cartilaginous fishes: sharks, skates, rays (Chondrichthyes, or Selachii): EVOLUTION AND CLASSIFICATION: Britannica Online. Http://www.eb.com:180/cgi-bin/g?DocF=macro/5002/34/27.html. Jan. 15, 1998.

Fishes: THE PRIMITIVE FISHES (LIVING REPRESENTATIVES): "The fleshy-finned fishes (Carcopterygii):Lungfishes (Dipnoi)" Britannica Online. Http://www.eb.com:180/cgi-bin/g?Doc F=macro/5002/34/29.html. Jan. 15, 1998.

Fortey, Richard (1997). *Life: A natural history of the first four billion years of life on Earth*. New York: Vintage Books.

Freske, Stanley (1980). Evidence supporting a great age for the universe. *Creation/Evolution, II*.

Freske, Stanley (1981). Creationist misunderstanding, misrepresentation, and misuse of the second law of thermodynamics. *Creation/Evolution, IV*, 13-14.

Fritz, William (1982). *The geology of the Lamar River Formation, Northeast Yellowstone National Park.* 33rd Annual Field Conference, Wyoming Geological Association Guidebook.

Gentry, Robert (1988). *Creation's tiny mystery.* (2nd ed.) Knoxville: Earth Science Associates.

Gilkey, Langdon (1959). *Maker of heaven and earth.* New York: University Press of America.

Gish, Duane T. (1978). *Evolution? The fossils say NO.* San Diego, CA: Creation-Life Publ.

Gish, Duane T. (1990). *The amazing story of creation from science and the Bible.* El Cajon, CA: Institute for Creation Research.

Gish, Duane T. (1993). *Creation scientists answer their critics.* El Cajon, CA: ICR.

Gish, Duane T. (1995). *Evolution: The fossils still say NO,* El Cajon, CA: ICR.

Godfrey, Laurie R. (Ed.). (1983). *Scientists confront creationism.* New York: W. W. Norton & Co.

Godfrey, Stephen J. (1989-90). Tetrapod fossil footprints, polonium halos, and the Colorado Plateau. *Creation/Evolution. XXVI,* 8-15.

Goldsmith, Tim & Zimmerman, W. (2001). *Biology, evolution and human nature.* John Wiley and Sons.

Gould, Stephen Jay (1991). To be a platypus. In *Bully for Brontosaurus* (pp. 269-280). New York: W. W. Norton.

Griffiths, M. (1988). The platypus. *Scientific American, 258* (5), 84-91.

Haught, John F. (1995). *Science and religion: From conflict to conversation.* New York: Paulist Press.

Haught, John F. (2000). *God after Darwin: A theology of evolution.* Boulder, CO: Westview Press.

Hearn, Walter T. (1997). *Being a Christian in science.* Downers Grove, IL: InterVarsity Press.

Huchingson, James E. (1993). *Religion and the natural sciences: The range of engagement.* New York: Harcourt Brace College Publishers.

Hughes, Liz Rank (Ed.). (1992). *Reviews of creationist books.* Berkeley, CA: National Center for Science Education, Inc.

Hughes, Robert B. & Laney, J. Carl (1990). *New Bible companion.* Wheaton, IL: Tyndale House Publ.

Hunt, C. Warren, Collins, L. G. & Skobelin, E. A. (1992). *Expanding geospheres:Energy and mass transfers from Earth's interior.* Calgary: Polar Publ. Co.

Isaak, Mark (1997). *Bombardier beetle and the argument of design.* The Talk. Origins Archive. http://www.talkorigins.org/faqs/bombardier.html

Isaak, Mark (1998). *Problems with a global flood* (2nd ed.). The Talk Origins Archive. http://www.talkorigins.org/faqs/faq-noahs-ark.html

Johnson, M. E. (1979). Evolutionary brachiopod lineages from the Llandovery series of eastern Iowa. *Paleontology, 22* (3), 549-567.

Johnson, Phillip (1991). *Darwin on trial.* Downer's Grove, IL: InterVarsity Press.

Johnson, Phillip (1995). *Reason in the balance: The case against naturalism in science, law, and Education.* Downer's Grove, IL: InterVarsity Press.

Johnson, Phillip (1997). *Defeating Darwinism by opening minds,* Downer's Grove, IL: InterVarsity Press.

Kitcher, Philip (1994). *Abusing science: The case against creationism.* Cambridge, MA: MIT Press.

Kofahl, Robert E. (1977). *Handy dandy evolution refuter.* San Diego: Beta Books.

Kofahl, Robert E. (1981). The bombardier shoots back. *Creation/Evolution, V*, 12-14.

Loftin, Robert W. (1988). Caves and evolution. *Creation/Evolution, XXIII*, 21-28.

Lubenow, Marvin (1992). *Bones of contention: A creationist assessment of human fossils*,Grand Rapids, MI: Baker Book House.

MacDonald, David (1988). The flood: Mesopotamian archaeological evidence. *Creation/Evolution, XXIII*, 14-20.

MacKay, Donald M. (1982). *Science and the quest for meaning*, Grand Rapids, MI: Eerdmans Publishing Co.

Marty, Martin E. & Appleby, R. Scott (Eds.). (1991). *Fundamentalisms observed: The fundamentalism project* (Vol. I). Chicago: University of Chicago Press.

Marty, Martin E. & Appleby, R. Scott (Eds.). (1994). *Accounting for fundamentalism* (Vol. IV). Chicago: University of Chicago Press.

Marty, Martin E. & Appleby, R. Scott (Eds.). (1995). *Fundamentalism comprehended* (Vol. V). Chicago: University of Chicago Press.

Miller, Kenneth R. (1999). *Finding Darwin's God: A scientist's search for common ground between God and evolution*. New York: Cliff Street Books.

Milner, Richard (1993). *The Encyclopedia of Evolution*. New York: Holt.

Mixter, Russell (Ed.). (1959). *Evolution and Christian thought today*. Grand Rapids, MI: Eerdman's Publ.

Montagu, Ashley (Ed.). (1984). *Science and creationism*. New York: Oxford University Press.

Moreland, J. P. (Ed.). (1994). *The creation hypothesis*. Downer's Grove, IL: InterVarsity Press.

Moreland, J.P. & Reynolds, John M. (Eds.). (1999). *Three views on creation and evolution*. Grand Rapids, MI: Zondervan Publishing House.

Morris, Henry (1963). *The twilight of evolution*. Grand Rapids, MI: Baker Book House.

Morris, Henry (1986). *Science and the Bible*. Chicago: Moody Press.

Morris, Henry & Parker, G. (1987). *What is creation science?* El Cajon, CA: Master Books.

Morris, Henry & Morris, John (1996a). *The modern creation trilogy: Scripture and creation* (Vol. 1). Green Forest, AR: Master Books.

Morris, Henry & Morris, John (1996b). *The modern creation trilogy:Science and creation* (Vol. 2). Green Forest, AR: Master Books.

Morris, Simon Conway (1998). *The crucible of creation*. New York: Oxford University Press.

National Academy of Sciences (1998). *Teaching about evolution and the nature of science*. Washington, DC: National Academy Press.

Nelson, Dwight (1998). *Built to last*. Nampa, ID: Pacific Press Publ. Assoc.

Numbers, Ronald L. (1992). *The creationists: The evolution of scientific creationism*. Berkeley: Univ. of Calif. Press.

Padian, Kevin & Chiappe, Luis M. (February 1998). The origin of birds and their flight. *Scientific American* (38-47).

Parker, Gary (1994). *Creation:Facts of life*. Colorado Springs, CO: Master Books.

Perutz, M. F. & Lehmann (1968). *Nature, 219*, 902.

Polkinghorne, John (1998). *Science and theology*. Minneapolis: Fortress Press.

Ramm, Bernard (1956). *The Christian view of science and scripture*. Grand Rapids, MI: Eerdmans Publ. Co.

Ratzsch, Del (1996). *The battle of beginnings.* Downer's Grove, IL: InterVarsity Press.

Ross, Hugh (1995). *The creator and the cosmos* (2nd ed.). Colorado Springs, CO: Navpress.

Ruse, Michael (Ed.). (1996). *But is it science? The philosophical question in the creation/evolution controversy.* Amherst, NY: Prometheus Books.

Ruse, Michael (1999). *The Darwinian revolution: Science red in tooth and claw* (2nd ed.). Chicago: University of Chicago Press.

Ruse, Michael (2001). *Can a Darwinian be a Christian?* New York: Cambridge University Press.

Ryan, William & Pitman, Walter (1998). *Noah's flood: The new scientific discoveries about the event that changed history.* New York: Simon and Schuster.

Schmitz-Moormann, Karl (1997). *Theology of creation in an evolutionary world*, Cleveland: Pilgrim Press.

Schopf, J. William (1999). *Cradle of Life: The discovery of Earth's earliest fossils*, Princeton: Princeton University Press.

"Sensory reception: SENSORY RECEPTION:Photoreception" Britannica Online. http://www.eb.com.180/cgi-bin/g?Doc F=macro/5005/71/56.html

Simpson, George Gaylord (1967). *The meaning of evolution.* New Haven, CT: Yale University Press.

Stefoff, Rebecca (1996). *Charles Darwin and the evolution revolution.* New York: Oxford University Press.

Strahler, Arthur N. (1987). *Science and Earth history: The evolution/creation controversy.* Buffalo, NY: Prometheus Books.

Stoner, Don (1992). *A new look at an old Earth.* Paramount, CA: Schroeder.

Taylor, P. S. (1989). *The great dinosaur mystery and the Bible.* Elgin, IL: Chariot Books, David C. Cook.

Torrance, Thomas F. (1981). *Christian theology and scientific culture*. New York: Oxford University Press.

Thompson, Ernest Trice (1973). *Presbyterians in the South: Volume Two: 1861-1890*. Richmond, VA: John Knox Press.

Wakefield, J. R. (1987-88). Gentry's tiny mystery – unsupported by geology. *Creation/Evolution, 22*, 13-33.

Wakefield, J. R. (1988). The geology of Gentry's tiny mystery. *Journal of Geological Education, 36*, 161-175.

Weber, C. G. (1981). The bombardier beetle myth exploded. *Creation/Evolution, 2* (1), 1-5.

Weber, C. G. (1981). Response to Dr. Kofahl (re: bombardier beetles). *Creation/Evolution, V*, 15-17.

Whitcomb, John & Morris, Henry (1961). *The Genesis flood*. Phillipsburg, NJ: Presbyterian and Reformed Publ.

Whitcomb, John (1988). *The world that perished*. Revised Edition. Grand Rapids, MI: Baker Book House.

Witham, Larry A. (2002). *Where Darwin meets the Bible*. New York: Oxford University Press.

York, D. (1979). Polonium halos and geochronology. *EOS Transactions of the American Geophysical Union, 60* (33), 616-619.

Young, Davis A. (1988). *Christianity and the age of the Earth*. Thousand Oaks, CA: Artisan Sales.

Young, Davis A. (1995). *The biblical flood*. Grand Rapids, MI: Eerdmans.

Yuretich, Richard F. (March 1984). Yellowstone fossil forests: New evidence for burial in place. *Geology*, Geological Society of America, *12*, 159-162.

Zeigler, A. M. (1966). The Siluraian brachiopod *Eocoelia hemisphaerica* and related species. *Palaeontology, 9* (4), 523-543.

Questions Addressed
to Young Earth Creationists

Chapter Ten

"One of the tragedies for individual or church is to start living in the past as though there were nothing more to learn. If the church doesn't keep its mind open to new truth it loses its hold upon the mind of the rising generation. . . Too many people feel that the church is moving away from them, when in fact they have ceased to move on with God."

Ernest Trice Thompson (1894-1985), Presbyterian Seminary Professor

Introduction

This chapter includes some of the questions that arise when beliefs in a young Earth (approximately 6,000 to 10,000 years), creation by fiat (an arbitrary order or decree), ex nihilo (out of nothing), in six solar (24 hour) days, and a global flood, are maintained. These are reasonable questions, most of which are not addressed in creationist literature. If they are discussed, the explanation usually requires miracle or supernatural intervention, or it is claimed that the mechanisms are no longer operating. These poignant questions explain why evolutionists have difficulty grasping why informed and clear thinking Christians, including those with training and degrees in science, hold to the creationism model. This is especially a problem since, for the most part, these questions are answered by the evolutionary model.

The questions in this chapter are particularly addressed to those who are committed to careful thinking, who seek to honor God with their minds, who search for grounds for belief, who attempt to consider all data and weigh it honestly, and who are fearless as to where truth may lead. Those who wonder why creationism is practically universally rejected by scientists, many of whom are Christians, should see from these questions that the creationist model, no matter how much it is desired, cannot stand up to reasonable inquiry. Theistic evolutionists respect the mind the creator God has given and joyfully employ this remarkable gift in searching for answers to universal questions. They are awed by what God has allowed us to understand about creation and seek the best means to integrate rationality with faith on this significant and interesting question.

Ever since modern science made its debut, sincere Christians have had to consider how the new scientific paradigms impact personal belief. The history of science presents these challenges, some of which have become conflicts. It is interesting and instructive to note how Christians through the centuries have dealt with what some have felt was the continual onslaught of science on their thinking. Some have responded defensively, refusing ever to change. Some have never understood the issues involved. Some understood, acknowledged the new insights, admitted they were wrong and courageously integrated and embraced the new paradigms. Change did not always come quickly or easily for many in the latter group. Fortunately, biblical scholars have constantly provided insight to help with these new perspectives. Alternate means of interpreting scripture were often required, God's progressive revelation.

If we are perceptive, we see ourselves paralleling their experiences. Only the subject matter varies. We see how they tenaciously clung to former beliefs such as a flat Earth or a geocentric (Earth centered) solar system and defended them, resisting change and believing with all their hearts that they were preserving the faith. They made valiant attempts to explain the new data in light of old belief but ultimately accepted heliocentrism (sun centered solar system) and a spherical Earth and acknowledged natural laws upon which they could depend. This dependability is beautifully expressed in a classic hymn of the faith: Great is Thy Faithfulness.

> Summer and winter, and springtime and harvest,
> Sun, moon, and stars in their courses above,
> Join with all nature in manifold witness
> To thy great faithfulness, mercy, and love.

> Thomas O. Chisholm, 1923, Songs of Salvation
> Copyright 1923, renewal 1951, Hope Publishing Co.

We, too, resist change, assuming we have arrived at the truth. We, too, have had esteemed, devoted, and scholarly teachers and have great difficulty conceiving that they may have been in error. We, too, reel when something new from science presents itself (genetic engineering and its potential for the manipulation of the human genome, in vitro fertilization, fetal and stem cell research, cloning, artificial intelligence, space habitation, the possibility of life on Mars, or even extra terrestrial intelligence....and what next?). We, too, wonder if our faith will be able to incorporate these new perspectives and we, too, have been known to defend treasured belief against overwhelming data. We, too, are apparently willing to risk the loss of respect to Christianity by the academic world because we fear admitting past error or doubt and wonder if our faith can stand these onslaughts. We hide our heads in the sand hoping the problems will go away. We, too, have failed in becoming informed of the discipline of biblical criticism, which can significantly help us in our understanding. We, too, comfortably cling to irrationality, calling all of it faith. We are convinced we are on higher ground.

Their story is our story. We humbly recognize a common ground of frailty, which is universal to the human condition. We saw it with the devoted Pharisees who also resisted a new idea. We deride them at this point for their narrowness, blindness, lack of faith, and petty defense of the status quo. But they were the most devout, the most tenacious in their respect for the law and in their sincerity. The humble Jesus as their Messiah was a new and shocking idea. It didn't make sense in light of their understanding of the canon. In fact, the thought was frightening. How could this illegitimate carpenter from Nazareth, who regularly eschewed the law and brought a revolutionary way of thinking be their deliverer, the Messiah? Many refused to receive him to the very end.

God continually calls us to new ideas. "Call to me," God said to Jeremiah, "and I will show you new and wondrous things which you have not known before" (33:3). Through the ages God has progressively revealed the truth. To Aristotle, Augustine, Aquinis, Bacon, Copernicus, Newton, Galileo, Luther, Mendel, Salk, Einstein, Darwin, Wegener, Hubble, Martin Luther King, and unnumbered scientists and theologians living today.

In spite of the new concepts and insights, the faith and the faithful have prevailed and have progressed! They will not fail in the future. If we continually cower and refuse to face facts in defense of a faith that we perceive is unable to withstand the facts, then we do lose. And Christianity loses. This is a serious concern to Christians who firmly believe that our faith can victoriously deal with whatever the world of natural law, which was designed by God the Creator, can present.

Questions Regarding the Noachian Flood

1. Since the people who wrote the Old Testament thought the extent of the world was the limited one that they knew, the present day Middle East, the term "worldwide flood" might have meant something very different to them than it does to us today. Is it not reasonable to consider the flood they refer to as possibly being a local flood? How do we rightly interpret

the scripture in light of these vast cultural differences? How do we *know* a literal interpretation is truth, especially when the geological record does not confirm it? The Hebrew word "erets" can be translated region or country, or land. Genesis 6:17 may well be appropriately translated "I am going to bring floodwaters on the region (or country or land); everything on the region or country or land will perish." Might the translation of "erets" as Earth be a mistranslation?

2. Where did Noah get shipbuilding knowledge to construct a 450 x 75 x 45 foot ark with all of the engineering problems and stresses, especially when it was solely made of wood and needed to be seaworthy for a year, with no opportunity to dock and repitch if it leaked?

3. How did a pair of all birds, terrestrial mammals, reptiles, worms, amphibians and insects get to the site of the ark someplace in the Middle East? Yak, musk ox, saber tooth tiger, *Tyranosaurus rex,* tree sloths, wolverines, land snails, *Archaeopteryx,* slugs, parrots, peacocks, penguins, pelicans, cobras, bison, grizzly, pandas, beavers, skunks, kangaroos, and burrowing animals such as moles or cave animals? How did nonswimming animals living on islands get to the ark site on another hemisphere? If the Earth was one land mass, as creationists believe it was immediately prior to the flood, what guided this astounding migration across this enormous continent? Divine guidance? Supernaturalism? Miracle? If so, it is not scientifically verifiable and is outside of the bounds of science.

4. How did Noah deal with monophagic animals (those who only eat one thing, such as pandas which only eat bamboo, koala bears which only eat eucalyptus leaves, anteaters which only eat ants, shrews and some snakes which only eat fresh prey; and hedgehogs which require insects) on the ark?

5. How could all the animals *plus* their food for a year fit in the ark? African elephants eat up to 600 pounds of grass, leaves and roots in one day! Suggesting that animals hibernated or aestivated (were dormant) most of the year requires supernatural intervention. There are no data to support the hibernation suggestion.

6. What did carnivores (meat eaters) eat? How did they keep the plant food on the ark from decaying or becoming moldy in the humidity generated by the flood? What did the humans eat and drink?

7. Many plant seeds die when immersed in water for any length of time. How did all the many plants that exist today survive the flood especially since the water was salty? Since layers of sediment supposedly were deposited during the year of the flood, from whence came the fresh olive leaf?

8. How were the hundreds of animals who needed it given exercise? How could eight people oversee that?

9. How did all the animals disperse from Mt. Ararat in eastern Turkey after the flood? What was there for them to eat? Wouldn't the carnivores gobble up the pairs of herbivores? What plants were growing for the herbivores to eat? Where did jungle animals go? How did the cave animals find caves? Where could koala bears find eucalyptus or pandas bamboo? How did kangaroos get to Australia, orangutans to the jungles of Southeast Asia, lemurs to Madagascar, jaguars to South America, moas (flightless birds, recently extinct) to New Zealand? It seems quite remarkable that the land mass they were on just happened to split and move to a longitude, latitude and environment that suited their specialized needs. Did Noah's family all split and go to separate continents to populate them? Genesis 10 doesn't seem to support that thesis.

10. What proof can be given to substantiate creationists' claims that continental drift occurred immediately after the flood, the separated continents and islands moving at speeds up to a half mile per hour? Has falsification of this hydroplate thesis, as it is called, been attempted? Are there *any* scientific data to support this idea? Is it just believed with no attempt at falsification or support?

11. How did aquatic (fresh water) life survive, being inundated by salty water during the flood?

12. How did marine (salt water) life survive in the diluted salt water during the flood?

13. How can a series of transitional trilobite genera from the Lower Devonian, which are tidily sorted in consecutive layers in Bolivia, be explained? Was this remarkable organization left after a catastrophic deluge? Is not this orderliness exactly what evolutionary theory would

predict and the antithesis of what a catastrophic flood hypothesis would predict?

14. Floods occur today and young and strong people die. During the Noachian flood young, old, and infirm could not all have run to high places and not all people had high places to run to. What is more, people can't run as fast as many animals. People would have died before many fast-running animals, who may have temporarily made it to high ground. Why then are all human skeletons found in upper strata and *none* found in any lower levels? Why are no extinct, fast runners found above humans?

15. There are dozens of species of kangaroo in Australia and its surrounding areas. They are quite varied, some being as small as rodents, some being arboreal, living in trees. Did they all originate from one pair, which came from the ark? This modification in just a few thousand years is much faster than evolution occurs. What mechanisms were operating to allow this? Or were all of these species on the ark, and all traveled to Australia? What would account for such an astounding coincidence? Also, there are many varied and extinct kangaroos in the fossil record in Australia. They would either have to be accounted for on the ark, or they went through very fast change prior to their extinction.

16. There are over 2,000,000 identified species of living things on the Earth today. Fossil evidence suggests there are millions of extinct species. Even if marine and fresh water species are removed, pairs of each of the flying and terrestrial forms both living and extinct could not fit in the ark according to the dimensions given in the Bible. If more generic "kinds" could fit then how could such diversity have arisen in the few millennia (4,500 years) since the flood? Are there any data to substantiate this thesis of rapid species radiation and diversification (evolution)? What mechanisms were operating? Wouldn't the gene pools be limited from having just two individuals of each kind? Where did all the diversity originate, especially in kangaroos and beetles?

17. If the sedimentary layers we find across the globe were laid down during the year of Noah's flood then why are dinosaur footprints, raindrops, river channels, worm trails, mudcracks, and sand dunes, all of which are formed on dry ground, in mud or in shallow water, found in some of the middle sedimentary layers, buried below many, many layers? How could

these fossils have been made in middle layers during the time of the flood when everything was under deep water?

18. Since Noah's flood is purported to have killed all terrestrial animals except those in the ark, and since this flood is also credited with depositing the layered sediments around the world, how can there be fossil trackways at *many different levels* (thirteen) within the Colorado Plateau? Furthermore, these footprints are not uniform. Following the evolutionary paradigm, lower strata generally have 4 and 5 toed amphibians and reptiles, whereas 3 toed dinosaur prints are found on more recent layers. Progressively younger rocks have added new and varied dinosaur prints. How is this explained by the flood model?

19. Varves are thin layers of rock that were laid down as silt in glacial lake settings, one thin layer of dark and light each year. They continue to be formed today. There are varves numbering in the millions in formations that are miles thick in Wyoming and Colorado. How can it be claimed that the Earth is just 10,000 years old when these annual records are there for all to see? How could these delicate and even strata have been formed in one year amid the swirling waters of the catastrophic flood? Creationists note that a fish or bird can be found buried among varves. Do they analyze for microscopic layers surrounding the bodies? Do they question whether the fish or bird was in an anoxic (without oxygen) setting? In such a setting the bodies would not decay, and they could then indeed be surrounded by the delicate layers of sediment over several years. Fish can be found, not buried in layers (if the layers were laid down faster than annually as is suggested by a flood model) but between layers, more in keeping with the annual sedimentation thesis.

20. How could the arctic fox with its tiny ears designed for heat conservation survive in the same environment, either in Eden or on the ark, as the large eared rabbit of the desert? How did other animals requiring specialized environments survive, such as cave animals or those who live in the tropics or in high trees? How could the yak and polar bear survive in the same setting as a desert Gila monster or rain forest cobra?

21. If the dinosaur fossils were laid down during the year of the flood why have *none* of the skeletons of any of the people who drowned during the flood been found in sediments contemporary with the dinosaurs? Why didn't even one dinosaur make it to the higher ground and become buried in sediments contemporary with the wildebeests or lions, mastodons and

camels, if indeed they were living at the same time? Why didn't even one moose, caribou, walrus or gorilla which was old and weak die earlier and be found with the dinosaurs? Why are *no* mammals found in lower layers???

22. If the Earth is only 6,000 to 10,000 years old and all living things were created at that time, then present day species would have been living at the time of the flood. Why are none of them found in the lower sedimentary layers that creationists believe were laid down by the flood? Why would *none* of them have died during the early weeks of the flood? Why are extinct species found exclusively at lower levels and most living species found toward the higher, more recent layers? What accounts for this very clean organization? Why are delicate organisms, which would not sink first, found in the lowest layers and heavier organisms such as conchs, clams, starfish, or six foot wide ammonites (coiled, chambered, enormous mollusks), which would be expected to sink first, not found in those layers? Why is a snail or fish *never* found with a trilobite?

23. If all sedimentary layers were laid down during the Noachian deluge, why have we found *no* remains of human civilization in these strata? The Bible speaks of cities, and the pre-flood inhabitants presumably would have had tools, pottery, metals, precious stones, writing tablets, weapons, grinding stones and other implements, which would have been buried. Why is there *no* trace of antediluvian (pre-flood) civilizations in lower sediments? Why are there no remains of humans who would have died and been buried hundreds of years prior to the flood? No place, anywhere, are there humans or their artifacts except associated with the most recent layers. Why?

24. The cartilaginous fish are seen earlier in the fossil record than the bony fish. How can this be explained by a flood model? If they had all been created and lived at the same time, then members of both groups would have died simultaneously in the flood. How is it that invertebrate sea creatures are found in lower rock strata, and then, predictably, the vertebrates in order: fish, amphibians, reptiles, birds, and finally mammals? Why are the whales only found in recent sedimentary layers?

25. On the ark, what was the behavior of animals like rats? They live only one year and begin to reproduce at two months of age. A typical litter is seven pups, which in turn are ready to reproduce in two months. If the

rats didn't reproduce, how was their survival assured for a year on the ark, assuming they were a few months old when they boarded the vessel?

26. Were amphibians, land snails, slugs, snakes and worms on the ark? How did they keep flying insects from escaping? Were they in larval form? If so, who collected all of them?

27. Explain why there is absolutely no scientific support for the following assertions from creationists:

    a)   The Earth tilted on its axis and that is what caused the rains which began the flood.
    b)   This tilting caused the Earth to wrinkle (mountain building) or caused change in climates.
    c)   There was only one ice age and it was within the past 4,500 years.

28. Every animal species has a whole consort of parasites: numerous tapeworms and other flatworms, roundworms, insects, bacteria, yeasts, viruses, or fungi. Did Noah and his relatives carry all of these organisms for the whole human species on their bodies? Did the pairs of animals house all the worms of that particular kind? What would keep the variety of parasites from reproducing and overwhelming their hosts? Some are deadly. How did all pairs stay healthy for the year? How could each species or kind have contracted all of these parasites prior to getting on the ark? Or did all of these parasitic organisms originate following the flood? How?

29. A flu virus lasts a week in humans before it is destroyed by the immune system. That virus would go extinct unless it were successfully passed to another host. If Noah's wife had such an organism, she would pass it to a daughter-in-law, who would keep it alive for another week, and she would pass it to her husband, etc. All eight aboard the ark would manufacture antibodies, which would render them immune to that virus. According to this scenario, that virus species would have a lifespan of about eight weeks aboard the ark and then become extinct. Where, then, did present day viruses (or all parasites) originate? All in the past 4,500 years? Much change over time! Multiply this for measles, polio, hepatitis, chicken pox, diptheria, smallpox, anthrax. Were they all aboard the ark? Did Noah and his family suffer from these diseases? Why not?

30. A single mating pair contain a limited gene pool. How are the tremendous variations within species today explained, such as with dogs, frogs, owls or horses? Wouldn't the limited gene pool and the subsequent inbreeding since the flood have resulted in deleterious and fatal outcomes?

31. If one catastrophe, the Noachian deluge, was responsible for all or most of the fossils, this means that all fossilized animals lived concurrently and died within a year of each other. There was not enough landmass to support these enormous populations, plus all the other animals that were not subject to fossilization but did die in the flood. We know there were a lot of the latter, for no humans were fossilized during the flood yet many died. Presumably many other species were not represented by fossil evidence either. The Karroo Formation in Africa alone has preserved 800 billion vertebrate animals. Did they all live in that part of Africa at the same time? Impossible!

32. Sedimentary layers are thousands of feet high in places. Where did all of that sediment come from if the flood occurred only about sixteen hundred years after creation? Soil takes a long time to be formed from rock. Do creationists have any theories as to where, in such a short time, all the soil came from to form the sedimentary layers?

33. How is the record of a great flood on ancient clay tablets from Sumer explained? The Babylonians expanded this story after they conquered the Sumerians in ~3,000 B.C. Two stories have been translated: Atrahasis and the Gilgamesh epic. A boat with pitch filled with representative animals and the king's family protected them from the flood. Birds were released at the end and two returned but the third did not. The Hebrew flood narrative was written about 1,000 B.C., about 2,000 years after these epics. Most scholars suggest that the Hebrew flood record was adapted from the previous stories. Can this thesis be disproved?

34. Why are there no records of a flood event in the literate and continuous Egyptian or Chinese civilizations, which existed uninterrupted before and after the supposed flood? The city of Ur was inhabited from at least 4,000 B.C. to approximately 400 B.C. Why is there *no* evidence that supports its being totally inundated by a flood in ~2,500 B. C.?

35. Why do many mollusks (snails, clams) occur in so many geological strata without any hydrodynamic sorting according to size or shape? How is it

explained that the brachiopods, which are similar in size, shape, and weight to the mollusks, are appropriately sorted according to their evolutionary state, and show anatomical progressiveness in the older to younger strata?

36. From whence did all that water come? Where has it gone? Can the explanation be scientifically verified?

37. How did white limestone chalk cliffs, hundreds of feet high, composed of skeletons of marine organisms laid down under water, form during Noah's raging flood? Did they form prior to the flood? There was not enough time between when the flood occurred and creation week (1650 years) for these enormous cliffs to be made.

38. Why are evaporites, such as gypsum or rock salt which are mainly formed from evaporating sea water, found in sedimentary layers hundreds of meters deep?

39. Earthworms and some snails are hermaphroditic, or self fertile. Just one of them would have been needed on the ark, not a pair. Also, parthenogenic females, those who produce viable progeny without fertilization, such as some beetles and salamanders, would not need a partner.

40. The scriptures say (Genesis 7:1-4) that Noah collected, in seven days, mating pairs of each of the "unclean beasts," seven pair of "clean beasts," and seven pair of each kind of bird. How did he get pairs of slow moving walruses, penguins, crocodiles, or sloths to the region of the ark that fast? If this is science, as in "creation science," then these claims must be credible, or capable of being falsified. Also, it is of interest that another flood account (Genesis 6:19-20) has God asking Noah to bring in two of every living thing. Nothing is said about seven pairs of some groups. How is this discrepancy explained from a literal perspective?

41. Why are leaves, pollen, and roots of the same plants found together in the same geological layers and other plants (with their respective pollen and branches) found in other strata? Why wouldn't all sorts of pollen and plant parts be mixed throughout all the layers if they had lived concurrently and all fell prey to this natural disaster simultaneously?

42. Why are there *no* remnants of vascular (veined) plants, the most recent plant forms, in the lower fossil layers? Why are there no pine cones or other fruits, pits, seeds, nuts, flower parts, or branches from these groups in lower layers? Wouldn't they have fallen into some lower sedimentary layers during the flood or initially have been buried in situ as the early floodwaters' sediment was laid down? Why are the plants so neatly separated in the fossil record, starting with the algae, then the bryophytes (mosses and liverworts), then ferns, horsetail rushes, and club mosses? Then came the vascular plants such as gymnosperms (conifers, cycads and ginkgoes), and finally the angiosperms, the flowering plants, toward the top layers. Why are there no fern trees, lepidodendrons or massive cycads found in upper levels? How can this remarkable progression of plant life and orderly sorting in the fossil record be explained in light of a catastrophic worldwide deluge? Is it coincidental that this organization follows the evolutionary progression of plants? Wouldn't the olive trees, grapevines and wheat of Palestine be covered with sediment and preserved at the bottom? No such vascular plants are found anywhere near the lower sedimentary strata.

43. Why have scientists found no records in tree-ring dating, which extend over 10,000 years, of the interruption of the flood that supposedly occurred about 4,500 years ago (Becker, B & Kromer, B., 1993. "The continental tree-ring record-absolute chronology, C-14 calibration, and climate-change at 11 KA" *Palaeogeography, Palaeoclimatology, Palaeoecology*, 103 (1-2):67-71).

44. Why has there been no evidence in sea bottom cores of terrestrial detritus, or human artifacts which inevitably would have been carried into the seas and dumped during a year-long global flood?

45. Ice cores contain 40,000 years of annual layers. They should also reveal a distinctive layer of sediments from the time of the flood. Why does no such evidence exist?

46. How are some alternating sedimentary layers explained by the flood model? Some layers with marine fossils alternate with layers with terrestrial fossils. Geologists explain this by the repetitive retreat over time of the continental shoreline or inland seas.

47. How are rat-gnawed fossil bones explained by the flood model? Or the *T. rex* teeth marks in a *Triceratops* pelvis? These events would have

occurred on dry land. If they were formed prior to the flood they should be in lower layers. In fact, they are found in upper layers.

48. How could the massive sedimentary layers that compose the mile-high walls of the Grand Canyon have (a) been deposited in one year, and (b) become dehydrated and hardened into rock within months, so that they could withstand the raging water which creationists claim cut through these layers to form the steep walled canyon? Wouldn't raging water have destroyed the recent, non-solidified strata, leaving the area a muddied plain, not a steep-walled canyon?

49. Did the worldwide flood succeed? Did it wipe evil from the Earth? Quite a waste, no? Much sorrow and pain, yet its agenda unfulfilled.

50. Isn't it more than coincidental that after a year-long deluge the ark ended up north of its origination in Mesopotamia, against the flow of water, which would be south? Also coincidental is the fact that it grounded in the general vicinity of the Middle East. It's a big world out there, and a year is a long time, and a flood covering all of the Earth would have been an enormously moving mass.

Other Puzzles

1. Yes, the eye is an awesome organ. Yet why do most of us need corrective lenses even as young people? If designed, why are they so imperfect? Might they be in the process of evolving?

2. Why do so many of us have allergies? If designed abruptly, why aren't our immune systems more perfect?

3. Why do males have nipples? Why do we have useless, buried teeth (wisdom teeth)? Why can some people wiggle their ears and scalps? Might it have some relationship to lower animals which have this ability? What is the function of irregularly occurring human hair on arms, back, chest and legs?

4. Why do animals such as crocodiles and some birds eat their own young? Why do female preying mantises and black widow spiders eat their mates? What about parasites such as worms, insects, bacteria, protozoa and viruses? Was this design?

5. How did a food web occur in the Garden of Eden? Why would carnivorous (meat eating) animals have been created if originally the plan was that there be no death? If all animals were to be herbivores (plant eaters) why were some made with sharp teeth and ripping claws? Why would an anteater be made to eat animals? Why would snakes have venom if they didn't need to kill prey? Why would animals such as lions and leopards be made to run fast if they only ate plants and didn't need to chase prey? Why would other animals such as antelope, rabbits and deer be made to run fast if they had no enemies from which to flee? What would be the necessity for the bombardier beetle's toxic defense?

6. How did all animals that have ever lived on the Earth, including dinosaurs, polar bears, and arctic terns as well as all plants, palms, sequoias, rubber trees, giant fossil ferns, and plants of the tundra fit in one environment: the Garden of Eden? Where were troglobites (animals which only live in caves such as blind salamanders, crayfish, and some insects) in the Garden of Eden? Were caves, which take long periods of time to form, part of creation or did they develop later?

7. How did all the animals disperse throughout the Earth to islands and other isolated places from that beginning in Eden? If the Earth was one huge continent, how did they disperse without being preyed upon first? Why did they just happen to end up in ecological niches that best suited them? In other words, how did the koalas know where eucalyptus trees grew to head in that direction? How did the polar bears know to head north? Was it luck that the land mass they were on just happened to end up in an arctic environment?

8. We are told by literalists that the siblings of Cain and Abel could intermarry and their progeny not experience deleterious effects because they had "perfect" DNA. What about Noah's sons and their children? Wouldn't intermarriage between those close relatives lead to genetic weakness? Whence came all of the variability seen in the human race in such a short time (4,500 years) and from just eight people, five of whom were blood relatives?

9. How are the data from astronomers which support the 13.7 billion years ago Big Bang such as (a) the present expansion of the universe, (b) an afterglow called cosmic background radiation, and (c) the abundance of hydrogen and helium elements left over from that explosion negated?

10. If the Earth was originally designed to have no death how would early humans in cold climates have clothed or warmed themselves without animal skins? Could early humans have eaten eggs? Was *that* death?

11. How is the biogeography of numerous animals and plants explained from a creationist perspective? For instance, how come mammals are poorly represented on islands? How can the preponderance of marsupial varieties in Australia be explained, when many occur in no other place? Why do only a handful of Madagascar's 267 species of reptiles exist elsewhere? Why is there no evidence that any of the many other species of reptiles on Madagascar inhabited any other place in the past? Might they have evolved there?

12. If Genesis 1 and 2 are taken literally, that is at face value, as a record of exactly how things occurred, then how are the following inconsistencies between the two creation accounts explained? Which is correct? How can they both be correct?

Genesis 1	**Genesis 2**
man and woman created last	man created first; then other living things; woman created last
humans created immediately out of nothing (by fiat) by the spoken word	man formed from dust; God breathed into him; woman formed from man's rib
name given God in Hebrew is Yahweh	name given God in Hebrew is Elohim

13. Why is it that the inventions and discoveries of modern scientists in medicine, pharmacy, dentistry, engineering (bridges, cars, elevators, refrigeration, airplanes, CAT scans, x-ray machines, roller coasters, and innumerable other kinds of machinery to which our lives are entrusted), food processing technology, electronics, and communications are fully affirmed and respected by creationists, yet scientists' findings in the fields of geology, paleontology, or astronomy are negated? A multitude of molecules (pesticides, detergents, fire retardants, inhalers, drugs, food preservatives, artificial flavorings, industrial fluids, artificial fabrics, etc. etc.) which scientists have devised are received willingly, yet a very clear line is drawn and certain data presented by astronomers, geologists,

310

biologists, and chemists are refused. All of these data are arrived at through identical processes and reasoning. Why are the data from astronomers that affect spacecraft activity recognized as reliable, yet their conclusions pertaining to the Earth's or the universe's age rejected? The data that geologists have gained with respect to oil and gas exploration are accepted as valid but if these same geologists, using the same scientific method, interpret the fossil record, their conclusions are categorically rejected. Upon what basis is it determined what will be accepted and what won't?

14. If a strict literalism with the scriptures regarding the six days of Genesis 1 and 2 and the story of the flood is taken, then how are scriptures which say the following interpreted?

> The sun stood still. (Joshua 10:13)
> As far as the east is from the west (as though the Earth were flat), for the east and west join. (Psalm103:12)
> God, who is spirit, *walked* in the Garden of Eden, and *"formed"* Adam and *breathed* into his nostrils; whose finger *wrote* on tablets of stone, who *smelled* the sweet savor of burnt offerings.
> The serpent talked, reasoned, even outwitted the woman! Snakes have no vocal apparatus or mental capacity to accomplish this. Was it ventriloquism as some creationists state?
> God made the rainbow so that he could remember his promise. Does God need help remembering? (Genesis 9:15-16)
> Let the rivers clap their hands. (Psalm 98:8)
> Jesus said, "I am the door." (John 10:9)
> Jesus said, "Out of his heart shall flow rivers of living water." (John 7:38)
> "His legs are alabaster columns, set upon bases of gold." (Song of Solomon 5:14)
> "Jews from *every* nation under heaven" (Acts 2:5)
> There were giants in the land. (Genesis 6:4). No data have been found to substantiate this.
> Language originating in one place. No data have been found to substantiate this.
> All animals vegetarian at one time. No data have been found to substantiate this.
> People living hundreds of years. No data have been found to substantiate this.

15. In light of all the scientific evidence, would it ever be considered that a literal interpretation of Genesis 1-11 might be inaccurate? Could it be conceived that perhaps it is the method of interpretation that is errant rather than the conclusions of multitudes of scientists, theologians, and other Christians? Do fear or pride interfere? Can it be seen that there are many varieties of literature in the Bible and they must be addressed and interpreted distinctly? History, love letters, song, prophesy, proverbs, biography, poetry? How can one be absolutely sure that this section is literal history and not some other form of literature?

16. Can it be seen that when the answer to all the difficult questions pertaining to the ark or the origin of life in the Garden of Eden is "Well, God performed a miracle and put the animals in a deep slumber during the year aboard the ark so they didn't need to eat so much; God modified their behavior, brought them two by two from the far reaches of the unicontinent, and took them back after the flood to their respective habitats through miraculous acts" that this is not science? God made a serpent speak and made a man from the dust of the Earth to appear mature all through miraculous, unexplainable, unrepeatable acts. Is this science? It may have happened but it can never be demonstrated through science. It may be some other truth but it is not scientific truth.

17. Why do flightless birds such as penguins, ostriches, kiwis, and the cormorants of the Galapagos Islands have wings and feathers?

18. Why do pigs, which use only two toes on each foot, have two additional and useless toes located above the ground on each foot? Design?

19. Why do some snakes, such as the boa constrictor, and several species of marine mammals, such as whales, all which do not walk, have pelvic bones and small, internally located hind-limb bones? Why do some even have external buds of hindlimbs?

20. Why do subterranean and cave-dwelling organisms, which need no eyes, have useless eyes under their skin?

21. Why do human embryos have pharyngeal pouches, a tail and six aortic arches, all found in embryonic fish? Why do the pouches of humans become glands and ducts instead of gill slits? Why does the tail disappear? Why do the aortic arches disappear or develop into various arteries?

22. Creationists often speak and write about the lack of transitional forms. There are a variety of examples of transitions in the fossil record. That there are not more has been explained in Chapters Seven and Nine. Interestingly, there are transitional examples alive today. How else is a two chambered heart in the fish, a three chambered heart in amphibians, a three and a half chambered heart in the reptiles and a four chambered heart in the birds and mammals, the most recent vertebrates, explained? Aren't warm blooded, hairy animals that lay eggs (such as the duck billed platypus) transitional between reptiles and mammals? Mammals, which are warm blooded and have hair, give birth to their young alive, except for these transitional examples where the organism has characteristics of both primitive and more advanced forms. Why do opossums, appearing among the first mammals in the fossil record, have scaly tails, similar to reptiles? Is it more than coincidence that birds, which presumably arose from reptiles, have scaly legs? Marsupials, mammals which complete fetal life in a pouch, are early in the fossil record. Are not these transitions?

23. Where did the soil come from to support vegetation in the Garden of Eden? Soil takes extensive time periods to form from the slow weathering processes on rock.

24. How could Adam name and then remember the names of all of the millions of species of animals? Genesis 2:19 tells us that "whatever the man called *every* living creature, that was its name." Is this to be taken literally? All marine creatures? Protozoa? Bacteria? Insects? Worms? Could he write? With what and on what?

25. Are creationists aware that in their July 1997 publication *Acts and Facts*, the Institute for Creation Research stated that most publications of young-Earth creationists have been somewhat simplistic regarding the problem of dating and have not addressed geochronology and radiometric dating thoroughly? What does that say about the assertions that were made to that point regarding the age of the Earth and how valid scientifically their much heralded young Earth position is? Upon what scientific basis could they have challenged the age of the Earth to that point?

26. If the Earth is a mere 10,000 years old, how can the supernova explosions, which were observed in the Andromeda galaxy 2,000,000 light years away, be explained? Did God create with that light already in

transit, giving the appearance of age? How are the images from the Hubble deep field telescope, which show galaxies billions of light years away, explained? The speed of light is constant and values can be calculated regarding distance.

27. If creationism is science, why are there so many references to religious tenets and supernatural intervention associated with this thesis?

28. If teaching creationism can be justified in the public school classroom then it would be subject to the rules of scientific inquiry. All miracles and supernatural events would be excluded. The rules of scientific inquiry limit study exclusively to what can be assessed, empirically demonstrated, or inferred by the senses.

29. Is it understood that evolutionary theory is distinctive from the discipline that studies the origin of life? No argument or discussion relating to the origin of life impacts or is relevant to or could possibly negate the theses of the theory of evolution, that there has been change over time.

30. The Second Law of Thermodynamics applies to a closed system, and life on Earth is in an open system, continually receiving energy from the sun. Is it clear why scientists hold that the claim that the Second Law contradicts evolutionary theory is therefore totally inaccurate and inapplicable? If greater complexity could not occur then photosynthesis could not take place.

31. Why are the only animals mentioned in Genesis the ones that were known in that limited region of the world? Why no mention of any planets except the Earth, the one that they could see with the unaided eye? No mention of microbes or dinosaurs. Doesn't this support the thesis that the authors were limited by their cultural and temporal setting? Can it possibly be read as a human story with a significant, eternal meaning, just as we interpret Jesus' parables?

32. The Bible states that God created cattle abruptly. How is this explained? Cattle were bred from wild forms hundreds of years before the Israelites were organized. They didn't start as cows, just as dogs didn't start as dogs but came from wolves.

33. Is it understood that when scientists disagree it is a sign of health in science? This is how science advances. It thrives on conflict and the peer

review that demands quality support for assertions. Unanimity on everything would be a sign of stagnation. Scientists discuss varying theses about how the process works and the significant factors for evolution, but they agree on the fact of evolution.

34. If the Earth is no more than 10,000 years old how can we account for coral reefs, which can be 5,000 meters deep? Reefs only grow in shallow water so they've been in a subsidence zone, where land such as a volcanic cone is sinking or where the water level has slowly risen as a result of the melting of Pleistocene ice sheets. Corals are attached to the sea floor and biologists estimate that some have been building for two million years. Fast subsidence would not allow the corals to grow, as they would sink too deep. Slow subsidence would allow them to grow but it would take a long time for them to build layers thousands of meters thick. Could these fragile structures have withstood a catastrophic deluge?

35. If one believes in an old Earth creation by fiat where each "day" in Genesis 1 represents thousands or even millions of years, how is it explained that plants were created on day 3, yet the sun wasn't created until day 4 to provide photosynthesis? Why would creation be backwards? Why would there be light on day 1 when the sun wasn't created until day 4? How can this be taken literally without a lot of imaginative explaining?

36. Who was it that Cain, the son of the first humans on Earth, feared (Genesis 4:14) would kill him as he wandered on the Earth? His own relatives (Genesis 4:17)? How did Cain build a city in a distant land? A population is needed for a city.

37. When during creation week were cherubim (Genesis 3:24) created? When were angels created?

38. Is it conceivable that there might be a connection between the first life forms and the anaerobic, methane-producing bacteria found presently in geothermally heated, mineral-rich waters near hydrothermal vents on the ocean floor?

39. What is meant by the biblical "kind"?

40. In light of such verses as Romans 10:9 (believing in your heart), Leviticus 11:6 (rabbits don't chew the cud), Leviticus 11:21-23

(grasshoppers and beetles have six feet), Genesis 1:24 (cattle created abruptly), how can the Institute for Creation Research museum assert in Exhibit #1 that there are no scientific errors in the Bible? How can the moon stop (Joshua 10:13)? What is truth?

41. Why would terrestrial salamanders experience a larval stage with gills and fins which are never used and then lose these features before they hatch? Doesn't it appear that they may have a relationship with aquatic ancestors that would have needed these structures? Descent with modification?

42. How could the Earth have been formed before the Sun and other stars? Are there any data which support this idea?

43. Can it be understood that theistic evolutionists have no problem believing in evolution and also acknowledging their need for a Savior in Jesus Christ? Theistic evolutionary belief does not negate the reality of sin. People still need a savior and guide for moral living. Humans sin, by definition, through rational consciousness and choice. We cannot choose correctly all the time or lead perfect lives. There will always be a need for deliverance from this condition, which is provided through Jesus Christ. Just because theistic evolutionists do not believe there was a flesh and blood Adam and Eve who sinned in a Garden called Eden does not mean that they do not recognize that they were born to sin and are in need of the sacrificial atonement of Jesus. Evolution does not negate the death of Christ or absolve anyone from his or her need for repentance before God. Honest humans recognize their need for forgiveness and do not require that blame for such sin be placed on anyone but themselves! Theistic evolutionists believe that the early Hebrews also observed the innate evil in humans and asked from whence it came. The culture in which they lived provided the answer in a colorful, poetic, powerful, poignant story.

44. Can it be seen that a story of a God who punishes all people because one couple disobeyed might have come from an early culture trying to understand the origin of evil? Is not a God who gave the gift of free will (which inevitably results in error), who provided a means of redemption, who calls us to holiness and continually forgives our shortcomings if we ask and helps us make right choices more in line with the loving, just, holy, and caring God whom Jesus reflected?

45. How do you explain the evidence that points to ancient continents such as Pangaea and Gondwanaland, and ocean basins (Tethys, Rheic), or the distribution of orogenic (mountain building) belts?

46. Is this issue on origins really worth the conflict among Christians? Is it worth the ridicule and loss of respect to the Christian faith by those who have studied science? Is rejecting the mind and rational data what God asks of us? Is it worth the pain our young people experience as they learn biology and geology in college? Is it worth the risk of losing them to the faith? Does the time and effort we spend on it keep us from living and loving in God's name?

Many of these questions can be explained through science, some through the evolutionary model. Many with biblical reference are clarified using modern historical and literary criticism scholarship. The literal biblical interpretation, the creationism model, cannot resolve the majority of these questions.

> Usually, even a non-Christian knows something about the earth, the heavens, and the other elements of this world, about the motion and orbit of the stars, and even their size and relative positions, about the predictable eclipses of the sun and moon, the cycles of the years and the seasons, about the kinds of animals, shrubs, stones, and so forth, and this knowledge he holds to as being certain from reason and experience. Now it is a disgraceful and dangerous thing for an infidel to hear a Christian, presumably giving the meaning of Holy Scripture, talking nonsense on these topics; and we should take all means to prevent such an embarrassing situation, in which people show up vast ignorance in a Christian and laugh it to scorn.
>
> St. Augustine

Creationist and Theistic Evolutionist Areas of Agreement

Chapter Eleven

I know that the Immovable comes down;
I know that the Invisible appears to me;
I know that he who is far outside the whole creation
Takes me into himself and hides me in his arms.

St. Symeon the New Theologian, theologian poet of the late 10th Century.[1]

I know that my redeemer lives! Job 19:25

There are significant and profound areas of agreement between Christian creationists and Christian theistic evolutionists. It is important to delineate and emphasize those areas. Since all of these people are committed in their faith and have a love for their Lord, it follows that they share many experiences, hopes, histories, goals, and theologies in common. Their mutual concern about the issues of origins and evolution springs from the fact that they all ardently care about Christ's kingdom and witness in this world.

All Christians affirm the existence of an eternal, immortal, omnipotent, omnipresent, omniscient, creator God. They are all theists. They believe that God is. This God is worshipped and acknowledged as creator and sustainer of the universe by both creationists and theistic evolutionists.

In addition, they all believe by faith that this same God became incarnate; that God became human, entering history as a babe in Bethlehem, in Judea, ~6 B.C. He grew up, apprenticed as a carpenter, and then for three years in his early thirties taught the Kingdom of God, and modeled loving, forgiving, and merciful, righteous living. This Jesus, Messiah, the Christ, the Son of God, willingly became their substitutionary atoner, their savior and redeemer by giving his life on a cross ~28 A.D., a sacrifice in their stead. He conquered death, rising from his grave three days after being entombed and several weeks later ascended from the Earth. He promised to return and give life in his presence forever to all who acknowledge him as their Savior and Lord.

---

[1] McManners, John (Ed.), 1990. *The Oxford Illustrated History of Christianity.* Oxford: Oxford University Press, p. 147.

God vowed to be with them in Spirit here on Earth and to guide and comfort them in all the vicissitudes of their lives. They all share his requirement of holy living and service to their fellow humans. They all have been given a call to love each other, esteem the other better than themselves, be kind and tender hearted, forgive one another, to be of one mind, and live in peace. They all received the great commission to spread the good news of God's redemptive and abiding grace throughout the world. Christ's selfless life is a model they all claim and attempt to emulate.

Another key agreement between these two groups is their mutual belief in the inspiration of the scriptures, the Holy Bible. Not all concur that the scriptures are without error (inerrant) but all of them respect these writings as being the word of God to humankind. They all believe the various authors were guided by the Holy Spirit in a divine, unexplainable way. They all trust this book in matters of faith and practice and see eternal truth expressed in its many literary forms. They have all witnessed its power to change lives, comfort, guide, encourage, rebuke, and instruct.

Both groups recognize the infallibility of scripture, which refers to its doctrinal (not necessarily textual or factual) reliability. They agree that the writings, with respect to faith (doctrine) and practice (ethics), are true and dependable. They set their lives and hopes on its promises and sincerely try to obey its precepts. They understand its cultural setting and can divorce that aspect from its universal verities. For instance, many Christian groups allow women to lead in worship (I Timothy 2:12). They do not greet each other with "holy kisses" (I Corinthians 16:20) nor do most require women to have their heads covered in church (I Corinthians 11:5) or suggest that long hair relates to level of devotion (I Corinthians 11:15).

A significant point of agreement between these parties with respect to the creationism/evolution controversy is that they mutually reject the evolutionary materialism/ evolutionary naturalism thesis. This atheistic stand, that the universe and all life, including humans and their self-aware brains, are the result of random factors having arrived by chance, is foreign and anathema to both creationists and evolutionary theists. They both attest to the design and purpose provided by a sovereign Creator.

They both are sorry that misinterpretations or perversions of evolutionary theory have spawned beliefs, such as social Darwinism, that are irrelevant to the basic evolutionary tenet of change over time but have resulted in harm to individuals and to the culture. They both regret that some have, out of ignorance, deceit, or lack of faith interpreted evolutionary theory as a denial of God, giving license for evil living. They see a social philosophy of survival of the fittest as contrary to Jesus' teaching that the meek shall inherit the

Earth (Matthew 5:5) and that the last shall be first (Matthew 19:30). All of this they share in common.

All Christians are aware of their need for repentance of sin before a holy God. They all recognize that they are innately sinful and prone to err. Whether that sin arose in a Garden with two humans eating a forbidden fruit or whether it is the result of free will that leads to self-centeredness, greed, conceit, deception, pride, and lack of love, all Christians have understood their need for a Savior. That is what it means to be a Christian: recognizing Jesus as the sinless, Lamb of God, sacrificial atoner, as savior. No beliefs on origins or whether there was a real Adam and Eve will hide the universal understanding that all were born sinners. It is important to note that free will also results in benevolent acts, the pursuit of truth, compassion, faithfulness, worship, altruism, sacrificial giving, love, and many other positive actions and qualities.

Christians who are creationists or theistic evolutionists all care about sharing the good news of their savior, Jesus Christ, in the world. There is no way evolutionary theory negates the significance and need for Christ's death for the sins of humankind. They all wish to honor him in all they do. Unfortunately, this creationism/evolution conflict is perceived by members of both positions as a necessary battle in achieving that honor.

Christians who are creationists or theistic evolutionists agree on these basic tenets:

> God is. God was in the beginning.
> God is apart from and prior to the material universe.
> God is eternal.
> God is creator, designer, sustainer.
> God is omnipotent (all powerful), omniscient (all knowing), omnipresent (everywhere).
> God is our heavenly father (parent).
> God is love.
> God is holy, just, merciful.
> God the Father Almighty as immanent, transcendent, King of Kings, Lord of Lords; The Alpha and Omega, the first and the last; the Creator.
> God is our rock, our hiding place; our ever present help in time of trouble.
> God's word is a truthful and dependable guide in faith and life.
> God's word was inspired by the Holy Spirit.
> God's word must not be idolized.

The preservation and unity of the scriptures, their prophetic accuracy, and their power to change lives speaks to their holy state and divine authorship.

God's word builds relationship between humankind and God.

Evolutionary materialism/evolutionary naturalism is rejected.

Why we are here, how we should live, and where we are going are key issues our faith addresses.

Jesus is the Son of God; Messiah; Redeemer; Substitutionary Atoner; The Christ; Son of Man; Mediator between God and humankind; the Word. Through him were all things made.

The Holy Spirit is the ever present Comforter.

The virgin birth of Jesus; the celebration of Christmas.

The bodily resurrection of Jesus; the celebration of Easter.

We were all "born in sin" and are capable of sinning. We all need to be cleansed from sin, redeemed, forgiven. We have all sinned and come short of the glory of God.

Sin separates us from God and from each other.

There is a power of evil in this world.

Jesus' death bridges us to God, enables us to fellowship with God.

Forgiveness of sin is accomplished by the substitutionary atonement of Jesus.

The church is God's family and witness here on Earth.

The return of Jesus is mutually anticipated.

The priesthood of believers.

The power and efficacy of prayer.

Death is perceived as the entrance to eternal life; to depart and be with Christ.

The purpose of our works is to say "Thank You," not to achieve our salvation.

The triune God; Doctrine of the Trinity. God the Father, God the Son, and God the Holy Spirit.

We've all been given the Great Commission: to spread the good news of Jesus to all people.

> We share the desire to spread the news of Jesus' love, to
> live lives which honor Christ, and to make this world
> a better place; to be salt and light.
> We acknowledge that God wills that all of his children
> dwell together in unity (not necessarily uniformity).
> We share the hope of eternity with God.
> We believe in the immortality of the soul.
> We all desire to worship God.
> We claim and are comforted by the promises of Jesus.
> We are in a covenant relationship with God.
> We are entrusted to be stewards of the creation.

In addition, Christians share a common religious history as seen in the Jewish faith of the Old Testament. Even though there have been divisions, such as the Western Church in Rome and the Eastern Church in Constantinople, Christians have shared much historically. While the Reformation set Protestants apart from Catholics in many ways, there is much fellowship between these groups today. Unfortunately, the division between creationists and theistic evolutionists became established in the 20th Century and continues.

Believers in evolution do not deny the universality of sin, the reality of a Creator, the responsibility to live a holy life, or the existence of a holy, creator God. In no way does a belief in evolution impact the necessity of Christ's death and the individual need for a savior. Such a belief does not make one an evolutionary naturalist/evolutionary materialist nor does it imply any affirmation of any kind of New Age philosophies or ideas. It only says that the individual believes God created through the processes of evolution over a long period of time, and that the Genesis accounts should be interpreted theologically rather than scientifically.

It behooves Christians to assess priorities and judge whether open conflict on peripheral issues is constructive and honoring to God and the holy kingdom here on Earth. Christians should also be challenged to look for all they have in common and to rejoice, rather than dwell on and magnify differences that can lead to pain, disillusionment, dissension, and dishonor to their Lord. Accentuating all that is shared in common edifies, elevates, increases the unity and love for one another, and powerfully witnesses to the unique and life-changing love of God to the world.

If Christians cannot agree on the peripheral issues they should resist conflict, exercise tolerance, allow God to be the judge, and meanwhile in humility and grace seek with all their hearts, minds and souls the unity and reconciliation so desired by Jesus. They should even consider whether such disunity is a device by the power of evil to separate and detract from larger, more important issues such as evangelism, environmental and social justice, peace, holiness, and mercy. Could it be that we have been innocently and unknowingly manipulated into this state of disunity to fulfill a function for the force of evil?

What should equally sincere Christians do when they disagree in various aspects of biblical interpretation? J. R. W. Stott, in *Understanding the Bible*, 1972, p. 219 suggests:

> We should be humble enough to re-examine them ourselves in the light of sound principles of interpretation. And we should be mature enough to discuss them with one another without rancour. If then we still disagree, we must regard such disputed points as being secondary in importance and respect one another with mutual Christian love and tolerance. We should also rejoice that in all the central doctrines of the faith we remain agreed, for in these the Scripture is plain, perspicuous and virtually self-interpreting.

By this all will know that you are my disciples, if you love one another.
John 13:35

Genesis and Evolution: Integration

Chapter Twelve

I take it now as self-evident, requiring no further special discussion, that evolution and true religion are compatible. It is also sufficiently clear that science, alone, does not reach all truths, plumb all mysteries, or exhaust all values and that the place and need for true religion are still very much with us.

Biologist George Gaylord Simpson,
The Meaning of Evolution, *p. 5*

All thy works with joy surround thee,
Earth and heav'n reflect thy rays,
Stars and angels sing around thee,
Center of unbroken praise.
Field and forest, vale and mountain,
Blooming meadow, flashing sea,
Chanting bird and flowing fountain
Call us to rejoice in Thee.

Mortals, join the mighty chorus
Which the morning stars began,
Love divine is reigning o'er us,
Leading us with mercy's hand.
Ever singing, march we onward,
Victors in the midst of strife.
Joyful music lifts us sunward
In the triumph song of life!

From "Hymn to Joy," Henry van Dyke, 1907

The Need for Unity and Humility

The subjects of creationism and evolution impacted American culture throughout the 20th Century, especially within the Christian church. Countless members continue to struggle to integrate the findings of modern science with their traditional faith. Some Christians have critically examined the origin and development paradigms in which they have been acculturated and have comfortably expanded their means of interpreting the universal and eternal verities of the scriptures. For others, traditional sources of authority remain unchallenged, as the beliefs they espouse have become cherished sources of solace and security. Their established authorities are unquestionably accepted as unimpeachable. The result is that Christians who think on these subjects have generally migrated either to creationism, as defined by creationists, or theistic evolution, which incorporates the knowledge provided by science. Other beliefs are also embraced or opinion is withheld on this subject.

In the minds of many, particularly within the mainline Protestant or Catholic milieus, having differing views on the subjects of origins and development is not cause for concern, division, or rancor. Tolerance for variable belief regarding peripheral issues is the norm in many Protestant churches. Baptism (how or when it is performed), communion (how often, who administers, or to whom it is given), varieties of worship and music, beliefs about future events, standards for ordination, philosophies pertaining to women's leadership within the church, attitudes toward war, homosexuality, abortion, or strategies for mission, and standards of appropriate social behavior vary among individuals and churches. Most of the differing bodies within mainline Protestantism have long recognized the God-given freedom of others to exercise their conscience within their unique and personal relationship with God.

To many, however, primarily within the more evangelical or fundamental wing of Protestantism, what one believes on the subjects of origins and development is extremely crucial and theologically significant, worthy of conflict and justifying division within the body of Christ. To them this is not a peripheral issue. It is central. Having what is determined to be inaccurate beliefs in this realm is so serious that it often warrants exclusion and loss of fellowship with other members of a particular Christian community. It justifies conflict within and without the church. It is serious because creationists believe that evolutionary belief denies the need for a savior. If there were no Adam who sinned, no original sin, then people are not sinners and Jesus as Savior is not necessary, so this thinking goes. Theistic evolutionists, however, along with affirming God as creator, believe that people sin as a result of free will and there is definitely a need for a savior providing forgiveness. Their sin generates from their own actions and choices. It is present, not because of Adam, but because of their own tendency to err.

As was discussed in Chapters Five and Eleven, there is strong theological base to assert that sin indeed is universally present in each one of us as a result of free will and choice. Our need to survive makes us selfish, conniving, greedy, deceptive and cunningly manipulative. Evolution with its drive for survival even helps explain our proneness to iniquity. It affirms a need for forgiveness, rebirth, renewal, cleansing, looking beyond ourselves and turning around.

It appears that many creationists are willing to risk the loss of professionals, particularly scientists, to the faith. They also risk the alienation of their own young people who, upon entering higher education and learning new paradigms, experience conflict and feel disloyal as they become aware of different belief systems. Many people have undergone considerable distress as they wrestled with alternative schemas. When and if they convert from a creationist to theistic evolutionist position the result often is guilt, anger, disillusionment, resentment, or estrangement from family and church community

The divisiveness that permeates some quarters of Christendom with respect to this subject matter is contrary to the love and unity Christ taught. This condition might be alleviated if Christians were more tolerant of the diversity and individuality that occurs within the church. Humility, recognizing that none of us possesses all truth, would help. Presently, creationists are pressured to take sides against their brothers and sisters in the faith, the stereotypically labeled "secular humanists" who espouse evolutionary theory. It becomes an "us" and "them."

As was discussed in previous chapters, careful thinkers are humble, fairminded, honest, and open to new ideas. They do not perceive themselves as having arrived at all truth. Furthermore, most Christians understand the Christ-like qualities of gentleness, kindness, caring, forbearance, compassion, humility, inclusiveness, and goodness. Thinking Christians are open to new truth, knowing that only God has all truth. The attitude that "only we have the truth" is an insidious, and destructive mindset within the Christian world. We only need to look at the church's history to see how this attitude has dishonored her Lord.

Listen to Henry Morris, President Emeritus, and John Morris, President, Institute for Creation Research, in their recent (1996) book *The Modern Creation Trilogy*, Vol. 1.

> Great denominations that were once sound biblically and warmly evangelistic are now thoroughly liberal and neo-orthodox, and their denominational schools, colleges, and seminaries are citadels of unbelief and worldliness.

Ever since the Scopes' trial in particular (i.e., 1925), even evangelicals and fundamentalists have largely ignored these basic creation issues, piously concentrating on "personal Christianity"--nowadays on such shibboleths as "self-esteem," and other forms of what has come to be called "psycho babble." Even their Bible study groups tend to focus almost wholly on inter-personal relationships instead of biblical doctrine and God's great purposes in creation and redemption (p. 169).

The writers deride those more "liberal" and manage to indict the conservatives as well. Who is left? Judgmentalism, criticism, and exclusion do not advance Christian unity, nor do they address Christ's prayer in the Gospel of John (17:11) "So that they may be one as we are one" (New International Version). Jesus did not pray for uniformity, which is mandated from without, but for unity, which germinates from within the heart and mind. His desire was not that his followers be carbon copies of each other, but that they be united in mutual respect and bonded by His love for them and their love for him. After all, we have *personal* relationships with him. We're all different! The goal is not that we are all alike or that our Bible studies concentrate on the same things. It is that we all love in his name, starting with each other! The love he modeled was the "in spite of" love, not the "because of" love. Christian unity can be expressed by love, humility, inclusiveness, longsuffering, and tolerance. It is easy to love those who agree with us and affirm our beliefs. It is godly to love those who disagree with us and challenge our beliefs. This unique love is Christianity's greatest witness to the faith and to her Lord. Christians must strive for unity and enjoy our diversity.

Christians don't love one another because they all agree on every point of doctrine and emphasize the same theologies. They love one another in spite of the fact that they disagree or have varying areas of mission emphasis, liturgies (forms of worship), or polity (church government). The household of faith is not homogeneous. Christians are united by the unmerited love and grace of their Savior and Lord, Jesus Christ, not by their beliefs on origins! This was the unique love that dumbfounded those in the 1st Century who watched the early Christians, and it is still commonly seen in many settings within the church, both locally and universally.

Jesus gave a new commandment in John 13:34, "That you love one another as I have loved you." This love for one another, according to Jesus, was how the world would know that they belonged to him (John 17:21 "That they may all be one; even as thou, Father, art in me, and I in thee, that they also may be in us, so that the world may believe that thou hast sent me"). Not

327

so much their doctrinal stands or good works, but how they treated each other would make the difference! Their unique love and unity would be the ultimate testimony that *he was sent from God!*

The Apostle Paul enjoins the Romans (12:10) to be devoted to one another in brotherly and sisterly love, honoring one another above themselves. Ephesians 4:32 states, "Be kind to each other, tenderhearted, forgiving one another. Romans15:5 has the same message: "May the God who gives endurance and encouragement give you a spirit of unity." Ephesians 4:3 encourages Christians to "Make every effort to keep the unity of the spirit through the bond of peace." Without doubt, unity should be a sought after quality within the house of God.

Scholtes composed the words and wrote the music to what has become a signature hymn in contemporary Christianity. No doubt all Christians who sing this hymn concur in theory with its message:

> We are one in the Spirit, We are one in the Lord,
> We are one in the Spirit, We are one in the Lord,
> And we pray that all unity may one day be restored.

> Refrain:
> And they'll know we are Christians, by our love, by our love,
> Yes, they'll know we are Christians by our love.

> We will walk with each other, we will walk hand in hand,
> We will walk with each other, we will walk hand in hand
> And together we'll spread the news that God is in our land.

> We will work with each other, we will work side by side,
> We will work with each other, we will work side by side,
> And we'll guard each one's dignity and save each one's pride.

> The Celebration Hymnal, 1997, #429, Word Music/Integrity Music

And over all these virtues put on love, which binds them all together in perfect unity. (Colossians 3:14)

How good and pleasant it is when brothers live together in unity. (Psalm 133:1)

Most specialists in the fields of creationism, evolution, and biblical criticism acknowledge that there remains much to be understood about the areas of origins, purpose, and destiny, and that some questions may never be answered this side of eternity. Humility is the appropriate attitude, for no one save God alone is privy to the exact historic events of the universe, and to the intricacies of cells and their complex molecular endowment. We are all on a search using the remarkable minds God has given us. Having learned the lessons of the past, we can admit limitations, and be open to new insights. This is the recipe for unity as well as for truth.

New and Hidden Things: A Dynamic Faith

Malachi (3:6) states: "I am the Lord and I change not." Hebrews (13:8) tells us that Jesus Christ is the same, yesterday, today, and forever. All of us gain great strength and comfort from the realization that our God remains faithful, dependable, constant. We realize that the creator God is our rock and anchor, our mighty fortress and never-failing bulwark. God is our firm foundation, our ever present help in time of trouble. We are secure that our God is not subject to the whim of historical impacts or scientific breakthroughs. God is constant, the I AM, the everlastingly faithful parent.

What we don't often think about is that this great God, while unchanging, is indeed active in our midst, sometimes surprising us, revealing novel concepts, sharing marvelous secrets, freshly inspiring awe, and often challenging us to new heights of understanding and behavior. While God does not change, God is actively involved in our midst and our ideas about God's actions, will, world, and word requires that *we* change. We have experienced this in the past: The Hebrews wrote about the God who was up in the heavens, who came into the Garden in the cool of the day, rested on the seventh day, needed a rainbow to be reminded of a promise he had made, smelled the sweet savor of burnt offerings, visibly appeared in a furnace of fire, and spoke out of a burning bush and whirlwind.

Today we describe God differently. In the 21st Century we refer to the incarnate, transcendent, immanent, omnipotent, omniscient, triune God; the risen Savior, Redeemer, Sacrificial Lamb; the God of the atom, of DNA, radioactivity, plate tectonics, quarks, light years, black holes, and the Big Bang!

When the fullness of time was come, the historical Jesus broke forth on our earthly scene. He represented something very new. *God had become flesh and dwelled among us!* He changed the tenet of an eye for an eye and replaced it with forgiveness, seventy times seven if need be. He defended the prostitute, had compassion on the blind beggar, and preached that we should love our enemies. He dined with publicans and sinners and elevated the status of women. He pointed out that the very stone that the builders had rejected would become the head of the corner. He turned everything upsidedown! Rather than seeing that this was the Lord's doing and should be marvelous in their eyes, the most devout of the time could not deal with this challenge to the status quo and responded with murder in their hearts (Matthew 12:14).

We, too, resist the new. Novel ideas are still not welcome to the church. Well did Copernicus, Galileo, Luther, Tyndale, Wycliffe, and Martin Luther King understand that! Darwin joined the group in the 19th Century. God reveals secrets through science and honors us by providing answers through that medium to the mysteries that have puzzled humankind from the beginning. We must allow God to continue to break into our lives with divine truth.

Similarly, while the scriptures also are dependable and authoritative, we see that our interpretation of them must be open to enlargement. When we understand that, the progressive revelation of God's work in this universe becomes clearer. This revelation has often been expressed through the scholarship of theologians, but modern science has mightily unveiled truths as well. Christians are continually challenged to integrate and interpret the scriptures in light of what is being revealed in God's amazing, dynamic creation.

Some Christians resist change of outlook and interpretation, because it often requires changes in behavior and beliefs. But many have been exhilarated by these disclosures, and like Piglet in Winnie the Pooh, they ask each day, "I wonder what's going to happen exciting *today?*" When the Pilgrim fathers left Holland in 1620, John Robinson said, "I am verily persuaded that the Lord hath more truth yet to break forth from his holy word."

We are on a spiritual journey. Journeys don't go around the block. That's known territory. Journeys infer distance and often take us to new, challenging, scary, surprising, beautiful and exciting places. Are we willing to go on this journey or do we want to continue circling the comfortable, dependable, maybe even boring block? Might we miss perceiving how the glory of the Lord can be expressed innovatively in this complex world?

The scriptures tell us Jesus went on a journey. He set his face as a flint and headed for Jerusalem. Sometimes our journeys take us where we don't want to go, but we know that a fellow traveler is with us and will guide us into all truth and even unto death. "Call unto me and I will show you new and hidden things which you have not known before" (Jeremiah 33:3).

330

The Role of the Church

The lack of higher order thinking has contributed to the conflicts that surround the fields of biblical interpretation, creationism and evolution. While efforts are in place to improve critical thinking skills in society as a whole, it will take some time for such change to be applied and manifest throughout the religious community. Authoritarian church settings may be fearful and not encourage the practice of such skills. It is possible and regrettable that they may never be as completely exercised within the world of religion. Jesus told the Pharisees that the greatest commandment was to love the Lord with all your heart and all your soul and all your *mind* (Matthew 22:37).

Training in seminaries helps disseminate these truths. Courses bridging science and faith, from seminary to conference center, summer camp, retreats, youth groups, and in adult education programs in churches would greatly enhance understanding and increase tolerance among God's people. Printed materials, videos, distance learning opportunities and field trips give insight. Bible study on unity and love would be an ongoing and undergirding foundation. Ecumenical events stressing our relationship to our Lord and giving a forum for thinking, sharing, and growth would foster inclusiveness and oneness. Do we fear such activity? Would it upset our status quo? Honestly, would it honor the Lord? That is the question! Intra, as well as inter-denominational study is encouraged.

The leadership in many churches have met these issues responsibly and carefully, but for a variety of reasons have not been able to reach all in the pew. Mainline denominations have published many educational materials and offered forums for discussion on creation and evolution. Church related colleges have courses and have sponsored lectures by some of the leading minds in these areas. There are many books available that help bridge these disciplines, written by theologians who are also knowledgeable in science and scientists who are informed on religion. It is possible that the laity are not aware of these readings and various study opportunities.

Many Christians are content to maintain the level of belief they established as children. They do not wish or thirst to grow. Some are not aware of the scholarly support for a more figurative interpretation of the Scriptures. The fear of the unknown, commitment to the traditional faith of the fathers, the assumption that higher criticism is a trend toward modernism and the unspoken threat that higher order thinking and biblical criticism may dictate change or shake their belief in biblical inerrancy has prevented many Christians from opening their minds to another means of assessing the scriptures.

The organized church cannot be blamed for individuals who allow an immature faith plateau to prevail. Belief change is difficult, stressful, costly, divisive, and jarring, and some avoid it at all costs. It must be remembered, however, that Christ never promised that it would be easy to follow. We must be determined to examine thoughtfully and carefully whatever impacts his Church.

In the 20th Century belief became of supreme importance to many Christians, far surpassing the sacrificial action of faith that was taught by Jesus and the New Testament writers. Action and self-sacrificial commitment often continue to take second place to belief in assessing spirituality. Belief becomes the standard for acceptance, and the basis for judging others' Christian depth and genuineness. This mentality somewhat absolves individuals from the responsibility of living their faith as long as their beliefs are in order. Belief, even on peripheral issues, becomes so critical that stereotypic labeling, a type of name calling, exclusiveness, and judgmentalism seem justified in the minds of many. The strong group ties within many Christian churches where members share homogeneous belief also do not always encourage original thought.

As all things come together for the Christian, there are two records that provide insight on origins: modern science and the Genesis record. These stories can be integrated as Christians hold to a God who is Creator, who has designed dependable laws and in wisdom has freed these laws to operate.

We can see the specific mechanisms of science yet perceive the broader overview of meaning and purpose provided by religion. Both are unified in the great Creator and inform each other. One speaks mainly to the heart and its human longings and the other to the mind with its deep curiosities and desire to understand. Light can be shed on the mysteries and wonders of each by the other. Spirituality needs intellectual foundations, yet it is a way of knowing beyond rationality. The mind regains homeostasis through the gifts of the spirit. Revelation proceeds both from the actions (science) and personal directions (religion) of God. They are consistent, not in conflict. God and natural law are both knowable, orderly, reliable, good. They are not whimsical or capricious, nor do they show favoritism or bias.

Science gives us insight as to origins: from whence we came and how. Faith tells us who and informs on purpose and destiny. Together there is wholeness. Science and faith are mutually enhanced and they relate time and eternity. Reason (science) reveals God at work and its free inquiry can lead to awe, worship, and humility. This synthesis answers our greatest, deepest, and most profound questions.

All that remains for a complete picture of our origins is the record in the rocks, cells, and stars which must be appropriately deciphered, and the record in the inspired word which must be read and rightly interpreted. As Harry Emerson Fosdick, referencing evolutionary theory in a 1924 lecture at Yale University declared, "Have no fear for the new truth. Let us fear only our own lack of wisdom, insight, courage, and spiritual power in using it for the redemption of the souls and societies of men."[2]

There is no doubt that God communicates through the written word, amazingly preserved through the centuries, as well as through his astounding works: galaxies, the stars, geological formations, the infinite variety of life, both plant and animal, and complex molecules. We are one with God as we contemplate all of these entities. We are enriched in our knowledge and appreciation of the God of the universe. Christianity must never fear what science will discover. It provides one more opportunity to know the Creator through the work of God's hands.

I have a good friend named Bryn who is six years old. She drew me a self-portrait, which reveals a lot about Bryn. It consists of a large, happy face. There are details such as eyebrows and dimples, and a hairbow is included. The use of color is varied and intense. The artist is reflected in her art. I know Bryn a bit better when I look at this portrait. She is a happy, confident, intelligent, sharing, detail oriented individual, who has flair.

In like manner when we scrutinize the handiwork of God, whether it is beholding an erupting geyser, the grandeur of autumn, a mountain's majesty, or observing Protozoan *Vorticella* through the microscope recoiling in pond water we get to know God better. Whether it is seeing a far off nebula through a telescope, analyzing a core from the ocean's depth, sequencing the nucleotides in a DNA molecule, or understanding the mechanisms of natural selection, we are learning about the Creator's magnitude, variety, secrets, all encompassing detail, and overarching plan.

Science must always be perceived as a friend of the church, an aid in the journey to God, a means of grace, a contributor to our understanding of God's glory. We must take our study of science seriously, recognize our limitations and humbly and worthily use science to better show forth its Originator. Responsible use of scientific understanding honors the Creator and furthers God's kingdom on Earth. Irresponsible use can bring great pain and could lead to ultimate annihilation of life on Earth. Society will always require the ethical guidance provided by religion to help define what is right and what is wrong.

Along with understanding the origins of the marvels in nature, Christians should recognize their role as responsible stewards of God's handiwork, as

---

[2] *The Modern Use of the Bible* (1958), p. 273. New York: Macmillan.

well as heralds of God's love and forgiveness. Only then is wholeness realized as science and faith intermingle and mutually affirm the other's necessary role in the plan of the ages.

> *Someday, after we have mastered*
> *Wind, waves, tides, and gravity,*
> *We will harness for God the energy of love,*
> *And then, for the second time in the world,*
> *Humanity will have discovered fire.*

> *Teilhard de Chardin*

> *The heavens are thine, the earth also is thine:*
> *As for the world and the fulness thereof, thou has founded them;...(Psalm*
> *89:11)*

> *Lord, thou has been our dwelling place in all generations.*
> *Before the mountains were brought forth,*
> *Or even thou hadst formed the earth and the world*
> **Even from everlasting to everlasting, thou art God.** *(Psalm 90:1-2)*

Know that the Lord is God.

It is he who made us, and we are his.

Psalm 100:3

APPENDIX A

Creation References in the Bible

Genesis 1
Genesis 2
Exodus 20:11
I Samuel 2:8
II Kings 19:15
I Chronicles 16:26
Job 9:8-10
Job 12:9-10
Job 26:7-14
Job 38:4-11
Job 39:26-27
Psalms 8:1-4:
Psalms 19:1
Psalms 24:1
Psalms 33:6-9
Psalms 74:16-17
Psalms 89:11-12
Psalms 90:2
Psalms 96:5
Psalms 100:3
Psalms 102:25
Psalms 104
Psalms 121:2
Psalms 124:8
Psalms 136:5-9
Psalms 139:1-17
Psalms 146:6
Psalms 147:15-18
Psalms 148:3-5
Proverbs 3:19
Proverbs 8:22-29
Proverbs 16:4
Proverbs 26:10
Isaiah 37:16
Isaiah 40:12
Isaiah 42:
Isaiah 43:1

Isaiah 44:24
Isaiah 45:12, 15-18, 21-23
Isaiah 48:13
Jeremiah 10:11-13
Jeremiah 31:35
Jeremiah 32:17
Jeremiah 51:15-16
Ecclesiastes 3:11
Ecclesiastes 12:1
Amos 5:8
Amos 9:6
Zechariah 12:1
Mark 10:6
Mark 13:9
John 1:1-4
Acts 4:24
Acts 14:15
Acts 17:24
Romans 1:20
Romans 11:36
I Corinthians 8:6
I Corinthians 15:38-39
II Corinthians 5:18
Ephesians 3:9
Colossians 1:16-17
Colossians 2:3
I Timothy 6:13
Hebrews 3:4
Hebrews 11:3
I Peter 4:19
II Peter 3:3-7
Revelation 4:11
Revelation 10:6
Revelation 14:7

APPENDIX B

History of Time Line

Years ago Billion	Event
13.7	Big Bang
13	Hydrogen and Helium atoms formed
12	Milky Way begins to take shape; stars
4.6-.59	**Precambrian Era**
	Solar system formed in Milky Way galaxy; Sun, Moon, Earth. Moon rocks from Apollo 11 and 12 are 4.5 billion years old
4.4-4.2	Oceans and continents formed
4.2	Primordial sea; Life? Wiped out over and over?
4.03	Oldest Earth rocks found, a result of cooling; NW Territories, Canada
~3.5	Earliest anaerobic bacteria and algae formed; stromatolites (blue-green algae and rock); photosynthesis liberated oxygen from water into atmosphere
3	Microfossils; Prokaryotes (cells without membrane-bound organelles)
2	Fossil algae in Gunflint Chert in Canada; oxygen-rich atmosphere; aerobic respiration
1.5	Gigantic land mass Pangaea begins to form
1.2	Worm-like trail found in Australia sandstone; oldest data of animal more than one cell
1	Eukaryotes (complex cells with membrane-bound organelles including multiple chromosomes in nucleus); development of sexual reproduction; bacteria on land: biocrust in Torridon region of Scotland
Million	
850	Bitter Springs Formation of Australia; diversification of nucleated cells!

700	Multicelled fossils abound; jellyfish, sea pens, wormlike animals soft corals, sponges; Ediacara Hills of Australia
600	Explosion of life; marine invertebrates abundant
580	First of many ice ages
550	Shell fossil remains, biomineralized shell reef, S. Namibia
590-505	**Cambrian Period**: rapid diversification of animal phyla; development of hard parts; shellfish, trilobites; Burgess Shale, Canadian Rockies; North America combined with Greenland formed the continent Laurentia, an island along equator; first known backboned animals, primitive fish called Ostracoderms
505-438	**Ordovician Period**: Corals, crinoids, bryozoans, starfish, nautiloids, graptolites, trilobites; spread of jawless fishes; large continent Gondwana consisting of present day Africa, Antarctica, Australia, South America, Southern Europe, much of the Middle East and India began to move over to South Pole region
438-408	**Silurian Period**: jawed and armored fishes (Placoderms)
420	Coral reefs
408-360	**Devonian Period**: lobe-finned fishes with lungs and gills; land colonizers (Rhipidistians); amphibians, insects; bony fishes; sharks (cartilaginous); ammonoids; Northern Europe collided with and joined Laurentia
405	First terrestrial plants

360-310	**Mississippian Period**: snails, Lepidodendron trees; trilobites, brachiopods
345	First fossil of animal which walked on land: *Pederpes finneyae*
340	First coelacanths; seas flood much of Europe and North America
320	Early trees
310-286	**Pennsylvanian Period**: Early reptiles appear
300	Coal swamp cycles ('trees', ferns, horsetails, club moss)
265	Separated continents joined to become Supercontinent Pangaea
286-248	**Permian Period**: Insects, amphibians; *Dimetrodon*; reptile radiation; dinosaur ancestors, crocodile-like Phytosaurs
250	Greatest extinction event in Earth's history; 95% of species thought to have disappeared; massive lava flow?? *Seymouria*, (amphibian/reptilian features)
248-213	**Triassic Period**: *Coelophysis*, small, bipedal reptile; first dinosaurs;mammal-like reptiles (Therapsids); origin of mammals; gymnosperms dominant
225	Continents begin to separate opening Atlantic Ocean
212	Three toed footprints in Argentina: bird??
213-144	**Jurassic Period**: Ichthyosaurs, Stegosaurs; abundant and diverse dinosaurs
180	Gondwanaland split; two large land masses: South America, Africa, India, Antarctica, and Australia pulled away from Europe and North America
150	Birds from Theropod dinosaurs; *Archeopteryx*

144-65	**Cretaceous Period**: *Triceratops, Pteranadon;* Flowering plants appeared
140	Modern sharks, bony fish, marine reptiles (crocodile)
135	South America and Africa split; India headed toward Asia from Africa
125	Flowering plants established; oldest placental mammal, mouselike, *Eomaia,* Northeast China
124-122	Feathered dinosaurs, Northeast China
100	*Tyrannosaurus rex* appears
85	Asteroid?
80	Late Cretaceous; Asiamerica (Asia and West Coast, USA joined); inland sea splits West Coast from East Coast; Euramerica (East Coast and Europe joined)
75	Triceratops roams Earth
67	Dinosaurs extinct; mammal age begins
65-2	**Tertiary Period:** mammals flourish but modern orders not yet distinguishable
65	Alps formed; Atlantic Ocean widens; South America and Africa are islands. North America, Europe, and Asia linked
62	Early primates appear; oldest: *Purgatorius* (Montana); good eyesight, grasping hands, large brain
60	Australia separated from Antarctica
58	Ancestor of horse, *Hyracotherium,* 30" tall
55	Temperature peak; subtropical forests into Arctic; global greenhouse warming
53	Bats
50	Mountain ranges of Earth emerging; India crashed into Tibet after 150 million year journey; continents similar to those of today
50-45	Opposable thumb, stereoscopic vision; tree dwelling primate-like lemurs, tarsiers, whales, giant birds.

40-30	Grass; *Ambulocetus*, whale missing link: Pakistan
37-24	Rodents, pigs, camels, rhinos, *Mesohippus* (horse); modern orders of mammals distinguishable
35+	Apes and monkeys diverge; sabre toothed tiger
25-24	Cattle, deer, elephants; proliferation of horse species
20	Apes; no tails, arms longer than legs
17	Formation of Himalaya Mountains
12	Africa joins Europe and Asia; modern elephants
10-7	Hominid to be branched off from ape common ancestor; Red Sea opened
8-6	Environmental upheaval; forests replaced by grasslands; new species, plain dwellers; earliest known hominid ancestor, *Sahelanthropus tchadensis,* Pakistan
7	Skull found of pre-human ancestor that walked upright: Chad
6	Bipedalism
6-5	First Hawaiian Island formed (Kauai)
5-2	South and North America joined
4.2	*Australopithecus anamensis*
4-3	Human precursors, Africa; limbs similar yet brain size; "Lucy," *Australopithecus afarensis* (bipedal ape-man, East Africa), *A. africanus* (South Africa), *Pliohippus* (horse)
4	Laetoli fossil hominid tracks
3.5	*Kenyanthropos platyops*: flat faced man, Kenya
3.7-10,000	**Quaternary Period**
2.5	*Homo habilis*; tool makers; chopping tools from Tanzania; human ancestor brain began to expand in size

2-11,000	Ice Age began: Glaciers advanced and retreated five times; glacials from 64,000 to 200,000 years; interglacials up to million years; mammoth extinction; modern horses, *Equus*
1.8-1	Choppers, scrapers
1.75	At least three types of early humans migrated from Africa to Eurasia, three skull types found in Republic of Georgia
1.5	Ice sheets cover 1/3 Earth's surface
1	Further dispersal from Africa
1.6-300,000	*Homo erectus*
Thousands	
800,000	Fire used (?)
600,000	Organized hunting
350,000	*Homo sapiens* "wise man"
230,000	Neanderthals
130,000	Last *Homo erectus, H. habilis* in Africa
75,000	Deliberate burial of dead
50,000	*Homo sapiens sapiens*
40,000	Bering land bridge; New World; Cro-Magnon man moves westward to Europe
35,000	Neanderthal (variant) burials; disappearance; humans to North America
33,000	Humans to Australia
30,000	Oldest writing; lunar marks on bone; Cave art (Europe); Cro-Magnon; hunters, wanderers, gatherers
28,000	Humans cross land bridge between Asia and North America
20,000	Bison hunters, North America
18,000	Maximum reach of last glaciation
12,000	Pottery (Japan);
11,000	Retreat of last ice age; Great Lakes formed; hunting to farming, herding; villages, civilization arrived

10,000	**Neolithic (New Stone) Age**
	Bow and arrow; dog domesticated in North America mass extinction: mammoths, woolly rhinos, glyptodonts, sabre toothed cats, mastodons; horses and camels disappeared in New World; first farms in Fertile Crescent
	Years Before Christ (BC) or Before Common Era (BCE)
9,500	Jericho (pre-pottery): oldest walled city in the world
8,000-4,000	Creation week occurred in here according to biblical literalists
7,000	First pottery in the Near East; beginnings of work with metals
5,000	Land bridge between Britain and Europe severed
4,600	Metalworking (Europe)
4,004	Bishop Ussher's date for creation week; sail propelled boats; horse domesticated in Russia; disastrous floods in Mesopotamian region
4000	**Chalcolithic (Copper-Stone) Age**
3,760	Earliest date in Jewish calendar; traditional date of creation
3,500	Sumer:first city-states in Mesopotamia; earliest numerals in Egypt; pictographic writing starts; then cuneiform; clay tablets; Epic of Gilgamesh
3,000	**Early Bronze Age**
2,800	Britain: earliest stage of Stonehenge begun
2,700	Egypt: Old Kingdom starts; Gilgamesh, legendary king of Uruk in Sumeria; first epic tales of Gilgamesh
2,600	Egypt: Great Pyramid built; dogs domesticated in Egypt; Pharoah, the god-king in Egypt
2,500	Sumerians: earliest law codes

2,500-1,800?	Stonehenge assembled showing mathematical sophistication (England)
2,400	Syria: Canaanite empire based on Ebla; settlement of Aramean nomads from Euphrates area and Semitic Canaanite tribes in Palestine
2,350	Sumerian empire founded
~2,100-1,900?	Abraham's journey from Ur (modern Iraq) into Canaan; Monotheism
2,100	Egypt: Middle Kingdom starts; discover use of papyrus
2,000	**Middle Bronze Age**
1,900	Beginning of Semitic alphabet
1,800-1,300	Patriarchal Period of Jewish history; oral tradition begins 1,750
1,750	Babylon: Old Babylonian Empire under Hammurabi; great Code of Laws
1,600-1,200	Greece: period of Mycenaean domination
1,550	Egypt: New Kingdom starts
1,500	**Late Bronze Age**
1,400-1,200	Canaan: Ugarit palace archives (Ras Shamra)
1,400	First alphabet: Syria
1,300-1,250	Mosaic Period
1300?	Hebrews; Moses; Exodus from Egypt; Monotheism Conquest of Canaan (some say this was 200 years earlier); Phoenicians spread alphabet
1,290-1,224	Egypt: Ramesses II (Ramesses the Great)
1,250?	Anatolia: fall of "Homeric" Troy
1,225-1,205	Egypt: Pharaoh Merneptah
1200	**Iron Age**
1,200	The Sea Peoples: Ugarit destroyed, end of Hittite Empire

1,190	Egypt: Rameses III defeats the Sea Peoples; Palestine: Philistines settle the coastal plain
1,150-1,025	Palestine: period of the Biblical Judges
1,100	Egypt: end of the Egyptian Empire; first Chinese dictionary produced
1,050	Palestine: Philistines win the battle of Eben-ezer, conquer Israel
1,025-1,000	Palestine: King Saul anointed by Samuel, last Israelite judge
1000-587	Palestine: David takes Jerusalem: Period of Monarchy; David king
965-920	Palestine: Solomon king; First temple built
920	Palestine: Divided kingdom-Judah and Israel; beginning of written tradition; Hebrew alphabet developed as opposed to Semitic alphabet; beginning of Hebrew literature; Song of Deborah
876-869	Israel: King Omri, founder of capital at Samaria
869-850	Israel: King Ahab, husband of Jezebel
842-640	Israel and Judah: King Jeroboam II, King Uzziah, King Ahaz, Fall of Samaria, King Hezekiah fortifies Jerusalem, King Josiah and religious reforms
800	Amos, first book of Old Testament, written (not first canonized)
753	Rome founded (traditional)
722	End of kingdom of Israel
626-539	Babylon: Neo-Babylonia Empire; King Nebuchadnezzar
621	Deuteronomy first book canonized; first Bible = 1 book
597	Judah: Babylonian invasion. The first deportation; Babylonian exile
586	Judah: the fall of Jerusalem. Destruction of the Temple; Nebuchadnezzar II of Babylon
586-538	Babylon: the Hebrew Exile

585	Thales of Miletus; geometry, solar eclipse predicted
563	Buddha born
551	Confucius born
~530	Pythagoras, father of mathematical physics
520-515	Palestine: the rebuilding of the Temple in Jerusalem
509	Roman republic founded (traditional)
500	Aramaic language begins to replace Old Hebrew in Palestine
5-4 centuries	Sophists; Greek lecturers, writers; traveled and taught
477	Athens starts rise to power
460	Hippocrates, Greek physician, father of medicine, born
445	Palestine: Nehemiah, the walls of Jerusalem rebuilt; Torah becomes moral essence of Jewish state
427	Plato born; becomes student of Socrates 407-399
400	The rest of the Law (Pentateuch) canonized
384	Aristotle, the first great biologist, born
336-323	Macedonia: Alexander the Great conquers the world; Egypt: Ptolemy I, Palestine under the Ptolemies
300	Euclid: mathematician, geometry
255	Writing of "Septuagent;" Greek version of Old Testament
250	Parchment produced at Pergamum
~220	Archimedes: mathematician, mechanics
200	Palestine: conquest by the Seleucids
~165	Book of Daniel
141	Jews liberate Jerusalem
~112	Rise of Pharisses and Saducees in Palestine

77	Pliny the Elder published *Natural History* about the nature of things, cosmology, astronomy, zoology, humans, botany, minerals, technology, some magic and superstition; this was authoritative science up to the Middle Ages
63	Palestine: Romans under Pompey capture Jerusalem
37-4	Herod the Great
23	Augustus becomes Emperor of Rome
5	Probable date of Jesus Christ's birth at Bethlehem
	Years After Christ (Anno Domini-AD) or Common Era (CE)
26-36	Pontius Pilate procurator of Judea
27	Baptism of Jesus
~30	Crucifixion and resurrection of Jesus the Christ
31	Martyrdom of Stephen
32	Conversion of Saul (Paul)
45	St. Paul sets out on missionary travels
50	Church in Corinth established
51 or 52	Paul's disputes with philosophers at Athens
58	Paul's letters to the Corinthians; imprisoned in Caesarea
60	Paul brought to trial before Festus; appeals to Rome
60-100	First three Gospels written; Mark first
64	First persecution of Christians by Nero; fire destroys Rome; Peter's martyrdom?
66	Palestine: the First Jewish Revolt against the Romans
~67	Paul's execution in Rome

70	Palestine: Jerusalem falls. Destruction of the Second Temple; Matthew written in this period
73	Palestine: Masada falls
75	Luke written
85	Gospel of John written
95	Revelation written
112	Letter of Pliny, governor of Bithynia to Emperor Trajan: The Christians are harmless!
~200	Formation of Neo-Hebrew language
200+	Persecution of Christians increases; martyrs revered as saints
250	Emperor worship compulsory; Ptolemy:mathematics applied to astronomy
Late 2C	Formation of the New Testament Canon
306	Constantine declared emperor
312	Constantine converted to Christianity
325	Nicaean Creed adopted; doctrinal clarification
330	Constantinople dedicated as "New Rome;" heart of Eastern Christendom; Orthodox Christianity; hub for 1100 years! (except 1204-1261) Byzantine era; monasticism, aceticism, charity
382	Pope Damasus holds council and identifies canonical books in Old and New Testaments
~386	Jerome translated Bible into Latin
395	Christianity only official state religion in Roman Empire
396	St. Augustine becomes Bishop of Hippo; his theological writings dominate western thought down to Aquinas; *De Rudibus Catechizandis*
4C	Churches built; icons; relics; holy ground.
432	St. Patrick to Ireland

476	Roman Empire collapses; papacy growth; 480-500 Christianity dominant religion in cities of the west; Boethius authors *Consolation of Philosophy*
~540	Benedict draws up monastic rule
~563	Columba leaves Ireland for Iona
570	Muhammad born; Muslims of Islam
597	Augustine arrives in Kent
	Middle Ages: Monk scribe; monasteries, manuscripts
~600-636	Isidore, Bishop of Seville, writes encyclopaedic works; source of knowledge for Middle Ages
620	Vikings invade Ireland
622	The hegira, year 0 on Muslim calendar
638	Arab conquest of Jerusalem
691-2	Muslims erect Dome on the Rock in Jerusalem on Mt. Moriah
700-1050	Monasticism; schools, libraries, gold relics, ritual, boys choirs, chants, episcopal majesty, illustrated liturgical books, organ
700	Psalms translated into Anglo-Saxon; Lindisfarne Gospels written
731	Bede completes *Ecclesiastical History of the English People* and biblical commentaries
771-814	Charlemagne; Monk scholar Alcuin of York headed palace school at Aachen; revival of learning in Europe: Carolingian renaissance
787	Second Council of Nicaea upholds veneration of icons
~800	Book of Kells, Ireland
814	Arabs adopt numerals 0-9, they pursue astronomy, invent algebra
909	Monastery at Cluny founded; becomes center of reform

932	Wood-block printing in China for mass production of classical books
978	Chinese begin compilation of an encyclopedia of 1,000 volumes
1009	Destruction of Church of the Holy Sepulchre in Jerusalem
1050-1200	Forests cleared, cities expanded, international trade; Gregorian Reform; applying principles of gospel to contemporary society; Cathedral schools;
1079-1142	Peter Abelard theologian: church's quest for a solid theological base
1099	First Crusade; Jerusalem captured
1146	Second Crusade: failed
1170	Murder of Archbishop Thomas Becket of Canterbury
1189-1192	Third Crusade
1204	Fourth Crusade, to Egypt
1200s	**Renaissance:** universities from cathedral schools: Bologne, Paris, Oxford; works of Aristotle on physics and metaphysics arrived via Arab world; interest in natural science stimulated; hard to correlate biblical story of creation with belief in the eternity of matter; devotion to Virgin Mary; suffering Savior
~1200-1250	Golden age of papal power, yet crusades failed; rise of nation states; growth of lay authority
1209	Francis of Assisi; Franciscan Order
1212	Children's Crusade
1215	Magna Carta
1217-1221	Fifth Crusade: to Egypt

1225-1274	St. Thomas Aquinas; scholasticism; *Summa Theologiae;* supporting Christian belief with reason; wrote commentaries on most books of the Bible
1228	Dominicans established; leading struggle against heresy
1278	Aristotle's works translated and circulated
1327-1347	Franciscan William of Ockham writes polemics against papacy
1348-1351	Black death ravages Europe
1375-1382	John Wyclif attacks clerical wealth, monasticism, authority of pope
1382	First English translation of the Bible (Wyclif) from Latin
1400s	Petrarch: classical learning and Christian spirituality compatible; beginnings of humanism; individualism, dignity of humans, reason; recovery of classical texts; classicism
1413	Czech reformer Jan Huss writes *De Ecclesia* encouraging church reform
1415	Huss burned
1453	Printing Press, movable type; (Gutenberg); Byzantine empire collapsed, captured by Ottoman Turks
1473	Sistine Chapel built
1492	Columbus crosses the Atlantic
1500s	High Renaissance; Italian artists: Michelangelo, Leonardo da Vinci, Raphael; British scholars Sir Thomas More, Elyot, Ascham, Shakespeare; Italian Erasmus: nature; love of learning

1517-1521	**Reformation:**
1517	Monk, priest and university professor Martin Luther posts 95 theses at Wittenberg; justification by faith; Bible to common man; denominations
1519	Luther denies primacy of pope and infallibility of general councils; Cortes attacks Aztecs in Mexico
1521	Martin Luther excommunicated
1522	First world circumnavigation by Magellan
1524	Franciscans arrive in Mexico
1525	Fugitive translator Tyndale's Bible available to laity; Hebrew and Greek into English
1530	Copernicus's *De Revolutionibus Orbium Coelesticum* published; heliocentrism
1534	Church of England separated from papal authority
1535	Execution of Thomas More
1536	Tyndale, Father of the English Bible, burned near Brussels; French jurist John Calvin arrives in Geneva. *Institutes;* theological basis of Protestantism
1539	Henry VIII's Great Bible printed
1543	Vesalius, anatomy
1549	The First Book of Common Prayer in England
1560	A reformed church established in Scotland by John Knox
1570	Tycho Brahe: Earth motionless
1588	Molina (Jesuit from Spain) publishes a work defending free will against predestination

1600-1800	**Enlightenment:** growing secularism, literacy; biblical criticism; denial of supernaturalism; fossils; hints of old Earth; attempts to interpret Genesis in light of new material; Bentham, Locke, Rousseau, Voltaire, Thomas Jefferson; natural rights and political democracy
1603	Pontifical Academy of Sciences founded, Rome
1607	Smith founds Jamestown
1609	Telescope invented
1611	Galileo's *Sidereus Nuncius* published, including observations on the moons of Jupiter; sunspots and Moon mountains noted
1611	King James Version of the Bible published
1620	Mayflower sails from Holland and England
1621	Kepler's *Epitome of Copernican Astronomy* published; planetary motion; science helped him learn about God
1628	Harvey established anatomy and physiology; blood circulation; organic phenomena subject to experimental assessment and can be reduced to mechanical systems
1630	Puritans found Boston
1633	Galileo convicted of suspected heresy; sentenced to life imprisonment
1644	Descartes' *Principia Philosophiae* published; considered the beginning of the "Age of Reason"
1650	Bishop James Ussher of Ireland proposes Earth created on October 3, 4004 BC
1658	Blaise Pascal mathematician, physicist, religious thinker: *Apology for the Christian religion*
1662	Royal Society of London for the Promotion of Natural Knowledge chartered
1666	Academie des Sciences of Paris established
1667	Milton's *Paradise Lost*

1678	Richard Simon *Histoire Critique du Vieux Testament* (the beginning of Old Testament criticism); John Bunyon's *Pilgrim's Progress*
1682	William Penn founds Pennsylvania on the basis of religious toleration
1687	Isaac Newton's *Philosophiae Naturalis Principia Mathematica* published; new physics and observation applied to terrestrial and celestial bodies; law of universal gravitation; universe divinely ordered; Catholics moved into Arizona and California from Mexico
1704	Newton's *Opticks;* experimental physics; heat, light, electricity, magnetism
1707	Isaac Watts: father or English hymns
1723-1750	Johann Sebastian Bach composes great religious works at Leipzig
1726	Beginning of Great Awakening in North American Christianity
1727	Conversion of Jonathan Edwards, leading Calvinist theologian in North America
1733	Flying shuttle for weaving; beginning of Industrial Revolution in England
1738	Conversion of John Wesley
1739-1752	David Hume's writings introduced skepticism: *Philosophical Essays Concerning Human Understanding (1748)*
1740s	Great Awakening arose from revivals; bequeathed spirit of freedom of religion in United States
1742	Handel's *Messiah* first performed, Dublin
1749-1804	Buffon worked on *Histoire Naturelle, Generale et Particuliere*, systematically presented natural history, geology, and anthropology in one publication
1758	Halley's comet returned as he predicted!

1769	Watt's steam engine patented
1776	Declaration of Independence
1778	Lamarck, botanist; wrote three volume flora of France; first concept of museum collection; invertebrate systematics
1780s	Augustin de Coulomb measured electrical and magnetic forces
1790	Hutton: rocks, sedimentation; "Present the key to the past"
1794	First great scientific school of modern world: Ecole Polytechnique in Paris
1796	Jenner: first vaccination against smallpox
1799	Schleiermacher publishes his addresses to 'the cultured despisers of religion'
1800	First electric battery; Christianity throughout the world from China to Peru; second Great Awakening; Protestant revival in US
1802	Lamarck first to use word "biology"
1804	British and Foreign Bible Society founded
1805	Cuvier published in comparative anatomy, and later (1812) book on vertebrate fossils
1807	First Protestant missionary to China
1809	Lamarck's theory of evolution
1817	Robert Moffat, missionary to South Africa for over 50 years
1821	Faraday's electric motor and generator
1825	Geoffroy wrote of evolution of crocodiles
1838	Charles Lyell's *Elements of Geology* published including geological succession; Schwann and Schleiden Cell Theory

1840	Bruno Bauer's *Kritik der evangelischen Geschichte des Johannes* proposing a new type of biblical scholarship, the "Historical critical method"; David Livingstone (son-in-law of Moffat) arrives in Africa
1843	Kierkegaard publishes existential view of Christianity
1844-1859	*Codex Sinaiticus* of Greek Bible from 4th C. discovered; Codex *Vaticanus* (4th C) released to scholars
1854	Papal bull establishes immaculate conception of Virgin Mary
1857	Pasteur set foundation for Germ Theory of Disease
1858	First edition of *Gray's Anatomy*
1859	Darwin's *On the Origin of Species;* denial of special creation of species; natural selection required much time
1870	Pius IX: dogma of papal infallibility "in doctrine regarding faith and morals"
1871	Darwin's *Descent of Man* published
1875	William Draper's *History of the Conflict between Religion and Science* published; Koch proved Pasteur's Germ Theory of Disease
1876	Bell invents the telephone
1878	Leo XIII, a friend of science, becomes pope; comes to terms with modern world, including Marxism
1880	Pavlov's experiments with conditioned reflex in dogs
1884	Pasteur's first inoculations against rabies
1889	*Lux Mundi* publication; a collection of essays by Christian evolutionists

1895	White's *A History of the Warfare of Science with Theology in Christendom*
1900+	Mission movement
1901	Identification of different blood groups
1902	Alfred Loisy's *L'Evangile et l'Eglise* published; "modernist" reconciliation of biblical criticism with Roman Catholic theology
1903	Mendelian genetics understood and appreciated; first motor powered flight by the Wright brothers
1905	Einstein publishes Special Theory of Relativity; successful direct blood transfusion between humans
1907	Pius X's encyclical, *Pascendi gregis*, condemning Roman Catholic "Modernist" trends in theology and biblical scholarship
1910	Fundamentalism; pamphlets; moderate; discovery of protons and electrons
1916	Einstein's General Theory of Relativity published
1919	World Christian Fundamentalist Association formed in U.S.
1920	Fundamentalism; more militant; holy war against evolution
1925	Scopes "Monkey" trial, Dayton, Tennessee; Hubble demonstrates existence of galaxies beyond our own
1920s	Oparin pioneers with coacervate (aggregation of lipid molecules) droplets, forming "membranes"
1930s / 40s	Haldane researches origin of life
1932	Reinhold Niebuhr's *Moral Man and Immoral Society*; symbolizes arrival of a new critical realist Protestantism
1945	First atomic bomb employed in war
1947	Discovery of the Dead Sea Scrolls at Qumran

1948	State of Israel established; World Council of Churches founded
1949	Billy Graham begins evangelism tours
1950	National Council of Churches founded
1953	Watson and Crick discover structure of DNA; Miller artificially synthesized amino acids, urea and fatty acids; prebiotic molecules
1957	Launching of Sputnik
~1960	Evolution returned to textbooks
1962-1965	Second Vatican Council; Catholics 'new opening' to the modern world
1963	First liver transplant
1964	Penzias and Wilson detected radiation, light and heat from the Big Bang!
1969	First moon landing; total artificial heart implanted in a human as a temporary measure
1977	Fox polymerized amino acids which formed proteinoid microspheres when in contact with water (protocells)
1978	First test-tube baby born
1980s	Genetic engineering; television evangelism
1981	First flight of US space shuttle; Act 590 "Balanced Treatment Act" became law in Arkansas
1982	Arkansas: U.S. District Court, "Balanced Treatment Act" struck down; Court denied that creationism may be taught as science in public schools
1984	Vatican commission admits error in condemning Galileo in 1633; Baby Fae receives heart from baboon and survives 20 days
1986	First successful double-lung transplant

1987	John Paul II's address, "The Church and the Scientific Community: A Common Quest for Understanding;" Supreme Court struck down Louisiana's Creationism Act
1989	Ban on chemicals destroying ozone layer agreed to by 80 countries
1990	International scientists appeal to religious leaders for cooperation in addressing ecological crisis
1991	U.S. National Institutes of Health awards grant to the Center for Theology and the Natural Sciences to conduct research on the theological and ethical implications of the Human Genome Project
1992	Earth summit on environmental concerns: Rio de Janeiro
1995	Baboon bone marrow transplant to humans
1996	Pope John Paul II asserts that the Theory of Evolution is "more than just a hypothesis"
1997	Successful cloning of mammals
1999	Kansas Board of Education eliminates evolution and Big Bang cosmology from state high school exams
2000	Kansas voters remove legislators who established 1999 tenets; evolution and Big Bang cosmology restored to classrooms
2001	Human genome completed First human embryos produced using nuclear transformation (cloning); First genetically modified primate via genetic engineering; Pennsylvania legislators assess the teaching of evolution and intelligent design in the public school classroom
2002	Ohio legislators assess the teaching of evolution and intelligent design in the public school classroom; Water detected in atmospheres of planets orbiting distant stars; water on Mars

Compiled from:

Benton, Michael (1986). *The story of life on Earth*. New York: Warwick Press.

Berra, Tim M. (1990). *Evolution and the myth of creationism*. Stanford, CA: Stanford Univ. Press.

Buttrick, G. A. (Ed.). (1962). *The interpreter's dictionary of the Bible: An illustrated encyclopedia* (Vol. 1). New York: Abingdon Press. (Inside front cover)

Cooke, J., Kramer, A. & Rowland-Entwistle, T. (1981). *History's Timeline: A 40,000 year chronology of civilization*. Barnes & Noble, Inc.

Dowley, Tim (Ed.). (1977). *Eerdmans' handbook to the history of Christianity*. Herts, England: Lion Publishing.

Encyclopedia Britannica (1994-1998). "The History of Science," Britannica Online.

God and science: Must we choose? A nine-part discussion series for adult Christian education, Leader's Guide (1993). Newton Center, MA: Center for Faith and Science Exchange.

Harrold, Francis B. (1990). Past Imperfect: Scientific Creationism and Prehistoric Archeology. *Creation/Evolution, XXVII*, 3.

Magnusson, Magnus (1977). *Archeology of the Bible*. New York: Simon & Schuster.

McManners, John (Ed.). (1990). *The Oxford illustrated history of Christianity*. Oxford: Oxford University Press.

Mt. St. Helen's Visitor Center at Silver Lake, Washington, 1997.

National Geographic Supplement, May 1998. Millennium in maps: Physical Earth. *New Revised Standard Version Bible*, 1989. Supplemental Resource Materials, Nashville: Thomas Nelson Publishers.

* * * * * * * * * *

It must be noted that many of the dates herein are, as sometimes noted, approximations. Also, different sources list varying dates for specific periods or happenings. Therefore these dates may well not agree with all of the above sources or with other experts.

APPENDIX C

Responses to Evolution

1. There is no use in saying that we do not like the changes forced upon us...Regarding a fresh revelation of God's truth, the question never is whether we like it, but how soon we shall make it a part of our life and thought.

> J. C. Swaim, 1953, *Right and Wrong Ways to Use the Bible*, p. 164

2. To the fearful and timid let me say, that while Evolution is certain to oblige theology to reconstruct its system, it will take nothing away from the grounds of true religion.

> Henry Ward Beecher, preacher at Plymouth Church in the 1880s In G. Kennedy (Ed.). *Evolution and Religion:The Conflict Between Science and Religion in North America*, 1957, p. 19

3. Theology would be corrected, enlarged, and liberated by evolution, but religion, as a spiritual fixture in the character of man, would be unmoved.

> R. Hofstadter, same source as #2, 1957, p. 13

4. Have no fear of the new truth! Let us fear only our own lack of wisdom, insight, courage, and spiritual power in using it for the redemption of the souls and societies of men.

> Harry Emerson Fosdick, in a series of lectures at Yale, 1924 From Fosdick, H. E., *The Modern Use of the Bible*, 1958, p. 273

5. Religious authority, like the medieval mind, looks always backwards, toward the past. Its wisdom, its mysteries, its experiences with God, its miracles, its revelations, all took place centuries ago.....But if God is the creative and controlling power of the universe, why confine His operations to the first few years of the Christian era?....Let us think out the interpretations for ourselves, untrammeled and de novo. Let us breathe the fresh air of this new morning without forever smelling the dust of obsolete libraries.

M. Shipley, quoting Parrish, in *The War on Modern Science: A Short History of the Fundamentalist Attacks on Evolution and Modernism*, 1927, p. 10.

6. The Bible assumes that the plants and animals with which we are familiar are part of the unalterable original state of the world as God created it. The findings of Natural Science....force us to give up this idea entirely. Whatever may be our attitude towards the theory of evolution....., at one point the discussion has been closed forever, namely, that most of the forms of life which now exist did not formerly exist at all, that many of those which used to exist no longer do so, and that between the earliest and the present-day forms of life....there were very many others, so that those which now exist prove to be one of the many worlds of forms which followed each other in orderly progression.

   Theologian E. Brunner in *The Christian Doctrine of Creation and Redemption. Dogmatics* (Vol. II) (O. Wyon. Trans.), 1952, p. 32-33.

7. The proper attitude for her, however, does not consist in always accepting the scientific and philosophical ideas. What I offer, she must say, is valid, whether Copernicus or Ptolemy, Darwin or Agassiz, is right. The gospel is and has no system of cosmology and biology; it preaches the kingdom of God which is to be realized in the heart of man.

   Philosopher Paulsen referring to the church; quoted by H. Lane in *Evolution and Christian Faith*, 1923, p. 26.

8. Why could not a creator work through the evolutionary process, his providence operating, as it were, on the installment plan?

   Asa Gray, Harvard botanist and Darwin's main supporter in the United States. From Kennedy, G. (Ed.). *Evolution and Religion: The Conflict Between Science and Religion in Modern America*, 1957, p. viii.

9. I have steadily endeavored to keep my mind free, so as to give up any hypothesis, however much beloved (and I cannot resist forming one on every subject), as soon as facts are shown to be opposed to it. Indeed I have had no choice but to act in this manner, for with the exception of the

Coral Reefs, I cannot remember a single first-formed hypothesis which had not after a time to be given up or greatly modified.

> Charles Darwin in Barlow, N. *The Autobiography of Charles Darwin 1809-1882 with Original Omissions Restored*, 1958, p.87.

10. Evolution (of itself) neither affirms nor denies a Creator. Evolution (of itself) neither validates nor negates creation. Evolution and creation are not essentially joined, nor are they mutually exclusive...Evolution is science; creation is faith (in a Creator); each is looking at the origin of mankind and the universe from its own perspective. A person may espouse science, faith, both, or neither.

> Kenkel, L. A. in "A case against scientific creationism: A look at content Issues. *Science Education, 69,* 1985, p. 62.

11. Religion had no right to insist on the scientific accuracy of its mythical heritage. from this position a retreat was necessary. That part of mythology which is derived from pre-scientific thought, which does not understand the causal relations in the natural and historical world, must naturally be sacrificed in a scientific age.

> Theologian Reinhold Niebuhr, "The truth in myths." In Kennedy, G. (Ed.). *Evolution and Religion: The Conflict between Science and Religion in Modern America.*1957, p. 89.

12. To de-mythologize is to reject not Scripture, which is the world-view of a past epoch, which all too often is retained in Christian dogmatics and in the preaching of the church. To de-mythologize is to deny that the message of Scripture and of the Church is bound to an ancient world-view which is obsolete.

> Theologian Rudolf Bultmann in Johnson, R. A. *Rudolf Bultmann: Interpreting Faith for the Modern Era*, 1987, p. 300.

13. Today, however, all the bibles of the religions are subject to the scrutiny of scientific criticism. The end result is that thoughtful men no longer believe any are infallible. This does not mean that sacred books have no value, or that they can be discarded without loss. Nothing could be farther from the truth. As sources of enduring religious insight, they are priceless; but they must be studied critically as well as devotionally if

they are to continue to contribute to the spiritual life of modern man.
Munk, A. W. *Perplexing Problems of Religion*, 1954, p. 35.

14. The Bible is not a book of science. If this fact had been acknowledged and remembered, many a conflict that has brought discredit on both science and religion could have been avoided. The 139th Psalm is true whether the earth is flat or round....Science, however necessary, is sensate, and cannot sound the depths. It is of the analytic mind, and therefore cannot serve the wholeness of man's nature. It can give some answer to "How?" but none to "Why?" Only faith can say why, and every man must live by some faith....The Bible is not a book of science. It has mightier business on hand.

> Buttrick, G. A. in "The Study of the Bible," *The Interpreter's Bible* (Vol. 4), 1952, p. 166.

15. The whole difficulty here lies in the fact that we try to use the Bible in ways for which it was never intended. The Bible as we know it is the work of many writers, writing at widely diverse periods in human history. The contributions of these multitudinous writers are almost inextricably mixed, although modern Biblical scholars have done much to untangle the intertwining strands. All of the writers had this in common: They were interested in religion, not science, and they did their writing long before anyone knew anything about modern science. If in writing of religion they had occasion to refer to science they inevitably did so in terms of the science known in their day. So if we piece together these scattered references to the physical world we obtain a picture of the world and solar system as these people thought them to be.

> Moody, P. A. in *Introduction to Evolution* (3rd ed.), 1970, pp. 492-493.

16. Biblical man, despite his undoubted intellectual and spiritual endowments, did not base his views of the universe and its laws on the critical use of empirical data. He had not, as yet, discovered the principles or methods of disciplined inquiry, critical observation or analytical experimentation. Rather, his thinking was imaginative, and his expressions of thought were concrete, pictorial, emotional, and poetic.

> Sarna, N. M. in *Understanding Genesis*, 1972, pp. 2-3.

17. Science (or at least natural science) is a body of knowledge painstakingly acquired by observation, experiment and induction. The purpose of God through Scripture, however, has been to disclose truths which could not be discovered by this empirical method, but would have remained unknown and undiscovered if He had not revealed them. For instance, science may be able to tell us something about man's physical origins; only the Bible reveals man's nature, both his unique nobility as a creature made in the Creator's image and his degradation as a self-centered sinner in revolt against the Creator.

Stott, J. R. W. in *Understanding the Bible*, 1972, p. 14.

18. At the time the Bible was written it was believed that the Earth was flat and that a sea lay under it (Psalm 136:6, Psalm 24:1-2, Genesis 7:11). The heavens are described as a tent or an upturned bowl above the flat Earth (Job 37:18, Genesis 1:6-8, Isaiah 40:22, Psalm 104:2). The Earth is described as stationary (Psalm 93:1, Psalm 104:5). A sea was above the sky (Genesis 1:7, Psalm 148:4). There were windows in the sky through which the rain came down (Psalm 78:23, Genesis 7:11). None of these images are accurate scientifically.

Fosdick, quoted in Moody, 1970, p. 493. The scriptures speak of the sun "rising" and "setting" as it appeared to them that it came up and went down.

19. The biblical writers were primarily, indeed exclusively, concerned with religion—with making known the ways of God to man. Consequently if the Bible is to be read aright, it must be read religiously. This is what is meant by saying...that in it we hear God speak.

Easton, W. B., Jr., in *Basic Christian Beliefs*, 1957, p. 36.

20. In the opinion of many theologians Darwin threatened the trustworthiness of the Scriptures by casting doubt upon the literal accuracy of the narratives in the book of Genesis....The traditional Christian definition of the image of God in man seemed to clash with the idea of his descent from earlier and lower forms of life.....Faith in the direction of divine providence over nature....could not stand if Darwin was right. Darwin's suggestions about the descent of man appeared to make the Augustinian doctrine of original sin through the fall of one human couple untenable....All of these Christian doctrines, and many others besides,

seemed to lose their moorings when Darwin cut the rope between man and Adam.

Pelikan, J. in *The Christian Intellectual*,1965, pp. 38-39.

21. That collision between the new teachings and the old tradition seemed at first as shattering as an earthquake. Multitudes of men and women reacted in panic or in defiance, supposing that if their confidence in the literal exactitude of the first verses of Genesis should go, then their whole religious faith would be gone with it. Yet the new teachings had come not to blight religion but to stimulate it to new growth. If they seemed at first to break up old patterns of belief, the result was to lift men's eyes to mightier perspectives of the majestic works of God.

> Simpson, C. A., Buttrick, G. A. (Ed.). in "Genesis," *The Interpreter's Bible*, 1952, p. 462

22. The first step toward nonreligion of the western world was made by religion itself. This was when it defended its great symbols, which were its means of interpreting the world and life, not as symbols, but as literal stories. When it did this it had already lost the battle.

> Theologian Paul Tillich, quoted in Dobzhansky, "The biology of ultimate concern," in Anshen, R. N. (Ed.). *Perspectives in Humanism*, 1967, p. 34

23. He never realized that it was a fight merely between a literal interpretation of the Bible and common sense. He rested religion on the precise verbiage of the Book and insisted that religion would fail if those words were not accepted literally. Instead of accepting the spirit of religion or of Christianity, he accepted words, many of them wrong words, many of them representing improper translations, all of them representing the ideas of men of thousands of years ago who spoke the language and expressed the ideas of their time. Such views lead to the downfall of religion, not to its growth. If to be religious one must believe things that his mind will not accept, he must, perforce by human reasoning reject religion.

> Hays, A. G. in *Evolution and Religion: The Conflict between Science and Religion in Modern America*, 1957, p. 36 In reference to the Scopes Trial. William Jennings Bryan, the prosecuting

367

attorney, felt that this was a fight between religion and atheism or agnosticism.

APPENDIX D

Geological Column

	Millions of years ago (mya)		
Pleistocene		First modern humans	
Pliocene	5	First cattle, sheep	
		First humans	
Miocene	24	First apes	
Oligocene	37	First monkeys, pigs	CENOZOIC
Eocene	58	First "dogs," "cats"	
		Elephants, whales, horses	
Paleocene	65		
Cretaceous	144	First flowering plants	
Jurassic	208	First birds	MESOZOIC
Triassic	245	First dinosaurs, mammals	
Permian	286		
Carboniferous	360	First reptiles, amphibians	
Devonian	408	First land plants & animals	
Silurian	438	Scorpions	PALEOZOIC PHANEROZOIC
Ordovician	505	Sea urchins, sea lilies, starfish	
Cambrian	570	First fishes, corals, mollusks, Trilobites, brachiopods	

~1500	Origin of complex cells with nuclei
2000	Low levels of oxygen in atmosphere
3100	Oldest fossils (blue-green algae/ Stromatolites)
3500	Origin of Life???
3800	Oldest known rocks Origin of oceans and continents
4600	Origin of the Earth

PRECAMBRIAN

APPENDIX D

Standard Geological Column

Era	Period	Epoch	Duration in millions of years	Millions of years ago
CENOZOIC	Quaternary	Holocene	0.01	0.01
		Pleistocene	1.8	1.8
		Pliocene	3.5	5.3
	Tertiary	Miocene	18.5	23.8
		Oligocene	9.9	33.7
		Eocene	21.1	54.8
		Paleocene	10.2	65
MESOZOIC	Cretaceous		79	144
	Jurassic		62	206
	Triassic		42	248
PALEOZOIC	Permian		42	290
	Carboniferous	Pennsylvanian	33	323
		Mississippian	31	354
	Devonian		63	417
	Silurian		26	443
	Ordovician		47	490
	Cambrian		53	543
PRECAMBRIAN				

APPENDIX D

Standard Geological Column

EON		ERA	Duration in millions of years	Millions of years ago
PHANEROZOIC		CENOZOIC	65	65
		MESOZOIC	183	248
		PALEOZOIC	295	543
PRECAMBRIAN	PROTEROZOIC	LATE	357	900
		MIDDLE	700	1600
		EARLY	900	2500
	ARCHEAN	LATE	500	3000
		MIDDLE	400	3400
		EARLY	400	3800
	HADEAN		800	4600

APPENDIX E

Excerpt:
Confession of 1967, Presbyterian Church (USA)

THE BIBLE (9.27 - 9.30)

The one sufficient revelation of God is Jesus Christ, the Word of God incarnate, to whom the Holy Spirit bears unique and authoritative witness through the Holy Scriptures, which are received and obeyed as the word of God written. The Scriptures are not a witness among others, but the witness without parallel. The church has received the books of the Old and New Testaments as prophetic and apostolic testimony in which it hears the word of God and by which its faith and obedience are nourished and regulated.

The New Testament is the recorded testimony of apostles to the coming of the Messiah, Jesus of Nazareth, and the sending of the Holy Spirit to the Church. The Old Testament bears witness to God's faithfulness in his covenant with Israel and points the way to the fulfillment of his purpose in Christ. The Old Testament is indispensable to understanding the New, and is not itself fully understood without the New.

The Bible is to be interpreted in the light of its witness to God's work of reconciliation in Christ. The Scriptures, given under the guidance of the Holy Spirit, are nevertheless the words of men, conditioned by the language, thought forms, and literary fashions of the places and times at which they were written. They reflect views of life, history, and the cosmos which were then current. The church, therefore, has an obligation to approach the Scriptures with literary and historical understanding. As God has spoken his word in diverse cultural situations, the church is confident that he will continue to speak through the Scriptures in a changing world and in every form of human culture.

God's word is spoken to his church today where the Scriptures are faithfully preached and attentively read in dependence on the illumination of the Holy Spirit and with readiness to receive their truth and direction.

The Book of Confessions, Presbyterian Church, (USA), 1991. The Confession of 1967, 9.27-9.30. Published by the Office of the General Assembly, Louisville, KY.

Excerpt: The Book of Common Prayer, the Episcopal Church, 1977

God of all power, Ruler of the Universe,
you are worthy of glory and praise.
Glory to you for ever and ever.

At your command all things came to be: the vast expanse of interstellar
space, galaxies, suns, the planets in their courses,
and this fragile earth, our island home.
By your will they were created and have their being.

From the primal elements you brought forth the human race, and blessed
us with memory, reason, and skill. You made us the rulers of creation. But
we turned against you, and betrayed your trust;
and we turned against one another.
Have mercy, Lord, for we are sinners in your sight.

The Book of Common Prayer, the Episcopal Church, 1977, p. 370
Kingsport Press, Kingsport, Tennessee

APPENDIX F

Excerpt From Erasmus Darwin's Evolutionary Epic

Then, whilst the sea, at their coeval birth
Surge over surge, involv'd the shoreless earth;
Nurs'd by warm sun-beams in primeval caves,
Organic Life began beneath the waves.

First forms minute, unseen by spheric glass,
Move on the mud, or pierce the watery mass;
These, as successive generations bloom,
New powers acquire, and larger limbs assume;
Whence countless groups of vegetation spring,
And breathing realms of fin, and feet, and wing.

Next, when imprison'd fires in central caves
Burst the firm earth, and drank the headlong waves;
And, as new airs with dread explosion swell,
Form'd lava-isles, and continents of shell;
Pil'd ricks on rocks, on mountains mountains rais'd,
And high in heaven the first volcanoes blaz'd.

In countless swarms an insect-myriad moves
From sea-fan gardens, and from coral groves;
Leaves the cold caverns of the deep, and creeps
On shelving shores, or climbs on rocky steeps
Cold gills aquatic, for respiring lungs,
And sound aerial flow from slimy tongues.

Thus the tall Oak, the giant of the wood,
Which bears Britannia's thunders on the flood;
The Whale, unmeasured monster of the main,
The lordly Lion, monarch of the plain,
The Eagle, soaring in the realms of air,
Whose eye undazzled drinks the solar glare;--
Imperious man, who rules the bestial crowd,
Of language, reason, and reflection proud
With brow erect, who scorns this earthly sod,
And styles himself the image of his God;

Arose from rudiments of form and sense,
An embryon point, or microscopic ens!

From: Darwin, Erasmus (1803). *The temple of nature, or the origin of society.* London: J. J. Johnson.

APPENDIX G

Some Religion and Science Organizations in the United States

American Scientific Affiliation (ASA)
Perspectives on Science and Christian Faith (Journal)
P. O. Box 668
Ipswich, MA 01938

*Answers in Genesis
P. O. Box 6330
Florence, KY 41022

*Bible-Science Association
2911 E. 42nd
Minneapolis, MN 55406-3194

*Center for Creation Studies
Liberty Baptist College
Lynchberg, VA 24506

Center for Process Studies
Newsletter of the Center for Process Studies
Claremont School of Theology
1325 N. College Avenue
Claremont, CA 91711-3154

Center for Theological Inquiry
Newsletter of the Center for Theological Inquiry
Princeton Theological Seminary
50 Stockton Street
Princeton, NJ 08540

Center for Theology and the Natural Sciences (CTNS)
Theology and Science (Journal)
2400 Ridge Road
Berkeley, CA 94709

Center for the Study of Science and Religion
Columbia University
405 Low Library
MC 4335, 535 W. 116th St.
New York, NY 10027

Cosmos and Creation
Loyola College in Maryland
4501 North Charles Street
Baltimore, MD 21210-2699

Counterbalance Foundation
2030 Dexter Ave. N, Suite B296
Seattle, WA 98109

*Creation Research Society
CRS Quarterly (Journal)
P. O. Box 8263
St. Joseph, MO 64508

Georgetown Center for the Study of Science and Religion
Georgetown University Theology Department
Washington, DC 20052

*Geoscience Research Institute
Loma Linda University
11060 Campus Street
Loma Linda, CA 92350

*Institute for Creation Research
Impact and Acts and Facts (monthly pamphlets)
P. O. Box 2667
El Cajon, CA 92021

Institute for Theological Encounter with Science and Technology
(ITEST)
ITEST Bulletin
3601 Lindell Blvd.
St. Louis, MO 63108

Institute on Religion in an Age of Science (IRAS)
P. O. Box 55
Bagdad, KY 40003

Metanexus Institute on Science and Religion
Spiral (Journal)
3624 Market Street, Suite 301
Philadelphia, PA 19104

National Center for Science Education (NCSE)
Reports of the NCSE
420 40th Street
Oakland, CA 94609

Tapestry
Institute for Philosophy, Religion, and Life Science
100 N. 6th Street, Suite 702
Waco, TX 76071

The John Templeton Foundation
Progress in Theology (Journal)
P. O. Box 8322
Radnor, PA 19087-8322

The New England Center for Faith and Science Exchange
Faith and Science Exchange (F&SE) Notices
Boston Theological Institute
210 Herrick Road
Newton Centre, MA 02459

Zygon Center for Religion and Science
Zygon: Journal of Religion and Science
1100 E. 55th Street
Chicago, IL 60615-5199

*Creationist

APPENDIX H

Excerpts from "The Epic Of Gilgamesh"

(A story of the third millennium B.C. about the notorious
king of Uruk in Mesopotamia)

I built the hulls of the ark one-hundred seventy-five feet high,
And the decks one-hundred seventy-five feet wide.
I constructed a top deck and six lower decks,
I separated the hull into compartments by nine bulkheads.
Then I caulked the ark with bitumen and asphalt thinned with oil.

...At dawn...the horizons turned black with clouds,
Adad, divine patron of thunder, roared.
Nabu and Sharru, the divine messengers flew before the wind.
Nergal, divine patron of the dead, unlocked the fountain of the deep.
Ninurta, son of Enlil, opened the dikes.
The divine assembly strafed the earth with lightning,
Adad turned the day into night; the land was smashed like a pot.
One person could not see the other, the heavens could not see the earth.
The flood ran the old Annunaki into the heavens,
Frightened the divine assembly like stray dogs against city walls.
Ishtar, divine patron of love and war, shrieked, cried out like a woman in labor,
"How could I kill my own people, conspire against those to whom I gave birth?
Their bodies float on the sea, swell like schools of dead fish.

From Matthews, V. H. and Benjamin, D. C., "Stories of Gilgamesh,"
in *Old Testament Parallels*, New York:Paulist Press, pp. 26-27.

Then I bowed low, I sat down and I wept, the tears streamed down my face, for on every side was the waste of water. I looked for land in vain, but fourteen leagues distant there appeared a mountain, and there the boat grounded; on the mountain of Nisir the boat held fast, she held fast and did not budge. One day she held, and a second day on the mountain of Nisir she held fast and did not budge. A third day, and a fourth day she held fast on the mountain and did not budge; a fifth day and a sixth day she held fast on the mountain. When the seventh day dawned I loosed a dove and let her go. She flew away, but finding no resting-place she returned. Then I loosed a swallow, and she flew away but finding no resting-place she returned. I loosed a raven, she saw that the waters had retreated, she ate, she flew around, she cawed, and she did not come back.

From page 111, *The Epic of Gilgamesh: An English version with an introduction by N. K. Sandars*, (1972). New York: Penguin Books.

Printed in the United States
40189LVS00006B/304-315